HERALDS OF HEALTH

The Saga of Christian
Medical Initiatives

i

HERALDS OF HEALTH

The Saga of Christian
Medical Initiatives

Edited by
Stanley G. Browne   Frank Davey
and
William A. R. Thomson

Foreword by
The Rt. Hon. The LORD PORRITT
Bt, GCMG, GCVO, CBE, FRCS

Published for the Medical Committee
of the
Conference for World Mission
by

 CHRISTIAN MEDICAL FELLOWSHIP

LONDON

© 1985 Christian Medical Fellowship

First published 1985

Christian Medical Fellowship
157 Waterloo Road
London SE1 8XN

Trade distributors:

Inter-Varsity Press
Norton Street
Nottingham NG7 3HR

ISBN 0 906747 17 1

Printed in Great Britain by

Wrights (Sandbach) Ltd
9 Middlewich Road
Sandbach
Cheshire CW11 9DP

FOREWORD

The Rt Hon The Lord Porritt, Bt, GCMG, GCVO, CBE, FRCS

President: ECHO (The Joint Mission Hospital Equipment Board)

Formerly: Governor-General of New Zealand; Sergeant-Surgeon to
H.M. The Queen; President, Royal College of Surgeons; President, British
Medical Association; President, Royal Society of Medicine

This is a very remarkable book – it could justly be described, in the truest sense of the word, as 'extra-ordinary'. Based on the ancient historical connection between religion and medicine, it is indeed a saga (again an apt description) of medical missionaries and missionary hospitals during the last century and a half.

Until the publication of this book has justly saved them from oblivion, these unsung heroes and heroines had a cause, and they had a faith; they believed that a patient was an individual, and if that individual needed care, it involved not only his physical well-being, but also his mental and spiritual health as well – irrespective of cult, creed or colour. For them, there was more to medicine than surgical technology and chemical pharmacology – important as these were, especially in establishing their initial credibility. How they achieved these objectives is the story of this book – an epic story of selfless devoted service to humanity. I suppose that this is essentially a medical book, though it is so much more because of the emphasis on people – both patient and doctor.

The story is told with a wealth of detail – historical, geographical, medical, anecdotal – but despite the multiplicity of authors it never becomes repetitive; it is in other words very well edited. Many of these authors are known the world over as authorities in their subjects and their contributions provide a fund of knowledge that I doubt is available elsewhere, and is of intense interest.

It becomes obvious as one reads the book that the seeds sown by the pioneers so worthily honoured in these pages have indeed borne good fruit. It has taken a century and a half of difficult, dangerous and devoted work, but the responsibilities so bravely shouldered by the early medical missionaries – particularly in China, the Indian subcontinent and Africa – are more and more being accepted by national governments and international organizations. But the WHO slogan 'Health for all by the year 2000' is still a dream, and there remains a vast field for the dedicated doctor pledged to help the millions of individuals still lacking ordinary medical care. The change in emphasis from curative to preventive medicine, and especially the concept of community medicine, the acceptance of 'holistic' medicine as a viable entity, together with the great improvement in communications and the provision of reasonable equipment and drugs – all offer immense scope in the immediate future to medical men and women, and nurses, willing to share their expertise and their faith.

This book should give such adventurous spirits great confidence and the assurance that their response to what is surely the greatest of all causes – the welfare of mankind – is still as vitally necessary as it ever was.

The fascinating story told in these pages – pragmatic, yet very moving – of how the early pioneers met the challenge, often against almost impossible odds, of illness, starvation and sheer human misery, makes compulsive reading. I am sure that it will, deservedly, find a far wider public than simply those involved and interested in medical missionary work. It is a fine book, and I wish it every success.

PORRITT

August 1985

PREFACE

This book is the brain-child of the late Dr Frank Davey. For years he had been concerned that many writers and publicists were apparently unaware of the real contributions made by Christians to advances in medical practice in countries comprising what is now known as the Third World. Out of his long experience as a medical missionary in Africa and India, interspersed by the administrative overview he gained when Medical Secretary of the Methodist Missionary Society, he became convinced that a wider public needed to be informed of the initiatives that had been taken by Christians in many medical activities abroad. As the co-author (with his wife) of an unpretentious little book entitled *Compassionate Years* (published by the Methodist Missionary Society in 1964), and as the author of numerous important scientific articles on leprosy, Dr Davey was uniquely qualified to suggest to the Medical Committee of the Conference for World Mission (of the British Council of Churches) that it ought to sponsor the preparation of a book that would inform the general public of the crucial part played by Christian medical workers in bringing health and healing to many parts of the world.

The Medical Committee enthusiastically welcomed Dr Davey's suggestion, and also his advice that Dr Wm. A.R. Thomson, formerly Editor of *The Practitioner*, and I should form with him an editorial team. Dr Thomson had made many notable contributions to medical literature, not least his *Faiths that Heal*, published by A. & C. Black in 1972. This team approached the contributors whose chapters appear in the present volume, and also numerous resource persons whose records and recollections of people and events have proved invaluable.

The chapter authors had to face the difficult task of selection and curtailment of an extensive documentation in order to limit the length of their contributions. Enough material was in hand to justify much longer chapters; for instance, the pioneering work of Christian doctors and nurses in medical education in China deserves more adequate treatment than is possible here. It is hoped that the references given may be useful in indicating sources.

Work on the preparation and editing of the scripts was well advanced when, in 1983, tragedy struck: Dr Davey, and then Dr Thomson, died. Thanksgiving services were held for Dr Davey at the Headquarters of the Methodist Church Overseas Division on 27 April, and for Dr Thomson in All Souls, Langham Place, on 1 December. At both services, fitting tributes were paid to the sterling qualities and many activities of these two co-editors.

A possible criticism of the coverage of the topics in the present volume concerns the apparent over-emphasis on British and Protestant contributions in the initiatives recorded. The chapter authors are well aware of this, but I should point out on their behalf that notwithstanding the recognized activities of non-British and non-protestant medical workers, the chapters do give in the main a balanced account.

The problem of financing the publication of such a book as this in these days of cash-flow difficulties was at length resolved by generous contributions from the respected drug firm of CIBA-GEIGY and from an anonymous donor. Grateful thanks are due to the Methodist Church Overseas Division for generously providing office accommodation and the services of secretarial assistance in the person of Mrs Valerie Coms.

I must express my personal thanks to the Christian Medical Fellowship for assuming the responsibility of publication, to Dr Ralph Schram for his editorial help and the preparation of the Indexes, and to the Rev John Rivers for assistance in the final stages of presenting the scripts for printing.

This book supplements the broader-based historical work entitled *The Influence of Christians in Medicine*, edited by J.T. Aitken, H.W.C. Fuller and D. Johnson, and published by the Christian Medical Fellowship in 1984.

Lord Porritt, well known for his sympathy with the object of this publication, has graciously agreed to write the Foreword.

I must express my real personal indebtedness to my late friends and colleagues over many years – Drs Frank Davey and Wm. Thomson – for their unremitting help, hard work and encouragement, and for their buoyant optimism (indeed, conviction) that the present volume should – and would – eventually see the light of day.

To all who have helped in any way, I express my deep thanks and appreciation.

Stanley G. Browne

September 1985.

CONTRIBUTORS

Josephine BARNES, DBE, DM, FRCP, FRCS, FRCOG, Hon DSc, Hon MD, Hon DM, Hon FRCPC, FRCPI
Consulting Obstetrician and Gynaecologist, Charing Cross Hospital, and Elizabeth Garrett Anderson Hospital, London
Vice-President, Royal College of Obstetricians and Gynaecologists
Past President, British Medical Association
Past President, Medical Women's Federation
Honorary Fellow, Lady Margaret Hall, Oxford

John T. BAVINGTON, MB, BS, D(Obst)RCOG, DPM, MRC Psych
Consultant Psychiatrist, Lynfield Mount Hospital, Bradford
Past Director, Mental Health Centre, Mission Hospital, Peshawar, Pakistan
Past Medical Superintendent, Mission Hospital, Peshawar, Pakistan

Peter BEWES, MB, MChir, FRCS(Eng), D(Obst)RCOG
Consulting Surgeon, Birmingham Accident Hospital
Hon. Senior Lecturer, Birmingham University
Surgeon, Kilimanjaro Christian Centre, Moshi, Tanzania
Surgeon, Mulago Hospital, Kampala, Uganda
Senior Lecturer, Makerere University, Kampala
Surgeon, Mengo Hospital, Kampala

William Roy BILLINGTON CBE, MD
CMS Missionary, Uganda
Medical Superintendent, Mengo Hospital, Kampala
Medical Superintendent and Physician, Church Missionary Society, London

Paul BRAND, CBE, FRCS
Orthopaedic and Rehabilitation Surgeon, National Hansen's Disease Center, Carville, Louisiana, USA
Director, Orthopaedic surgery, The Leprosy Mission International
Professor of Orthopaedic Surgery, Christian Medical College, Vellore, India
Chairman, World Committee for Leprosy Rehabilitation of the International Society for the Rehabilitation of the Disabled

Stanley G. BROWNE, CMG, OBE, MD, FRCP, FRCS, DTM, FKC, KLJ
Moderator, Medical Committee, Conference for World Mission, London

President, International Congress of Christian Physicians
President, Medical Missionary Association, London
President, Ludhiana British Fellowship
Past Director, Leprosy Study Centre, London
Consultant Adviser, Department of Health and Social Security, London
Secretary-Treasurer, International Leprosy Association
Past President, Royal Society of Tropical Medicine and Hygiene
Medical Consultant, The Leprosy Mission International
Senior Specialist Leprologist and Director of Leprosy Service Research
    Unit, Uzuakoli, Nigeria
BMS Medical Missionary, Yakusu, Zaïre

Frank DAVEY, CBE, MD, MSc
Editor emeritus, Leprosy Review
Author (joint) of 1964 edition of Leprosy in Theory and Practice
Medical Secretary, Methodist Missionary Society
Leprosy Adviser, Federal Government of Nigeria, and Senior Specialist
    (leprologist) Nigeria Leprosy Service
Director, Leprosy Service Research Unit, Uzuakoli, Nigeria
Director, Victoria Leprosy Hospital, Dichpalli, India

Herbert M GILLES, KOSJ, MSc, MD, FRCP, FFCM, FMCPH(Nig),
    DTMH, DSc(Karolinksa Inst), DSc(Malta)
Professor of Tropical Medicine, Liverpool University
Past Dean, Liverpool School of Tropical Medicine
Professor of Preventive Medicine, Ibadan University, Nigeria
Visiting Professor of Tropical Medicine, Lagos College of Medicine,
    Nigeria
Visiting Professor, Khartoum University, Sudan

Philip E. Clinton MANSON-BAHR, FRCP, MD, DTMH
Consultant Commonwealth Development Corporation, London
Past Consulting Physician, Overseas Development Administration,
    London
Senior Lecturer, Clinical Tropical Medicine, London School of Hygiene
    and Tropical Medicine
Professor of Tropical Medicine, Tulane University, New Orleans, USA
Senior Specialist, Colonial Medical Service

David MORLEY, MA, MD(Cantab), FRCP
Professor of Tropical Child Health, Institute of Child Health, London
Reader in Tropical Child Health, London University
Senior Lecturer, Department of Human Nutrition, London School of

Hygiene and Tropical Medicine
Paediatrician, Wesley Guild Hospital, Ilesha, Nigeria
Associate Lecturer in Paediatrics, University College, Ibadan, Nigeria

Jean McTavish McLELLAN, RGN, SCM, ONC (British Orthopaedic
Nursing Certificate, Nursing Administration, Royal College of
Nursing, Edinburgh)
Tutor (In-Service Education), Princess Louise Scottish Hospital,
Bishopston
Past Director of Nursing Services, Christian Medical College, Ludhiana,
India
Theatre Supervisor, Ludhiana
Nursing Administrator, Ludhiana
Director of Nursing, Institute of Post-Graduate Medical Education and
Research, Chandigarh, N.India (Seconded to Govt. of India)
Senior appointments at Glasgow Royal Infirmary and Glasgow Western
Infirmary

James Clifford McGILVRAY, BA
Past Director, Christian Medical Commission of the World Council of
Churches, Geneva, Switzerland
Superintendent and Secretary, College Council, Christian Medical
College, Vellore, S. India
Director, Inter-Church Commission of Medical Care, Philippines
Director, Christian Medical Commission, National Council of Churches
of Christ, USA

Ralph SCHRAM, MA, MD (Cantab), DPH, DIH, FFCM, AFOM,
FMCPH(Nig.)
Medical Adviser, Africa Evangelical Fellowship, London
Past Director, Bureau of Hygiene and Tropical Diseases, London
Senior Lecturer, Ross Institute, London School of Hygiene and Tropical
Medicine
Reader, Ahmadu Bello University, Zaria, Nigeria
Senior Lecturer, Makerere University, Kampala, Uganda
Visiting Professor of Community Health, Lagos College of Medicine,
Nigeria

William Archibald Robson THOMSON, MD, FRCPE
Medical Consultant, The *Daily Telegraph*
Author, *Dictionary of Medical Ethics and Practice*
Past Editor, *The Practitioner*
Chairman, Leprosy Study Centre, London
Foundation member, British Academy of Forensic Sciences

Harry WILLIAMS, OBE, FRCSEd, FICS
Commissioner, The Salvation Army
International Secretary and Medical Adviser, The Salvation Army
Chief Medical Officer and Head of Reconstructive Surgery,
Catherine Booth Hospital, Nagercoil, India

CONTENTS

CHAPTER 1

INTRODUCTION

T.F. Davey

Throughout the world, and from time immemorial, medicine has been linked with religion. It could scarcely be otherwise when both are concerned with matters of life and death. In many places the physician was also priest, and in early times there were examples of this in Greece. The Greek physicians were also as a guild related to temple worship, but religion in Greece did not share in the invigorating developments which were rapidly changing medicine and indeed all the sciences. Across the Mediterranean, in Palestine, and far to the east in India and China, things were different.

In India, Gautama, the gentle Buddha (563-483 BC) taught a concern for all life, and hospitals for the sick arose over a wide area as an expression of his religious philosophy, along with an assiduous study of medicinal plants, and expertise in some branches of surgery, from which the Greeks benefited. These developments reached their zenith in the time of the Emperor Asoka, but thereafter the vision faded, and compassionate concern for the sick and needy became encapsulated within the rigid structures of the caste system. A denial of reality to the physical world and a prohibition on necropsies proved serious hindrances to progress. In China, as well, philosophy and medicine were developing together at the time of Hippocrates, but there, too, development was arrested through worship of the past and similar prohibitions. On the other hand, in Palestine from the 5th century BC onwards, tentative movements began to arise within Jewish monotheism which had a bearing on medicine with their perception that the divine compassion extended beyond Israel to the people of other races. Such ideas had important implications, but they never seem to have won the whole-hearted acceptance of the Jewish people. Thus in these widely different parts of the world promising developments in medical and philosophical thought arose and then gradually became

1

arrested, but in Greece they continued to expand and became a living inheritance to future generations.

There are wide areas of the world where the Greek heritage appears to provide the only necessary philosophical basis for modern medical practice. This, however, is not true of Western Europe, and those parts of the world where Western European influence has been profound. Here, another factor becomes evident. In these countries for over a thousand years medical practice and indeed the common mind have been infused with a breadth of compassion, a responsible concern for the sick which go far beyond that found in ancient Greece and even in some modern societies.

Let it be said at once that no culture or religious system can claim any monopoly of compassion. This is a precious quality of the human race as such. Its flowering into practical action is another matter. As actually encountered throughout history and across the world, compassion is expressed predominantly within the limits of the family or group and only in emergency situations outside these limits. The European heritage has a broader vision, which has moulded the traditional image of the family doctor and has expressed itself in the concept of the caring society.

Both these aspects were clearly illustrated in the inception of the National Health Service in Britain in 1948. Visions of a healthful society have been conceived at various times in history, but in 1948 vision was translated into practice in a Service remarkable for its comprehensiveness. A nation, through its government, expressed its conviction that access to health care is the birthright of every citizen, regardless of ethnic origins or social status, and, at considerable cost to the entire community, it set up the machinery whereby free medical care became available to all. Sir Winston Churchill commented on it at the time in the following words:

> 'The discoveries of healing science must be the inheritance of all; that is clear. Disease must be attacked whether it occurs in the poorest or the richest man or woman, simply on the ground that it is the enemy; and it must be attacked in the same way that the fire brigade will give its assistance to the humble cottage as it will give it to the most important mansion . . . Our policy is to create a national health service, in order to secure that everybody in the country, irrespective of means, age, sex, or occupation, shall have equal opportunities to benefit from the best and most up-to-date medical and allied services available' (Ross, 1952).

This noble concept did not arise in a vacuum. It was not a natural product of civilization One may seek in vain for anything comparable among civilizations more ancient and just as rich in culture and the arts as Western Europe. The human race does not grow more tender-hearted, more concerned about the welfare of the underprivileged by a process of natural selection; indeed the reverse is more often the case.

Equally, no modern political party could claim to have inspired the principles underlying the National Health Service. They are far more fundamental and long-standing than that, and Greece cannot claim the honour of inventing them. At the very time when Hippocrates and his followers were practising medicine there existed large numbers of slaves in Greece whose human rights were minimal, and were simply non-existent in the Roman times that followed. Any social philosophy that suggested that such people had a right to compassionate medical care would have been regarded as both outrageous and dangerous.

Medicine, like democracy, was primarily for the free-born, and related in general to the patient's ability to pay for the services rendered. Furthermore, the social philosophy of Greece, as everywhere else in the world, favoured the physically perfect, youth, beauty and athleticism. 'Clear the way for the strong, the healthy, the young' was the order of the day. The Roman poet Juvenal's 'sound mind in a sound body' left little room for the disabled, the aged, the weak and the underprivileged.

In contrast to this, the energies of the caring society, instead of ignoring such people, are *actually directed towards them*. This is an unusual phenomenon, the product of a social consciousness sensitized to suffering and need. It is clear that the world of 400 BC had no understanding of this kind of social responsibility. It was a quality that human kind had still to discover.

There is a personal and professional aspect of this. Quite fundamental to the success of the National Health Service was the outlook of the members of the medical profession who were expected to operate the Service, the kind of doctor-patient relation regarded as natural and proper. It is clear that the general public expected that the existing popular image of the family doctor in Britain would continue into the Health Service and be a normal and permanent feature of it. This image is of great importance. For the older generation at least the family doctor is expected to be something more than a skilful scientist and a man of integrity. He adds to these qualities a kindness, a combination of wisdom and compassion which enables him to enter personally into the situation of his patients and their families, whatever their social standing, and seek their health and well-being, even at some sacrifice of leisure and comfort on his own part. These are not qualities expected of the medical profession in many parts of the world, but these qualities associated with the medical profession made the concept of a National Health Service in Britain acceptable. The nobility of the medical profession owes much to this strain in our heritage.

Greece cannot claim responsibility for these attitudes. The Greek physicians were humane and compassionate men within the limits of the social mores of their day, but their primary concern was nevertheless with the *disease* rather than the person suffering from the disease, and only with *curable* disease: hence their concern with prognosis. Phyllis Garlick (1952) expresses this very clearly:

'The limitations of the Greek view become very apparent when we consider the position of the sick man in society. The burden he carried was not a sense of sin but of inferiority. Disease, weakness or any physical disability which deprived him of perfect health and soundness, made of him an inferior being who had fallen short of the accepted ideal of perfection. Only if his condition showed likelihood of improvement could the sick man hope for the continued care of the physician or any consideration from society. A hopeless case could expect neither the one nor the other. Thus in exalting the healthy and sound, the Greek world showed neither compassion nor organised care for the weak and disabled.'

There can be no doubt that in the first century AD new and important ideas arose in the spheres of religion and social ethics. Stephen Verney, Bishop of Ripon, refers to the period as the great evolutionary leap (Verney, 1976), while John Taylor, Bishop of Winchester, describes it as 'that extraordinary springtime of the Spirit' (Taylor, 1972). Peripheral to this was the introduction by the Roman military authorities of hospitals for their sick and wounded, but central to it stands the unique figure of Jesus of Nazareth, who, in a short ministry of at most three years, shattered universally held concepts of human responsibility and social behaviour. He re-established the association between medicine and religion at a new and profound level. His life, teaching and example relate to all concerned with health in at least five important ways.

Firstly, Jesus was himself a healer, 'The Great Physician'. It was a commonplace in those times for aspirants after greatness to claim miraculous healing powers as a boost to their authority. Certain Roman emperors and kings did this. The healings of Jesus are very different. In not a single instance is there any suggestion that he undertook healings for his own glory. It is recorded that he specifically rejected such behaviour. Again and again he told patients not to advertise his cures. Quite often he withdrew after an act of healing in order to avoid publicity. The reason for his healings was more fundamental. In brief, *he healed because he could do no other.*

The New Testament gospels describe twenty-six healing occasions and refer to many more. These are not to be considered in isolation; they are inseparably linked with a remarkable series of conversations, interviews, discussions and stories, through the whole of which the healing redemptive theme is evident, the whole presenting a spectrum of healing which was new in the world of his day. His primary concern was always with the patient's restoration to wholeness of health in body, mind and spirit in an ongoing social context. The curing of specific diseases was only part of this wider picture. He never considered the patient in isolation from other people. It was continuing relations that mattered. He had a total disregard of barriers of race, class, occupation, sex, age or religious custom.

The compelling motivation for his healing work came from his own religious faith, in which there were highly original elements. As a devout Jew, Jesus inherited the noble monotheism of his people. He clearly pondered long and deeply on their sacred Scriptures and allied himself with that thin strain of inspired prophetic thought that declared that Israel was not the only recipient of the Divine mercy, love and compassion. Jesus took this thought to its ultimate conclusion and made it immediately and intensely practical when he declared that every human being is the personal recipient of the love of God, and that the Creator's purpose is fulfilment and wholeness in every life. 'God so loved the world . . .' These are uniquely Christian words. Jesus proclaims God's reign as realized wherever the sick are healed, the oppressed and underprivileged relieved, the rejected accepted, the brokenhearted comforted, the wrongdoers forgiven. 'It is not the will of your Father in heaven that one of these little ones should perish' (Mt. 18-14).

Our second point of contact concerns the vocation of medicine. Jesus believed very clearly that the human race is under the continuous beneficent creative energy of God, operating now and always for higher and more fulfilled expressions of humanity; the evolution of the human spirit. He saw himself and all who are working for healing and wholeness, both in the individual and in society, as aligned with the divine purpose, working with God in the overthrow of negative, evil forces – in short, all healing is God-inspired, whoever is undertaking it. Thus for him, medicine is a sacramental vocation, a visible expression of the present healing activity of God.

There are several references to this in the Gospels. 'My Father has never yet ceased his work and I am working too' (Jn. 5.17). 'If it is by the finger of God that I drive out the devils, then be sure that the kingdom of God has already come upon you' (Lk. 17.22). 'Master, said John, we saw a man driving out devils in your name, but as he is not one of us we tried to stop him. Jesus said to him, Do not stop him, for he who is not against you is on your side' (Lk. 9.49). Very striking, too, is the way in which repeatedly the minds of the onlookers and the patient were turned towards God, so that they gave thanks to God for what they were seeing. Jesus encouraged this. The profession of medicine in all its branches, including medical research, can have no higher dignity than that of cooperating with the Creator for the good of mankind.

In the third place, Jesus opened up new dimensions in the doctor-patient relation. His concept of the universal love of God for mankind means that every person is precious, every person matters, and merits a care in sickness which is not only skilful but sensitive, supportive and comprehensive. The teaching of Jesus is expressed with great clarity in the incomparable parable of the good Samaritan, a story timeless in its relevance. He personifies it in one incident after another.

This, and many other incidents in the Gospels, reveals depths of compassion that are uniquely to be associated with Jesus. He has a sensitivity to suffering, an empathy that enables him to enter into the experience of the patient and his family and see the problem from their side. He is courageously persistent in seeking the patient's health and wholeness. He accepts personal discomfort, self-denial and self-sacrifice for the sake of the person in need. These are the qualities that Jesus understood when he talked of 'love of neighbour', and for him they were not just a response to sudden emergency, but a way of life embracing even enemies. Here, surely, is an elevated understanding of the doctor-patient relation, and one given by him the highest authority when he placed love of neighbour in the centre of religion, side by side with love of God. Here indeed is the standard by which love towards God is to be measured.

In the fourth place, Jesus reversed the social priorities of his day by demonstrating and teaching a special concern for the poor, the disabled, the outcast and the underprivileged. Such people had no claim to attention until Jesus became their champion. He saw his mission as particularly directed towards such people. He rejected the idea of almsgiving as a means of acquiring religious virtue for oneself. Compassion for the poor, weak, helpless and destitute, as he saw it, was to be offered purely for their own sakes, and without hope of reward, because this is a reflection of the nature of God. The quality of medical care is not to be regulated by the ability of the patient to pay. In all these matters Jesus went far beyond the thought of his Greek antecedents. One cannot imagine Hippocrates showing much interest in a prostitute in trouble, a blind beggar, the slave of a soldier of the occupying power, a psychotic foreigner clearly with no money, an old woman with a chronic spinal condition. Jesus not only did so, he expected his followers to do the same. Hans Kung (1977) puts it very clearly:

'Jesus turns with sympathy and compassion to all those to whom no one else turns, the weak, sick, neglected, social rejects . . . He has no cult of health, youth or achievement. He loves them all as they are and so is able to help them . . . Are not these actions, though they do not infringe any law of nature, very unusual, extraordinary, astonishing, marvellous and wonderful?'

Our fifth important point of contact with Jesus is in his attitude towards death. He did not believe in the finality of death. For him it was no inexorable curtain coming down to end the otherwise meaningless play which we call life, but rather a door into a different dimension of existence with God. His own understanding of the love of God enabled him as his last words to pray amid extreme anguish: 'Father, into thy hands I commend my spirit.' This peculiarly Christian prayer is applicable to everybody and gives Christians a particular ministry of comfort and hope to the dying. At the same time Jesus believed that life is the Creator's gift, to be treasured and not abused. In his understanding, the best preparation for death is a quality of life in which there is growing richness and maturity, and this is

fostered only in responsible community relations and community service. The ideas of Jesus were beautiful, but they were
also dangerous. No-one with his outlook could expect to live
very long in the world of the first century AD, with its callous
attitude to suffering, its oppression, its disregard of human life.
Jesus knew his time was limited. He died a criminal's death as a
political revolutionary, the manner of his dying displaying both
the depths of depravity to which mankind can sink, and the
quality of love for others that Jesus displayed to the very end, the
unconquerable love of God. That was not the end of the story, it
was just its beginning, for the ideas of Jesus have continued to
ferment in the world ever since, and continue to do so, their far-
reaching implications the inspiration for all self-denying service
for others. If Greece provided the mind of medicine, here is its
heart.

It might well have been expected that with such origins the
Christian community in every land and in every age would form
the spearhead of social reform, the exemplars of the caring
society. The truth is not as straightforward as that.

For three centuries there was no obvious problem. The
church from very early days was international in outlook and
compassionate in practice. There are numerous references to
Christian compassion for the needy and service to the sick
during this period, a particularly splendid one relating to an
epidemic of bubonic plague in Alexandria in 256 AD, when
Christians, instead of fleeing the city as most other people were
doing, stayed behind to nurse the sick and dying, and many of
them gave their own lives in the process. That was authentic
Christianity. Hans Kung (1977) comments as follows:

'The message of Jesus culminates in love of neighbour . . . In
this light the young community of faith from the very beginning
recognized active care of the suffering as a special task. Hence
systematic care of the sick became a specifically Christian affair,
distinguishing that religion from the world religions.'

The motivating power of this was not simply the memory of a
wonderful leader, however treasured. From the beginning
Christians have believed passionately that in Jesus, God the
Creator was showing mankind eternal and universal truth
essential to the future well-being of the race. Such truth is
indestructible, and so was Jesus, who, living and glorified, continues his gracious work wherever self-sacrificing service is
offered to those who suffer. Whatever theological language is
used to describe this, many of those who engage themselves in

such service see Jesus actually challenging them in the person in need, their service an act of devotion to the Lord rather than just 'do-gooding'. At the same time they feel that they are being given reinforcing graces from beyond themselves: a sensitiveness that perceives human need not evident to others; the ability to love the unlovable; illumination in penetrating difficult problems, the urge to action, and a courageous persistence against all odds in the pursuit of healing.

The 4th century brought a change of emphasis. With the conversion of the Emperor Constantine the Christian church had to adapt itself to becoming part of the establishment of imperial Rome. The taste of acceptance and authority was sweet. Little wonder that the personal, devotional, and doctrinal aspects of the faith all too often were given precedence over its uncomfortable challenges to social reform: in short, a religion in the last resort egocentric, and far removed from the total self-forgetting self-giving of Jesus, to whom the need of others always came first. Surely the most elementary demand on an organization believing itself to be the Body of Christ must be Christlikeness. Unfortunately, the same process of betrayal has been repeated on many occasions since, when loyalty to the State has taken precedence over the basic principles for which Jesus lived and died, and when rigid doctrinal emphases have destroyed the unity of Christians so dear to Jesus. Thus it comes about that today, when there is a greater volume of practical Christian concern for all kinds of disabled people than at any time in history, when most people at least admire Jesus as a wonderful person and great social reformer, he is not automatically associated in the public mind with the Christian Church, which was indeed founded to be his living body in every age. The Bishop of Winchester (Taylor, 1972) has put it like this:

'Once Christians had begun to think of the church as a structure to be compared with and related to other structures in society, it became one of the very principalities and powers that the gospel was supposed to withstand ... the Christian service of men in their need so quickly embodies itself in church controlled service institutions on which the churches come to rely for their status, and which compete with similar institutions under other authority. Unable to lose its life in order to save it, the community of the New Man seems willy-nilly to have become just one more of the establishments which are innately predisposed to crucify any new man.'

Fortunately, this is only part of the truth. Whatever may have been going on at official level, many Christians in every generation remained loyal to their Lord. Fabiola, who founded and endowed the first general hospital for the poor and needy, is a classic example. Wherever Christianity has been carried in the world, there have flowered many expressions of Christian love for the sick and needy such as previously were not only nonexistent, but had never even been imagined.

Two other things remain to be said. We have to thank Christian monastic institutions for the preservation and transcription of many of the classical Greek medical manuscripts, clear proof of the medical concern of Christians in the early Middle Ages. At the same time, the history of official Christianity has been punctuated by reforming movements within the Church, some of them of great importance, which have recaptured the spirit of Jesus and recalled the Church to its social responsibilities. The Franciscans, the Cluniac reformers, the Moravians; women's healing orders, both Protestant and Roman Catholic; in the 19th century, the Salvation Army; and nowadays, the World Council of Churches. These are all important examples. The light lit by Jesus has never gone out.

In Britain, the unknown Christians of the fourth century who cared for the leprosy sufferer were followed by monastic orders to whom the care of the sick was part of their calling. In 1224, Francis of Assisi sent Agnellus of Pisa, one of his close associates, as an emissary to Britain, seeking to recall the Church in Britain to the simple and practical devotion to Jesus, so characteristic of their beloved and saintly leader.

The next two centuries witnessed a remarkable outpouring of charity and benevolence towards the sick poor. Several well-known hospitals date their origins from that period. There are records of 326 homes for leprosy sufferers in Britain and 2,000 in France, almost all of them benefactions by Christians. While strict laws of isolation against leprosy were enforced, they were administered with a degree of compassion which is uniquely Christian and in sharp contrast with what has prevailed in some other parts of the world right into modern times (Richards, 1977).

The Reformation brought little joy to the underprivileged in Britain. Across England, hospitals and charitable institutions established by Christians for the sick, destitute, orphans, the blind and mentally deranged were confiscated by Henry VIII and in many places closed. Trevelyan (1946) puts it thus:

'The disendowment of hospitals was more injurious to the
poor than the disendowment of monasteries. The hospitals had
been founded to help the poor and had been placed where they
were most needed.'

The evangelical revival of the 18th century once again
sparked off a wave of concern for the underprivileged. John
Wesley's insistence on Christian benevolence by precept and
practice is well known. In 1745 he opened the first free dispensary in Britain for the sick poor. His *Primitive Physic* was
published the following year, aiming to give health hints to
people too poor to avail themselves of the services of a family
doctor. Between 1700 and 1825 no fewer than 145 new hospitals
and dispensaries were established in Britain. To quote
Trevelyan (1946) again:

'These were not municipal undertakings – municipal life was
then at its lowest ebb; they were the outcome of individual initiative and of coordinated voluntary effort and subscription.'

In 1786 William Wilberforce wrote in his diary, 'Today I
committed my soul to God and my fellow men.' The ending of
slavery had begun.

At the same time the minds of many Christian people began to
turn towards the needs of people farther afield. Some medical
care for the American Indians and slaves already existed before
1800. There and elsewhere the early social concerns of the new
missionary societies were channelled towards literacy and
education rather than towards medicine, and for this they have
deservedly been castigated. Their choice, however, is not surprising. It is a debatable point just how much, prior to the mid
19th century, Western medicine had to offer to the people of
Asia and Africa which was superior to their own systems.
Furthermore, in an age when little social responsibility was felt
for the bodily needs of the poor, when many could afford only
rare visits to a doctor and in any case life was often short, it was
easy to concentrate on elevating the mind and saving the soul.
Indeed at that time one well-known Society actually recruited
doctors, ordained them and sent them overseas with specific
instructions that they were not to practise medicine. It was the
heavy loss of life among workers overseas and their families,
combined with pressure from abroad, that finally opened the
eyes of British mission boards to the appalling health situations
in many countries. Advances in western medicine created a new
sense of responsibility, and honourable amends were made.

Every decade after the mid-19th century brought with it new discoveries, fresh developments, new branches of medical science. Many of the famous pioneers of that age were Christians who were encouraged in their work by their faith, and whose discoveries are a vital part of the history of modern medicine. By the turn of the century medical workers from Europe had valuable treasure to share with the rest of the world, treasure that increased with every passing year. The trickle of medical workers going overseas soon became a flood.

Developments in medicine in the last few decades have challenged the Christian church as never before in its history to re-examine its role in the world in relation to health. The first stimulus to this has come from the dramatic advances in technology and therapeutics which have given the medical profession a new authority, a new power over life and death, with enormous enhancement of the status of scientific medicine everywhere in the world. The demand is universal that these new facilities, regardless of their cost, should be available at least to those who can afford to pay for them. This demand has important social and ethical consequences.

During the same period a widespread process of secularization has taken place in medical institutions with long-standing Christian traditions as these have been taken over by governments and absorbed into national health services. The process may be inevitable and indeed right, but it easily becomes associated with diminished standards of responsibility and the equation of medical practice with nothing more than the application of scientific knowledge, a concept that ignores a whole range of values intimately concerned with health.

Much study is being given to these issues, especially through institutes of religion and medicine, but none has been more productive than that stimulated by the World Council of Churches from 1964 onwards. This is concerned not so much with non-medical aspects of health as with the foundations of health and medical practice, and is very much concerned with the implications of the teaching and practice of Jesus for the current world situation. The following are among the principles that have received wide acceptance in Christian circles.

1. *All healing is of God* – Healing in the cell, the tissues, healing by scientists, healing by spiritual healers and counselling groups, healing by compassion and love; all are expressions of the one gracious, saving redemptive energy of the loving Creator,

a breaking into human life of the powers of the Kingdom of God and a dethronement of the powers of evil. All healing vocations are thus sacramental.

2. *Health and wholeness* – The technical medical model of health as essentially physical well-being, the absence of detectable disease, is only part of the full picture of health, just as the curing of specific diseases is only a part, and often a minor part, of healing. Health must involve the whole personality, body, mind and spirit in co-ordinated, joyous, serene and purposeful living, in full awareness of the problems of human guilt and meaninglessness and the shadow of death. Faith is at the centre of health.

3. *Health and openness* – Health is not a static wholeness; it has to grow and develop through constant openness of mind and heart to new understanding and new demands. This truth is highlighted when experience in one culture is imposed on another, when health planners seek to introduce scientific medicine into communities unfamiliar with it. Both sides need to learn from and respect one another.

4. *Health and community* – Health is not a private matter. It cannot be enjoyed in isolation, and can only be experienced in its fullness through community relations, community service. The real battle ground for health is not in institutions, but in the community, and in comprehensive health care. This is an objective with broad implications and wide ramifications, but it is nevertheless the only acceptable goal. The corporate fellowship of Christians, the congregation, has an important role to play in healing, by its prayer, its shared insights into the needs of others, its loving and self-sacrificing actions, and its role in recruiting health workers. Experience has already proved that, granted cooperation and dedication, great progress is possible even with limited resources.

5. *Health and responsibility* – The preciousness of every life inexorably demands that privilege must be linked with responsibility. A responsible commitment to promoting world health is mandatory for Christians. This involves the taking of initiatives in promoting health at individual, community and world level, and in championing the cause of the underprivileged and oppressed, working for a just distribution of the resources available.

Here the followers of Jesus are back again where they belong, combating with him the destructive forces that, in a flawed world, operate against the creative and health-giving purposes of God, cooperating with all who seek similar objectives, and doing it from the profoundest theological and philosophical motivation. Never again can the Church ignore its healing role in the world. The Christian Medical Commission of the World Council of Churches is supported by churches around the world and works in close liaison with the World Health Organization, concentrating on the health concerns of underprivileged urban and rural populations.

Modern medicine has had thrust upon it enormous responsibilities in the life of mankind, but when regarded purely as a science, it is not equipped to explore and express these imponderables. In *The Healing Church* Erling Kaiser (1965) says:

'The predicament of modern medicine is that it is only a natural science and not at the same time a science of the spirit *(Geisteswissenschaft)*. It is open to experiment and investigation only, and not to the word of God'.

The wheel has gone full circle. Once again the outlooks of the ancient Greeks are dominant in many minds, concentrating with great skill and penetration on disease, but unable to consider the patient suffering from disease with any comparable understanding and consideration.

Without the penetrating Christian understanding of love of neighbour, not only is medicine less effective than it should be, but the practitioner himself loses that enrichment of his own personality that comes only in the interpersonal relations between himself and his patients that Jesus personified. Christianity will always be a spur to dedicated service, and one that we lose to our enormous impoverishment. The exercise of compassion, the readiness to share creatively in the experience of people in need involves some loss of personal pride, some self-sacrifice, but there comes in its place a richer treasure, a sense of fulfilment, a deep content that are at the heart of health, because one becomes sustained by love.

Early in the 19th century individual doctors began to look with compassionate eyes beyond the shores of their native land to countries where disease was rife, the span of life short and the benefits of scientific medicine were unknown. There was great ignorance in the West concerning the actual conditions prevailing in Africa and Asia, but the mortality among foreigners was shocking enough. Missionary societies becoming established at that time tended at first to see their primary function as concerned with elevating the mind and saving the soul. Pressure from their own workers overseas, backed up by factual accounts of tremendous disease problems, began to open the eyes of Mission Boards to the most obvious spheres of Christian service which were awaiting them overseas on a global scale. The era of medical missions had begun.

Between 1850 and 1950 at least 1500 doctors and as many nursing sisters left the shores of Britain to offer their skill, dedication and personal experience to the underdeveloped world. Many scarcely knew what they were going to. Few realized on their departure that it would fall to their lot to introduce scientific medicine over wide tracts of land where it was hitherto unknown, and be responsible for the development of medical services that have become a vital part of national life in country after country, but so it was. Many made the supreme sacrifice. Many suffered extraordinary privations; not a few had to return, broken in health, overwhelmed by the mass of human need around them against which they were lonely pioneers. Some had to face suspicion and misunderstanding, regarded as interfering in the status quo that reactionary forces wanted to preserve. Today almost everywhere they are thought of with gratitude, and in many cases with affection, the builders of modern medicine.

They are together one of the most noble groups in the entire history of medicine, their exploits largely forgotten, and indeed often grossly misunderstood and even maligned. This book seeks to tell the story of at least some of them, When Dr Porter Smith, the first Western and missionary doctor to central China opened the first small hospital in the great city of Hankow, he had an inscription painted over the entrance, which, translated, read as follows:

Hospital of Universal Love

This was an extraordinary idea to the people who read it, but those few words epitomize the meaning and purpose of the whole vast Christian medical enterprise.

References
1. Ross, Sir James (1952) *The National Health Service in Britain* Oxford University Press.
2. Garlick, Phyllis L. (1952) *Man's Search for Health* London: The Highway Press.
3. Verney, Stephen (1976) *Into the New Age* London: William Collins.
4. Taylor, John V. (1972) *The Go-Between God* London SCM Press Ltd.
5. Kung, Hans (1977) *On Being a Christian* London: William Collins.
6. Richards, Peter (1977) *The Medieval Leper* D.S. Brewer, Roman and Littlefield.
7. Trevelyan, G.M. (1946) *English Social History* Second Edition, London, Longmans, Green & Co.
8. World Council of Churches (1965), *The Healing Church* Geneva.
9. Kaiser, Erling (1965) 'Medicine and Modern Philosophy: an Introduction', *In The Healing Church* Geneva: World Council of Churches.

CHAPTER 2

THE CHALLENGE AND FASCINATION OF TROPICAL MEDICINE

W.A.R. Thomson

The unknown has intrigued mankind from time immemorial. It has been the stimulus that has led his searching mind to explore all the mysteries of life as they have slowly revealed themselves to him – whether for good or ill. At times the mysteries unveiled may have been beyond the comprehension of the human mind, but the Christian could always console himself with the thought as expressed by J. Russell Lowell in *The Present Crisis:* 'Behind the dim unknown, Standeth God within the shadow, keeping watch above his own.'

Or, more eloquently, in the Words of Minnie Louise Haskins in *God Knows* as quoted by King George VI in perhaps the most memorable of all the Royal Christmas Broadcasts, that of 1939:
'And I said to the man who stood at the gate of the year: "Give me a light that I may tread safely into the unknown". And he replied: "Go out into the darkness and put your hand into the hand of God. That shall be to you better than light and safer than a known way" '.

And so, hand in hand with the Almighty, those missionaries of old trod into the unknown. They were, of course, following in the footsteps of the ancient Phoenicians who, it is said, circumnavigated Africa in the 6th century BC under the orders of Pharaoh Necho II. The evidence here may be somewhat equivocal, but there seems to be little doubt that the Carthaginians had sailed down at least part of the West African coast in the 4th century BC.

A millenium later we are in the realms of hard fact, with Prince Henry establishing the first European settlement in Africa since Roman times. Among the reasons for these pioneer exploratory journeys were 'the conversion of the pagans to Christianity, the discovery of a sea route to India, the search for the legendary Prester John who was said to reign over a Christian kingdom in the heart of Africa' (Hibbert, 1982). Before the end of

17

the 15th century Vasco da Gama had set out on his journey round
the Cape of Good Hope which was to open up India for the ever-
adventurous citizens of this island home of ours.

The sea has ever had an appeal for British people, exemplified by that apparently inveterate landlubber, William Cobbett
(1763-1835) who, on first seeing the sea as a boy, exclaimed:
'No sooner did I see it than I wished to be a sailor'. By this time
the British were well settled in India; whether for good or ill was
still an open question as poignantly epitomized by Roy Porter
(1982):

'In the second half of the 18th century, British India offered a
pukka England where nabobs – officials of the East India
Company – could enact their plundering fantasies before a cap-
tive audience of natives: young William Hicky, in London a
ne'er-do-well, had 63 servants as an East India Company clerk in
Calcutta. Successful nabobs could hope to bring back a couple of
hundred thousand pounds with them (though up to two-thirds
perished through tropical diseases).'

When Edmund Burke indicted Warren Hastings for misrule
in India in 1783, he complained: 'England has created no
churches, no hospitals, no palaces, no schools, England has built
no bridges, made no highways, cut no navigations, dug out no
reservoirs.' But native society was not spared much longer. By
the early 19th century it was succumbing to the white man's
mission, to Evangelicals and utilitarians. 'Europeans lord it over
natives with a high hand', wrote Byron's friend Edward
Trelawney about India, 'every outrage may be committed with
impunity.'

Simultaneously Africa was attracting the attention of the
adventurous and the commercially minded British citizens. In
1788 was formed the African Association, the progenitor of the
Royal Geographical Society. 'Their work', Hibbert (1982)
records, 'would be in the national interest. "Gold is there so
plentiful", a member of the Association's committee wrote of
Timbuktu, "as to adorn even the slaves . . . If we could get our
manufacturers into the country we should have gold enough".
The Association's work would also be in the interests of learning
and "in the pursuits of these advantages", Beaufoy emphasized,
benefits would at the same time be "imparted to natives hitherto
consigned to hapless barbarism and uniform contempt".'

One of the sequels of this uprising of interest in the 'dark
Continent' was the Niger expedition of 1832-34 organized by
the African Inland Commercial Company primarily as 'an

ambitious trading expedition', but also in the hope that 'it would help to strike a blow at the slave trade and to import "tracts of Christianity" to peoples abandoned to paganism'.

The national conscience may at last have been awakening to the blight cast upon it by the slave trade, but it was still to take an unconscionable time abolishing its ravages. British slave traders transported 1½ million Africans during the 18th century, and, in spite of the Somersett ruling of 1774, the rights to own Negro slaves in England remained practically unaffected throughout the century. Typical of the trade at its height was the fact that in the 1710s and 1720s over a hundred ships were leaving Bristol every year on the slave trade, with a capacity of around 30,000 slaves.

Equally apposite are the views of Sir Rider Haggard:

'It was the country squires of Britain and their sons who were the administrators of Victoria's expanding empire. Their attitudes born of their inherited position as benevolent rural despots determined the methodology of colonial government . . . Their traditionally paternal treatment of their labourers and servants was easily extended to subjugated races; their enthusiastic interest in their own rural traditions and heritage was transferred to the indigenous cultures of the lands they colonized; their unswerving belief in the natural justice of the legal system they administered at home as magistrates, barristers and judges allowed them to enforce it unquestioningly on the people they governed, and the moral superiority derived from their privileged position in the Established Church encouraged their disdain of the infidel and heathen savage, while making them suspicious of the zeal of evangelical missionaries' (Higgins, 1982).

So far as China is concerned, the picture is a very different one. At a relatively early stage in what might be described as modern history, its western frontiers were penetrated. Prominent among these early pioneers is to be found the name of Marco Polo, though modern historical research casts doubt on whether he ever visited China at all. As Craig Clunas (1982), of the Far Eastern Department of the Victoria and Albert Museum, has commented:

'Marco Polo's fame has unjustly eclipsed that of all other medieval European travellers to East Asia. These included missionaries, papal envoys, craftsmen and merchants. The Christian gravestones excavated in China in recent years bear witness of their presence'.

Notable among these were the Jesuits who, by virtue of their traditional skill as diplomats, were able to maintain contact, though at times tenuously, with the governors and rulers of a country that was for long to remain an enigma to the West. The final breakthrough did not take place until the 19th century when, in spite of their strong evangelism, the Protestant missionary societies of the West adopted the Jesuit motto of the end justifying the means, by penetrating the Celestial Empire on the crest of the despicable Opium Wars.

Such then is the background to the glorious epoch of Christian missions initiated around the turn of the 18th century. It epitomizes the fascination – often literally fatal – that the mysterious East had for the inhabitants of this island home of ours – as well as others. Primarily – some might say primitively – it was the call of the sea, adventure, the unknown. Superimposed on this – and all too often prostituted to selfish gain – was the age-old search for gold, so long regarded as the elixir of life. Merchants and entrepreneurs, soldiers and sailors, explorers and diplomats, scientists and doctors – a motley, and often goodly (and godly) crowd – set out to explore the great unknown.

Notable among these were those men and women of God who answered the call of their Maker: 'Go ye into all the world, and preach the gospel to every creature' (Mk. 16.15). Initially they were evangelists, ordained or not, sent out with the aim of winning souls for Christ. Only gradually was it accepted that the doctor could be a man of God as well as the ordinand. Indeed it was not until the formation, in 1841, under the inspiration of Dr Peter Parker, of the Edinburgh Association for Sending Medical Aid to Foreign Countries (two years later to become the Edinburgh Medical Missionary Society), the first medical missionary society in the British Isles, that missionary societies began to realize that the beloved physician was an integral part of the Christian ethic.

From this time flowed the great company of doctors and nurses who left their homelands in Western Europe and America to serve the sick and needy. They include some 1500 doctors, over 200 of them women, and an even larger number of nurses, who went overseas from the West for missionary service between 1850 and 1950. Together this 'medical partnership in the Church overseas', as Phyllis Garlick (1952) aptly describes it, in the course of a year copes with around one million inpatients and 23 million outpatients. In the 1840s, by contrast, according to Phyllis Garlick, there were only 40 medical missionaries at work in the whole world: 26 from USA, 12 from Britain, one from France and one from the Near East.

Two typical examples of the state of affairs so far as personnel is concerned may be quoted. According to the *World Mission Atlas* of 1925 there were then 66 nursing training schools and 1032 nurses. Figures issued by the London Missionary Society in 1923 show that from 1796 to 1923 the Society's Register lists 1482 missionaries (1159 men and 323 women). Of the men, 103 were doctors, while of the women, 17 were doctors and 44 were nurses. Numbered chronologically, No 13 in the Register is John A. Gilham, who was appointed as a surgeon to the South Seas in 1796.

In passing it is of interest to note that the name of David Livingstone does not appear in the Register. Apparently the Society never forgave him for resigning before setting out on his Zambesi expedition. Yet he stands out as a classical example of the many attractions that the tropics had for a Christian doctor, as admirably epitomized by Michael Gelfand in *Livingstone The Doctor* (1957).

'. . . He had received a letter from the Society clearly stating that it was unable to undertake projects that might involve the risk of those participating of malaria and death from the bite of the tsetse fly, both of which might prove unsurmountable obstacles. The Society would have to move cautiously in such untried, remote and difficult fields of labour. Livingstone suspected that in these circumstances the Society was more than likely to transfer him to some other field away from the temptation of Central African exploration and his plans for this part of Africa would come to nothing. Rather than allow this to happen he decided to dissolve his connection with the Society and continue with his project as a private individual . . .'

'Although he was severing his connection with the Society his missionary zeal was by no means abated. He still hoped through his travels to open Central Africa to missionary influence. He outlined his aims in his letter to Sir Thomas Maclear the Cape Town astronomer, and one of his most loyal supporters, written on the 17th August, 1856: "If I had opportunity, I might do something by investigation of fever, 31 attacks of which I've had myself – for the commerce of Africa whose future in the way of raw materials I conceive to be of immense importance to England – and to the inhabitants both white and black by diffusing a knowledge of Christ's Gospel, the best antidote for the wars of the world".'

'. . . The country was so stirred by his mission that his friends, University bodies and the Government itself, saw fit to elaborate

a plan by which something positive could be achieved to uplift
the heathen of Central Africa, to assist in spreading the Christian
Faith and last but not least, to stamp out the slave trade. No doubt
the Government was influenced by Livingstone's reports of a
territory possessed of possibilities for trade and commerce,
although at the time England had neither the wish not the intention of annexing so vast and unhealthy a part of the world'.

So important is this association between Christian missions –
and particularly medical missions – and the opening of Africa
that it is of more than passing interest to quote yet another
example of how persisting was this tradition initiated by one of
the leading characters in the history of medical missions.
V. L. Cameron, a clergyman's son and naval officer, was the first
European to cross the African Continent from East to West,
starting off in Zanzibar in charge of the expedition to find
Livingstone. On his return to London, according to Hibbert
(1982), he was received

'as an explorer whose name was worthy to be ranked with
Livingstone . . . He can be considered a leading expert on African
affairs and an influential advocate of Livingstone's view that
"commercial enterprise and missionary effort" must do their best
to assist each other. "Wherever commerce finds its way", he
maintained, "there missionaries will follow, and wherever missionaries prove that white men can live and travel, there trade is
certain to be established".'

To which Hibbert adds the interesting epilogue.

'Before 1880 their [European] colonial possessions had been
few and were nearly all limited to coastal regions. A few years
later national rivalries, the need for African raw materials for
European industries, and genuine belief in the virtues of bringing
civilization and Christianity to the backward and heathen, had
brought about the scramble for Africa'.

Wanderlust may not have been responsible for many medical
missionaries accepting the call of the wild, but undoubtedly it
was a call that played at least a part in many cases, combined
with the desire to serve the sick and to do something to help to
conquer the diseases that ravaged the tropics, such as malaria,
yellow fever and sleeping sickness and the like. It was a call
more than tinged with danger, a factor enhancing for many the
urgency of the call, at least where doctors were concerned, but
not necessarily their ecclesiastical colleagues, as illustrated by
the following instructions of the American Board of Missions to
a missionary being sent to West Africa in 1833.

'Let it be remembered that the sacrifices made by you and your friends, the privations and hardships to which you will be subjected, and the dangers which you will have to encounter, and which appear so formidable to many, are extraordinary only in the history of missions. In the history of Commerce and of Science, they are common and familiar scenes . . . Commerce had no difficulty in procuring her missionaries for any portion of the earth; and even now they are "going forth into all the world" . . . It is lamentable that the Church should make so much of personal sacrifice endured for the glory of Christ and the salvation of men, when the World accounts them so little endured for the sake of wealth and fame'.

To the medical missionary this was a challenge to his medical knowledge to do what he could to alleviate the morbidity and mortality of these killing diseases. To him disease was an integral part of life and its alleviation his purpose in life. The mere fact that he might himself fall victim to it was no more than a passing consideration – if even that. And one cannot help wondering, incidentally, to what extent this reaction to disease enhanced the defence mechanisms of his body and gave him a degree of protection. It would be interesting to know the relative morbidity and mortality of medical and non-medical missionaries in West Africa in those early days. But, whatever the findings, few, if any, would deny that faith played a part in maintaining life and health in these pioneering missionaries.

Not the least significance of this increasing interest in medical missions shown by doctors is the part it played in persuading the missionary societies that body could be neglected no more than soul. It was a long struggle as exemplified by the fact that, in the words of Phyllis Garlick (1952),

'the Church Missionary Society, which was founded in 1799 and from which was to develop one of the largest medical missionary organizations in the world, let nearly a century pass before it gave official recognition to medical missions as an established part of its work'.

Typical of the Society's almost childish reaction to medical missionaries who had not been 'redeemed' by ordination is the following extract from the official history of the Society.

'The CMS Annual Report of 1847-1848 reported the sailing of Mr Ashwood in 1847 as the first "Medical Adviser to the Mission", and described him as "an experienced surgeon who has gone out not only to afford the benefits of his professional advice and attendance to the Mission families, but also to give elementary instruction to some of the Natives on the theory and practice of Medicine." He was given no missionary training, and does not seem to have been regarded even as a catechist. When he died in Freetown in April 1850, only brief mention was made of the bare fact in a couple of lines in the Annual Report; whereas a clerical missionary of similar seniority, who died a few months later, was eulogized in several hundred words!'

The Baptist Missionary Society, probably the diehards in this matter, were even slower to change. In the centenary history of the Society there are few references to medical work, and nearly all of them show that medicine was still regarded as a subsidiary tool. When Dr Vincent Thomas offered his services to the Society in 1894, there was not a single male doctor on the Society's staff in India, and only one woman doctor, Dr Ellen Farrer, on the staff of the Baptist Zenana Mission.

The Roman Catholic Church was even more dilatory in admitting the medical missionary to the full membership of Christ's mission to evangelize the world. For example, differentiating between what he described as the Protestant concept of the 'medical missionary' and the Roman Catholic concept of the 'mission doctor', Floyd Keeler (1925) wrote:

'The one is looked upon as a real missionary – one called to aid the salvation of souls through the exercise of his professional skill, the other as a mere lay member of a mission staff, one engaged as any other efficient labourer is engaged to render a certain service for a stipulated remuneration'.

In reviewing Keeler's book, a United States Roman Catholic writer commented:

'Strange to say the truth that man needs assistance in mind and body as well as in soul seems to have been more clearly brought out in practice in Protestant missions than by our own. Among them the medical missionary is given a place of prominence; with us he has hitherto been a negligible quantity'.

As Phyllis Garlick points out, however: 'In recent years there has been a notable advance in Catholic medical mission work; it has received encouragement from Rome and support from Ireland and the United States. A number of doctors have entered religious orders and there has been a development of midwifery nursing among nuns'.

Among the many attractions that might finally be added to those of tropical medicine for the medical missionary is that of research. A classical example is Sir Patrick Manson who originally went out to China in 1865 at the age of 21 to assist an overworked missionary in Amoy. Here he came in contact for the first time with filariasis, which seized upon his imagination and led in due course to his momentous discovery that the mosquito

was the carrier of the causative parasite, thus laying the foundation for his reputation as the Father of tropical medicine. Many
other names could be added to the honourable list of medical
missionaries, such as Sir Clement Chesterman in trypanosomiasis and Dr Robert Cochrane in leprosy, who, by satisfying
their professional curiosity in tropical medicine, made outstanding contributions to the service of the Church to suffering
humanity.

As Phyllis Garlick (1952) has pointed out:

'Any fair-minded study of the progress of medicine must
recognize, as a matter of historical fact, that the credit for introducing the benefits of western medical science to Africa and Asia
belongs to the religious organizations of Europe and America . . .
Within the span of little more than half a century, organized
medical missions have led the way in a creative achievement –
not only in the life of the Church, but in the development of
western medicine in Africa and the East. Among primitive and
eastern peoples, ignorant of the laws of health and hygiene, and
subject to a crushing burden of preventable suffering endured
with fear or fatalism, medical missionaries have sought to establish modern medical and surgical practice as an expression of
Christian love in action. In teeming centres of oriental life, they
have combated with scientific weapons the terrible scourge of
epidemic disease'.

Such was, and is, the fundamental challenge and fascination
of tropical medicine for those members of the medical and
nursing professions who were also members of the Church of
Christ. It was a challenge to their professional skill and to their
Christian faith, and the results are to be seen in the pages of this
book, which record the outstanding contributions that these
modern successors of 'Luke, the beloved physician' (Col. 4.14)
have made to the physical, mental and spiritual welfare of so
many of their fellow beings scattered over the continents of the
world.

References

Clunas, Craig. 1982. *The Times*, April 14.
Garlick, Phyllis. 1952. *Man's Search for Health*. London: The
    Highway Press.
Gelfand, Michael. 1957. *Livingstone The Doctor*. Oxford:
    Blackwell.
Hibbert, Christopher. 1982. *Africa Explored*. London: Allen Lane.
Higgins, D.S. 1981. *Rider Haggard: The Great Storyteller*. London:
    Cassell.

Keeler, Floyd. 1925. *Catholic Medical Missions*. New York: Macmillan.
Porter, Roy. 1982. *English Society in The Eighteenth Century*. Harmondsworth: Penguin Books.

CHAPTER 3

FIRST STEPS IN HEALTH

Harry Williams

The contribution made by Christians to world health knows neither geographical bounds nor limitations of race or sex. Rich and poor, the educated and unschooled, and all races figure in it. As disease and calamity are no respecters of persons, neither is God. The Christian has no monopoly of love for his brethren, but he has usually been in the van in the fight against human misery. The story will take us to city slums, to lonely mountain villages and to isolated Pacific islands, but also into the operating theatres of leading hospitals and laboratories in all parts of the world. The story goes back to Peter and John, in the 1st century AD, in fact to days when the Galilean prophet, Jesus, was a lively memory in Palestine. Christ was their life, and their calling was to be his life in society. Of what that life was like they had vivid memories, and in hindsight they saw its purpose and principles more clearly. In simple terms, it could be said that he went about doing good, and this doing good had included many happenings that transcended normal experience and could only be termed miracles. These had included numerous acts of healing. With a strange new boldness, the disciples remembered his promise that these and greater miracles would be theirs in the power of the Holy Spirit. The cripple begging at the gate of Jerusalem's Temple was cured – the first recorded instance of healing by Christian compassion. What inspired the desire and gave the ability to help a crippled beggar in this way?

People in their thousands came from town and village alike to enjoy the assurance of his teaching about God and to seek mental and physical healing. The two aspects of Jesus' mission were indivisible; both were to reveal the true nature of God and particularly his relation with men. Christ did not use his healing miracles only as evidence of his divinity. In fact he was often at pains to prevent the enthusiasm of his patients detracting from the impact of his teaching. 'Tell no man . . .' (Lk. 5.14) is his injunction on a number of occasions. He did, however, point to the total programme as authenticating his claim to be the Messiah.

When from prison, John the Baptist expressed some doubt and asked, through his emissaries, 'Are you the Christ or look we for another?' (Mt. 11.3), Christ's answer was: 'Go and shew John those things which you hear and see; the blind receive their sight, and the lame walk, the lepers are cleansed, and the deaf hear' (Mt. 11.4,5). His message was that the kingdom of heaven had come. The healing miracles were the signs of the new age, to be expected in the new order that Christ initiated. Understood in this way, Christ's acts of healing were natural to him. When he sent his disciples out in pairs, he said: 'As you go, preach, saying, the kingdom of heaven is at hand. Heal the sick, cleanse the lepers . . .' (Mt. 10.7,8).

That those who followed him were to show compassion to all in need is clear in Christ's story of the man robbed and assaulted on the lonely road from Jerusalem to Jericho. (Lk. 10.25-37). The Good Samaritan has a lesson so clear that every age and every race has grasped it. The hero of that tale reacted immediately and at personal inconvenience and expense, and he used the best medical knowledge available.

Concepts of disease current then are still held by some today:

1. That disease and disability are divine punishment for sin committed by the sufferer. The ancient book of Job wrestled with this problem.
2. That the parents' sin is visited upon innocent children, grandchildren and even great-grandchildren.

Modern medicine can accept the fact that some forms of illness are the result of a person's ignorance, folly or bad habits. It would even see in congenital syphilis the child paying for the parent's promiscuity. But there is no acceptance of a divine judgement acting personally. Where did Christ stand? John records the incident of the congenitally blind man brought to Christ by his parents. As so often in the Gospel narrative, there was no privacy of the consulting-room. There were hostile on-lookers, intent on finding their own theology in each incident. 'Master, who did sin,' they asked, 'this man, or his parents, that he was born blind?' (Jn. 9.2). Christ rejected the whole concept of God issuing rewards and punishments by direct physical inter-vention. 'Neither has this man sinned, nor his parents' was his answer, 'but' (he added as a rider that lies at the heart of his medical programme) 'that the works of God should be made manifest in him' (Jn. 9.3). His final comment is the raison d'être for medical missionaries. On occasion he associated infirmity with the devil. He denied explicitly that suffering is the will of God. This feature is seen in most of his healing acts – an evident love for the person on Christ's part, and usually a genuine response of trust and faith on the part of the patient. The woman who had repeated haemorrhages illustrates this point well (Lk. 8.48).

The acts of healing cover a wide spectrum of disease, physical and mental, but there are certain common features in Christ's response to all those he healed.

1. His reaction was always emotional. He was 'filled with compassion' is the reporter's constant comment. Often he specifically underlined the truth that his reaction is God's reaction to human suffering. He was expressing a divine imperative.

2. He made it clear that he was not courting popularity – sugaring the pill of his ethical teaching. One telling example is that of people with leprosy (Lk.5.12-15; 17.11-19).

3. His cures were miracles: i.e. they were beyond scientific explanation then and even now. Some could be understood by any 20th century doctor. Take, for example, the moving story of a paraplegic's friends, so determined to get Christ's assistance that they remove the tiles and lower his mattress under the Teacher's nose. Here Jews related the tragic impotence to the patient's guilt and, in identifying this and pronouncing divine forgiveness, the man was liberated, rose from his bed and walked. Hysterical palsies do react in this way. The cures of some epileptics could have a similar explanation.

4. These miracles show Christ as a fine diagnostician: John says cryptically that 'he knew what was in men'. It also exemplifies Christ's holistic concept of health. A rightness of spirit is as vital as rightness of mind and body. That all three interrelate is the basis of modern concepts of psychosomatic medicine. Weatherhead (1964) comments that Jesus Christ had more in common with a modern surgeon than a modern faith healer, for Christ always knew the nature of the patient's trouble and why it had befallen him, and he varied his techniques accordingly.

Of all these common features, the first is the most important; in the birth of the Christian church, a new dynamic entered the doctor's world; it was compassion.

Here is how a modern theologian puts it:

'More important than number and extent of the cures, expulsions of devils and wonderful deeds, is the fact that Jesus turns with sympathy and compassion to all those to whom no one else turns; the weak, sick and the social rejects. People were always glad to pass these by. Weaklings and invalids are burdensome. Everyone keeps his distance from "lepers" and "the possessed" . . .

'Jesus does not turn away from any of these. He rejects none of them. He does not treat the sick as sinners, but draws them to Himself to cure them. "Clear the way for the strong, the healthy, the young"; these are not the words of Jesus. He has no cult of health, youth and achievement. He loves them all, as they are, and so is able to help them; to the sick in body and soul he gives hope, new life, confidence in the future. And are not all these actions – even though they do not infringe any law of nature – very unusual, extraordinary, astonishing, marvellous and wonderful?' (Kung, 1977).

Compassion has flowered wherever the Gospel has been accepted. It has influenced those with medical training, but in particular it has involved the whole community, including administrators and teachers. But the illiterate and poor who have meekly inherited the earth have had their part too. Compassion is a must for every Christian, and the care of the sick an authentic part of the Church's work in all the world. This struck first the pagan Romans. Neill (1980) quotes the Emperor Julian (332-363)

'Atheism (i.e. Christian faith) has been specially advanced through the loving service rendered to strangers, and through their care of their burial of the dead. It is a scandal that there is not a single Jew who is a beggar, and that the godless Galileans care not only for their own poor but for ours as well; while those who belong to us look in vain for the help that we should render them'. (Neill, 1980).

The history of the Church prior to Constantine's edict of toleration is not confined to stories of martyrs but includes accounts of Christian social work.

'The spirit of love and pity in the church of the first four centuries is equal to the courage and endurance of the martyrs . . . The record of practical philanthropy and relief of distress is a very remarkable one. Generous help was given to travellers and those thrown out of work, whether for conscience's sake or through economic causes and churches were labour unions finding work for those who needed it.' (Schiff, 1960).

The fact that many Christians were thrown into jail meant

that visiting in prisons became a work of mercy and the social work of widows as described in the New Testament led to the foundation of Orders of Deaconesses.

It was particularly in the treatment of the sick that Christians shone, and help was not confined to the sect. In the years when the Gospels were written and the canon of the New Testament took shape, many miracles were recorded. The Christian community – the church in the house – had responsibility for the health of its members. Thus James writes: 'Is any sick among you? Let him call for the elders of the church; and let them pray over him, anointing him with oil in the name of the Lord; And the prayer of faith shall save the sick . . .' (Jas. 5.14-15). Paul explained that the one Spirit was active in human affairs in many ways: 'In each of us the Spirit is manifested in one particular way, for some useful purpose . . . one man through the Spirit has the gift of wise speech . . . another gifts of healing' (1 Cor. 12.7-9 NEB).

From the writings of Tertullian (AD 155-230) we learn that through the Christian communities many attested cases of healing were to be found covering a wide range of physical and mental disease. The methods used were holy anointing and prayer.

The Greek fathers of medicine from Hippocrates onwards set up their hospitals, comparable to modern nursing homes, catering for paying patients and providing a lucrative business for the physician (Weatherhead, 1968). The early Christian hospitals provided not so much a system of medicine, as careful nursing based on the ideal expressed by Christ: that service given to a needy man was a service given to him. This nursing care was probably given in the home initially, but there are records of specific institutions created for such a purpose. The very name 'hospital' reminds us that, primarily, hospitality was given to travellers and particularly the infirm. It is noteworthy that such expressions of Christian practice were found when epidemics such as plague and cholera decimated communities. Here is a report from Alexandria in AD 259.

'Plague is raging in the city of Alexandria. Most of those who have the means to do so have left, but some remain.' Bishop Dionysius wrote:

'Most of our brethren did not spare themselves and held together in the closest love of their neighbour. They were not afraid to visit the sick, to look after their need, to take care of them for Christ's sake and to die joyfully with them . . . Many of them

lost their own lives after restoring others to health, thus taking
death upon themselves . . . in this way some of the noblest of our
brethren died . . . some presbyters, deacons, and highly esteemed
lay people . . . but the heathen did exactly the opposite. They cast
out any people who began to be too ill, threw the sick, half dead,
into the streets and left the dead unburied.'

A measure of specialization developed even in the first century, and as medical science slowly grew through the next
thousand years its exponents were moulded in a society based
on Christian teaching and values. Nowhere was this more true
than in the development of monasticism after the fall of Rome
and the disintegration of its empire which Christian teaching
had permeated. Many a monastery had its infirmary, and its
library would likely contain medical manuscripts. Many developed herb gardens from which infusions and tinctures were
made.

The greatest advance in the art of nursing the sick took place
in the monasteries. In the Roman tradition, the monastic orders
were pioneers in the provision of good water supply, effective
sanitation and sound nutritional standards. Above all, however,
they provided not only loving care, but peace and quiet.
To generations nurtured in the Christian faith, the distant sound
of Gregorian chants from the abbey church must have been a
balm to the sick in the infirmary. The great of the land retreated
to them when themselves sick or dying. Particularly in orders for
women the art of nursing has been practised to the present time,
the nuns imbibing new ideas and methods as medical science
has advanced. In Roman Catholic countries, famous hospitals
are still provided with nursing staff in this way.

Notable characters people this story. St Francis had no medical knowledge. To express a Christian solidarity with the sufferers he ignored the possibility of contagion, and his example
led to the establishment of leprosaria all over Europe. Francis
did not contract the disease, but his example to fellow Christians
did prove contagious. 'Dominus conduxit me inter leprosos et
feci misericordiam cum illes' (the Lord led me among those who
had leprosy and I suffered with them), he wrote.

'The words of St Francis provide the key to the extraordinary
heroism and dedication with which it has inspired others. The
things which divide one group of Christians from another have
no meaning here, for the same motivating power in Catholic and
Protestant alike issues in qualities of service common to them
all' (Richards, 1971).

When St Francis embraced his first leprous sufferer, Europeans had for nearly two centuries been in contact with the Middle East through pilgrimages and crusades. To the reservoir of leprosy already in Europe, was added a stream of fresh cases contracted in the Holy Land. It was the period when Europe became most conscious of leprosy and the hospital that Francis built on the plain below Assisi was one of many built and maintained by Christians. In England the first Norman Archbishop of Canterbury, Lanfranc, had built a hospital near his cathedral even earlier than Francis. Other early institutions were at St Leonards, near Northampton and at Sherburn in Durham. All were staffed by monks.

Through the long line of Christian writers from Tertullian at the end of the 2nd century, Jerome, Ambrose and Augustine and up to Bede in Northumbria at the beginning of the 8th century, the story of healing continued, associated with holy oil and the laying on of hands. The Church, however, was losing its broad understanding of healing using all knowledge available; this attitude culminated with Pope Innocent III in 1215 condemning priests who practised surgery. Scientific enquiry was banned until the Renaissance and the Reformation brought theology and medicine into the open again.

With the Reformation, particularly in Britain after the dissolution of the monasteries under Henry VIII, the study of medicine and theology developed separately, but for centuries the influence of the Christian Church remained strong in moulding society. Unfortunately, with the dissolution of the monasteries some of the established hospitals (St Bartholomew's and St Thomas's in London) lost most of their endowments. The wave of concern for the sick poor, particularly in London in the early 18th century, is an example of the Church's continuing stimulus to physicians: the chain of voluntary hospitals which resulted providing the setting for medical education which has persisted into the 20th century.

As the political pre-occupation of the Reformation waned, the era of exploration and European colonization led to a rediscovery of Christ's command to his disciples, 'Go into all the world and preach the Gospel to every creature'. This resulted in missionary endeavour first by Jesuits, notably in the person of Francis Xavier, and much later by Protestant missionary societies. With this development, a sense of a specifically Christian medical responsibility for all the world slowly emerged.

Initially, the theologically-minded leaders of missionary societies did not encourage such medical endeavours but the compassion of evangelists (mostly lay, in medical terms) led to notable
service to the sick. In 1680 a slave ship from West Africa came
into the Port of Cartagena to discharge its tragic cargo – hungry,
naked, distracted with fear and apprehension, and some sick
and near death. No-one thought anything of it, but on the quay
there was one man, Peter Claver, who for 38 years met such ships
and brought a spark of humanity into a revolting scene, as, with
clothing and medicine, a word of comfort and a touch of pity, he
put himself on the side of the slaves.

The world that was being opened up by European exploration
and colonization impressed the newcomers in two ways. There
was a vast need for the medical knowledge and compassionate
care that they had in their homelands, but they were also confronted by cultures more ancient than their own, containing
knowledge of disease, drugs and surgery worth investigating.
With these new and intimate contacts with alien cultures, a missionary humble enough to learn from what was commonly considered to be more primitive concepts of disease and treatment,
could make discoveries that would enrich the West. The Jesuits
learned of quinine in Macao and S. America. In Nigeria,
Methodists and Anglicans found that most fractures were dealt
with satisfactorily by village healers; India's Ayurvedic pharmacopoeia was found to contain effective herbal remedies, however empirical the dosage might be. Opium, gentian, capsicum,
castor oil and a dozen more had long been imported from Asia,
but rauwolfia was to open a new chapter in the treatment of
hypertension.

These products enriched the pharmacopoeia, but there was
little to cast light on the basic sciences of anatomy and physiology. A little lore from the golden era of Indian Buddhism remained as craft secrets. Susruta's surgery was rediscovered in
the rhinoplasty performed by the potter caste, but there were few
medically qualified missionaries in the first centuries of world
evangelization sparked by the Reformation. The lay missionaries
in Asia, Africa and South America were confronted by appalling
medical needs. The precariousness of life in many parts of the
world before the advent of modern medicine is well brought out
by simple population surveys which are available from various
places; even as late as 1938, in Eastern Nigeria, only about one
child in four reached adult life (Davey, 1964).

One of the earliest records of a response to human need in the
Third World comes from the story of the Society for the Propagation of the Gospel in the West Indies. General Codrington, who
died in 1770, left his estates in Barbados to the Society with 'the
intent that the estates be maintained by at least 300 negroes
supplied with professors and scholars . . . under the vow of
poverty and chastity and obedience who shall be obliged to
study and practise phisick and chirurgery as well as divinity'.
In the event the Rev. Joseph Holt, who appears to have been a
converted alcoholic from the colony of Virginia, was appointed,
his commission 'including care of the sick and maimed negroes
and servants'. By 1818 this dispensary had become a hospital,
with an apothecary and a nurse, and broke new ground by
opening a creche for the children of working mothers. The
mothers 'were examined and excused from work before and after
childbirth', and given a supply of linen for each baby. Is an early
attempt to reduce neonatal mortality indicated in the added
words 'and the present of a dollar when it is a month old'?
(Thomson, 1951).

In Sierra Leone in 1826 a CMS missionary, Trimmell, who
had been a doctor before ordination, does not appear to have
practised medicine. Three years later, however, Henry Graham,
(who had been an apprentice to Dr Whiting), was appointed for
educational work but reported 'my labours in my medical capacity . . . have taken up so much of my time, that very little of it
has been given to the schools'. In the same territory in 1923 the
wife of the missionary at Segbwema began to treat patients on
the verandah of her house, and from this a good hospital was to
develop.

Help was to come from Africa's own sons, uprooted by
slavery. The Church of Scotland began missionary work in
Jamaica in 1800, and soon Jamaicans were organizing their own
missionary outreach to Calabar. The Rev. Hope Waddell was
despatched with a catechist, a teacher, a carpenter – and a
dispenser.

Before British colonization began in New Zealand, the CMS
had opened missionary work in the Bay of Islands of the North
Island. The Home Committee commended to William Williams
the need 'to make yourself well acquainted with the proper
method of treating all the ordinary diseases.' Twelve years later,
Williams reported: 'According to our ability we have administered the medicine required . . . following the instructions of

the Rev Williams and by paying attention to Thomas's *Guide to Health.* Some very stubborn cases have been completely cured . . . we have long thought it desirable to have a small medical chest and some surgical instruments which might be used as occasion required.' In 1802 Mr Yate wrote: 'Had seventeen applications this morning to visit the sick. I attended personally on eleven of them and sent medicine to the others'.

In India, from the CMS mission station at Tinnivelli, Rhenius wrote in his journal in 1834: 'It is again most gratifying to see our catechists diligently employed in administering medicine to the sick of whatever description.' Farther south at the CMS mission station at Dohnavur, Mrs Winckler was treating the sick in 1831: 'The Lord hath hitherto blessed our means though they were very simple – either a purgative or an absorbent medicine'. She adds: 'This the people look on as nearly miraculous'. And at Satankollan in the same district of Tinnivelli in 1908 it was Mr Ross, primarily concerned with education, who was employing the little knowledge he had in medicine for the relief of many sick persons who asked him for help.

Village dispensaries were opened by CMS and SPG missionaries in other parts of India. It was Victorian individualism and self-help at its best, but it lacked continuity. From this period, comes the record of the Rev M.H. Cooksley, an Anglo-Indian with medical training, whose dispensary at Mengmanapuram received an annual Government grant of R200 for 6000 outpatients.

All the records refer to an itinerant outreach. The Rev. J.A. Sharrock (1895-1900) reported to SPG headquarters from Trichinopoly that 'in one year 600 villages were visited and 4000 patients treated.' From Nasik, too, in Western India Mrs Farrar wrote in 1836: 'A little girl who has been very ill with fever, and who was regularly supplied with medicine I am thankful to say is recovered. Her mother carried her to school this morning . . . I went yesterday to see a widow to whom I had sent medicine; she was nearly well, and wishing to thank me said, "You have given me the great gift of life; you are my god; your righteousness is very great.".'

Every missionary has similar stories to tell. At Secunderabad, the Methodist publication *Compassionate Years* recorded in 1887 'Mrs Pratt has a large and successful dispensary . . . 360 patients have been treated.' The Rev C.W. Posnett, appointed to Medak, was saddened and appalled by the poverty and sickness he saw when he arrived from his comfortable home in England. 'How can I preach the Gospel in these circumstances?', he wrote. His sister, Emilie, was training in England as a doctor. He wrote to her and begged her to leave her studies and come to him in India at once. She and a friend, Sally Harris, obeyed. From Medak they trekked to the surrounding villages, distributing simple medicines. Incidentally, they travelled by camel. At Ramayampett, they treated the wife of the patel (headman) who was seriously ill. She died but the patel was so moved by their loving care and attention that he asked to be instructed in the Christian faith. That was the beginning of the church there.

Some of these amateur physicians were great characters. In 1913, a 60-bed hospital was opened in Chickballapur in Bangalore district, and grew rapidly. Its inception as a dispensary goes back to the appointment by the London Missionary Society (LMS) of Richard Hickling, who worked there for forty years. He had no medical training; indeed it is uncertain how much theological training he had. He seemed to take some pride in the fact that he had never been ordained by any church, though he was often spoken of in the area as 'the Reverend Hickling'. In these days he would be regarded as a most unlikely candidate for missionary service, yet he was one of the most able missionaries ever appointed by any society. Of outstanding versatility, he was a compassionate man greatly loved by Indian villagers whose language and music he shared. Moved by the physical suffering he saw all around him, he established a highly popular dispensary which eventually developed into a hospital, in the erection of which he shared the manual labour.

One of the raciest of these human stories is that of Harry Andrews (Richards, 1971). His father, a foreman in a packing case factory in the East End of London, was a convert of the young Salvation Army. With the death of his wife, his large family of small children posed practical problems. Bramwell Booth took the youngest to the Booth home where his mother, and particularly his sister Emma, brought up Harry. When Emma married Frederick Tucker and went to India, Harry – in his teens – went too. By 1895 he was an Indian-trained Salvation Army Officer on the staff of a new divisional headquarters at Nagercoil near Cape Comorin. His bedroom in the bungalow, which housed the staff and the office, had a small bathroom opening into the garden. With the simplest of cheap medicines on the shelf, Andrews was soon holding daily clinics at the bathroom door. On leave in Britain, he was given a six months' course as a dresser at the London Hospital and, by 1897, opened a hospital which was to grow eventually to a 360-bed general hospital. Andrews had the confidence of patients wherever he was. His colourful life ended when he was killed on the Afghan border in 1919; his exploits there brought the posthumous award of the Victoria Cross.

Most of this extensive network of rural health programmes was based on small static dispensaries from which the missionaries toured the surrounding area on foot or by horse or bullock cart. Some were mobile like that at Krishnagar in Bengal. This waterside mission had a dispensary boat. The 'doctor' was the Rev J. Hall, who had begun some medical studies while a divinity student in Islington. He sought further studies in Calcutta, and day after day crowds of sick people came to the boat 'undeterred by the rain which often drenched them, nor by the long delay which could not be helped, seeing that Mr Hall had to act as doctor and dispenser'.

The cost of these simple medical services by men such as Andrews and Hall was extremely modest, as is clear from the CMS account of pioneering in Onitsha, Nigeria. What is now a modern hospital was then 'an ultra-simple medical work where almost allcomers were treated alike with carbolic acid externally and salts inwardly'. From the Baptist Missionary Society's China story comes this account of the contemporary scene told by Dr Fletcher Moorshead, who speaks of the wonderful results obtained by the administration of castor oil or Epsom salts. He continues:

'One day when Mr Smyth was busy in the dispensary he was asked to see a boy who had swallowed his mother's brass ring 5 days before. A native doctor had "needled" the boy's neck all around with the object of setting up counter irritation. This it undoubtedly did, but not sufficiently to produce the ring. Another doctor had ordered the head to be shaved and a blister applied, which he hoped would draw the ring out. This treatment also failed. As a final hope he brought him to Mr Smyth, who administered an emetic and went on with his dispensing. In a few minutes, and before a crowd, the boy was violently sick and brought up the ring'.

How the recipients of such service felt is illustrated by a recent account. In 1979, Dr Harry Bennett, a retired CMS medical missionary, visited the scene of his father's life's work in Nigeria and was taken to the local Chief who brought out a book written by his own father in the local dialect.

It spoke of Bennett's pioneer medical work based on a Livingstone College course, and gave this as a prime factor in winning
the first converts. Dr Bennett's comment is:

'The medical work was not started with this in mind but out of
compassion . . . and, perhaps, for that reason it had a strong missionary effect. Christianity has always made little progress in
Muslim lands; undoubtedly medical missions have been the
most effective.' The following excerpt from the CMS records tells
of 'an adventurous journey into the Kaffiristan district of
Afghanistan of two Christian evangelists Fazal Huq and Nurallah
from Peshawar in 1864.'

'The former knew the dangers he would meet with for he had
been discovered there to be a Christian. The other, also a
Eusufzdi, who had himself been a mullah and a hafiz (one who
knows the whole Arabic Koran by heart) courageously agreed to
accompany him. From the Medical Mission Fund, these two
travellers were supplied with ordinary medicines and little presents for the people. A missionary's wife gave them two hours of
most intensive instruction in the use of these: a short medical
course indeed but in the outcome it proved effective enough, perhaps because they had been prevailed upon to write down all
that they had been taught. From their Mohammedan background
as well as from their own Christian experience they realized, too,
that prayer was the essential concomitant of all healing in God's
name.

'At the end of their first day's travel they fell in with a man
who proved suspicious. Finding that he was ill with dysentery
they gave him medicine which relieved him, and he took them to
his uncle's house and gave them food. The next night no-one
would take them in or give them either shelter or food, even for
money. They sat down by the wayside; after a little while they
heard a man telling another that his wife was ill. They asked what
her sickness was and sent her medicine by the husband, praying
earnestly that it might be blessed to her recovery. The woman's
pain abated and the grateful husband brought loaves and beds
and hospitably entertained them, and procured four guards on
the following morning for their onward march.

At a subsequent stopping-place nothing could be obtained to
eat, and here again their medicines came to their aid. A man was
ill with fever, they gave him an emetic and then quinine which
cured him, and he then brought out both bread and cheese. Then
a woman with sore eyes recovered and immediately the whole
village brought out their sick to be healed. Six out of eleven men
were cured of fever with quinine and the people became more
friendly.' 'So', says the missionary narrator of their journey, 'we
observe the great importance of medical missions amongst these

mountain clans.'

The CMS records move from Afghanistan to the Turkish dominions in the Middle East. Prior to their entry into Abyssinia, the Revs. Gobat and Kugler had spent a short time in Jerusalem. Of the latter, his companion (later Bishop in Jerusalem) said, 'having successfully administered medicine to a sick person he was very soon known in the whole city as a skilful physician; and thus he had the opportunity of going from house to house and of exhorting people . . . Mr Kugler's reputation obtained for him constant access to the house of the Governor of Jerusalem.'

In Southern Arabia, following a visit in 1885, the Hon Ian Keith Falconer reached the conviction that medical work should form a prominent part of any new Mission enterprise in the area. He died at Aden in 1887 at the age of 31. Within twenty years there was a well-appointed mission hospital in the town.

Reference was made earlier to the compassionate work of Peter Claver for African slaves in the 17th century. In 1873, the CMS established a settlement for freed slaves near Mombasa and before the turn of the century, three successive doctors had maintained a hospital of bamboo and palm-leaf branches for 60 patients.

In the first decade of the 20th century, at both the LMS Mission Hospital at Neyyoor, and the Salvation Army Catherine Booth Hospital at Nagercoil, medical schools had been opened and recognized by the Maharajah's government, where medical assistants were trained to run village hospitals. In a three years' apprenticeship-cum-academic course, these men were prepared for a life-time service in either mission or government medical service.

Between 1907 and 1920 Frederick Booth-Tucker, the Salvation Army Commander, assumed responsibility from the Government of India for thousands of criminal tribesmen. Humble couples, mostly from Britain, lived in settlements with these nomadic trouble-makers. In each settlement primary schools and cottage industries were developed, but the service that drew even the villagers from outside was the dispensary, superintended by the missionary's wife. A St John's Ambulance Brigade Home Nursing Certificate, provided in Training Colleges, became a normal qualification and slowly nursing qualifications, such as the local Certificate of Salvation Army hospitals in Canada, or the midwifery diploma obtained at the Mother's Hospital, Clapton, London, were found to be good training for village dispensaries.

Harley House was also equipping missionary candidates with a short course in obstetrics. Emily Stevens was one of those who, after a course of midwifery training at Doric Lodge, established a clinic for women in Taiyuanfu in China, maintaining an obstetric programme for thirty years. A little later, also in China, the Rev and Mrs Douglas Thompson (she a nurse and ex-matron) had a scheme for 'local healers' – on the principle of the Methodist local preacher. They gave simple training, supplied selected people with boxes of appropriate medicines and sent them out to the villages with their good gifts – and good news. When we read today of China's barefoot doctors, we should remember the Thompsons in Hunan – the home province of Mao Tse Tung himself.

Shorter periods of medical training were provided for missionaries from Britain by the opening of Livingstone College, in Leyton, in the East End of London. This college was founded by Dr Harford in 1893 to give a basic medical training for missionaries going to areas in the world where there were few if any qualified doctors. The staff were fully qualified and had experience of service in tropical countries. The students gained practical experience at Bethnal Green Medical Mission and at the Islington Mission. Courses were flexible. Its graduates wrote back from all parts of the world giving details of the medical service they were providing in addition to their evangelistic or educational responsibilities. Every issue of the College magazine is full of these accounts. Of the hundreds of Livingstone College students who graduated and sailed from Britain between 1893 and 1939, we take as an example Ralph Ladlay from the 1920 class. Equipped with a medicine chest, he was sent from his home Methodist Church in Leeds as assistant to the educationalist building a college at Uzuakoli in East Nigeria. The missionary's wife was running a verandah dispensary which Ladlay took over. The small dispensary was a boon to many and his amateur efforts were well rewarded. He treated minor complaints, fevers, injuries from machetes or falls from palm trees, worms, stomach upsets and tropical ulcers. The missionary's wife wrote:-

'Tropical ulcers were a well-known speciality of my husband, and we were able also to help mothers with their children's complaints. He handles simple surgical procedures as taught in Leyton. In his first year there was a major tragedy at Uzuakoli. Men working on an outlying farm were attacked by bush cows. The most seriously injured was a man so severely gored that his stomach and intestines had been torn. R.L. sought the help of a local "doctor" whom we had come to know and they replaced the organs and stitched the wound. Years later at Uzuakoli, a man who had been clawed by a leopard was brought to his home. While R.L. was treating him he told the story of the bush cow attack. Some days later, a man came to see us and pulling up his singlet, displayed a long mark where the skin had been stitched and proudly pronounced that he was the former patient!'

Those Livingstone graduates who went to the Belgian Congo often took further courses at the Tropical Medicine Institute in Brussels (later moved to Antwerp). The control of sleeping sickness was prominent in these courses and missionaries undertaking responsibility for control measures in their district received a salary. The Baptist, A.G. Mill, was one who did pioneering work in the Stanleyville area and trained others to help him.

Many non-Christians were happy to facilitate the development of Christian medical work. The Sultan of Zanzibar gave the land for the CMS hospital in Mombasa and the Maharajah did the same at Srinagar. At Yezd it was a Parsee who gave a caravanserai for the hospital and, in China, the Dowager Grand Empress provided 10,000 tolas of silver for the Union Medical College in Peking and the promise of Government backing for its medical courses.

In India, many Hindus and Muslims gave support. The CMS hospital at Jandiala near Amritsar was built by a local Brahmin, while Clara Swain's hospital at Bareilly, the first for women, was given by the Nawab of Rampur. In some cases the populace joined in when they saw the good work. Shikarpur on the road from Quetta to Sukkur, famous for Sir Henry Holland's eye camps, is an example.

Care of plague victims, which featured in third-century Alexandria, broadened to include cholera in the modern missionary enterprise. Cholera camps, even malaria camps, were regular events in India, the staff being trainee nurses and medical students from the 'barefoot doctor' schools operated by the London Missionary Society at Neyyoor and The Salvation Army in Nagercoil – both in Travancore State. A number of missionaries died in these activities, including Booth Tucker's wife. Others had hair-raising experiences.

An early public health programme was reported from Sarawak in 1870 where at Undop the Rev. W. Crossland, urged by the Headman, vaccinated 700 of the tribe. A transformation

sionate Christians and many continue to be a faithful expression of Christian involvement.

In Gujerat in West India, for example, in 1899, both monsoons failed, and 20,000 starving people crawled into Ahmedabad. The city closed its gates and the Government relief depot could cater for no more than a sixth of the number. Before long Colonel Nurani (Clara Case), the local Salvation Army commander, organized a programme which was soon feeding 30,000 a week. Work was found, cottage industries set up and orphanages opened by this indefatigable woman (Rendle Short and Gauntlett, 1946). The Anglican missionary, Rev J. Fayer, was moved to the Ghond region at Patpara in this famine. With timber and bamboo supplied by the Government, he built two hostels for famine orphans and one for leprosy patients.

It was from famine relief that the CMS church in Iran originated. In 1869 the Rev Robert Bruce, after eleven years in the Punjab, was returning from furlough overland. Reaching Isfahan he stayed there, doing famine relief, for which he collected £15,000 privately. In 1879 he was joined by the Rev Dr E.E. Hoenle, son of a Basle missionary working on the borders of the country. Dr Hoenle established a dispensary; the only contributor was Robert Bruce but by 1887 the work was flourishing.

In 1918, Colonel Charles Jeffries visited Tientsin where the Salvation Army had a hundred huts for relief work among the peasants who were flood victims. 'Hearing one poor woman muttering something as she stared at us I asked what she was saying . . . her words meant . . . "Here are people who love their fellow men" ' (Claughton, 1946).

The latest expression of Christian compassion is a response to the appalling death rate among children in the Third World. It has been the Christian emphasis on loving human relations that has brought the most striking success. The mushrooming of primary health centres in rural and urban jungles in the poorest countries is the distinctive feature of Christian work today. They are run in the main by a special breed of Christian nurses who combine clinical diagnostic ability with traditional nursing skills. The following extract from a Rhodesian letter is a fair example:

'As soon as we returned from England (17 July 1963), we were besieged by sick people. It was the wet season and most of the trouble was malaria . . . we could not sit there with our own personal box of 500 pills while babies were brought to us, children carried on bicycles, and messages from those who had collapsed

on the way. We started to give out our malaria pills. In a month
they were gone. We begged another 500 from a Roman Catholic
nun running a small hospital 48 kilometres away. In another
month those were gone. Fortunately the malaria season came to
an end, but now we had ulcers, conjunctivitis, coughs, diarrhoea,
burns, and mostly it was children who came with their parents or
alone. We often have a group of five or six children aged from 2 to
7 who have come all by themselves with bad ears, bad eyes,
ulcers and coughs; they all reel off their own ailments, or else a
child of 5 will speak up for one too small to talk'.

These simple health centres provide preventive inoculations,
a curative programme on a simple pharmacopoeia, obstetrics
and a practical instruction programme in the care of children,
based on the fundamentals of hygiene and diet. In many instances they are linked with agricultural schemes, intermediate
technology and provision of a piped water supply. All this
instruction is given in a form, and at a level that illiterate women
can assimilate. And if this makes a big dent in infant mortality,
then the same centres are family planning centres too.

In the 19th century the Church began to recruit doctors both
for home and abroad. This was partly in response to the inadequate free care available for the poor in Britain and the urgent
appeals from established missionaries in what we now refer to as
the Third World. Added to this was the ever-increasing volume
of evidence to show that health care opened hearts to the Gospel.
Some who responded were not certain where their priorities lay.
Sierra Leone and the CMS provided an example.

The prodigious mortality rates among missionaries indicated
that there was in fact a crying need for doctors: 53 missionaries
or their wives died in the first 20 years of the CMS. In 1823 the
Church Missionary Society sent 12 missionaries to Sierra Leone.
Within 18 months ten of them were dead.

'The Committee', it is recorded, 'were for the moment crushed
by all this overwhelming sorrow. They gazed in one another's
faces across the table, they knelt together at the footstool of the
Divine Mercy; and the tradition is that one leading lay member,
on the day that the news came of the several deaths, rose and said
in a tone of deep feeling and resolve, "we must not abandon West
Africa"' (Stock, 1899).

The Society resigned itself fatalistically to a seemingly irre-
mediable situation, and felt justified in challenging its missionaries to donate their blood to be the seed of the Church. In the 13
years beginning in 1840, when they sent their first fully-trained
doctor to West Africa, five doctors died of the six sent. The

history of this period prompted a later generation to ask whether it might not have been better to have combined with the local Government in a challenge to the British medical profession to survey the causes of its failures rather than to make this desperate but unsuccessful frontal attack on the deadly dangers of tropical conditions.

Many of the appeals for medically qualified staff could not be met. The CMS records:

'For 80 years Nursing Sisters have carried much of the burden of medical mission work overseas, particularly in its formative stages. Many of them left comfortable homes and well-equipped hospitals to serve their fellow-men under conditions sometimes as appalling as those which confronted Florence Nightingale at Scutari. But like her, they were undaunted, and with indomitable spirit, great ingenuity, and enduring courage, they started hospitals, conducted mobile dispensaries under wayside trees, and visited the homes of the sick, all the time displaying a skill and a winsomeness that won the hearts of the people and prepared the way for the large hospitals of today. All too often the Nursing Sister was the only exponent of modern medicine over a wide area, with no one else to consult as day by day she was confronted with immense obstetric and surgical problems. If she survived, the result was a wisdom and experience that made her professionally unique, her influence extending far beyond the locality where she lived.'

The stories of these compassionate, enterprising women are legion, but this example from Southern Rhodesia will suffice:

'One of my first patients was the child of our African minister – a baby girl of about fifteen months old. When I reached the hut where the child was living, I found her in a very collapsed condition and I knew the only hope for her was proper nursing. The problem was where she was to be nursed. The village was too far away for me to visit her every day, so the only thing to do was to bring the child to my own house and nurse her in my bedroom. Many of my friends would have smiled to have seen the wonderful steam tent which was erected. We have no cot, but a wicker chair, with broom handles and walking-sticks and an umbrella, answered our purposes very well. The sheets were pinned round with a professional touch, and we used an ordinary kettle with a piece of an old watering-can to lengthen the spout. This was kept boiling on an oil stove. Within a few days the child greatly improved and I was able to send her back to her mother strong and well, much to the parents' surprise.'

These pioneering ventures by nurses led not only to the establishment of hospitals but, more pertinently, the development of nurses' training schools and the provision of indigenous nurses. In many countries, though girls from any religious background were eligible, nursing became a specifically Christian art (see chapter 13). Other paramedical workers joined the missionary teams as new specialities developed. Each group quickly entered into the training of indigenous colleagues. Initially this was by simple apprenticeship but gradually training courses were set up and external examinations undertaken. The best example of this is from India, where after World War II the Christian Medical Association established a paramedical training committee, setting standards, inspecting hospitals, conducting examinations and issuing diplomas. It covered courses in pharmacy, laboratory technology, radiography, physiotherapy and hospital administration. All of these developments resulted from pioneering by individual enthusiasts.

This is true of the first course undertaken by the Rev Barton who trained laboratory technicians at the Christian sanatorium at Arogyavaram in South India. The first full training in physiotherapy was given at the Salvation Army Emery Hospital at Anand in Gujerat. Stanley Beer, appointed as administrator, felt the greater need for doctors and studied with Indian students at the College of Physicians and Surgeons in Bombay. After a few years work as a doctor, he went blind. His compassionate zeal led him to take a St Dunstan's course which enabled him to pass the examination for MCSP. He returned to Gujerat and established a training school. His first graduates set up modern departments in medical college hospitals of India.

Before closing this general survey of the mind of Christ permeating Christian thought and practice in the care of the sick, one particular branch of modern medicine requires special mention. Psychiatry is a relatively new speciality, but the treatment of the sick in mind has been a specifically Christian field since Christ's Galilean ministry. His healing ministry is worth analysis. Pre-eminently it was a demonstration that God desires wholeness in man. The foundation of the concept of psychosomatic medicine can be found in Christ's miracles. In particular, the role played by guilt and faith is clearly exemplified. Thus, faith healing became a part of the ministry of some Christians. Confession and faith were requisites for salvation, and the practice of confession, whether in secret or a priest's confessional, has been a potent agent for mental health and the requirement of honesty and restitution a healing balm in human relations. One other category of patient was dubbed by Christ as demon-possessed – a group that appears to have included both manic psychotics and epileptics. The Church in diminishing degree has considered exorcism as a legitimate function, and a contact with African native medicine underlines the potency of such thinking.

Christianity has thus been fertile soil for the advance of medical science and more particularly in the development of the caring services. It is no accident that the words 'whole', 'healthy', and 'holy' have a common root in Anglo-Saxon. Christians through two millenia have been spurred to activity in thought and action by this perceived oneness in the purposes of God.

References

Claughton, Lilian (1946) *Charles H. Jeffries*, London: Salvation Publishing & Supplies

Davey, T.F., and Davey, K. (1964) *The Compassionate Years*, London: Methodist Publ.

Kung, Hans (1977) *On being a Christian*, London: Collins

Neill, Stephen (1980) *A History of Christian Missions*, Harmondsworth: Penguin Books

Richards, Miriam (1976) *It Began with Andrews*, London: Salvation Publishing & Supplies

Richards, Peter (1971) *The Mediaeval Leper*, D.S. Bremer, Rowman & Littlefield

Schiff, L.M. (1960) *The Christian in Society*, Madras: The Christian Literature Society

Short, A. Rendle, & Gauntlett, S.C. (1946) *Clara-Case-Nurani*, London: Salvationist Publishing & Supplies

Thompson, H.P. (1951) *Into all Lands*, The History of the Society for the Propagation of the Gospel in Foreign Parts, 1701-1950 London: SPCK.

Weatherhead, Leslie (1968) *Psychology, Religion & Healing*, London: Hodder & Stoughton

CHAPTER 4

INITIAL MEDICAL SERVICES

R. Schram and W.A.R. Thomson

Medical missions in the modern sense of the term are a relatively recent development in the long history of the Christian Church. David Livingstone is sometimes considered the first medical missionary, but in fact there were many before his time. Mar Sergius, a physician from Samarkand, was appointed governor of Chiakiang, China, in 1277 or 1278. The first Christian hospital in Japan was built in Kyoto in 1568 by two Jesuit priests 'well versed in the practice of medicine'. There was even some evidence of a Christian physician at the court of Japan by the 8th century (Robinson, 1915). Bernard Rhodes, born in Lyons in 1644, studied medicine and surgery, entered a religious Order as a lay brother and eventually went to China where he lived for 16 years, dying near Peking in 1715. The Franciscans arrived in 1731 but they employed no qualified doctors. However their missionaries provided medicines and wrote books on treatment (Wong and Lien-Teh, 1932). The Society for the Propagation of the Gospel (SPG) was the first Protestant medical missionary society, thanks to the generous bequest of General Christopher Codrington, Commander in Chief of the Leeward Islands. In his will, dated February 11, 1703 he gave his two plantations in Barbados to the Society, on condition that a number of professors and scholars should be maintained. By 1712 sick and maimed negroes and servants were being cared for by a missionary skilled in physic and surgery, the Rev J. Holt. Medical training at Codrington College continued for a number of years. This was the only organized medical effort by the SPG in the 18th century. By 1730 Dr Schlegelmilch, a Danish Lutheran, was at work in India and by 1747 two Moravian doctors, Dr Christina Frederick William Hocker, and Dr John Ruffer in Persia. Later Dr Hocker spent many years in Egypt trying to contact the Ethiopian Copts; he died there in 1782. Dr John Thomas went out with William Carey to India in 1792, under the Baptist Missionary Society that Carey had just founded, but he did little medical work and after a while he became mentally ill. He died in 1801.

China

In 1805 Dr Alexander Pearson of the East India Company introduced vaccination at Canton, and this has been described as the first step toward medical missionary work in China. The modern missionary movement in China really begins with Robert Morrison of the London Missionary Society (LMS). He opened a dispensary in 1817 and three years later, together with Dr Livingstone, opened another in Macao. These provided Chinese drugs only. Pioneer doctors to China laboured under special difficulty. China despised all foreigners, regarding them as 'foreign devils'. Missionaries were in competition with a sophisticated traditional health care system. They had no status, and had to win their way by their integrity, their scientific success, and above all their loving and self-sacrificing lives.

Before 1850, however, there were a few such to be found. Perhaps the best known was the American, Dr Peter Parker (1804-1898), sent to Canton by the American Board Mission in 1834, but he was not the first. Apart from Pearson, a St. Thomas's surgeon with the East India Company, Thomas Richardson Colledge, founded in 1827 the first institution ever opened in China to bring western medicine to suffering Chinese, the Macao Ophthalmic Hospital. Although Colledge was not a medical missionary in the professional sense, he is regarded as the originator of medical missions in that most ancient civilization. Half a century later he said of his hospital, and more particularly of the Medical Missionary Society of China which he founded with Dr Parker ten years later, 'That was the one good thing in my life' (Balme, 1921). When Dr. Parker landed the two struck up a great friendship, and united to launch the Society that would 'waken the dormant mind of China . . . place a high value upon medical truth, and seek its introduction with a good hope of its becoming the handmaiden of religious truth' (Brook, 1985).

In 1838 William Lockhart FRCS (1811-1896) arrived, followed in 1839 by Benjamin Hobson (1816-1873), both of the LMS. Lockhart opened the first hospital in Shanghai in 1844 and in Peking by 1861. Hobson spent most of his life translating Western medical textbooks into Chinese, the first 'medical bookmaker of China' his *Outline of Anatomy and Physiology* appearing in 1850 (Wong and Lien-Teh, 1932). Lockhart was the first medical missionary to Hong Kong. He moved on to

Shanghai, opening the first hospital there in 1844. Still not satisfied, he reached Tianjin (Tientsin) and Peking, where a hospital was opened in 1861 (Lockhart, 1861). Dr. John Kerr of the American Presbyterian Mission, who came to Canton in 1854, was credited with over 1000 operations for stone in the bladder; he had more than 100 students and translated or compiled 27 books.

Mention must be made of an interesting Prussian missionary, Karl Friedrich August Gutzlaff. After training with the Moravian Missionary Institute in Berlin, since there were then no German missions, he was adopted by the Netherlands Missionary Society, trained as a doctor, ordained, and sent to Batavia in the Dutch East Indies. Having what has been described as an 'uncanny knack with the language' he soon learnt Chinese and Malay. He became largely Anglicized, and married the first lady missionary teacher in Malacca, Miss Newell. Sadly she died a year later and Gutzlaff signed on as a crew member of a 250 ton junk, arriving at Tianjin on June 18 1831. Later he was based at Macao, and travelled widely on the coast and practised medicine. In 1832 the East India Company recruited him as a surgeon and interpreter on the Lord Amherst which, like all the Company's clippers, was secretly carrying opium. He became well known in Europe and influenced, among others, both David Livingstone and Hudson Taylor. When he visited Herrnhut, the headquarters of the Moravian mission, he inspired them to launch a mission to Tibet in 1853. Unfortunately he was taken in by several scores of Chinese workers whom he paid to distribute the Bible and while he was in Germany, one of his colleagues discovered that almost all were frauds, opium addicts and criminals (Neill, 1964), but he was undaunted on his return and started other projects. The Chinese Evangelisation Society which eventually sent Hudson Taylor to China, was also founded as a result of his inspiration. Gutzlaff spoke and wrote Cantonese fluently, and mastered other local dialects. He was thus of immense value as an interpreter. Even though, as already noted, he did this for an opium-running ship on one journey, his influence along the China coast in distributing Bibles and medicine was wholly beneficial.

Oceania
Farther east in the Pacific, Christian missions were beginning among the Polynesians and eventually led to many thousands

becoming Christians on a great number of islands. The Rev. Dr Burdsall Lyth spent a short period in Tonga, and then joined a group on the island of Fiji in 1839. He became exceedingly busy and medicine had to take second place, but as 'the carpenter of illness' his fame was wide. Lyth was a Methodist, but the LMS and the Church Missionary Society also sent out missionaries. The story of John Williams and many other LMS missionaries to the South Seas is one of the great annals in the history of Christianity. Eventually chief after chief, island after island, rejected cannibalism and war and accepted the peace and forgiveness of Christ. By 1836 the CMS were at last able to send out to New Zealand Dr S.H. Ford, one of the first to be specifically set aside for medical work. He was given no extra money for this, and was not allowed to charge any fees (though gifts in kind were permitted). The Committee did suggest that he might select and train a few intelligent youths to assist him, a forward-looking move at this time. Ford's first major task was the treatment of victims of a serious influenza epidemic with a high mortality, together with tuberculosis.

'At least 800 natives', he reported, 'have been under my care during the last six weeks, whose cases for the most part have not only been seen but followed up, and generally to a happy result.'

He was stationed at Paihia, and built a house with a surgery at Horolatu. Later he talks of being 'busy with patients from morning to night, a hundred a day'. He withdrew from the mission in 1840 but not from medical help to Australasia.

Africa

African missions began at the Cape and on the West Coast. The LMS sent their first missionary to South Africa in 1798. He was Dr John Van der Kemp, a Dutch doctor who had spent sixteen years as an army officer and then studied at Leiden and Edinburgh where he qualified. He came to personal belief in Christ following the loss of his wife in a drowning accident in Holland, and volunteered for work among the Hottentots. After many difficulties as a liberal-minded Dutchman sent by a British mission to a country governed alternately by the Dutch and the British, he established a Christian mission at Bethelsdorp and did some medical and literary work, though he did not found any medical institution as such. He had considerable knowledge of Greek, Hebrew, Armenian, Persian and Syriac. He has been vilified by Boer historians but, although eccentric, he certainly did good work for many years in defence of simple African peoples (Burrows, 1958; Schram, 1971).

In 1835, a party of missionaries, sent out by the American Board of Commissioners for Foreign Missions, arrived in Cape Town. They included two doctors, the Rev Dr Alex Wilson and Dr Newton Adams, but the Board of Commissioners made it clear that these two doctors were sent to do ordinary evangelistic work and to make their medical practice 'subservient to the grand object of the mission . . . Their first care is of the missionary families, but they expected to exert a conciliating influence among the natives by their kindly office of their profession'. That the missionary families were at risk is indicated by the tragic death of Mrs Wilson soon after their arrival, her grave being marked by a monument to the first white woman to be buried north of the Vaal. Soon afterwards Dr Wilson returned home.

Although he died in 1851 at the relatively early age of 45, Dr Adams made history by being the first white doctor to settle in Natal. A jack of all trades, as all missionaries had to be in those days,

'he rose very early and donned a little jacket while he supervised the milking of the cows, feeding the horses, cleaning the stables, cutting wood and clearing the paths . . . After breakfast he put on a white coat to receive and treat his patients . . . in the evening he wore a dark coat. The Zulus therefore called him "umfundisi yamabantyi amatatu" – the teacher with three coats' (Gelfand, 1983).

His reputation as a skilled physician and surgeon rapidly spread among both whites and blacks who flocked to consult him from all over Natal and the Free State. He also established a school and printing press, and, after a slow start (he had to wait eleven years for his first convert), anything up to a thousand Africans would attend the Sunday services he held under a wide-spreading wild fig tree.

The fourth medical missionary in South Africa was Dr David Livingstone, although his first years (1841-1852) were spent at Kuruman near the Kalahari desert under Robert Moffat. Livingstone's aim was to explore and open up new territory to Christianity and commerce, thus both defeating the slave trade and bringing medical succour to enormous areas of Southern Africa. Although he founded no hospital or dispensary, he was in every way a doctor, being keen to use both the latest knowledge and to discover what was good in traditional herbal medicine. He would ask witch doctors to reveal their cures and undertook trials of herbal medicine himself. He realized the importance of gaining the witch doctors' friendship in the community. He was one of the first to use a clinical thermometer (1852), while in 1854 he observed the relation of relapsing fever to the bite of a tick. He also described maggot fly boils, tropical ulcers, *Onchocerca volvulus* in the eye, scurvy and schistosomiasis, and he associated swarms of mosquitoes with malaria. He was convinced of the efficacy of quinine, and encouraged the Niger expedition to use it (Gelfand, 1957). After his period of exploring the Zambesi he encouraged other missions to start, such as that of the Free Church of Scotland, under whose aegis Dr. James Stewart laid the foundations of Lovedale which became one of the great missionary centres in South Africa, and the Universities Mission to Central Africa in Nyasaland. Later the Church of Scotland established work of permanent value at Livingstonia in Malawi.

In West Africa early beginnings were in connection with the slave trade and the founding of Sierra Leone and Liberia. The CMS were pioneers here and in later years in Nigeria. In 1847 a surgeon, Dr J.N. Ashwood, was sent out to Freetown and founded a dispensary the next year. He employed Samuel Crowther and Thomas Smith from the Fourah Bay Institution. Thus, early on, West Africans began to take a hand in medical care and by 1859 three, including James Africanus Beale-Horton, had qualified in London and two were awarded the MD in Scotland.

Borneo
One further field was opened before 1850 in the Far East. In November 1847, two missionaries with their wives and children sailed from London for Kuching. One was the Rev Francis Thomas McDougall, a skilled surgeon as well as a minister. He reached Borneo in June 1848 and was faced at once with a difficult language and serious outbreaks of cholera and malaria. Many died. McDougall developed a painful rheumatic knee and was often unable to work. They lost five children, four almost at birth, the fifth of diphtheria at Singapore. But he stuck to his post, teaching simple treatment methods to all his assistants. In 1855 he was consecrated Bishop of Labuan and Sarawak (Thomson, 1951).

The first phase of missionary healing enterprise, up to 1850, ended with a handful of hospitals and dispensaries scattered in India, the China coast, Africa, and in the islands of the South Seas.

1850-1880

The earliest missionaries could provide little in the way of scientific cures, and in many ways were little in advance of much traditional practice. They had some understanding of the importance of good diet, of cleanliness, of the usefulness of smallpox vaccine, but many of their practices were still actively harmful, such as the giving of excessive mercury and blood letting. In the 1840s and 1850s came the discovery of anaesthetics (ether, nitrous oxide and eventually chloroform) and in the 1860s some conception of the vital importance of antiseptic techniques, following the use of carbolic by Lister. These advances allowed safer surgery to be practised.

Two other major events stem from this period. One was the revolution in nursing introduced by Florence Nightingale, first from her reforms at base hospitals in the Crimean war (1854) followed by the founding of the School of Nursing at St Thomas's Hospital, London (1860). The second was the creation of the General Medical Council of Great Britain to regulate the training, practice and standards of the medical profession (1858). Serious and complex surgery now became possible, with reduced mortality from neglect and infection, and western medical care became far more worth sharing with the rest of the world.

At this time most missionary societies regarded the evangelistic and theological side of their work as by far the most important, if not their only real function. They did not grasp that Christ's approach to men and women lost in sin was to bring loving care and forgiveness to the whole man, body, soul and spirit: that all aspects of his salvation were inextricably bound up together; and that he did not divide up human beings into separate entities and put the purely spiritual side on a pedestal. Missionary societies of those days were therefore suspicious of a man or woman who made much of the healing ministry.

China

Dr William Welton was one such. After twelve years of practice in Woodbridge, Suffolk, he was accepted as a medical missionary by the CMS and posted in 1849 to Foochow, one of the Treaty ports. In many ways he may be reckoned as the first authentic medical missionary of the Society. He lived in the city, opened a dispensary which was attended by large numbers, and did some surgery. Day after day crowds thronged his rooms and verandahs. Opposition to Christianity faded away; he was welcomed into the homes of the mandarins, and was able to distribute scriptures and tracts freely. He saw some 2000 to 3000 patients annually. In due course he was persuaded by his Bishop to accept ordination, and the CMS Annual Report for 1856/7 illustrates the official attitude:

'Mr Welton having been an experienced medical practitioner before he was ordained, has made his former profession auxiliary to his missionary duties by improving the large opportunities which his medical skill gives him of intercourse with all classes to their instruction in scriptural truth'.

What indeed had be been doing before ordination but just that?

The official attitudes altered eventually. Welton was only 40 when he went to China, but his seven years at Foochow wore him out and he returned to England where he died two years later in 1858. Dr James H. Young was the first medical missionary of the English Presbyterian Mission. He left an extensive practice in Hong Kong and on May 18 1850 he started work at Amoy on the mainland, concentrating on opium addicts. In 1852 he married a missionary who died the following year leaving two children. He never recovered from the shock, and was invalided home where he died in 1855. The work at Amoy began again in 1859 with the arrival of Dr and Mrs John Carnegie, and in 1863 they reported that 1356 patients had been admitted, with 5160 attending the dispensary. Local residents raised all the necessary funds for the work and this continued until 1879.

On September 18 1863 Dr William Gauld arrived at Swatow, 120 miles south of Amoy, an unsavoury port engaged in both opium and 'coolie' traffic, the latter being a form of press gang in which young men were seized, loaded on junks, and shipped overseas as cheap labour. Since coolies were paid a bounty this was not technically slavery, but it was in all but name. They were crowded under hatches in appalling conditions without medical care. Usually only two-thirds survived the voyages to the South Seas, Cuba and elsewhere.

'The services of Dr Gauld are a great blessing, and beginning to tell already. At one place Mackenzie and I were stopped by a band of lawless fellows and soon surrounded. We were asked if we belonged to the same party of foreigners as Dr Gauld and on replying in the affirmative we were allowed to pass without annoyance.'

Dr Gauld treated the Tau Tai (Governor) at Chao-chow-fu,

who was desperately ill with dysentery and ten years later he granted a new site for Gauld's hospital.

It is important to realize what was meant by the term 'hospital' then, and no better description can be given than that by Dr Harold Balme in his book *China and Modern Medicine* (Balme, 1921):

'Neither ventilation nor cleanliness was a marked feature of these old hospitals. The furniture of the wards was of the scantiest description, and probably consisted of nothing more than a few Chinese beds (wooden or bamboo). Everything else was provided by the patient who brought his own clothes to sleep in, his own bedding to lie on, and his own friends to nurse and feed him. It is perhaps well to draw a veil over that bedding and clothing, and to bury its entomological contents in a decent silence!

A small lean-to shed with a primitive stove served as a kitchen. Here the patient's friends, or the hospital cook, prepared whatever the sick man fancied. It was almost impossible for the medical staff to maintain adequate control over the patient's diet and as likely as not, a man suffering from severe dysentery would surreptitiously procure a solid meal of dumplings, or slake his thirst with a hard pear. An ill-furnished but well-kept operating room, where some remarkably successful operations were performed, usually completed the hospital plant. Under such conditions the doctor could not do much for cases that required skilled nursing or elaborate medical treatment, but he usually succeeded in building up a large practice, especially on the surgical side, and in obtaining some very striking results. In time he might be able to build a new hospital specially adapted for the purpose'.

The early hospitals were only adapted Chinese buildings, and at one period this meant a simple courtyard with small rooms, and the use of paper for windows. Mission after mission opened such small hospitals and dispensaries. Some of the hospitals were for sick missionaries. In 1879 Dr Hudson Taylor opened a sanatorium at Chefoo, alongside others in that town, which did much to succour overworked and ill missionaries of the China Inland Mission, which he himself had founded. This intrepid evangelist and doctor was determined that the Gospel should be taken to the innermost regions of Imperial China where, in the words of Professor Latourette (1929),

'in the distant and often lonely stations of the CIM the dispensary and the hospital were equally a part of the regular programme, and the pioneer missionary was often both evangelist and physician'.

In 1880 Dr Gauld of Swatow returned home for his second furlough, but his health never allowed him to return. For the next thirty years he served as medical superintendent of the Mildmay Mission Hospital in London, replacing Dr Lyall who became his successor at Swatow, where in 1881 1000 operations were performed; and in 1886 306 were cured of opium smoking.

In those days there was no waiting for ideal conditions before making a start. Thus in 1881, after a period of language study, Dr Grant settled in Chuan Chow in rooms attached to the church, and in the old preaching hall. Small rooms behind this served as consulting room and dispensary. Waiting patients listening to preaching in the hall, while dressings were done in the chapel courtyard, where a large slab of granite did duty as an operating table. In 1882 a dark, black, filthy malodorous house was transformed into a thirty bed hospital.

Dr F. Porter Smith, posted by the Wesleyan Missionary Society to Hangkow, arrived there in 1864 with not the slightest knowledge of the language. He began treating patients in his own home but was soon able to rent a small shop on the street, with the Rev. Josiah Cox acting as interpreter. Eight days later he hung a signboard showing four Chinese characters, a sign used ever since by Wesleyan hospitals at Teian, Suichow, Tayeh, Anlu, Wusueh and others in Hunan and South China. He spent much time learning Chinese, and was soon able to manage on his own. By the end of July 1864 he was able to accommodate inpatients in two small rented houses, the first mission hospital in Central China.

His patients included not only villagers, beggars and soldiers, but also Tartar officials, mandarins, literary graduates, and other influential people. His family still possess a gorgeous scroll which an official gave him for curing his little daughter. Another patient was a mullah of the principal mosque in Hangkow, who even placed in the mosque for public use a copy of the New Testament that Dr Smith had given him. But trouble was soon coming. Hangkow was threatened with Nein Fei rebels and the whole district was unsettled; shops closed and businesses stopped. Dr Smith had to give up the two houses he had rented for hospital work, but he used this opportunity to expand. A large plot of land was bought on which was erected a modern hospital to Dr Smith's own plans, 78 by 30 feet, capable of accommodating 20 patients (12 male and 8 female) with a built-in dispensary and large waiting room.

This small hospital, opened on April 21 1866, was, however,

only his base. He began by educating the neighbourhood in public health, and wrote leaflets on hygiene and sanitation. These were freely and widely distributed by the Commissioner of Customs – the first such health education material in all central China. Within four years he wrote a book, *Notes on Materia Medica and Natural History of China,* later widely read by missionary doctors and medical students. This was but one of a stream of serious academic publications including *Creeds of China, Chinese Proper Nouns, On Chinese Slang,* and *Orientalism of Russia.*

His successes led to great opposition through the jealousy of local indigenous healers, but he overcame this by his friendliness and willingness to learn from them, to spend days visiting them, and prescribing their drugs with them in such settings. Like Livingstone with the herbalists of central Africa, Smith did not despise the indigenous skills and drugs and his work began to be appreciated even by those who once regarded him as a competitor, spy, or usurper of their rights. Such labours were not without their strain, and Dr Porter Smith's health was gradually affected, as was that of his wife and family living in Wu-Shen-Miao through six long hot summers. In 1870 Dr E.P. Hardey was recruited by the mission to assist him, and eventually Dr Smith was able to hand over to him after a few months together. The intention was a short leave in Britain, but his health had been so seriously affected that he was never allowed back to China. He lived in Somerset until he died eighteen years later in March 1888.

Dr Hardey continued for five years, nearly always on his own, until he in turn had to be invalided home, broken in health. He was not allowed to return. The hospital had to be closed but the story ends happily in that the Rev. David Hill (who entered China in 1864 when Smith landed) found a Dr Sidney Rupert Hodge who was able to work there for twenty years and who won the love and admiration of many.

India

One of the most notable medical missionaries of the period was Dr William Jackson Elmslie. He was recruited to Kashmir by Christian officers in the Punjab who would not wait for the CMS although they had appealed to them for a doctor. Instead they contacted the Edinburgh Medical Missionary Society who found Elmslie, a Scot and a Presbyterian. The denominational difficulty was overcome provided he would agree to work within the rules of CMS which he happily accepted. He already had his FRCS(Ed) and sailed in 1864 for India. From Calcutta he went to Lahore, and on to Srinagar in Kashmir, at that time only open to Westerners for six months in the year. He arrived in May 1865 and established a dispensary on the verandah of his bungalow, and eventually one also at Amritsar where he spent the rest of the year. The Maharajah was hostile but gradually numbers rose. He had already begun to train Indian assistants, and these helped him with operating. During 1868 opposition began to lessen but accusations were put about that he made his medicine from swine's flesh and blood. In all he was asked to set up eight medical missions in the Punjab. He returned to England on furlough in 1870. His last period of work in Kashmir involved a severe outbreak of cholera, and he died soon after in November 1871, only 40 years of age (Stock, 1899). The day after his death the government gave permission to Europeans to live all the year round in Kashmir. The Bishop of Calcutta wrote: 'I quite believe that Dr Elmslie is knocking at the one door which may through God's help be opened for the truth to enter in'.

Workers in the Punjab were not all expatriates. Dr John Williams, later ordained, was an Indian, and a man of great influence with all the Afghan neighbourhood. He worked long days with great crowds of patients in the town of Tank and preached faithfully (with little obvious result) for many years. When the Waziris attacked and destroyed this town they spared the CMS hospital because of their regard for him. Unfortunately, the government dispensary was not spared.

In South India the appointment of the Rev. Dr Strachan to Nazareth in Tinnevelly in 1870 was the start of a regular medical mission by the SPG. The results exceeded the most sanguine expectations. By 1872 the number of patients treated annually had risen to 40,000 – Muslims, Christians, Brahmins, Vellarers, Channers, Rheddies, Naiks, Pariahs, and Pallens from as far afield as 80 miles. The number of district dispensaries and hospitals steadily increased until there were seven. In 1869 a small hospital was opened at Nasik by the Rev. W.S. Price for a village of freed slaves whom David Livingstone had brought from East Africa. He later employed the Rev. James Bunter who for eighteen years had practised medicine as an apothecary to a native regiment, and was allowed to obtain drugs from the deputy inspector of hospitals.

The Jalna Mission in India deserves mention. It was founded
and carried on for 27 years by a brilliant Brahman convert,
Narayan Sheshadri, who had mastered English so ably that he
was invited to speak at Church of Scotland meetings all over
Britain and at the Presbyterian Alliance in Philadelphia in 1880.
He established a Christian village three miles from Jalna at Bethel,
involving himself in the building of roads, the sinking of a well,
the building of schools and a church. Although an outstanding
Christian evangelist, he was allowed to purchase 800 acres for
his village from the Nizam's Arab prime minister, and at Indapur
he persuaded a rich Hindu to support a girls' school. Money
poured in from Scotland and North America. During the famine
of 1877-78 he accommodated 66 orphans at Indapur and 70 at
Bethel. He was not only a good organizer but a teacher himself,
holding children spellbound. He ran courses for catechists and
taught European ladies at Mahableshwar twice a week in literature, metaphysics and theology. He taught trades to the Mangs,
the lowest caste folk, and provided them and the orphans with
medical care through adding to his staff at Indapur a fully
trained apothecary with twenty-one years' experience. His
bungalow became a 'miniature hospital'. He did not reject Hindu
culture and music, but brought them into Christian worship –
obviously a man way ahead of his time. In 1890 it was decided to
split his huge district into two, and a European doctor, the Rev.
Dr A. G. Mowat, was appointed to one part. While crossing from
America to Scotland on his third visit, Sheshadri died at sea in
1891 and Mowat had the whole area to supervise. He established
several dispensaries and in 1898 a new hospital (Hewat, 1960).

1880-1980
Queen Victoria's Golden Jubilee in 1887 marked not only an era
of imperialism on an almost unparalleled scale, but also an even
more impressive development in medical knowledge. On this
floodtide of imperialism and medical research what we now
know as the developing world became of immediate, and often
pressing, interest to the citizens of the West. To Christians this
interest meant an increasing emphasis on missionary effort.
Primarily this was evangelistic but, gradually, most of the major
missionary societies accepted that the cure of souls should not
be separate from the cure of bodies.

China
The highlight of the initial period of this era was the setting up of

medical schools by the various societies. The first medical school on a modern basis was founded in 1881 by Dr Kenneth Mackenzie at Tientsin, which in due course became the Peiyang Medical College, Tientsin. Another pioneer in this field was Dr Dugald Christie of the United Presbyterian (later United Free Church) Mission, who arrived in Manchuria in 1892. His medical school in Moukden rapidly achieved a high reputation. But perhaps the best known of all was the School of Medicine established in Peking after the Boxer Rising by Dr Thomas Cochrane of the London Missionary Society. Not the least of its claims to fame was that it was an early, if not the earliest, example of what would now be described as a combined operation. It was, in the words of Harold Balme (1921), 'the first medical college to be established in China by the combination of both British and American men, and through the cooperation of missionary societies representing different religious denominations'. Dr. Cochrane even succeeded in securing the patronage and financial support of the Dowager Empress. In due course it was taken over by the China Medical Board of the Rockefeller Foundation (Aitchison, 1983).

Whether or not the chromium-plated, modern research-orientated medical school financed with the aid of the Rockefeller dollars was in accord with the Christian ideals of Thomas Cochrane may be debatable, but the Christian record of some of the other medical schools is well illustrated by figures quoted by Balme (1921).

'Of 115 men who completed their medical training between 1906 and 1919 at the Union Medical College, Hankow, no less than 110 have served for longer or shorter periods in mission hospitals, and the great majority are still doing so in spite of the fact that only a comparatively small percentage of them were under any obligation to return to such work'.

In 1887 the Church of Scotland established a mission at Ichang, the most westerly treaty port on the Yangtse, and the following year sent out Dr Macfarlane. In spite of it being a most conservative area antagonistic to foreigners, he treated over 4000 patients in his first ten months.

'But', as Elizabeth Hewat (1960) writes, 'the strain and exacting nature of a doctor's profession in 19th century Ichang bore hardly on the health of a succession of medical men in the Mission. Of the first four doctors who served in Ichang, three and a half years was the maximum period of service, the first two men being invalided home, and the third and fourth dying at their posts'.

This feature of missionary life in China is further illustrated by the experience of the Methodist hospital at Chaotung in Yunnan, founded in 1903 Dr Savin, the founder, and his two successors all died of typhus. Such also was the fate of Dr Harold Schofield, the brilliant young physician who abandoned his prospects of a notable academic career in Britain and, at his own charge, went to China in 1880 under the China Inland Mission to be the first medical missionary in Shansi. He survived for only three years.

Four other names from this era call for mention: Dr Duncan Main of the Church Missionary Society, Dr Harold Balme of the Baptist Missionary Society, the Maxwells – father and son – of the English Presbyterian Church Mission, and Dr Main also of the Baptist Missionary Society. Dr Main arrived in China in 1881, and the large hospital he founded in Hangchow was a lasting memorial to a long and honoured career in the service of Christ. Dr James L. Maxwell I arrived in China in 1865. His main claim to fame is his work in Formosa, where he was held in affectionate memory for many years by the Chinese. So much so that they referred to all mission doctors as 'Ma Iseng' (Maxwell Doctor). His son, James L. Maxwell II, who arrived in Formosa in 1901, was outstanding for his research activities which he stimulated in others through his membership of the China Medical Missionary Association which held its first meeting in 1890. It has been described as

'the pioneer national organization of modern physicians in China . . . It conducted a journal and discussed and laid plans for the promotion of medical education and of public health, the preparation of medical literature, the fixing of a uniform terminology, and the conduct of research'.

Notable among the medical literature was *The Diseases of China, including Formosa and Korea* by W. Hamilton Jeffreys and James L. Maxwell, published in 1914.

The main contribution of Harold Balme, who first went to China in 1906, was in the field of medical education (see also chapter 18). In 1912 he joined the staff of the Christian Medical College at Tsinan, a unit of Shantung Christian University, of which he became President in 1921. For sixteen years he played a leading part in the development of what became one of the major medical schools in China, distilling his wisdom for the benefit of others in *China and Modern Medicine*, published in 1921. Among the developments for which he was largely responsible were the establishment of a school of nursing and the

opening of the medical college for women students in 1923-24.
In this context it is of interest to note that, a decade earlier, the
North China Union Medical College for Women, Peking, had
awarded its first diploma to a class of two, these two graduates
thus becoming the first women in North China – if not the whole
country – to become qualified as doctors. Balme's retirement for
family reasons in 1927 was, it has been recorded, 'a matter of
keenest regret to the Society . . . No-one can overestimate the far-
reaching character of Dr. Balme's contribution to the cause of
missions in China' (Moorshead, 1929).

Statistics can be dull – and by no means tell the whole story.
On the other hand they do give some idea of what is happening.
For the period after the onset of the civil war that preceded the
Japanese invasion and the subsequent communist take-over
statistics are few and far between, but those for the earlier years
are enlightening. In 1874 there were 10 medical missionaries; by
1876 there were 16 hospitals and 24 dispensaries treating 41,281
patients, and by 1881 there were 19 medical missionaries. In
1913 there were 435 European and American doctors (300 men,
135 women), 94 qualified Chinese doctors and over 10,000
Chinese medical students. In 1915 out of 5338 missionaries, 525
were on the medical staff and the number of hospitals had
increased to 330, with in-patients 104,418 and outpatients
1,535,841.

Impressive as these figures are, however, their contribution to
the physical welfare of the teeming millions of China is indeed
pathetic with less than two million of this vast population
accounted for. On the other hand, as has been commented, 'in no
part of the mission field have medical missions done so much to
break down opposition and to commend the Christian Faith as
in China' (Robinson, 1915).

India
In India, or the Indian subcontinent as it is now known, all the
many missionary societies took increasing advantage of the part
that doctors could play in introducing and commending the
Christian faith. 'By their deeds shall ye know them' took on a
fresh significance. Even the Baptist Missionary Society, the most
reluctant of the societies where medical missions were concerned, 'saw the light', and in due course added a number of
distinguished names to the roll of honour of medical missionaries. In 1894, however, when Dr Vincent Thomas offered his

services to the Society, there was not a single medical man on the staff of the Society in India, and only one medical woman, Dr Ellen Farrar, who was serving in the Baptist Zenana Mission. According to Dr Fletcher Moorshead (1929), the historian of the Society and for many years its medical secretary, Dr Thomas was accepted reluctantly by the Candidate Committee and only 'subject to there being no undertaking for a hospital', and 'he had to wait eleven long years before he had his first hospital' in North India. In spite of such an inauspicious beginning, his work grew from strength to strength until he retired in 1921 with the award of the Kaiser-i-Hind Medal.

The extent to which medical missions developed in this era is well exemplified by the following figures, which include Sri Lanka and Burma, taken from the *Year Book of Indian Missions* for 1912: 204 hospitals, 405 dispensaries, 278 qualified doctors, 126 'without medical degrees', 294 trained nurses.

In this development the ladies played an outstanding part, overcoming the otherwise impenetrable barriers that shut off the women of the subcontinent from the help of male doctors (see chapter 13). Equally impressive is the part medical missions played in the development of medical and nursing schools as recorded in Chapters 13 and 18.

The highlights of this era are best delineated by brief pen pictures of three of the leading medical missionaries of the period. 'Since Pilkington was killed in Uganda in 1897, no missionary career and no death in the field have so appealed to the mind and sympathy of the whole Church as Pennell's' (Stock, 1916). Dr T.L. Pennell, after a brilliant undergraduate career, volunteered for service under the Church Missionary Society and was posted to the Punjab. Here he rapidly acquired what has been described as 'a rare influence over the wild frontier tribes that resorted to his hospital at Bannu; and many converts from Mohammedanism were the result' (Stock, 1916). His methods were often unconventional though effective as, for instance, the journey he took by bicycle through North India, 'in ascetic garb and living like a fakir on what people gave him unasked'. His services were appreciated by the powers that be, as well as the tribesmen among whom he worked, as exemplified by his being awarded the Kaiser-i-Hind Medal (1st class, gold). Alas his career was cut short in 1912 by his death from blood poisoning, acquired while operating. His own book, *Among The Wild Tribes of the Afghan Frontier*, and his 'Life' written by his

accomplished wife (one of the Sorabji family of Poona) constitute a valuable record of unique service. Following his death, his
wife, who graduated in medicine at London University, continued with the work among women which she had carried out
during her husband's lifetime.

As well known, and perhaps rather more conventional, was
another Church Missionary Society doctor in the Punjab, Sir
Henry Holland. He was a brilliant surgeon who, according to the
official history of his Society (Stock, 1916), 'performed operations at the rate of 100 a day', and his services were particularly
appreciated for his success in coping with the problem of cataract as described in chapter 11.

Perhaps best known of all the medical missionaries to India is
Dr Howard Somervell (1890-1975) who, according to Sir Francis
Younghusband in his introduction to Somervell's autobio-
graphy, *After Everest* (1936),

> 'is no mean mountaineer. He is one of the five who have
> reached the 28,000 feet level (he was a member of the 1922 and
> 1924 Everest Expeditions). He is no mean painter: his painting of
> Everest adorns the walls of the Royal Geographical Society's
> House. He is no mean musician: he has transcribed Tibetan songs
> and played them in England. He is no mean surgeon . . . He is no
> mean lover of men: he has given up a lucrative practice and devo-
> ted his life to alleviating the bodily suffering of Indians and put-
> ting new spirit into them. Above everything he is a Christian'.

At the end of the 1922 Everest Expedition, he recorded in his
autobiography, 'with three months of spare time and sixty
pounds as my immediate possessions, I set out to see as much as
possible of the architecture and the customs of India'. His final
port of call was Neyyoor in Kerala to visit his old friend, Dr S.H.
Pugh who was in charge of the hospital there, part of the
Travancore Medical Mission founded in 1838 by the London
Missionary Society. There, he wrote:

> 'I saw the thing which changed the entire plan of my life,
> something far more impressive than the mighty Himalayas, that
> something was the unrelieved suffering of India . . . I decided
> without hesitation that this should be my life's work. If I had not
> then gone to India at the call of suffering I should never have
> dared to look God in the face, or to say prayers to Him again'.

Before the end of 1923 he was back in Neyyoor as a medical
missionary of the London Missionary Society, of which his
father was treasurer. What he sacrificed is worth noting – not
because it is unique but because it illustrates the sacrifice made
by so many members of the medical profession in deciding to
devote their lives to the service of God in the mission field.

When he got back to London from his tour of India he found that he had been appointed to the surgical staff of University College Hospital, London. With his reputation as one of the first two men to get within a few hundred feet of the summit of Everest, and an appointment on the staff on one of the leading teaching hospitals in London, a great future lay before him. But he never hesitated. The call had come, he answered it and, in his own words, 'a great peace of mind, and a contented feeling that things were all right, came over me'.

After a little over a quarter of a century at Neyyoor, in 1949 he moved to the Christian Medical College at Vellore, whence his fame as a surgeon spread, and where he stayed until his retirement in 1961. He was undoubtedly one of the most brilliant surgeons of his time, according to Sir George McRobert, Professor of Medicine in Madras University, 'a real mentor in the field of abdominal surgery and an outstanding orthopaedic surgeon'.

Of the many mission hospitals of which India can now proudly boast, two may be selected as typifying the admirable work they are all doing. One is St. Luke's Hospital in Hiranpur, Bihar, a town situated some 200 miles north of Calcutta. It owes its origin to a judge of the Indian Civil Service, whose retirement gift to the Province in which he had served was a 12-bedded hospital. This was opened in 1929 under the aegis of the Church Missionary Society. It is now under the wing of the Church of North India. Under the inspiring leadership of Dr. H.C. Edmunds it steadily grew until now it has 150 beds and a staff of 72. Typical of its growth is the fact that in 1978 it dealt with 646 maternity admissions compared with 12 in 1929.

Plans for the future include the building of a Community Health Centre as a development of the hospital's plans to reach out to the people in the surrounding villages. No longer, it is felt, can a missionary hospital work in isolation, it must carry its mission to the people, and only bring the people to the hospital when their condition requires the facilities only available in a hospital (see chapter 16).

Another interesting development of recent years is the presence almost continuously of medical students from the United Kingdom and elsewhere who come for their three month 'elective' periods. Almost as a corollary to this is the experiment the hospital was asked to undertake of bringing into its fellowship pairs of Jesuit novices from their neighbouring seminary.

'Both these experiments', it is recorded, 'give their partici-
ants an experience of life different from anything they have
known before, and have brought them into close contact and
indeed friendship with each other. Both have proved most
successful'.

But perhaps the most moving item in *For Such a Time as
This*, the booklet published to commemorate the hospital's
diamond jubilee, is the photograph of the hospital's senior
woman sweeper opening a new hospital block named after her,
by cutting the traditional tape. Here at long last is Christianity
in practice, recognizing neither caste nor social distinction. All
are God's children and all are equal in his sight. In the words of
one of the British medical students who had spent his elective in
the hospital, as recorded in the diamond jubilee booklet:

'The St Luke's of today is a living testament to the love of
Christ, and to the dedication of those who have been connected
with it throughout the years'.

The other hospital is the Khasi Hills Welsh Mission Hospital
situated on the pine-clad hills on the outskirts of Shillong in
Assam. It was opened as a 90-bedded hospital by Sir William
Marris in 1922, the Governor of Assam. The Presbyterian Church
of Wales first sent its missionaries to the Khasi Hills in 1846.
From its very early days it stressed the importance of the care of
the body as well as the soul. Dr Gordon Roberts, the founder of
the Shillong Hospital, was in the words of Sir William Marris
'responsible for the extraordinarily munificent response of the
people of Wales to the appeal for the building and endowment
fund' of what he described as 'a hospital of which any province
in India might be proud'.

For many years it was one of the very few institutions in
Assam in which major surgery was performed, and more major
abdominal surgery was done in it than in all the government
institutions of the province. The Japanese advance to the
frontiers of Assam in World War II gave it much extra work.
During this period over 3000 military patients passed through its
hands. It also played a vital role in providing nurses for the
armed forces. Many of the nurses trained in the hospital joined
the army nursing services and more than 50 auxiliary nurses
were given their preliminary training there before entering on
their military duties. For his services Mr R. Arthur Hughes, the
senior surgeon, was awarded the OBE.

In a personal communication he throws an interesting light
on some of the problems facing the medical missionary. One of

the points to which he draws attention was the failure to diag-
nose rickets until bony deformity had occurred. In his opinion it
could be easily recognized at a much earlier stage, characterized
by fever, sweating, floppiness, irritability and irregular stools.
At this stage the child could be returned to normality by one
injection of vitamin D_3, or by the shark liver oil preparation
freely available. He comments:

> 'One of our most popular selling items in the travelling dis-
> pensary was a frightful looking mixture of equal parts of shark
> liver oil and compound ferrous phosphate syrup diluted with
> peanut oil'.

A not uncommon condition was what he describes as chronic
diarrhoeal hypoproteinaemia, which responded satisfactorily to
a diet containing adequate protein. The non-Christian Khasi
people, he reports:

> 'recognised this condition – especially if it came on fairly
> quickly – and attributed it to a poison given by evil-principled
> people in market places as part of ritual murder. We could cure it,
> and many times we were told that we had beaten the devil'.

Even more intriguing was his recognition of hyperventilation
tetany as the basis for the lay diagnosis of spirit possession,
and he recalls:

> 'Lecturing ministers and elders in a General Assembly on the
> recognition of tetany and giving them grounds to believe that
> they were not enchaining the spirit by refusal to accept the evi-
> dence presented by the possessed. A shot of calcium gluconate
> could exorcise the most persistent "spirit".'

Incidentally he notes that the hospital set up the first blood
bank in Shillong, which for long served all the hospitals in the
area.

Africa

The opening up of Africa by David Livingstone and other
explorers presented missionary societies with a challenge
which they willingly accepted though their means were
stretched by their activities in Asia. Outstanding in this era are
Sir Albert Cook and Sir Clement Chesterman.

Sir Albert Cook (1870-1951) was one of the founder fathers of
Uganda, where he arrived in 1897, along with eleven other CMS
missionaries (including his future wife, a trained nurse named
Katharine Timpson (see also chapter 13). Within three weeks he
had a dispensary in action and in two months a simple hospital.
Over the next six decades it was rebuilt several times. The 1904

hospital still stands with its characteristic impressive cruciform design but it is now being added to in a concrete two storey hospital on a neighbouring site in Kampala. In spite of his intense devotion to the job in hand in the care of patients, he never lost touch with the long-term view, and one of his outstanding contributions was the founding during World War I of a training school for medical assistants – the forerunner of Makerere University Medical School. Equally significant was the training school for midwives founded by Lady Cook, a model of many such schools throughout the continent. Unlike so many missionaries he did not retire to England. Uganda had become his home, and it was there he died – a beloved physician and an honoured senior citizen. His memory is preserved in the Albert Cook Memorial library in the Makerere Medical School which houses his masterly clinical notes and his large library of medical books (Foster, 1978).

Sir Clement Chesterman (1894-1983), for long the Grand Old Man of medical missions, went out to the Congo under the aegis of the Baptist Missionary Society in 1920, a posting that was 'hailed with delight by missionaries and Africans alike' (Moorshead, 1929).

'His ability and experience' it has been recorded, 'soon marked Yakusu for notable development in medical missionary work, and by 1924 plans were in hand for at least three major ventures – for a new hospital, for the training of African assistants, and for the opening of a series of district dispensaries in the Yakusu area, to be manned by the qualified Christian medical trainees from the hospital, known as 'infirmiers' (Causton, 1951).

Evidence of this is the speech made by the Governor of the Eastern Province of Belgian Congo when he opened the new hospital in Yakusu in 1925. In this he

'emphasized the happy relations between the State and the Baptist Missionary Society and spoke of the village dispensaries which were to be built and financed by the Government, but which he asked the Mission to staff and control through the infirmiers trained at the medical school' (Moorshead, 1929).

Unlike so many official openers he backed up his words with deeds. The following day he sent the Mission a cheque for 1000 francs.

In West Africa one of the outstanding hospitals is the Nixon Memorial Hospital in Segbwema, Sierra Leone. A Methodist foundation, it has 180 beds. Its outgoing philosophy is represented by the statement in its 1959 policy declaration: 'We should not be content with the establishment of a well-equipped modern hospital at Segbwema, but we feel we should expand farther outwards towards the people in the villages, into the houses.' Carrying this policy into effect it is now the organizing centre for a large-scale and efficient rural baby care programme and a rural ophthalmic service (see chapter 11). It was the first hospital in Sierra Leone to be recognized for the training of state enrolled community health nurses. It is also the field centre for the study of Lassa fever and has a nutrition rehabilitation unit.

The first Methodist medical missionary in West Africa, Dr J.R.L. Stephens, arrived in Lagos in 1912. The way had been prepared for him by John Bond, a lay missionary who in 1906 opened a dispensary at Igbo-ora. One cannot but admire his courage in tackling the medical problems in an area where doctors were completely lacking, yaws was universal, and malaria and yellow fever took an appalling toll of life. 'From these small beginnings', the Society's historian records, 'there was destined to develop the medical work that has made the Methodist contribution to Nigeria so outstanding'. The first step was the setting up of the hospital at Ilesha by Dr Stephens, one that has been totally rebuilt since David Morley's time (see chapter 6). A smaller hospital developed at Oron near the Cross River (Schram, 1971), and another at Ituk Mbang in the east.

The Church Missionary Society was equally active in the medical field in Nigeria with three hospitals, Ado Ekiti, Wusasa, and their main hospital at Iyi Enu near the Niger River, the foundation stone of which was laid by Lord Lugard, the governor-general, in 1913. It is a general hospital but the emphasis is on midwifery and training staff. Since 1933 the nurses it has trained in midwifery, and who have passed the government examination, have been placed in small maternity homes in the surrounding villages (Roseveare, 1946; Stephens, 1961). Iyi Enu hospital was rebuilt after civil war damage. Wusasa hospital in Zaria in the north started in 1905 as a dispensary in the old walled Muslim city in Dr Walter Miller's home, but grew to a well known hospital in the suburb of Wusasa in 1927, now linked to the Ahmadu Bello University complex of teaching hospitals. It has an active under-fives outreach programme (Miller, 1936; CMS, 1930).

Several other large societies ran medical programmes in Nigeria, the Presbyterians (whose Mary Slessor hospital at Itu was the best known, but was destroyed in the civil war), the

American Southern Baptists, at Eku, Ogbomosho, Kontagora, Shaki and Joinkrama (Sadler, 1950; Pinnock, 1918), and the two sister interdenominational missions, Sudan Interior (SIM) and Sudan United (SUM). Dr P.W. Barden founded Vom hospital in 1924, and Dr Bronnum (of Denmark) the Numan hospital in 1914. Other SUM doctors were recruited from the United States, Europe and South Africa (Maxwell, 1953). SUM were the first to begin medical work on the shores of Lake Chad (Carling, 1964; Moles, 1973). Dr Andrew Stirrett, SIM's first doctor, arrived in 1901, built a hill station near Jos at Miango in 1914, engaged in bible translation with Walter Miller, and died in Jos aged 83. SIM built hospitals and leprosy centres in Jos, Kano, Egbe and Patigi (Hunter, 1961). In Angola, Dr Walter Fisher of the Brethren was the best known of their many medical missionaries (Fisher and Hoyte, 1948). Other societies included the Church of the Brethren, several Catholic societies, the Salvation Army and the Seventh Day Adventists, all of whom carried on extensive medical work (Maule, 1977). Outstanding too was the work of the Scottish Presbyterian churches in South Africa, Malawi, and Kenya. Dr Robert Laws, perhaps Livingstone's most distinguished successor, after a brief stay in Cape MacClear on Lake Nyasa, established a first-class group of institutions at the northern end of the lake, a printing press, trade school, schools and teacher training college, clerical polytechnic and a hospital. He worked there from 1875 to 1934, and named it Livingstonia. He was the first to introduce chloroform to medical practice in Central Africa. His iron-hulled steamer, the *Ilala*, could be dismantled, and surmounting cataracts he eventually got it on to the lake and up the Zambesi and Shire rivers, something Livingstone failed to achieve (Laws, 1934). The Scottish missions attracted a wealth of unusually capable medical missionaries, such as Kerr Cross, John Chisholm, Walter Elmslie, Mrs Fraser, George Prentice at Bandawe, MacVicar of Blantyre, Henry Scott and William Affleck Scott, all in the period 1880 to 1905 (Elmslie, 1899; Gelfand, 1964). Dr James Stewart also created what might be termed a missionary college campus when he founded Lovedale Institution in South Africa in 1867 (Schram, 1981; 1985). Until the days of apartheid it was one of the most admired institutions of its kind in the country (Wells, 1904; Gelfand, 1983).

A few medical missionaries have been elected to positions in national governments in Africa. In Swaziland, Dr Samuel Hynd, medical superintendent of the Raleigh Fitkin Memorial Hospital of the Church of the Nazarene, and son of the founder who built the hospital in Manzini in 1925, had a period as Minister of Health. In Tanzania, Julius Nyerere appointed Dr Leader Stirling as Minister of Health, after he had worked since the 1930s with the Universities Mission to Central Africa at Lulindi and Masasi (Stirling, 1977). In 1966 the first speaker of the National Assembly of Botswana was Dr Alfred Merriweather, whose Scottish Livingstone Hospital at Molepolole was not only a place of healing and evangelism in a town, but the centre of an extensive medical outreach into the Kalahari by flying doctor services. He became a senior medical officer of the Botswana government in 1975 when the hospital was handed over (Merriweather, 1969; 1977).

In Egypt and the Sudan the pioneer work was done by the Church Missionary Society. Here, in a strongly Muslim area, proselytizing was sometimes forbidden and it was the work of medical missionaries which paved the way for a more sympathetic approach to the Christian faith (Gwynne, 1939).

The last word on the progress of medical missions in what used to be known as the Dark Continent may best be left to the Rev Dr David Milton Thompson who spent 29 years at St Luke's Hospital, Kaloleni, in Coast Province, Kenya. From his retirement as a clergyman in Essex he writes:

'My wife and I were posted to Kaloleni by the Church Missionary Society in 1952 to the hospital and its six outlying dispensaries. Both hospital and dispensaries were hardly out of the pioneer stage. There was no training school; no mattresses, sheets, pillows, or mackintoshes. There was no night staff, and it seemed revolutionary to put girls in men's wards . . . With the backing of CMS a change of policy ensued . . . In 1955 we embarked on two mobile dispensary units. One was concerned with treating schoolchildren for bilharzia . . . The other was manned by a doctor and nurse and was concerned for village health. This unit was out for 10-14 days at a time each month . . . We travelled up to 150 miles from the hospital . . . The unit reached remote parts cut off by lack of roads and transport . . . visits were welcomed . . .

During my time at Kaloleni, four diseases virtually disappeared: smallpox . . . cancrum oris, common as a complication of measles thirty years ago, has not been seen for ten years . . . Yaws and tropical ulcers have also virtually disappeared . . . Over the years we have witnessed a steady rise in standards of health and a steady passing of taboos and customs . . .

Why do we go? Because the "love of Christ constrains us". Not very often but every now and then a patient, or nurse, is converted and commits his or her life to Christ. This is perhaps the overall objective of our work. And it is work which calls for a life-long commitment to a country, a district, a tribe, to bring to them medical aid, and above all a knowledge of the saving power of our Lord Jesus Christ.'

References

Aitchison, Margaret (1983) The Doctor and the Dragon, Basingstoke: Pickering and Inglis

Anderson, G (c.1950) CMS Medical work, unpublished MSS in CMS library

Balme, Harold (1921) China and Modern Medicine, London: United Council for Missionary Education

Brook, Simon (1985) Unpublished MD thesis on Peter Parker of China. Cambridge: Still in progress

Broomhall, A.J. (1981) Hudson Taylor and China's Open Century, Book 1: Barbarians at the Gate, London Hodder & Stoughton and OMF

Burrows, E.H. (1958) A History of Medicine in South Africa up to the end of the 19th century, Cape Town and Amsterdam: Balkema

Carling, David (1964) Mobile Medical Work ashore and afloat, Saving Health, 3, 41

Causton, Mary I.M. (1951) For the Healing of the Nations, The Story of Baptist Medical Missions 1792-1951, London: The Carey Kingsgate Press

CMS (1930) Ina Za Ka? Written by CMS Hausa missionaries of Zaria. London: CMS

Elmslie, Walter A (1899) Among the Wild Ngoni, London: Cassell

Fisher, W. Singleton and Hoyte, Julian (1948) Africa Looks Ahead, London: Pickering and Inglis

Foster, W.D. (1978) Sir Albert Cook, a missionary doctor in Uganda (1870-1951) Macclesfield: Privately published

Gelfand, Michael (1957) Livingstone the Doctor, Oxford: Blackwell

Gelfand, Michael (1964) Lakeside Pioneers, 1875-1920, Oxford: Blackwell

Gelfand, Michael (1976) A Service to the Sick, (Southern Rhodesia 1890-1953) Gwelo: Mambo Press

Gelfand, Michael (1983) Christian Doctor and Nurse, a history of medical missions in South Africa from 1799-1976, South Africa: Published privately by the Aitken family

Gwynne, L.H. (1939) These Fifty Years. The story of the Old Cairo Medical Mission from 1889-1939, Old Cairo: CMS

Hewat, Elizabeth C.K. (1960) *Vision and Achievement*, Edinburgh: Nelson

Hunter, J.H. (1961) *A Flame of Fire, The life and work of R.V. Bingham*, Slough: Hazell, Watson and Viney

Latourette, K.S. (1929) *A History of Christian Missions in China*, London: SPCK

Laws, Roberts (1934) *Reminiscences of Livingstonia*, Edinburgh: Oliver and Boyd

Lockhart, William (1861) *The Medical Missionary in China*, London: Hurst and Blackett

Maule, Henry (1977) *Moved with Compassion, Evan den Hartog in Zaire*, London: Souvenir Press

Maxwell, J. Lowry (1953) *Half a Century of Grace, a jubilee history of the Sudan United Mission*, London: SUM

Merriweather, Alfred (1969) *Desert Doctor*, London: Lutterworth Press

Merriweather, Alfred (1977) *Desert Harvest*, London: Lutterworth Press

Miller, Walter R.S. (1936) *Reflections of a Pioneer*, London, CMS

Moles, Margaret (1973) *A Place called Vom*, Sidcup: SUM

Moorshead, Fletcher (1929) *Heal the Sick*, London: The Carey Press

Neill, Stephen (1964) *A History of Christian Missions*, Harmondsworth: Penguin Books

Pascoe, C.F. (1901) *Two Hundred Years of the SPG*, vol 2 London: Society for the Propagation of the Gospel

Pennell, T.L. (1909) *Among the Wild Tribes of the Afghan Frontier*

Pennell, A.M. (1914) *Pennell of the Afghan Frontier*

Pinnock, S.G. (1918) *The Romance of Missions in Nigeria*, Richmond, Virginia: Foreign Mission Board of Southern Baptist Convention

Roseveare, Margaret P (1946) *High Spring, the story of Iyi Enu hospital*, London: CMS

Sadler, George W (1950) *A Century in Nigeria*, Nashville, Broadman Press

Schram, R. (1971) *A History of the Nigerian Health Services*, (from 1450-1960), Ibadan: Ibadan University Press

Schram, R. (1981a) Modern Medicine, chapter in: *Cambridge Encyclopedia of Africa*, pp.392-396 Cambridge: CUP

Schram, R. (1981b) Britain's contribution to health and medicine in tropical countries through medical missions *Trans. Roy. Soc. trop. med.* 75, 56-58

Schram, R. (1985) A history of community health in Africa, chapter in: Sofoluwe, G.O. and Bennett, F.J. (1985) *Principles and Practice of Community Health in Africa*, Oxford: OUP

Somervell, T. Howard (1936) *After Everest*, London: Hodder and Stoughton

Stirling, Leader (1977) *Tanzania Doctor*, London: C. Hurst

Stock, Eugene (1916) *The History of the Church Missionary Society*, Vol. 4. London: CMS

Tatford, Fred A (1984) *Light over the Dark Continent*, Bath: Echoes of Service

Thomson, H.P. (1951) *Into All Lands, the history of the Society for the Propagation of the Gospel*, London: SPCK

Wells, James (1908) *The Life of James Stewart*, London: Hodder and Stoughton

Wong, K. Chimin and Lien-Teh, Wu (1932) *History of Chinese Medicine*, Tientsin: The Tientsin Press

CHAPTER 5

MATERNITY SERVICES

Josephine Barnes and T.F. Davey

The human race for many thousands of years has been acutely aware of the mystery and the dangers surrounding pregnancy and childbirth. What basically is the most wonderful and natural of all living processes can suddenly, mysteriously, and in a most devastating way become fraught with peril to the life of mother and unborn baby. Here we are at the centrepoint of human existence. Any threat to the continuity of the family, race or class is a matter for deep community concern, and long ago the whole sequence of events in human reproduction was a primary matter for folklore and became enshrined in religious beliefs of great tenacity.

It is difficult for people in affluent countries to enter into the struggle for survival that over the centuries has been the lot of many communities in Africa, India and other parts of the tropical world. Climate and nutrition are obvious factors. Even more serious, however, is the range of infective disease, long since controlled in Western countries, but still prevalent and lethal over huge areas of the developing world. The naming ceremony for a new-born babe is a joyous event everywhere, but the actual names given are often a sad reminder of the bitter experience of the race. Here are some boys' names common among the Ibos of Eastern Nigeria:

Chikwe – God grant (continuing life)
Onwubiko – Death, *please* (pass me by)
Ndudirim – May my lot be life
Chinasiokwu – It is all in God's hands (literally, God says the word)

There are many other names in the same category, all of them condensing into a child's name the sombre history of a race, where until very recently no first-born child was expected to live, and where half of the children born would be dead before they reached the age of five. These people have a rare gift of gaiety and humour, given perhaps to compensate them for an all too familiar acquaintance with death.

Until recently, among these people, the husband was vigorously excluded from the mysteries involved in his wife's confinement. By ancient right, his mother and mother-in-law very firmly took charge, and would call in the village midwife as need arose.

Truth has long exploded the myth that African women automatically have easy labours. If many do, this is largely due to the healthy active life considered normal for women throughout pregnancy. Complications encountered in Europe apply everywhere, aggravated in developing countries by malnutrition and anaemia.

From time immemorial the traditional midwife has been an important member of society. The position was often passed from mother to daughter, and in many countries these women possessed considerable skill and knowledge. The handywoman was still a feature of the British scene in 1930s, but she has largely disappeared thanks to the arrival of the professionally trained midwife and the fact that the National Health Service is available to all.

There are still many places in the world, however, where the majority of deliveries are conducted by unqualified birth attendants. They are known by a variety of names: dayas in Egypt, nanas in the West Indies, dukun beranak in Indonesia. They are usually older women who have borne children themselves, but in a few societies men also act as birth attendants. This group should never be disparaged, since they represent the ancestors of the profession of midwifery and the speciality of obstetrics.

In some societies, traditional midwifery practice is simple, natural and safe in the context of normal labour, but it may include dangerous customs. The use of cow-dung as a lubricant to the birth canal, or as an application to the umbilical cord is an important cause of tetanus in the newborn. In many parts of the world the tradition that no drop of water should pass the mother's lips until she was safely delivered increased the problems, especially in the heat of the tropics. Fortunately, normal and rapid labour is the setting of most deliveries, but outside this enormous problems may arise.

In Eastern Nigeria, the first object of the local midwives seems to be to make labour as short as possible. When conditions are entirely normal and the mother is in excellent physical condition, abdominal pummelling may not cause much harm, but again and again one has encountered most serious complications that could be traced to this custom. The same anxiety betrays itself in the need to complete matters rapidly once the child has been born. A mother being brought to hospital gave birth unexpectedly in the hospital grounds before the reception-room could be reached. Called urgently, the doctor arrived to find the two grannies pulling on the umbilical cord for dear life, and not at all pleased when he took over from them.

Ignorant midwifery meant the loss of many mothers. It was only when labour had been obstructed for some time, or the appalling disaster of twins was suspected, that the midwives would wash their hands of the case and hand the unfortunate mother over to the distracted husband, saying they could do no more, and it was now up to him. With local variations this situation could be parallelled over much of Asia and Africa. In China, the early Christian workers found themselves confronted with the additional problems of a depressed womanhood, and in 1868 Dr Porter Smith referred to the wide extent of female infanticide. Obstructed labour usually spelt death to both mother and babe, usually after meddlesome midwifery had first done its best – or worst.

Obstetrics played a minor role in the work of government hospitals in the developing world for many years, and it was largely left to Christian missions to introduce this important branch of medicine to the general public. This took place on a large scale, and is one of the great contributions of medical missions to the health of mankind. Christian doctors and midwives brought with them scientific training and knowledge and challenged ignorance and superstition. Progress followed that in the developed world, though they found traditional systems of obstetric care still deeply entrenched; indeed in many countries to this day traditional birth attendants provide the major part of obstetric care.

The first impact on the entrenched position came in the treatment of obstetric emergencies. In an obstructed labour a point will be reached where the traditional midwife will declare the case hopeless. In her opinion the unfortunate mother will have reached such a state through her own fault or through offending some ancient taboo. She is no longer acceptable to the tribal deities and her body is fit for nothing but to be thrown away. Now, and for the first time, her husband is allowed on the scene, and he may take her as a last resort to the Western doctor. Alas, by the time she reached skilled help, it is likely that the baby will be dead and, if the mother survives, she will be seriously injured.

Many such scenes occurred in Eastern Nigeria. Although theoretically a full-time leprologist at a large leprosy hospital, one of the authors (Davey) was repeatedly the only Western-trained doctor available to a surrounding population of at least 100,000. Inevitably, obstetric emergencies began to arrive at the hospital. A distracted husband and his friends would appear carrying on a bed his wife in extremis, with the undelivered baby already dead, and she herself with only a few hours left of life. Sometimes she was already beyond human aid, but there were occasions when a destructive operation on the impacted dead baby secured its speedy delivery, and then skilled nursing care could restore the life and health of the mother, to the amazed delight of all concerned.

Right across the developing world, this is where modern midwifery began, dealing with the terrible complications of midwifery which one reads about in old text books, but which are only rarely seen in modern midwifery practice in the developed countries. These were situations of total helplessness in the eyes of the husband and relatives of the patients concerned, who had invariably turned to the Western doctor as a last resort. Every success was thus a miracle in their eyes. Even though only one mother in three might survive, a powerful blow had been struck against age-old fears and prejudices. The power of malignant spiritual forces had been challenged and broken, and the first rays of a new dawn had appeared. Needless to say, such situations challenged all the skill, patience and resource that doctors and midwives could summon.

Midwifery practice thus constituted an immediate challenge to any Western doctor or trained nursing sister going into a pioneering situation anywhere in the developing world. Dr Porter Smith, the first Western doctor in Central China, opened the first hospital in that part of the world at Hankow in 1866. It consisted of a ward for twelve male patients in the rear portion; a patients' waiting-hall, consulting-room and dispensary in the front portion, together with two small rooms for female patients. Here obstetrics could be practised. Chinese women and children were greatly attracted by Dr Porter Smith's courtesy, gentleness and skill, and he built up a considerable practice among them, only terminated by his own failing health and return to Britain in 1871. Maternity work was resumed at a new level with the appointment of a trained nurse and midwife in 1886, and the opening shortly afterwards of the first hospital for women in Central China.

The same kind of experience occurred in numerous places, first in Asia and later in Africa. At first, it was exceptional for a male doctor to be allowed to look after a woman in labour, and indeed in places under Muslim influence, in any sickness whatever; but the arrival of Western trained women doctors and nursing sisters changed that situation and led to an enormous increase in maternity services. At first the maternity facility was attached to a women's ward, but soon separate accommodation was seen to be necessary, and substantial maternity units began to arise and develop into major departments in all large mission hospitals.

Some of the most important hospitals in Asia began in this way. One of the most famous of them all, the Christian Medical College and Hospital at Vellore in South India, owes its origins to an encounter between Ida Scudder, a carefree young American woman, and a desperate young Indian at her father's home near Madras. He had come to the home seeking medical aid for his 14-year-old wife who was dying in childbirth. She told him it was her doctor father he needed, but no, only a woman doctor would be acceptable. So she went back to the United States, trained as a doctor and returned to found the hospital in 1900. At least four other major hospitals in India:- St Stephen's, Delhi; the Christian Medical College, Ludhiana; the Christian Medical College, Miraj; and the Holdsworth Memorial Hospital, Mysore – all began with emphasis on midwifery.

Miss Elsie Ludlow, FRCS, writes:

'I shall never forget the first five maternity cases after my arrival at the Wesley Guild Hospital, Ilesha, in 1931; the first patient died on the way to the hospital as she was being carried in a hammock from a nearby village after several days in labour. The carriers requested the removal of the already dead baby, as it was not good to bury a mother with the child inside her. The second patient breathed her last at my feet on the hospital verandah, before she could be admitted. The third arrived in a state of shock, with no pains and an impacted head after five days in labour, and died before she could be delivered. The fourth was delivered of a stillborn baby and developed vesico-vaginal fistula after a prolonged labour before admission; the fifth was delivered of a healthy baby and after a very stormy puerperium recovered. At that time a normal case was rarely brought to the hospital. This experience taught me dramatically the need to get out into the towns and villages around Ilesha and carry out preventive medicine including antenatal care, and to teach mothers to come for help in time. This need was re-confirmed when, as a result of questioning one thousand mothers, it was established that the mortality rate in the first five years of life was over 70 per cent.

In the developing world, antenatal care began to be accepted as the direct result of the success of Western doctors in treating the complications of childbirth. It was natural for doctors and midwives to say to their patients: "If only we had been able to look after you during your pregnancy, these dangerous complications could have been avoided," and gradually the concept of antenatal care became accepted. This was indeed extremely important, because causes of ill-health during pregnancy in many developing parts of the world are more diverse and widespread than in affluent countries, especially as the result of tropical infective diseases, malnutrition and anaemia.

A crucial point in the development of modern maternity services in Eastern Nigeria arose when one or two far-seeing missionary nursing sisters encouraged women to come for antenatal care without demanding that anyone receiving it must come for delivery in hospitals. The hospital facilities were available, and patients were welcome to make use of them, but this was not mandatory. To more conservative foreign medical staff, this was a dangerous innovation, but it paid off in a remarkable way. Soon, antenatal clinics at these hospitals were crowded, and a popular movement developed which spread across the country. No matter how reluctant individual doctors and nursing sisters may have been, they were swept along with the movement and within a few years many thousands of women availed themselves of this service. Antenatal care had become fashionable: it was quite the done thing to meet one's friends at the clinic, receive the personal attention of the foreign midwives (and before long their national trainees), listen to a talk on health matters, and go home with a bottle of medicine, having spent an agreeable and invigorating day.

The longer term results were predictable. The traditional midwives may have gained in standing to some extent, as there were fewer abnormal labours, but in the villages some catastrophies inevitably continued. What really mattered was that a spirit of unrest had entered the women's world in the Region. Many now wanted to have their babies in hospital, and facilities began to be stretched. Simultaneously, a popular demand began to spread across the country for local maternity homes supervised by mission hospitals. The possession of a 'Maternity' began to be seen as a prestige symbol by one clan after another.'

The speed of change in Nigeria is well brought out by the

following statistics from Methodist hospitals:

Hospital	Women Outpatients		
	1940	**1950**	**1960**
Ilesha	3,420	4,833	22,401
Ituk Mban	1,866	4,166	6,140
Ama Achara	1,182	3,953	6,386
Oron	2,486	3,565	1,325

	Deliveries		
	1940	**1950**	**1960**
Ilesha	426	1,554	3,041
Ituk Mbang	38	1,247	1,442
Ama Achara	117	423	476
Oron	176	817	668

This experience was common to all mission hospitals in the country. It epitomizes the situation that develops as the concept of antenatal care becomes accepted widely by the people.

In former days in China, it was usual for the wives of Government officials to spend their lives in seclusion, many of them never to be seen by the public eye. The medical care of such women had thus to be exclusively on a domiciliary basis. Quite early this became an important feature of the life of many a missionary doctor, even before the days when women doctors began to be available. Here is an interesting first-hand report of such a visit made in 1905 by the doctor in charge of Fatshan Methodist Hospital:

'An encouraging feature of the twelve months' work was the continued increase in the number of visits paid to the homes of patients. These exceeded three hundred, in addition to sixty occasions on which the doctors were requested to attend cases of difficult labour. In Fatshan a professional visit is a much more ceremonious affair than in England. To a newcomer, indeed, it is most embarrassing. The journey itself, made in a sedan chair, is a novel experience.

When the patient's home is reached, the doctor is invited in by the head of the house, and some time is wasted in each trying to make the other sit down first. According to the Chinese Classics, the rules of ceremony are 300 in number, and those of behaviour 3,000; and one can well believe that it is so. Tea has to be drunk first, and much conversation entered into before the suggestion is thrown out at last that perhaps the doctor might like to see a case of sickness in the house. In the meanwhile, if the patient happens to live in a distant village, the whole population will turn out and form such a crowd outside the house as to block the street. After the patient has been seen and any necessary operation performed, a small feast is prepared, and perhaps arrangements are made to spend the night in some ancestral temple. It is then that abundant opportunities present themselves for friendly conversation about the gospel.'

Fatshan Hospital was founded in 1881. From small beginnings, it developed into an important teaching hospital, and probably continues in that capacity today. Gradually, midwifery became an important part of the work. Reviewing progress made up till 1908, the following statistics were recorded:

Outpatient cases	194,000
Inpatients	8,100
Midwifery cases	960
Operations upon the eye	1,400
Operations for stone	480
Total operations	6,800

Comment on the midwifery figures was as follows: 'Nearly one thousand cases of midwifery are included in our list. The Chinese have no knowledge as to what ought to be done in times of difficulty. As a rule, in any seriously abnormal case of childbirth the mother dies. The large majority of those who come under our treatment require operation.'

In India, domiciliary midwifery became a feature of a number of city hospitals. Khammanuet is a large industrial town in Andhra Pradesh. Domiciliary midwifery was introduced by Sister Watson at the 128-bed Church of South India Hospital in 1960. It was a moving experience for a visiting doctor to join one of the several teams of two midwives at work in the town and follow them during a busy morning. In one street, a wealthy home was visited where the young mother and babe had every comfort. A number of homes of respectable white-collar workers and artisans followed. Then came a slum, where precisely the same skilled care was offered with the same courtesy to the wife of a beggar. Everywhere the midwives went, their uniforms were recognized and respected, so that they could travel unharmed, much in the same way as their counterparts in England were able to do in the earlier years of this century. The effect of their work in terms of friendship and Christian witness was remarkable.

Palwal is a small town about 40 miles (64 km) to the north of Delhi. Here the Baptist Missionary Society has maintained a hospital for many years, but in 1956 it was decided to branch out with domiciliary midwifery. The Society appointed a trained European health visitor to the staff. The town was surveyed and a street plan prepared. The cooperation of traditional midwives, or 'dais' as they are called, was seen to be essential, and a proposal was made to pay to any who cooperated the going rate for every delivery: 2 rupees for a girl baby, 5 for a boy. One dai accepted this, and the project opened in her area of the town, the dai introducing the nursing sister and pupil midwife to expectant mothers, who were then visited regularly and a relation of trust established with at least some of them. In spite of much prejudice and several setbacks, the reputation of the midwifery service gradually grew and other dais began to call the midwives out, so much so that the hospital staff were soon fully extended.

A baby clinic, initially for mothers who had been delivered at home, was an obvious next step and became very popular, to be followed by an antenatal clinic. Both at clinics and in patients' homes, health talks were given, and before long the project began to spread into the villages around the town, a visible demonstration of the love of God for all.

A very remarkable example of domiciliary midwifery comes from Dhampueram in South India. The long-established Church of South India Hospital was a recognized major centre for midwifery, but it was felt that its impact on village life was inadequate. In 1960 a European nursing sister with an Indian nurse and midwife went to live in an Indian setting in a large and very conservative village, creating what was really a local health centre, following up patients from the hospital and encouraging all seriously sick people to seek help from the hospital. These brave women suffered initial persecution, but soon won overwhelming support from the women of the village, and it was then discovered that there existed a caste of people so conservative and so depressed that they had never availed themselves of any health services whatever, either from government or voluntary agencies. A woman in the village from this caste went into labour which became obstructed. By then, the little Christian group had become accepted, and they were invited to attend her. Both mother and baby survived, with a consequent accelerating acceptance of new standards of health care and hygiene.

In several parts of Africa extensive domiciliary midwifery

services developed not only in relation to city hospitals but also in rural areas where the key to the organization was the local maternity home. These maternity homes were developed in the first instance by medical missionaries as the only practical solution to the problems created by a mass demand by women for skilled medical care during pregnancy and labour. Some began as church-related institutions. Others were developed by local government authorities, but in both cases it was mission hospitals who trained the nurses and midwives so essential to the organization.

The Niger Diocesan Maternity Service, built up through the inspiration of Dr Sybil Batley in the Niger Anglican diocese, is a good example of a church-related organization. Local maternity homes were built to a simple standard plan in centres where they could be supported by local Christian congregations and receive oversight from the local pastor. Each home was in the care of a trained Nigerian midwife, who kept in touch with the major base hospital at Iyi Enu and was visited regularly by a doctor from that hospital. The early maternity homes were of simple design, built of mud and thatch in order to gain the confidence of the people; but these were gradually replaced by better and more permanent buildings. In some cases, voluntary labour was given by the townspeople, and maintenance grants were received from a few local authorities. Thirty-one such homes were established, and 6565 births were recorded in a single year with only four maternal deaths. In the same year there were nearly 13,000 new patients, so that almost 50 per cent had their babies at the maternity homes.

Infant welfare clinics were a feature of these homes, followed up in some cases by visits to the mothers' own homes. At Ata where 167 mothers were visited regularly over a period of six months, not a single baby died – a remarkable achievement in Nigerian conditions (Jewitt, 1950).

The development of modern maternity services in countries where they were previously unknown provided many opportunities for original work, both in relation to the facts discovered concerning the complications of pregnancy and childbirth, and also in relation to the problems surrounding the delivery of modern maternity care. The *Journal of the Christian Medical Association of India* has been an important forum for the publication of original articles. For example, it published the article responsible for the introduction into India of the modern lower segment Caesarean operation by the surgeons of the Presbyterian Hospital at Shillong, one among many important matters investigated in India. Three further examples may be selected from an extensive list of contributions to advances in this field by workers at mission hospitals.

Neonatal tetanus carries a high mortality in the newborn child. The causative microorganism, *Clostridium tetani*, is transmitted to the newborn infant via the umbilical cord, infected by the dirty knife or scissors with which the cord is cut, and the dressing which the traditional midwife then applies to seal the cut, which may consist of cow-dung. An alternative popular dressing in Nigeria is the juice of a young banana shoot. Such young banana shoots originate from the parent stem below ground level where they are liable to be heavily infected with various microorganisms, including that of tetanus.

In a series of 114 consecutive cases treated at the Nixon Memorial Hospital, Segbwema, Sierra Leone, Dr J.L. Wilkinson (1961), the medical superintendent, reported that the mortality rate fell from 72.7 to 48.6 per cent following the introduction of a new method of treatment.

Hydatidiform mole is a dangerous complication of pregnancy which tends to be particularly common in parts of Asia. The success of therapy depends predominantly on its diagnosis and removal. Satisfying evidence of its successful management is a report from the Holdsworth Memorial Hospital, Mysore, South India. This showed successful recovery in 13 out of 14 cases seen in 1939-41. In all who recovered, the successful outcome was predominantly due to early diagnosis followed by removal of the mole.

The maternity village at Ituk Mbang in Nigeria represents an important example of medical research in field conditions. Here the problem was how best to reduce maternal and neonatal mortality where many mothers were coming to hospital already in labour. Dr Harry Haigh decided to try the experiment of inviting mothers to stay in a model village for some weeks before their confinement in surroundings where they would feel at home, but which provided the opportunity for malaria prophylaxis and medical oversight before delivery, and made possible teaching in hygiene and infant care. During the first year (1961) the statistics of the hospital showed:

	Maternity village patients	Other patients admitted in labour
Number of deliveries	775	448
Number of children born	807	469
Still births	16	98
	(19/1000)	(209/1000)
Delivered spontaneously	723	349
	(93%)	(78%)
Ruptured uterus	nil	7
Destructive operations	nil	29

Christian medical work does not begin in the crowded outpatient department: it begins in research directed to the prevention of disease.

Almost everywhere in developing countries, the doctors and nursing sisters who founded maternity units soon found themselves engaged in midwifery training. The taxing demands of midwifery, much of it at night, imposed a considerable burden on workers whose days were already crowded with large numbers of medical and surgical cases, some of them of great complexity. Reliable help was essential to relieve this burden, and was to be found in the person of some young widow with a smattering of education, some orphan girl for whom there was no husband, or the wife of a teacher or pastor. In some places, unmarried girls were unacceptable to the general public as midwives, but almost everywhere some suitable person could be found, and midwifery training schools began to develop widely. Standards of training varied, and sooner or later governments regulated the situation by establishing National Midwifery Boards side by side with developing nursing services. Voluntary agencies were represented on these Boards, which had authority to standardize curricula, conduct examinations, award diplomas, and set midwifery on a firm professional basis.

A classical example of an achievement in this field is the Maternity School established in Uganda in 1918 by the CMS missionaries Albert (later Sir Albert) and Katharine Cook. It was named the Lady Coryndon Maternity Training School after the wife of the Governor who presided over the committee, and which included representatives of the government and Missions, both Roman Catholic and Protestant. In January 1919 the first eight students followed Katharine to church dressed in their most becoming uniforms of black cape with badge, white dresses with black collars. Six of these first students graduated a year later by passing a written and practical examination set by a government doctor, Dr Collyns. One of the students was the daughter of the Katikiro, Sir Apollo Kagwa (Foster, 1978).

The practice of midwifery in Uganda was revolutionized in the 1920s largely due to the energy of Katharine Cook; some of the problems reveal the difficulties encountered by this courageous venture. Thus it was at first almost impossible to attract students of an adequate educational standard, but the major problem was a moral laxity that led to a number of dismissals. The training scheme, originally one year, was extended to two years, and two schools, one Protestant and one Roman Catholic, were founded. Expansion inevitably took place, and in February 1931 Princess Alice opened the Lady Stanley Women's Hospital and Maternity Training Centre.

'The fame of Katharine's maternity training scheme soon spread beyond the boundaries of Uganda. Lady Gregg, the wife of the Governor of Kenya, was enthusiastic to start similar maternity centres in that country and she made a start with 2 Bagande girls specially sent to her at Mombasa by Katharine. A senior official of the Union of South Africa, hopeful of initiatives to start a similar training scheme, came to visit the Midwifery Training School, as did Prince Leopold, later to become King of the Belgians, who wished to start something similar in the Belgian Congo.'

These heroic enterprises indicate some of the many problems that the mission hospitals encountered in their endeavour to add to their Christian mission by bringing the advantages of modern midwifery training to the developing world and to the desperate needs of women.

References
Foster, W.D. (1978) *The Church Missionary Society and Modern Medicine in Uganda. The Life of Sir Albert Cook, KCMG. 1870-1951* Newhaven: Newhaven Press
Jewitt, Dorothy (1950) *West Africa*, January 28
Partridge, Alan B (1962) Medicine in the Church Missionary Society Niger Mission *Saving Health* 1, 44. London: Medical Missionary Association
Wilkinson, J.L. (1961) Neonatal tetanus in Sierra Leone *British Medical Journal*, i, 1721

CHAPTER 6

CHILD HEALTH

D. Morley

The authors of an account of the Health Services in Ghana start their report with these words: 'It is now widely accepted that in most countries of Africa, Asia and Latin America, the government health services have failed to meet the needs of the rural masses. Far too many children, in particular, die of preventable illness.' This criticism can be applied to both government and voluntary health services. Both have emphasized high standards, but have failed to ensure that *all* the population – and particularly children – have minimum services.

UNICEF have produced figures of life expectation of children from rich and very poor countries:

	Born in a rich country	Born in a very poor country
Chances of dying before age one year	1 in 66	1 in 5
Life expectancy	70 years	50 years
Chance of seeing a health worker	100%	10%
Probable years at school	11	2

Many in the West have become inured to this situation, but we need to examine the reasons for it. In less developed countries child health is dominated by the twin problems of nutritional deficiency and infectious disease. The blanket of illness affecting so many children is of great importance in social terms. In the past medical workers and planners have often assumed that any large reduction in child mortality must await an improvement in socio-economic conditions and environmental hygiene. But we now realize that health workers with appropriate training in child health can organize a service that will prevent more than half of the deaths in infancy and early childhood before any great change in the environment has taken place (Gwatkin et al., 1980). Such comprehensive care cannot wait for local conditions to approach those that now exist in more

91

developed areas of the world. Improvement, if any, in the per capita income of less developed countries is likely to be slow. The per capita expenditure on health, estimated in 1970 at only 1% of that of developed countries – is unlikely at best to more than double or treble by the end of this century.

While demographers predict that world population will stabilize around the middle of the next century, the number of children in the less developed countries is still increasing at the rate of 200,000 every decade. This increase comes at a time when resources are almost certainly not increasing as rapidly. Therefore those who are planning and providing services have a particular problem now, and Christians and others concerned for the future of mankind will need to give special emphasis to the care of children between now and the end of this century. The demand for services will far exceed what is available at a time when the health and intellectual development of those who will be the labour force and decision-makers of the future is at risk.

Church-related agencies
The history of the provision of health care in developing countries over the last fifty years cannot but take account of the work of the church-related agencies. In some countries they have provided one half of the medical services, measured in terms of hospital beds, and have developed and provided most of the care available in rural areas. It is less easy to assess the extent to which the reorientation of medical care towards preventive and primary health services has been achieved through church-related institutions – a change which is of more importance to children than to any other section of the population.

There is good evidence that Christian organizations have at least influenced this change. In many countries indigenous health workers, often supported by expatriate missionaries working in innumerable small hospitals, have explored and developed appropriate technology and health programmes suited to the needs of the area and the limited financial resources available. Few of the large number of these projects have been written up, and even fewer evaluated, but as an expression of Christian compassion they have done much to bring about a change of approach and greater concern for the health of both mother and young child.

The experience gained has been brought to bear at national

and international levels by the Christian Medical Commission of the World Council of Churches, a body brought into being in 1963 at a meeting in Tübingen hosted by the German Institute for Medical Missions. From its earliest days the Commission was responsible for many local and international meetings, and through its publications proposed considerable changes in the orientation of health care systems with a view to achieving greater justice in the distribution of medical resources. Many of the ideas and approaches antedated similar decisions by WHO and the UN General Assembly.

The fact remains, however, that the major contribution to improvements in the health of children in developing countries has, and will, come from changes outside the health field. For example, the work of Christian missions in setting up educational services, particularly for girls, has been more important than any efforts in the health field. The World Bank has stated that for every year of girls' schooling the infant mortality rate (IMR) – that is death in the first year of life – falls by nine points. This means that in the many countries with an IMR of 100/1000 live births, five years of schooling for all girls could be expected to reduce the rate from 100 to 55/1000. A new project being developed jointly by church-related workers in health and education is the CHILD-to-Child programme, which teaches and encourages older children to concern themselves with the health and development of their younger brothers and sisters.

Church-related workers are also helping to encourage the development of appropriate agricultural techniques to provide better family nutrition. By raising the economic ability of the family, particularly the mother, the children are the ones most likely to benefit.

An important Christian initiative in child health has been the positive example and influence of the Christian home. Through their home-making, family life, and care of their children's health, education and general welfare, pastors, teachers and other Christians have shown what can be done in many different circumstances. Through the influence of Christian wives, local women have been taught the importance of such things as washing hands and the care of the umbilicus of the newborn. The need for such a message is shown by a recent report that in parts of India more than 50 out of every 1000 newborn babies die of neonatal tetanus.

McKeown (1976) has suggested that the widespread and easy

public access to family planning services in Europe and North America has been a public health development of major importance, allowing parents to decide for themselves the number of children they wish to have. Here again, the church-related missions in developing countries, including Roman Catholics, have played a major part in making planning services, seen in the context of family health, understood and widely accepted. Their emphasis has been on child spacing rather than family limitation and by this means they have improved child health and educational potential (Morley and Woodland, 1979).

Specialist paediatric services

The UK lagged behind other countries in Europe and the USA in developing specialist paediatric services. Few British universities had a chair of paediatrics before World War II, whereas they were by then common in Europe. During the whole period of the British Empire no paediatrician was appointed to the Colonial Medical Service. Many Christian workers, however, saw the special needs of women and children. Ida Scudder at Vellore as far back as 1900, and others such as Amy Carmichael, devoted special attention to girls who are rejected in so many male-orientated societies. Dr. Betty Cowan at Ludhiana has shown how to teach young Indian doctors to identify female infants in Harijan families who are particularly at risk of undernutrition and early death. In 1917 Sister Tomkinson of the Holdsworth Memorial Hospital, Mysore, said that a nurse was not thoroughly trained unless she could care for children in health and sickness. The children's ward of that hospital, built in 1925, was a pioneering effort, as was the important step in separating children's outpatients in 1943. In 1955, when the foundations of the new hospital in Mysore were laid, the Maharajah of Mysore said:

'Dr. Gillespie . . . has rightly stressed the high priority that should be given to the development of medical work among children, for indeed the future of a nation depends on the welfare and strength of the rising generation, and the establishment of a hospital of this kind is one of the first steps towards nation building.'

Such statements, of course, are only too true. In some developing countries one half of all deaths occur in children under five, mostly from preventable or easily treatable conditions. Unfortunately such statements are seldom followed up by the necessary action in terms of deploying resources to improve child health. Nor are many of the child's needs met by hospital wards or hospital outpatient departments. For example, there has been much misunderstanding as to the major cause of the malnutrition that underlies and greatly increases the severity of the majority of children's diseases in these countries. It used to be assumed that lack of protein was at the root of the trouble, but we now realize that the major deficit in most diets is low energy (calorie) intake; in other words, most children do not have enough to eat. The unrefined foods which make up their diet are too bulky in relation to the small size of a child's stomach, so that even a 'full belly' twice a day (and many children eat at most twice a day) is not enough to provide all the energy required.

Doctors working in developing countries are faced with a blanket of malnutrition and the common infections. In a children's ward they are likely to see one or two deaths each day, and they soon come to realize that they will not prevent these deaths while they remain within the hospital environment. Paediatricians, especially those working in church-related hospitals, have therefore moved out into the community more than any other medical specialists, and they have found great encouragement and assistance from their colleagues in nursing and midwifery. No country could hope to provide curative services for so many sick children. The only practical solution was for the health services to move out to small centres, and, more recently, into homes, particularly those homes from which the high risk groups of children are seldom brought for help.

Community health care
Church-related medical work in the 1940s and even earlier had started in small dispensaries or other units in the vicinity of church-related hospitals. These were usually run by locally trained nurses under the supervision of expatriate sisters. These nurses proved popular, and some efforts had also been made with mobile clinics, such as that run from Vellore in India.

The Imesi study
In the early 1950s the Ilesha Hospital in Western Nigeria had built new premises and it was there that the surgeon, John Wright, who was in charge of the children's ward, recognized the ineffectiveness of existing curative services and appreciated the need for village studies if more appropriate care was to be offered to children. The West African Council for Medical

Research was approached and a small grant arranged which allowed Margaret Woodland, a trained health visitor who had had experience in Papua New Guinea, and myself, a paediatrician, to start the first and still one of the few major longitudinal studies of children growing up in village surroundings. Just over 400 mothers and their infants were recruited either in pregnancy or soon after birth. The study started in January 1957 in the village of Imesi-Ile. Margaret Woodland lived in the village for the next ten years and gained from the people their respect and love. She was able to gather a mass of information from which we could describe why common diseases such as measles and whooping cough took such a heavy toll of young lives. The experience gained there and in the associated Wesley Guild Hospital enabled a concept of comprehensive care through under-fives clinics to evolve.

As health workers in the village of Imesi, Margaret Woodland and I believed that we were introducing medical care as something new. As our knowledge grew we came to understand that we were not so much introducing something new as introducing an alternative system to that to which the people had been accustomed. Medical care at primary level, unlike that in hospitals, is a social and religious activity present to some extent in every community that has been studied worldwide. The mother appreciates the many dangers that arise for her small child in the early years of his life. She seeks to overcome and perhaps obviate these. For example, the mothers regularly used a medicinal tea for their children and placed around their necks neatly sewn leather necklaces in which they put material which, they hoped, would protect their children from what they saw as the cause of disease. With the advent of Western medical care, the preparation of these teas and the use of such necklaces declined.

In primary medical care the health worker must realize that she is offering an alternative. Whether these alternatives are acceptable will depend both on their success and her approach, particularly her sympathy to the child and his mother. To achieve this the medical worker needs to know, understand and sympathize with the peoples' beliefs, and particularly the beliefs of the mothers as to how disease is caused.

Recent trends
During the 1960s in East Africa, Maurice King was moving away from his microscope and laboratory bench and worked for a time

in a church-related hospital at Amudat. An invitation from him to join the symposium out of which came his outstanding book *Medical Care in Developing Countries* (King, 1966) was the start of a close collaboration and friendship. This book allowed the under-fives clinic to become well known and in particular suggested to workers around the world the advantages of simple growth charts (Fig. 1). These have now been widely adopted,

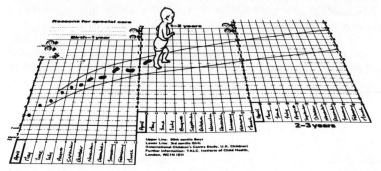

Fig. 1. – The simple growth chart successfully used in many church-related hospitals has been accepted by many Governments, but only in a few small countries is it used by three-quarters of the children.

modified in many ways, and are in use in almost every developing country as well as finding acceptance in many industrialized countries.

At Segbwema in Sierra Leone a mobile child clinic was started by Sister Edith Milner in 1959. This programme was taken over in the following year and developed over the next seven years by Sister Olive Smith. Her work became known throughout Sierra Leone and far beyond. Each year, at the height of the programme, two teams were coping with 45,000 attendances in the villages they visited.

During the 1960s there were important developments in India. The Children's Department at Vellore under John Webb, with Sheila Perera and Malati Jadhav, were undertaking important research in the common diseases of Indian children and in nutrition. Such conditions as undernutrition, diarrhoea, meningitis and rheumatic fever were studied in conjunction with the Indian Council for Medical Research. Both in urban and rural programmes the emphasis was on prevention. The influence of these studies was spread by the medical graduates trained at Vellore who are now working throughout India. Perhaps even more influential are the nurses who since 1950 have graduated BSc and now hold important positions as tutors and deans of nursing schools across the sub-continent.

William Cutting, coming from a family whose Indian medical service had spanned over 70 years, showed that under-fives clinics could be successful if appropriately modified to meet the different needs of a village in Andhra Pradesh. He also developed, for the first time in India, a residential nutrition rehabilitation centre on the model of those which had been pioneered by Michael Church at Makerere in the 1960s. In Ludhiana, Northern India, with support from Johns Hopkins University, Carl Taylor, who came from a family of missionaries, undertook the important and well designed Narangwal study which demonstrated that good nutrition was of greater relative importance than health care in improving the wellbeing and health of children in a group of villages in the Punjab.

In the 1960s a group of Methodists in the Ivory Coast set up an orphanage. From this the Methodist Missionary Society of the UK went on to develop their last major hospital, in Dabou. From its earliest days this hospital had a special concern for children.

In Zaire, from 1936 to 1958, a group of doctors and nurses including Dr Stanley Browne, Dr Raymond Holmes and Sister Mary Fagg, organized baby clinics and toddler clinics – 'kilos' as the locals called them because the children were always weighed. In these clinics mothers were trained in infant feeding and disease prevention. When pyrimethamine became available, deaths from cerebral malaria were reduced from 200 to zero in less than a year. The Yakusu area where this took place was one of the first where specific illnesses were identified for local campaigns. Hookworm was prevalent and caused child deaths from anaemia. Stool examination and haemoglobin estimations were made on 26,000 children by local auxiliaries and treatment given. The result was a rise in the haemoglobin level and complaints from the teachers that the children were becoming more mischievous.

An innovative programme has been developed by Jacques Courtejoie in Mayombe, Zaire. In the 1960s, with his help, the nurses there came to realize that the parents and relatives of children had little understanding of the causes of disease. They developed teaching aids and booklets and employed schoolchildren to produce them. Many of these children later became involved as health teachers. Their colourful teaching aids are now widely used in francophone and anglophone areas. For them health education has been a success story.

The work of the Christian Medical Commission in influencing international health policy has already been mentioned, but the Commission also had its effect on both Roman Catholic and Protestant church-related work throughout the world. To achieve this the Commission developed a policy of multiple local workshops in a developing country, in each of which the local hospitals were asked to redefine their policy and objectives. This was followed by a national workshop. As a result of these discussions, and particularly with the guidance of individuals such as Hakan Hellberg from Finland, the various mission groups were helped to a better understanding of the need for primary health care, and within primary health care the particularly urgent needs of children at village level.

The latter half of the 1970s saw the development around the world of a number of excellent village health programmes using part-time health workers from the community. Several of these started from church-related hospitals led by dedicated indigenous doctors. In India Raj and Mabelle Arole set up the Jamkhed programme which won for them the President Magsaysay Award, which has been likened to the Nobel laureateship. In Indonesia Gunawan Nugroho developed a health cadre in Solo. As a missionary in Korea, John Sibley was one of many surgeons who have become involved in setting up community health programmes. Across the world these programmes have particularly emphasized nutrition, immunization and the management of common conditions such as diarrhoea.

In Zimbabwe Dr Richard Stoughton at the Victoria Hospital developed such a programme among local farmers. Five of them were given practical training and were supplied with bicycles. They spent two to three days a week visiting outlying hamlets, treating minor conditions, advising the mothers on their children's nutrition and encouraging them to attend the next under-fives clinics. The 'health scouts' are but one of the many variations of health workers around the world.

Perhaps for the first time leaders of such programmes have been able to change the national approach to health care either by working through national governments, who have begun to recognize their achievements, or by joining and working through international organizations such as WHO.

The 'community compassion' for children demonstrated in many of the programmes described has grown from a fundamental compassion for the individual. This caring love has often been inspired by Jesus Christ who recognized the physical needs of children by healing those who were sick. He stimulated the intellectual development of his hearers with imaginative stories and real life parables. He encouraged their social consciousness, for example by accepting and sharing the food offered by a small boy, and he indicated that their attitude of personal trust was the highest example of God's kingdom on earth.

The influence on political decision-making in Christian countries has, however, been small compared with that achieved by Marxist teaching in socialist countries. In Marxist societies particular attention is given to the health of mothers and children. Countries such as Russia, Cuba, North Vietnam and China have surpassed capitalist societies in their ability to improve the health and development of children with limited but justly distributed resources. We need to accept this even if we cannot accept other facets of their ideology. If we are prepared to learn from them, we now have a wide choice of initiatives from which we can select appropriate items to include in our programmes. The choice in future may be made by the community or parish itself as to how their children will be cared for. The Christian church can muster its members engaged in health, education, agriculture and other disciplines to break down the barriers between them and further the care of children who are the future of the nation. Those who wish to be involved in this movement need, perhaps, to carry with them the words of Lao-Zi (c. 500 BC):

Go in search of your people.
Love them.
Learn from them,
Plant with them.
Serve them.
Begin with what they know.
Build on what they have.
When their work is done they will be satisfied if it can be said:
But of the best of leaders,
When their task is accomplished,
Their work is done, the people all remark
"We have done it ourselves".

References

Gwatkin, D.R., Wilcox, J.R., Wray, J.D. (1980) *Can Health and Nutrition Interventions make a Difference?* Monograph 13. Washington, D.C., Overseas Development Council.

King, M. (1966) *Medical Care in Developing Countries.* Nairobi, Oxford University Press.

McKeown, T. (1976) *The Modern Rise of Population.* London, Edward Arnold.

Morley, D. and Woodland, M. (1979) *See How They Grow.* London, Macmillan.

CHAPTER 7

EPIDEMIC DISEASES

C. Manson Bahr

Epidemic diseases have been a major cause of mortality in historic times and have greatly affected history both military and social. The Black Death, for instance, as plague was known, reduced the population of Europe by half in the 14th century. The Church has been intimately involved in many of the epidemics in the past as a source of solace and care, but not always in a caring role. Five epidemic diseases have been chosen to portray the Christian initiative – smallpox, plague, cholera, African trypanosomiasis and haemorrhagic fevers – and to show how the attitude of Christians has changed and developed.

Smallpox

Down the ages, smallpox has been one of the most serious scourges of the human race. The greatest boon to humanity was the discovery by Edward Jenner in 1796 of a strain of cowpox which over the years has been modified to produce the vaccinia virus. When introduced through the skin this gave rise to a permanent immunity to smallpox without causing any harm other than a single pock at the site of inoculation. The practice of vaccination enabled a massive herd immunity to be built up in most of the developed world, which led to control of the disease. Later, thanks to technological developments in the production, storage, and transport of the vaccine, and a beautifully organized worldwide campaign, the total eradication of smallpox from the world was achieved through the World Health Organization in 1980.

The part played by Christians, both medical and non-medical, has been instructive. The first achievement was to define smallpox and distinguish it from other pestilences, the second was to organize care of the victims and the third was to exploit the discovery of protective inoculation (vaccination) by Edward Jenner. The introduction of vaccination to what are now known as the countries of the Third World was a great boon since the procedure was simple, did not need to be repeated, and illiterate people could be trained as vaccinators. The success of its introduction depended upon its acceptance by the people and in this the Christian initiative has been prominent. In 1805, Mr Alexander Pearson (a missionary) introduced the practice of vaccination to China and, before he left the country in 1832, established a large vaccine institution in Canton with a Chinese surgeon in charge. A pamphlet on the subject had been translated into Chinese and distributed widely (Lockhart, 1861). Lymph sent from Macao in 1845 to the London Missionary Society Hospital in Shanghai was used successfully on the colonel in charge of the Chinese garrison; this ensured its acceptance by the general population. Many other examples exist of missionaries, both medical and non-medical, using their relation of trust with their flocks to persuade them to accept vaccination.

In Borneo, Bishop McDougall of the Society for the Propagation of the Gospel, who ministered to the Malays, Chinese and mixed races of Borneo, was faced with an outbreak of smallpox. At Undop the Rev. W. Crossland vaccinated 700 Dyaks whom he looked after, only 10% of whom died of smallpox. The usual Dyak custom was to run away leaving the sick to die and the dead unburied, but as a result of Crossland's example they began to show great care for the sick and dead.

In Africa the Christian initiative was largely responsible for the successful introduction of vaccination and its acceptance by the people. David Livingstone early attempted to produce vaccine from a heifer which he inoculated with smallpox (Gelfand, 1957) and later wrote to England for vaccine to deal with an epidemic in what is now Tanzania.

Sir Albert Cook introduced vaccination into Uganda in an ingenious way. In those days, with no refrigeration, vaccine rapidly lost its potency. He used some nine-month-old vaccine to inoculate some Africans who then ran away. Luckily he spotted some of them later with obvious vaccination scars. He therefore established a vaccinial lesion on the arm of an individual from which he obtained material with which he was able to vaccinate over 800 people in a day. Vaccination then became very popular and vaccination centres were opened up throughout the country and were readily accepted.

In Zaire vaccination against smallpox was not so easily accepted and as late as 1940 Dr Stanley Browne relates that in Yakusu an outbreak of smallpox occurred which was introduced by a man from Stanleyville who died from the disease. Although the vaccine in vacuum flasks and vaccinators was ready, the people were reluctant to have their arms scratched. Those who had been vaccinated often exposed their arms to the sun so that the vaccine would not take. The doctors vaccinated themselves in front of crowds many times until it was seen that no harm came to them and in fact that nobody who had had a sore on the arm developed smallpox. About 45 people did in fact die of smallpox before the population of 105,000 had all been vaccinated. Cases of smallpox were isolated in huts where they were attended by Christian medical auxiliaries. The power of the god of smallpox (the most powerful of evil spirits) was broken and vaccination became generally accepted as a result of a Christian initiative. As a sequel to efforts in Africa and India people everywhere began to accept vaccination against smallpox so that when the World Health Organization launched its campaign to eradicate smallpox from the world in 1967 people did not refuse to be vaccinated. The disease was finally eradicated ten years later in 1977, when the last case of smallpox occurred in Somalia.

Plague

Initiatives in dealing with plague, which used to be a fearsome disease, were first concerned with attitudes to the disease and the establishment of an atmosphere of care of the sick and restoration of the morale of the population. Later, following the discovery of the cause, *Yersinia pestis*, (the plague bacillus), and the role of the rat and rat flea in the spread of infection, the control and prevention of epidemics became possible, but this had to be put over to large populations of illiterate and ignorant people. Bubonic plague, an infection of wild and domestic rodents and transmitted by fleas from rodent to rodent and man has been known and feared for centuries.

Since the first pandemic in the year AD 542, the Plague of Justinian, there have been two further pandemics. The Black Death in the 14th and 15th centuries halved the population of Europe (all Christendom at that period) and more recently the third pandemic which started in China in 1892 reaching Bombay in 1896 caused a major epidemic in India. From this grew the work of the Plague Commission. In addition to these pandemics there were several lesser epidemics such as the Plague of London in 1665, and the Manchurian epidemics of 1910-1911 and 1917-1918.

Bubonic plague has been the most feared of all epidemic diseases, killing large numbers of the people and spreading relentlessly through the countryside to cause famine and depopulation. Christian doctors and lay Christians have contributed greatly, at first to the care of the sick and raising of the morale of the population, and later to the establishment of the cause and ultimate control of the disease until now it no longer threatens health anywhere to any great extent.

Until the discovery of Y. *pestis* as the cause of plague and the role of the rat flea in transmission little could be done to prevent the ravages of the disease and the Christian Church at first did little to help. In the early years of the Christian era the appearance of a great killing disease naturally led the people to turn to the Church to alleviate their misery. At first this help was in general unskilled and consisted in little more than sheltering and feeding the victims. Until the beginning of the 17th century the opinion was prevalent that God inflicted plague on man as a punishment for his sins and this view found particular support in the Church. In Italy, in 1348, the clergy were seized by the general terror of death and thousands of the populace perished without receiving the Holy Sacrament. In France the host was offered on a pole by the clergy to the dying. In 1180, the Brothers of the order of St Eloysius carried plague corpses in their arms to burial and during the plague of Marseilles in 1720 the Capuchins and Jesuits placed themselves at the service of those attacked by the plague, and monks who had recovered from the disease heard the confessions of the dying. St Rochus who was born in the middle of the 13th century nursed those sick with the plague and it is said that he healed many by signing them with the Holy Cross. He himself contracted plague but recovered and converted a nobleman to his views. His relics and a procession in his honour were used to quell epidemics in the Middle Ages, and an order was founded to tend those sick of the plague. In England in 1666 in the Derbyshire village of Eyam, 254 of the 300 inhabitants of the village died of the plague and the Rector, William Mompesson, and his wife Catherine, nursed the afflicted day and night. Catherine herself died of the disease (Scott, 1939).

The cause of plague and its transmission by rats and fleas were not discovered until the age of microscopy. A Jesuit priest, Athanasius Kurcher (1602-1680) using a simple compound microscope, said that he saw organisms in the blood of plague victims (Hirst, 1953), but although this raised the idea of a causative organism it was not until 1894 that Yersin discovered the plague bacillus. The demonstration of its association with rats followed shortly afterwards. In January 1884 Dr Mary Miles, a missionary doctor in Canton, saw the first case of plague recorded by a European physician in Canton and noted that the Chinese had remarked on the death of rats in the infected houses. Dr (afterwards Sir Patrick) Manson, who had worked in a mission hospital in Amoy in 1873, believed that plague was rat-borne and that the destruction of rats was the most important prophylactic measure (Hirst, 1953). Following the appointment and findings of the Indian Plague Commission in 1902 it was clear that rats were the reservoir of infection and that rat fleas transmitted the infection from rat to rat and to man.

In the winter of 1910-1911 Manchuria was struck by a terrible epidemic of pneumonic plague. Mrs Dugald Christie wrote that of 43,942 cases, none recovered. It wiped out entire families and hamlets. Dr Dugald Christie of the United Free Church of Scotland Mission in Mukden was appointed Honorary Medical Adviser to the Government. This epidemic brought to light a remarkable man, the great Dr Wu Lien-Teh who achieved fame as a world authority on plague, and worked in association with, amongst others, assistants who were graduates of the Peiyang Medical College which had been created by Dr Kenneth Mackenzie of the London Missionary Society (Wu Lien-Teh, 1959).

The approach of the plague to Peking caused alarm in government circles and a promise of early help came from the Imperial Army Medical College, Tsientsin (where Dr Wu Lien-Teh was vice-director). The Peking Union Medical College (a missionary institution founded in 1903) together with several missionary doctors from Tsinanfu, Chefoo, Paotingfu, Kirin, Changchun, Mukden and Asheho volunteered for duty as did Dr Dugald Christie. An international plague conference was convened in Mukden in April 1911. Dr Graham Aspland, a missionary doctor from Peking, who had done yeoman service on the antiplague staff, was appointed secretary because of his empathy with the Chinese doctors. Other delegates who attended were Dr R.A.D. Hill, lecturer in the Union Medical College Peking and Dr Dugald Christie, director of the Mukden hospital and adviser to the Manchurian Government. This conference established the important role of the marmot, or tarabagan as the reservoir of pneumonic plague and reported that the plague originated in the crowded huts of marmot trappers in the winter. Infection spread by aerial conduction from victim to victim by the respiratory tract. These discoveries led to a means of prevention and control of the epidemic by controlling overcrowding and the introduction of the protective masks which are such a feature of Chinese life today.

Dr Hill submitted reports showing the effect of temperature on mortality, and the experimental work elucidating the role played by the marmot was performed in Mukden partly within the compound of the missionary medical college. It was during this epidemic that Dr Jackson, who had recently arrived from Scotland to join the United Free Church of Scotland Mission at Mukden, made the supreme sacrifice. He had been given charge of the plague operations on the north China railway running between Mukden and Shanhaikuang. His duties lay in inspecting labourers in extremely crowded conditions and he was not protected by the masks introduced by Dr Wu Lien-Teh. Although he had been vaccinated, he contracted the plague and died on January 25, 1911.

During the winter of 1917-18 pneumonic plague broke out again – this time in Shansi – and spread until it threatened the whole of north China. Practically the whole of the Baptist Missionary Society staff in Shansi together with medical and other missionaries from Peking and elsewhere responded to the appeals for help and with the help of Christian Chinese succeeded in stamping it out. This so impressed the Governor Yen Hsi Shin that he introduced a campaign of social reform in the sphere of popular education and public health alongside other measures. These resulted in marked improvement in social conditions and Yen Hsi Shin was lauded as a model Governor. He consulted the missionaries on many occasions and they could not but contrast their lot with that of their massacred predecessors in the 1900 Boxer troubles (Williamson, 1957).

Following the introduction of the plague to India in 1896 via Bombay there were many widely spread epidemics which killed about 6 million people. The plague was at its worst in Western India, where word came to Dr Robert Gohur, a Christian at Venguila on the west coast, that rats were dying. He promptly obtained rat poison and encouraged young school children in the area to spread the poison around, so that the threatened epidemic was cut short. This was a great success story since the young students had to break with their traditions and respond to the challenge (Hume, 1959). In November 1897 Miss Bertha Fulcher, who had joined the missionaries (Zenana and Bible Medical Mission) at Malegaon, together with Miss Clark the senior missionary, persuaded the terrified women of the zenana to leave their homes and go into camps. To Miss Fulcher fell the task of nursing the attendant British doctor when he fell a victim to a severe attack of the disease, during which he became delirious. These actions greatly impressed the local people and led to many conversions.

Cholera

Although cholera has existed for centuries in its homelands, the Yangtse basin in China and what is now Bangladesh, it is only comparatively recently that it has appeared as a pandemic. Cholera first invaded Europe in the early 19th century, reaching England in 1831. There were two major developments in the removal of this dreaded threat to life: the first was the discovery of the connection between water supplies and the spread of cholera by John Snow in 1849, and the second was the discovery of the value of intravenous solutions (followed more recently by oral solutions) in treatment, which has reduced the mortality from over 70% to as low as 1%. Provided organization is undertaken and there is no panic, epidemic cholera can no longer wipe out populations. In China and India cholera has always been a threat and many fearsome epidemics occurred in the late 19th century with the increased movement of people, pilgrimages in India and the Middle East (Mecca) being specially vulnerable to epidemics.

In 1900 in Srinagar, Kashmir, Dr Arthur Neve was in charge of the Church Missionary Society hospital and was invited by the Government to participate in measures to deal with a severe cholera epidemic. In the six villages for which they were responsible, the mortality from cholera was reduced to 30%. Dr Neve noted that as a result of their efforts and the satisfactory proportion of recoveries, a favourable impression was created which greatly helped the missionaries' work. The benefit of organization was shown in Travancore State when cholera struck in 1912. Drs Steibel and Turner of the Salvation Army worked out a plan and erected a special ward in twelve hours with other temporary structures. They directed the work of 30 medical students who organized a safe water supply and counteracted village practices that tended to spread the infection (Richards,

1971). The benefit of organization and pressure on high places was shown in Peking in 1903 when Dr Thomas Cochrane of the Union Medical College obtained an introduction from the British Ambassador to Prince Su. Dr Cochrane then drew up a list of precautions to be taken in every house in the city regarding the contamination of food and drink and gave orders for the disposal of contaminated clothing and bedding. He called on Prince Su with a request that the Imperial seal be affixed to the document he had drawn up so as to make it authoritative. His request was granted. This was probably the first public health campaign ever carried out by order of the Imperial Government.

The discovery of the *Vibrio cholerae* as the cause of cholera by Robert Koch was a great triumph but little could be done about reducing the mortality rate until the real benefit of intravenous fluids was shown in 1915 by Sir Leonard Rogers (a dedicated Christian and a member of the Indian Medical Service) who added bicarbonate of soda to the intravenous solutions and reduced the mortality among treated cases of cholera by over 70%.

Sleeping sickness

Trypanosomiasis has been known from ancient times in West Africa, where it was called 'the negro lethargy' and was responsible for much morbidity and mortality among slaves shipped to the New World. It is caused by a trypanosome parasite. Christian doctors have played a major role in describing the effects of the disease and establishing its cause, as well as in finding a suitable treatment, controlling epidemics and eradicating it from some areas.

David Livingstone described the effects of sleeping sickness on his return to Central Africa from Luanda in Angola in 1856, and brought the subject to the notice of the world. At the turn of the century in 1906, Sir Albert Cook (Foster, 1978) diagnosed the first case of sleeping sickness in Uganda where it had not previously been known, and with his brother Mr John Cook drew attention to the great loss of life caused by the epidemic which then developed. In a letter Albert wrote:

'We met several men carrying large bundles of twigs to the Fort and they told us that every twig meant a death. Mr Grant, the Government Officer informed us that no less than 11,000 twigs were handed in and that he expected that the total death roll would be not less than 20,000 . . . We get the appalling total of 68,000 for Uganda and Bugosa since the onset of the epidemic.'

This was just a drop in the ocean since it has been estimated that 2 million people died in the epidemic of sleeping sickness in Uganda at the beginning of the 20th century.

Sleeping sickness then became an important cause of much social and economic disruption both in Uganda and the Congo where in the early 1920s Sir Clement Chesterman found that 25% of the riverside population west of Stanleyville had the disease and would die within two years. Although sleeping sickness had been encountered in Tanganyika during the 1914-18 War by two German doctors attached to Von Lettow's forces, cases were few in number and mainly in the southern half of the country. In 1922, however, Dr George Maclean, who later served in a mission hospital on an island in Lake Malawi, described the first cases of sleeping sickness round the lower end of Lake Victoria in Maswa district. These were to be the heralds of a major epidemic in Tanganyika (McElvey, 1973). He later showed the important relation between economic development and sleeping sickness, apart from the effect of nagana upon cattle.

Although trypanosomes had been found in the blood of an African in West Africa, the importance of this finding was not recognised at the time. In 1901 Sir Albert Cook, with his brother John, found microfilariae of *Dipetalonema perstans* in the blood of sleeping sickness patients and forwarded the slides to Sir Patrick Manson (Foster, 1978), who had found similar microfilariae in a patient in London. It was Sir Patrick who helped to arrange the Sleeping Sickness Commission set up in 1902 with the Foreign Office and the Royal Society to investigate the disease. Manson in 1897 saw a tadpole-like structure swim across the field in the blood of a sleeping sickness patient but was unable to follow up the observation. Following Sir David Bruce's discovery of trypanosomes as the cause of nagana, trypanosomes were demonstrated in the cerebrospinal fluid of patients with sleeping sickness in Uganda under the auspices of the Sleeping Sickness Commission in 1903.

At first the different forms of the trypanosome were not recognized but later three subspecies were identified: *Trypanosoma brucei* (found only in mammals), *T. rhodesiense* (found in game and man) and *T. gambiense* (found mainly in man and to a lesser extent in pigs). In 1909, Dr W.A. Murray at Mwera Mission Hospital (in what is now Malawi) found the first case of sleeping sickness in the country and by careful observation demonstrated that the disease in Malawi and Zambia was caused by a different trypanosome from that of the Congo and Uganda. This trypanosome proved to be *T. rhodesiense* as opposed to the form *T. gambiense* which was responsible for the disease in West Africa, the Congo and Uganda. This was to have a great importance in later studies on the epidemiology and control of the disease.

David Livingstone made an extraordinary early contribution to our knowledge of the tsetse fly, its biology, feeding habits, effects on cattle and the severe economic effects on the population. There was a long tradition known to both the cattle-owning Boers and Africans that the bite of the tsetse fly could be fatal to horses and cattle. Livingstone first recorded in 1856 the relation between the tsetse fly and the disease nagana in horses and cattle resulting from its bite. He also recognized 'fly belts' in Central Africa and recorded the presence of *Glossina palpalis* where it is not now found and described the severe economic effects of the fly. He noted that the country was heavily infested with tsetse fly which extended northwards from the Limpopo as far as Abyssinia and that large tribes were unable to keep cattle because the tsetse fly bites were fatal to the cattle. He described the mechanism of its bite, how the proboscis was thrust through the skin and the abdomen rapidly filled (with blood). Cattle so bitten lost weight and strength and died after two, three or five months, and he gave a surprisingly accurate account of the post-mortem appearances, noting that game animals were unharmed.

After the main tsetse, *Glossina palpalis* and *G. morsitans*, had been described, Dr George Maclean helped Dr Swynnerton to establish the existence of a new species, *G. swynnertoni*, which with *G. pallidipes* was the species responsible for the outbreak in Masawa district round Lake Victoria, an observation that has an important bearing on the present day epidemiology of sleeping sickness round Lake Victoria where it has become of increasing and menacing importance.

Treatment
Little was available for many years to treat what was an invariably fatal disease. At first attempts were made with arsenic. Livingstone administered liquor arsenicalis to horses with nagana without much success, but Sir Albert Cook having read of the use of injections of sodium arsenite in cattle trypanosomiasis in Nigeria gave it in human cases of sleeping sickness. He used it by mouth in a case with trypanosomes in lymphatic

gland juice and saw the patient alive 20 years later. (*T. gambiense* can sometimes be very mild and self-healing). In the early 1920s, Clement Chesterman used tryparsamide in the Congo and obtained successful results; this became the mainstay in the treatment of advanced cases until after the 1939-45 War. He later organized what came to be known as mass chemotherapy which was used extensively in francophone Africa to control the disease almost to vanishing point. Teams of 'fly boys', injectors and medical assistants undertook a systematic survey of all the riverside villages near Stanleyville in the Congo, and developed a programme of 'prevention by cure' using the drug suramin which, by sterilizing the blood of everyone suffering from the disease, prevented the tsetse becoming infected so that the incidence of sleeping sickness fell almost to zero.

Two major measures of control are practised today. One is the removal of the reservoir of infection by mass treatment already described which is only of use in the West African form *T. gambiense*. In the *T. rhodesiense* form the man-fly contact must be broken and this has been done by concentrating the affected population in new settlement areas which the fly cannot penetrate because of bush clearance. The pioneer of this form of control was Dr George Maclean who organized the first agricultural settlements in Tanganyika in the late 1920s and early 1930s. These became the model for the successful Anchau project in Nigeria after the 1939-45 war, when all the political, social and economic problems that arise were dealt with successfully.

Other fevers

The older epidemic diseases such as smallpox, plague and cholera have now lost their capacity to inspire terror since modern methods of treatment and control have led to their disappearance and, in the case of smallpox, complete eradication from the world. A new threat, partially old and partially new, has appeared – that of virus haemorrhagic fevers which result from man's disturbance of the tropical ecosystem. The oldest and best known of these is yellow fever or 'Yellow Jack' which used to terrify the eastern coasts of North and South America and the Caribbean. The newest is an arena virus, Lassa fever, which has arisen in West Africa and is an addition to two other similar viruses known in South America.

Yellow fever was probably introduced to the New World from

Africa. The first epidemic occurred in Yucatan in 1648 and in Cuba in 1649. From then onwards until the early years of the 20th century the New World and Caribbean were terrorized by outbreaks of yellow fever, often with a very high mortality. It was not until 1881 that Carlos Finlay suggested that a mosquito carried the infection from man to man and this was proved by the Yellow Fever Commission led by Major Walter Reed in 1900. This discovery permitted control work to be carried out and led to the control of urban yellow fever in the New World. The second most important advance was the demonstration of a viral cause and the development of a vaccine in the 1930s by Drs Hindle and Theiler. Christian institutions became involved in the work of inducing immunity which was known for many years to follow a natural infection and, in an experiment conducted in Cuba, Dr Finlay tested his theory that immunity to yellow fever could be obtained by allowing mosquitoes to bite healthy people after they had fed on a patient with yellow fever. Between 1883 and 1890, in a by no means perfect experiment, he inoculated 33 Jesuit and Carmelite Fathers in this way and allowed 32 others to act as controls. During these years five of the controls died of yellow fever whereas none of the inoculated subjects did (Scott, 1939). Otherwise, apart from the care of patients, little other active work is recorded.

Thanks to the vigilance of a missionary doctor, Raymond Holmes (of the Baptist Mission Hospital at Yakusu), a European planter who died of a febrile illness accompanied by jaundice was shown to have succumbed to yellow fever – the first case in Central Africa. Specimens of liver obtained by viscerotomy from Africans dying in similar circumstances showed that the disease was sporadically endemic in the area. The identification of the first case led to a thorough investigation by a Rockefeller Foundation team from Nairobi. Mouse protection tests indicated that several waves of subclinical infection had swept through the villages in the Bambole Forest in the preceding decades. Morning temperatures were taken in thousands of villagers in an attempt to discover any possible hidden febrile infections among the population. Yellow fever vaccination was made available throughout the district. One of the striking features of the investigation, according to the Rockefeller workers, was the reliability of the Christian medical auxiliaries (trained in the government-recognized school at Yakusu) who cooperated in the researches, and their excellent relations with the local tribesfolk.

Lassa fever is caused by a member of a recently discovered group of viruses known as arena viruses. They are normally carried by rodents and excreted in the urine, passing from man to man by limited aerial spread and contamination causing limited outbreaks. Although, as with yellow fever, there are many asymptomatic cases, the mortality in overt cases can be high. The Nixon Methodist Hospital in Sierra Leone initiated and played a major part in the elucidation of the cause and epidemiology of this haemorrhagic fever.

In 1969 an undiagnosed infectious disease caused two deaths and a severe illness among missionary nurses working in the village of Lassa in northeast Nigeria. In 1970 a new virus was isolated from an outbreak at Jos, Northern Nigeria, in which there was a 52% mortality in hospital cases, including a physician who had performed a necropsy on a fatal case. Following this outbreak localized epidemics occurred in Onitsha (E. Nigeria), Zorzor (Liberia), Panguma, Tongo and Segbwema (Sierra Leone). Among those who died in these outbreaks were two African nurses on the staff of mission hospitals. Further investigation on material supplied by missionaries has established that the virus was probably present in Guinea in 1952 and that an epidemic of 'Yanguma fever' described by Dr J.R. Rose at the Nixon Methodist Hospital in 1955/56 was probably an epidemic of Lassa fever. A recent survey of 104 returned missionaries from the Ivory Coast, Mali and the Central African Republic has shown some to be seropositive.

Now that the virus has been isolated and its main reservoir host the multimammate mouse (*Mastomys natalensis*) identified, the disease can be controlled and a vaccine prepared. This is all due to the early work of mission institutions and missionary doctors, at no small cost to themselves in lives laid down.

References

Chesterman, Sir Clement (1940) *In the Service of Suffering*. London: Livingstone Press

Foster, W.D. (1978) *The Church Missionary Society and Modern Medicine in Uganda. The Life of Sir Albert Cook, KCMG 1870-1951*. Macclesfield: Privately published

Gelfand, Michael (1957) *Livingstone The Doctor* Oxford: Basil Blackwell.

Hirst, L.F. (1953) *The Conquest of Plague* Oxford: Clarendon Press.

Hume, E.H. (1950) *Doctors Courageous, Christian Doctors and Nurses in Africa and Asia.* Harper and Sons.

Lockhart, W. (1861) *Medical Missionary in China* London: Hurst and Blackett.

McKelvey, J.F. (Jnr.) (1973) *Man Against Tsetse* Ithaca and London: Cornell University Press.

Richards, M.M. (1971) *It Began with Andrews* London: Salvationist Publishers and Suppliers.

Scott, H. (1939) *A History of Tropical Medicine* 2 vols. London: Arnold

Wu Lien-Teh (1959) *Plague Fighter* Cambridge: W. Heffer.

CHAPTER 8

GENERAL AND TROPICAL MEDICINE

H.M. Gilles

For many years most mission hospitals were situated in rural areas or in townships where environmental conditions were rudimentary, and most of their patients either belonged to the lower socio-economic strata of society or came from villages surrounding the hospitals within a remarkably wide radius. Indeed, the mission doctor often acted as primary health worker at village level as well as general factotum at the base hospital. As a pioneer of Western medicine, he had to prove himself professionally by results that were more dramatic and more permanent than those of the local traditional practitioners. Moreover, he was often faced with the medicine man's failures or rejects, as well as the latter's undoubted skills in dealing with certain conditions such as uncomplicated fractures. The traditional practitioner with his intimate knowledge of his own society and social environment offered a particularly difficult challenge in the field of psychosomatic medicine and mental illness.

The missionary doctor had to learn a completely new world of symptomatology, mediated through a dresser-interpreter who would often embellish the complaints to make them unusually picturesque or attempt to pre-empt the diagnosis by unconsciously exaggerating a symptom likely to be understood and acted upon. The relation between Western doctor and dresser-interpreter (until such time as the doctor learned enough of the local language to enable him to take histories himself) became one of the most interesting and challenging of human experiences, ranging from imperfectly concealed antagonism and distrust to mutual respect and affection. Many other adjustments had to be made, such as respecting desperate anxiety among relatives that a patient should not die in hospital; the firm belief that the quality of the treatment given would be dependent on the fee available; that medicine could only be effective if it had drastic and self-evident physical consequences; that manipulation had to be painful.

The missionary doctor had to be 'Jack of all trades' both professionally and in every other respect. Physician, anaesthetist, surgeon and obstetrician, with the certainty that he would have to deal with extreme conditions and emergencies which long ago had ceased to occur or were exceptionally rare in Europe and for which his Western training was in many respects deficient. Add to this village visits, ordering drugs, keeping accounts, maintaining property, supervising new buildings and counselling staff, and one has the perfect recipe for chronic overwork and mental illness.

Yet these dedicated men and women, armed with life-saving medical resources hitherto unavailable in the areas concerned, invariably gained the confidence of the people they served. They quickly learnt to understand and respect their customs; to treat everyone with courtesy and consideration, and in return they were soon accepted as trusted friends and part of the community in which they lived. The satisfying richness of these new experiences and relations made them feel at home in what was initially a strange and even hostile environment, and many of them lived a long and peaceful life after leaving their pioneer stations, yearning to be of service again.

The range of diseases and types of patients dealt with at mission hospitals is exemplified in the annual reports of three fairly characteristic ones for the geographical areas concerned: (1) The Methodist General Hospital (Hankow, China), (2) The Nixon Memorial Methodist Hospital (Segbwema, Sierre Leone), and (3) The Holdsworth Memorial Hospital (Mysore, South India).

The majority of patients attending the Methodist Hospital in Hankow were fee-paying, but on the top floor of the men's hospital was a twelve-bedded ward known as *san ping* which bore on the side of its entrance door a brass plate commemorating gifts from some friends in Dublin. This was the Samaritan Fund ward, and its English name was 'The Alfred Crawford Memorial Ward': here none of the patients admitted paid any fees. The diagnoses ranged from tuberculosis of the spine and *Schistosomiasis japonicum* (known to the Chinese sailors in the Yangtse fleet as 'Sister Soma') to extensive burns and accidents. Interesting entries appear such as: opium habit (61 cases), lead poisoning (38 cases), 198 patients with a variety of eye diseases and 31 with cirrhosis of the liver.

The 1954 report of the Nixon Memorial Methodist Hospital in Sierra Leone highlights some of the clinical material seen during the year; trypanosomiasis, yellow fever, blackwater fever, the dysenteries, filariasis, goitre, heart disease and kwashiorkor. Some of the cases of yellow fever could well have been Lassa fever, now well recognized in the Segbwema area, and it was in this very hospital that I was shown some patients in 1976 (Keane and Gilles, 1976). The comment that some of the patients died within a week with widespread haemorrhagic manifestations while others made a rapid recovery is revealing in the light of modern experience of the natural history of Lassa fever in the area.

The Golden Jubilee Report of the Holdsworth Memorial Hospital in Mysore in 1956 is noteworthy for the fact that the pattern of disease as diagnosed in the hospital had remained remarkably constant over a period of fifty years with some minor exceptions. Sixty cases of cholera in 1955 is not too unexpected.

The medical missionary pioneers would have been surprised and dismayed at the magnitude of the problems that still confront us today in relation to some of the diseases that they encountered, described and sometimes died of many years ago. They would have been equally disappointed had they been able to foresee how the description of these diseases has altered little over the years, and that despite substantial therapeutic advances little impact has been made on them at the village level.

Malaria remains a major global problem with millions of people at risk and a mortality of around 1%, mainly in childhood. It is estimated that over 1618 million people are exposed to one or other of the species of parasite infecting man, i.e. *P. vivax*, *P. falciparum*, *P. malariae* and *P. ovale*. In 1897, Ronald Ross working in Secunderabad (India) found a developing form of the malaria parasite in the body of a mosquito that had previously fed on a patient with the plasmodia in his blood, and thus finally elucidated the actual mode of transmission. His strong sense of personal dedication to the solving of this problem was akin to that of the many missionaries working in India and elsewhere at the time who were only too aware of the ravages that the disease caused. Thus Livingstone's instructions to Kirk as economic botanist and medical officer to the Zambesi expedition were accurate and in some sense also prophetic:

'It is intended that the Expedition should pass through the malarious district at the lower portion of the Zambesi River as quickly as possible, and it will be necessary for you to put into practice those precautionary measures against fever by the use of quinine which the experience of the Niger Expedition, and your own judgement, may suggest as likely to secure the health of your companions' (Faskett, 1964).

In the light of the recent finding of a Chinese anti-malarial drug derived from a 2000-year-old medicinal plant, quinghaosu, the following passage from Livingstone is more than pertinent:

'Your attention is particularly requested to the discovery of dyestuffs, gums and medicinal substances, in the hope that should either of these or fibrous tissues exist in quantities sufficient to warrant commercial enterprise, you may aid in the great work of supplanting by lawful commerce the odious traffic in slaves' (Gelfand, 1952).

Dr Patrick in Rajishahi, India (1948-1971) writes as follows:

'The commonest tropical disease was of course *malaria*. Benign tertian, and quartan cause few problems and were treated locally with quinine and regarded much as a common cold in Britain. Malignant tertian malaria was an entirely different story. We saw on average one case per month of cerebral malaria caused by malignant tertian. These patients were brought in comatose and amongst my Bengali colleagues the use of intravenous quinine was regarded as equivalent to malpractice as, by the method then used, it could cause immediate collapse and death. However, Manson-Bahr advises the use of adrenaline before a very careful and slow intravenous infusion of quinine. Using this method we were able to save *all* of the cerebral malaria patients admitted over the next few years.'

Acute gastrointestinal infections, as characterized by the dysenteries, are one of the principal causes of morbidity in the developing countries, and missionary doctors have been confronted with their presentations for many years. Most of them are now readily treated with a combination of rehydration and antibiotics.

A description of the patient with 'chronic diarrhoea' and the problems he presents to the physician given by Hughes (1955) bears so many reminiscences as well as basic truths in today's setting in the tropical world that it is worth quoting as well as paraphrasing:

'They more often than not bring sheaves of prescriptions and laboratory reports, and when one examines these papers one wonders what form of treatment is left to try out on the patient. The majority of them have already been treated several times for amoebiasis with injections of emetine, and many also with a representative collection of all the latest drugs which are described as being efficient. They present a problem to themselves, for they have often reached the stage of chronic invalidism and of intense preoccupation with the state of their bowels; they also present a problem to the doctor because they are so often treated without success. Most of them are hoping for a cure of immediate and

dramatic nature, and they expect the cure to be permanent.
Their invalidism, or their preoccupation with the state of their
bowels, converts them into people who are very far short of being
efficient – many attribute their failure in life to their "dysentery",
or explain and excuse themselves from responsibilities because
of "chronic dysentery". Their cure is therefore a matter of serious
concern to their doctors and the diagnosis and treatment concerns the whole man.

The means of investigating their cases involves first a careful
taking of the history, if possible from the very first attack.
Following this an examination of the abdomen and an attempt to
assess the psychological status of the patient. The routine of
laboratory and other investigations includes microscopic examination and very occasionally culture of the stools. Sometimes fat
analysis of the stools, and a full investigation of the blood picture
may be necessary.'

Hughes then goes on to describe several types of patients
fairly fully to emphasize that chronic dysentery is commonly
not a symptom of true intestinal disease, but is simply a method
of expression of the body's reaction to stress in different types of
individuals, in which the initial acute attacks of dysentery have
simply acted as localizing factors for the symptoms. He further
makes the pertinent yet often forgotten point that the mere presence of Entamoeba histolytica in the stools does not necessarily
mean that they are responsible for the patient's condition, and
quizzically ends his presentation with the following sentence:
'I can but hope that something I have said will help us all to
realize the fascination of such a tedious condition as chronic
dysentery.'

Around 200 million persons are thought to be infected with
the four species of human schistosomes: S. mansoni, S. haematobium, S. japonicum, and S. intercalatum.

Dr Clement Chesterman was intrigued by the clinical manifestations of Schistosoma intercalatum, and found almost all the
schoolchildren at Yakusu and the surrounding villages to be
infected. Dr A.C. Fisher (1934) obtained a fellowship to enable
him to investigate the disease. In the early 1930s he pursued his
researches at Yakusu, put S. intercalatum on the nosological
map, and suggested means for control. Charles Fisher was a large
man, both physically and spiritually, who inspired great confidence, respect and love among his many patients of all races. His
father was called by the Lunda peoples Mwanta Ndotolo – 'the
great doctor.' After qualifying, Charles was named Nxwana
Ndotolo – 'the doctor's heir': after his father's death he was

elevated to Mwanta Ndotolo. His generosity and great sense of humour endeared him to his many friends. In 1936 100% of schoolchildren at Yakusu were infected. Attempts to control the snail intermediate host by molluscicides were unsuccessful: they survived buried deep in mud. Every child who showed some sign of infection was treated actively and energetically by the Christian medical auxiliaries. The result was that when Dr Swetz, the Belgian specialist, came to Yakusu in 1952 to try to infect some mice with the parasite, he was unable to find a single case of stools containing the eggs of the parasite.

The history of schistosomiasis in Sierra Leone was summarized by Wilkinson and Campbell (1965) as follows:

'This was one of the diseases studied by workers in the Sir Alfred Lewis Jones laboratory in Freetown (1921-1941). The earliest recorded survey was carried out by Blacklock in 1923. He noted that the vector snail of *Schistosoma haematobium* was only found under three conditions: in streams with slow moving water and a muddy bottom, in the presence of weeds or grass in the water, and in the shade. Although the snail could be killed by seven days' drying in the open air, most snails could survive for thirteen days in soft mud, in the shade. In an investigation of the Eastern Province he found that the Mende and Kono people were more affected than the Limbas and Korankos and that the incidence was higher in the female than in the male (most of those examined were children). No *Schistosoma mansoni* was found.'

In 1930, Blacklock noted that in Sierra Leone in the area between Pujehun and Mongheri, 5% of urines examined contained eggs of *Schistosoma haematobium,* between Rotifunk and Kenema 9% were positive, and between Pendembu and Segbwema the incidence was 68%. About the Segbwema area he wrote:

'From the educational point of view I cannot imagine a more profitable form of Nature Study for Protectorate schoolboys than a properly organized and conducted survey for physopsis (the vector snail). The results which could be obtained in a single year would prove of incalculable assistance to the Medical Department in their task of eliminating Schistosome infection in the schools and villages. Boys who habitually bathe in the local streams could be allowed to take part in the search.'

In the Northern Province of Sierra Leone 578 urines were examined but only four were infected. Most of the infected cases originated from the Eastern Provinces.

Occasional clinical cases of infection by *Schistosoma*

mansoni were seen in Sierra Leone but the source in this country was not then known. In 1930, however, Mass and Vogel reported that 68% of the population of some Guinea villages close to the common frontier was infected. In 1931 an outbreak of *Schistosoma mansoni* infection occurred in the Kabala area and this was described by Peaston (1933). In 1938 Lightbody stated that 'Schistosomiasis is limited in its distribution and at present does not present a grave problem.' In 1952, Gerber investigated the town on Bajibu and found that 93% of children, 12% of women and 6% of men were infected with *Schistosoma haematobium*. Out of 7221 urines examined in Segbwema hospital in 1965, 1552 (i.e. 47 per cent) contained ova of *S. haematobium*. Fortunately, schistosomiasis is far more easily cured now than it was in 1965.

The most prevalent of the filarial parasites affecting man is *Wuchereria bancrofti*, and at least 300 million people across the world are constantly exposed to infection, while onchocerciasis, which causes untold misery with the prevalence of blindness as high as 30% in the worst infected villages, affects more than 30 million people in the savanna and rain forest areas of Africa. Browne's (1959; 1960) classical studies in Central and West Africa are perhaps the most noteworthy example of the opportunities available to missionary doctors and of how, despite an almost superhuman workload, the enquiring mind and dedicated heart can find the time and the extra energy to make meticulous scientific observations of the highest calibre.

One of the most influential of the medical missionaries who began work in the years following World War I was Sir Clement Chesterman. After a distinguished war record in which he did good work on malaria control in Palestine under Dr Philip Manson-Bahr, Chesterman began his service with the Baptist Missionary Society in Yakusu in the former Belgian Congo (now Zaire). When passing through Kinshasa, he was given a sample of a new drug (tryparsamide) for use if he came across any cases of sleeping sickness in the area he was going to. He found a prevalence rate of 30% in the riverside villages near Yakusu, and used the drug to such effect that the epidemic was controlled (Chesterman, 1922-3). This experience determined his thinking about the role of medical missionaries in countries now called 'developing'. He coined the phrase 'prevention is better than cure'; he believed in co-operation with the government health authorities; he began to train medical auxiliaries (Browne,

1975); he laid the foundations of a community health service covering a district of 10,000 square miles, with eighteen health centres and thirty-five dispensaries. This programme, called a model of its kind in Africa, was instituted years before the concept became accepted or fashionable. In addition to the eventual eradication of sleeping sickness (in 1947), endemic diseases like yaws and leprosy were controlled, cerebral malaria became just a memory, onchocerciasis was controlled by interrupting the life-cycle of *Simulium neavei* by disinfecting the breeding sites, and the health and nutrition of the whole population was improved out of all knowledge (Browne, 1971). Subsequently by his persuasive advocacy of the principles of preventive medicine and community health care, Chesterman exerted a wide influence on medical missionary thinking and practice.

There are two groups of soil-transmitted helminths: those in which the infective stage is swallowed, e.g. *Ascaris lumbricoides, Enterobius vermicularis, Trichuris trichiura,* and those in which the infective stage penetrates the skin, e.g. *Ankylostoma duodenale, Necator americanus,* and *Strongyloides stercoralis.* Annual statistics of mission hospitals throughout the world abound with the number of patients seen and treated for these soil-transmitted helminths, essentially the result of poor sanitation and poor personal hygiene. It is estimated that one billion people are affected throughout the world, and in many instances multiple infection is the rule. In the Golden Jubilee 1979 report of the Nixon Memorial Hospital, Sierra Leone, for example, 3348 persons were found infected with hookworm, 1897 with ascaris, 298 with trichuris and 450 with strongyloides.

A 1913 report from Cairo, Egypt, quotes: 'Lord Kitchener visited the hospital. He was so much impressed with the method of dealing with hookworm patients en masse that he advised the Egyptian Government to adopt it.'

The Yakusu team saw 9000 cases of yaws every year in the mid-thirties and were controlling its spread before the Global Eradication Campaign against yaws under the sponsorship of WHO/UNICEF was instituted. This campaign proved to be a great success, and despite a recent temporary resurgence, especially in West Africa, the disease is now rare and the logistics of control are clearly established. In the 1930s missionary doctors were only too familiar with the scourge.

In earlier days the Yakusu missionaries gave out 'blue-stone' (large crystals of copper sulphate) to rub on the florid excrescences of secondary yaws. This coagulated the surface, and helped the cicatrization of the individual lesions – but at the cost of severe pain. The decks of the mission steamer, The Grenfell, were crowded with parents bringing their children for a 'rubbing with the stone'. Then neoarsphenamine became available. With three magic injections the yaws lesions miraculously disappeared. Everybody began clamouring for 'the needle' for every imaginable disease, but often the lesions returned, and a full course of intravenous neoarsphenamine was supplemented by intramuscular injections of an oily suspension of bismuth salicylate. The successors of Sir Clement Chesterman superintended the making and sterilizing of many litres of this oily suspension, which was distributed to the dispensaries in sterile bottles containing 250 ml. The results were very gratifying. Long before the availability of long-acting penicillin (PAM) as advocated by the WHO/UNICEF combined programme, they had reduced the 9000 cases annually to a mere trickle.

In 1958 Burkitt gave a classical clinical description of the tumour in Uganda that now bears his name. This was a remarkable example of clinical epidemiology coupled with determination, dedication and astute observation at its best. The geographical distribution of the tumour in high prevalence is controlled by two climatic parameters: temperature and humidity. Thus it is most common in those areas of tropical Africa where the mean monthly temperature is over 15.5°C (60°F) and the relative humidity is high (Burkitt, 1962). A careful survey in Uganda showed that in lowland areas along the Nile the tumour was twenty times as common as in the mountainous regions (Burkitt and Wright, 1966).

The tumour is rarely seen under the age of two years and in endemic areas it is uncommon over the age of 15 years. It is most often seen in the 5 to 9-year age groups with a median of approximately seven years both in Africa and in the relatively few cases reported in the United States, whereas in the mountainous areas of Uganda where the tumour is not common, the average age of onset is said to be 16.2 years (Burkitt and Wright, 1966). The tumour is not uncommon among adult immigrants to Uganda coming from the mountainous districts of Rwanda and Burundi, where the disease is almost unknown. Boys are affected about twice as often as girls, and no race would appear to be exempt. It seems to be relatively rare among the higher socio-economic group of Africans living in endemic areas.

The apparent climatic influence on the incidence of Burkitt's tumour and its striking age distribution has led to a variety of hypotheses relating to its aetiology. It would now appear that high prevalence of the tumour in a population is associated with two factors: (1) the presence of stable malaria due to P. falciparum infection and (2) the presence of the Epstein-Barr virus (EB virus).

Superficial fungal infections, scabies and other skin diseases are so common in the tropics that most missionary doctors become quite expert in the diagnosis and treatment of these conditions. Indeed, those with a specialized interest in leprosy and onchocerciasis become excellent general dermatologists (Browne, 1960a).

In the Annual Report of the Nixon Memorial Hospital, Segbwema, Sierra Leone, 1954, Rose and Suliman showed a high prevalence of sickle-cell trait in the Mende tribe and a definite decline in the number of positives found with increasing age: 41.7% in the 0-2 years; 37.0% in the 2-8 years old, down to 27.4% in adults. They remark quite correctly: 'It is thus probable that sickle-cell anaemia is a major cause of death in small children.'

Missionary doctors at Lassa, Jos, Zazor, Zonkwa, Panguma and Segbwema were among others in the forefront when Lassa fever erupted on the medical world front. With minimal precautions and great courage they looked after more patients between them than anyone else in the world (Keane and Gilles, 1977).

Such is but a brief and selective summary of the many valuable contributions that medical missionaries have made over the last century and a half to our knowledge of disease, its prevention and treatment. The roll of honour is a distinguished one, of which the Christian Church has every reason to be proud. To mention names may seem invidious, but pride of place justifies the mention of one who may be described as a pioneer in this field: Dr William Lockhart (1811-1896) who was appointed by the London Missionary Society as the first European medical missionary in China (Lockhart, 1861).

Between 1839, when he arrived in Canton, and 1857, when he returned home to take his FRCS he had opened three hospitals — in Chusan, Hong Kong and Shanghai, and had treated 200,000 patients. On his return to China in 1861 he was appointed senior physician to the British Legation, becoming the first to practice

Western medicine in Peking. Here he founded yet another hospital in which 30,000 patients were treated for all kinds of disease in its first 2½ years before he finally returned to England in 1864 for family reasons. It was clinical experience such as this that was responsible for the many contributions and astute observations made by missionary doctors all over the world, some of which have already been recorded. Nor was this experience devoid of its lighter and memorable moments, as recounted by Miss Bullock in the early days of the Welsh Mission Hospital at Shillong, India:

'Another great event in the early days was when the Senior Maharani of Gwalior came to Shillong seeking relief from a serious illness. She belonged to a very orthodox Hindu caste and had been to several States and seen various doctors and surgeons, but could not make up her mind to be treated by any of them. The fame of the Welsh Mission Hospital had spread and the fact that there were good Khasi nurses, so she arrived in Shillong with all her entourage and took a whole boarding house for the summer.

Her senior physician came to the Hospital to consult Doctor Roberts and finally, together with other Senior Government Doctors, he was allowed to see the Maharani and to examine her: Only a very small portion of her anatomy being exposed – a very difficult way to make a diagnosis. She consented to have the operation under certain conditions which necessitated a good part of the private wards being set apart for her use, together with accommodation for the 'Ajibhai Saheb' (a grandmother) and the physician, the ladies in waiting and the Minister of State. The latter came during the day and sat in a large room in the lower block. Added to this, the astrologer used the summer house on the lawn to predict when things were to take place. Doctor Roberts informed the physician that the prediction regarding the time of the operation would have to be at a time convenient to him and it was agreed to do it at 9 a.m.: a hen had been killed and hung up in the Maharani's room. All went well and the Maharani was very pleased with the way the Khasi nurses attended to her.

At this time, it was found that the white ants had eaten away the wooden beams in the front wards of the hospital. To replace these would be very costly, but the large fee obtained from the Maharani's treatment sufficed to put this matter right. The civil surgeon of the Khasi and Jaihtra Hills District was very helpful and ready to give assistance at any time in various ways and when Doctor Roberts went home on sick leave in 1931, he made himself available for help whenever called upon, especially in dealing with private patients.'

Not the least of the medical missionaries' contribution is in the field of clinical research.

Livingstone's medical observations are among the earliest records on the diseases of Africa. Thus, in 1854, he observed for the first time the association between relapsing fever and the bite of the tampan (tick). This must be one of the earliest records of an arthropod-borne disease. This outstanding medical explorer remarked that pneumonia was a prevalent disease in the African producing sudden changes of temperature; he commented and described tropical ulcer and in 1872 recorded near Lake Tanganyika the presence of an insect (filarial worm) in the chamber of the eye of one of his men which moved about the eye and was very painful – probably loaiasis. He gave an excellent account of 'earth eating' (pica) and recorded that many of his men developed a haematuria which he (erroneously) attributed to the iron content of the water of Lake Dilala (Gelfand, 1952).

For more than 50 years, members of staff of the Neyyoor Hospital in South India have been interested in cancer, especially cancer of the mouth, particularly common in this part of South India, which has the highest prevalence of oral cancer in the world. Out of this special interest has grown a separate institution called the International Cancer Centre. Dr Derek Jenkins, who has been Medical Superintendent of the Medical Mission, took a great interest in this new development.

At the Manorom Christian Hospital in Thailand an interest in intradermal human diploid cell rabies vaccine has led to prophylactic and post-exposure treatment facilities being established since 1978, predating the therapeutic use of intradermal vaccine elsewhere.

As far back as 1913 Dr James Maxwell wrote: 'Research is essential to the progress of medicine in any branch and especially to medical mission work in China at the present day.' He claimed that the members of the Medical Missionary Association of China showed (1) that hookworm was one of the commonest parasites in China, (2) that *Schistosomiasis japonicum*, fasciolopsiasis and kala azar were also common and that splenic puncture was not the only, or indeed the safest, method of making a diagnosis of visceral leishmaniasis. Under Maxwell's supervision, research was expanded to include: (a) examination into diseases or pathological conditions which are local or circumscribed in their distribution, and (b) the causation of fevers of an obscure nature.

Maxwell later became Head of the Department of Field

Research, Lister Institute, Shanghai, and in 1931 summarized his findings to date as follows:-

1. Smallpox is universal and very frequently fatal
2. Malaria is unusual in the Southern and Central provinces
3. Kala azar is appallingly common in certain districts, one hospital having admitted 2500 cases in 1930
4. Tuberculosis is very common
5. Syphilis has spread because of the ubiquity of undisciplined and unbridled troops
6. Beri beri is found in many parts of the country
7. Osteomalacia extends as a wide band across the north of China
8. Goitre is extraordinarily common in some districts
9. Serious eye conditions (due to lack of essential elements of food) are found everywhere, and an appreciable amount of the blindness in China is due to this cause

The spirit of medical research within a Christian setting is clearly enumerated by Hughes (1951) in the following extract:

'If we are the kind of people with whom patients will not feel shy to tell of any new found joy or sorrow, or any cause for wonder, which a day in hospital has brought, then we also will be the kind of people who have no hesitation or embarrassment in sharing with others those same causes for wonder which we have found, and the joys we have experienced. Most important of all, if we would publish our findings to men and especially to our patients, we ought to try to give them the joy of being always able to share this wonder with One whose fellowship cannot be destroyed by anything in life whether it be joy, health or disease. This delight and wonder of ours can be made perfect in fellowship with Jesus Christ.

'Our child-likeness can be nurtured in the atmosphere which we shall later recognize as the Kingdom of Heaven itself.

'I have spoken of all this as though it were a scientific experiment and that advisedly, because the fundamental conditions for wakening us into that state of mind which gives entrance into the Kingdom of Heaven are: discipline which will make us humble in the field in which we are researching and reveal to us wonders; expectation which makes keen our eyes and mind and sharing which brings us into fellowship with God and man.

'Let us then work as scientists, and better still with a child's simplicity and purity of heart, exploring the goodness of God in the life of men, and see the wonders which He effects, revel in them, share them, and we will find ourselves walking in the Kingdom of God.'

In a paper given before the Royal Society of Tropical Medicine and Hygiene, Browne (1979) summarizes the contributions made by the Medical Missionaries to the science and practice of medicine.

A few examples may now be given of the adjustment of missionary centres and hospitals to changing conditions over the years.

The Methodist General Hospital in Hankow, founded in 1864 by Dr Porter Smith, was the first hospital in Central China and was later to become a large teaching hospital with specialized departments. It was taken over *en bloc* by the communist Chinese government in 1951 and is still flourishing. Dr A. Pearson, one of the medical staff at the communist take-over, was welcomed there on a visit in 1981.

The history of St Anne's Hospital, Barisal, Bangladesh, can be dated back to 5 February 1902, when four women missionaries arrived in Barisal, then a small riverside town in eastern Bengal. The four women had come to join two Brothers of the Oxford Mission Brotherhood of the Epiphany, with the intention of forming a Sisterhood of the Epiphany. They were committed to work among the people of Bengal, especially the women and children, as this was a Muslim area where men could not work with women and vice versa. Fanny, one of the Sisters-to-be, was a nurse. On February 13 the first medical call was received from a family needing help. This was the first of many such calls, which gradually increased in number, as confidence in the newcomer grew. Such calls, it is recorded, often entailed 'slow journeys by bund-gari to the outskirts of the town, and nights spent in bustees or across the river in the jungle. For many years tall lads would greet a Sister with a smile and say "Sister Fanny gave me birth".'

This medical ministry did much in laying the foundation for the acceptance of the other work done by the Sisterhood.

In 1903, a bamboo hut, with thatched roof, was erected in the Sisters' compound as a dispensary. Here Sister Fanny would see, on an average, 15 patients a day. Great interest was shown and many came, not for treatment, but to watch and comment. From such observers future patients were drawn. The patients paid for their treatment, though not always in cash, rather in kind, giving fruit, eggs and Bengali sweets. At this period the drug bill was about £2 a month. In March 1904, a Hindu family asked if the Sisters would nurse their daughter, who was very ill, her baby having died. This was something of a test case. Thankfully the girl recovered and as a result many homes were open to the Sisters from then on. 1905 saw an extension to the dispensary to accommodate children from the girls' school, which the Sisters had started, whenever they might need nursing.

The next big step forward was in 1914, when a new dispensary was built. In February 1918 a doctor, Sister Dorothy, came to join the Sisterhood, the first doctor to come and stay. The same month saw three Sisters going out to help in a nearby village, where plague had broken out. They lived in the village, cared for the patients and saw that all contaminated objects were burnt. They got little help from official sources as everyone was far too scared of plague to come into the vicinity. Thanks to the ministry of the Sisters, the epidemic stopped and did not spread to other villages.

The succeeding years saw a steady growth in the medical work, with more and more calls to cases in the town and nearby villages. At the same time more patients came to the dispensary for treatment. The work within the compound had also grown until the medical staff, now a doctor and two nurses, was responsible for the health of approximately 300 people resident in the institutions run by the Sisters. In 1934 a small 8-bedded maternity ward with labour room and nursery was built and named St Anne's Ward. The ward was in the special care of a nurse who had seen a number of years' service in Assam. She took Bengali girls, mostly of little education and trained them to carry out the deliveries. By the end of the year, a total of 13 patients had been delivered in the ward. Next year there were 40 admissions with 39 deliveries. From then on the number rose gradually, till by 1955 it had reached 288 admissions with 277 deliveries. From 1940 the girls in training were prepared for the Red Cross nurse dai's certificate. (Nurse dai was the name for the local midwife). As the examination was oral and practical only, even the illiterate could take it. These girls knew enough to read a thermometer and chart a temperature.

The medical work of the Sisterhood was never an isolated piece of work, but a part of everything they did. Patients who came to the hospital were followed up and visited in their homes, this often leading to evangelistic opportunities among the women. Sister Mary especially used to visit the patients in the ward, lending books to those who could read and having a talk with each one. Then, in the afternoon, she would set out in a cycle rickshaw to visit the old patients, always taking her bag of books with her. Wherever she went, a crowd of women quickly collected. She continued with this ministry until she was well into her 90s, and was often spoken of years after her death.

As the hospital had so obviously been accepted by the local community, who had overcome their fears of foreign staff and foreign medicine, and was being amply used, it was decided in 1956 to extend it. The bed strength was increased to 14, an action that was justified as that year 355 patients were admitted, bringing the total since the ward had been opened to 4143. In the autumn of that year another doctor joined the Sisterhood.

In the early 1960s the Community received a large legacy, part of which was allocated to St Anne's. As the children's ward was only corrugated iron and bamboo, and by no means waterproof, and the original St Anne's ward was showing ominous cracks in the walls, it was decided to rebuild the whole as one connected unit. The first wing was opened by the District Commissoner on December 6 1963 and the final block was blessed and opened on July 26 1964, the whole now being known as St Anne's Hospital.

At about that time another doctor joined the Sisterhood. The hospital staff was also considerably strengthened by two Japanese nurses and later by a third, some of whom were members of a Japanese Sisterhood. One or more of them stayed till well into 1968 and did a great deal to see that the training of midwives reached a good standard. All the girls taken for training were now educated, a minimum standard of class 8 pass being required. There was no difficulty in attracting trainees, in fact there were always many applicants from whom to select.

Once the inpatient department was re-opened, there was no lack of patients. There were 310 in the first year, and 402 in the next. The outpatient attendances also increased. The antenatal clinic had never closed but the numbers had been small. They now grew rapidly until, instead of one clinic a week, three were held, one of these being for private patients. Quite a number of the latter attended, including at one time the District Commissioner's wife. This part of the work helped the hospital finances considerably, so that eventually it reached its aim of being self-supporting. A postnatal clinic was begun and a fair number of mothers appreciated this period of extra care for themselves and their babies.

Gradually the outpatient work has been extended as new needs arose. The 1969 report summarizes the outpatient services as follows:-

1. Care of the health of the Community, school children, residents of St Mary's Home, domestic staff, nurses, a total of about 400 people. This included immunization against smallpox, cholera and the typhoid group.
2. A welfare and curative service for parish mothers and children extended to others as recommended.
3. Antenatal clinics for those of any creed, class or caste and a postnatal clinic for those who had attended as antenatal patients and wished to avail themselves of this further six weeks' care.
4. A domiciliary tuberculosis clinic, started three years previously, and treating an average of 10 patients at any one time.
5. Through the years an unofficial service had grown up to meet the medical needs of other missionaries in the town and their families. This has increased a great deal in recent years, due to the establishment of the Bengali language school in the town.

In 1969 there was a total of 2537 inpatients with 16,413 attendances. In 1976 the decision was taken to discontinue the inpatient maternity service while continuing all the outpatient clinics. The extra space gained by closing the wards was given to outpatients, whose conditions had become very cramped and congested. The private wards were used for some of the staff who wished to be resident.

Once again St Anne's changed its name and became St Anne's Medical Centre, with an increasing emphasis on community health, though a certain amount of curative work was maintained. The nurses were already being trained to give health talks on subjects such as breast feeding, diet, hygiene, family planning and so on. This continued, each outpatient clinic being preceded by a health talk. Also teams began visiting in some of the more congested areas of the town to study conditions and suggest improvements. An example will show the kind of conditions existing in many places. In one 'bustee' there was one latrine shared by 20 families, averaging seven members per family. This worked out at about ten minutes per person per day for the use of the latrine. This was quite apart from the fact that anyone using it had to go out-of-doors, a thing no woman or child would dare do at night.

Gradually a number of sub-centres were opened in different parts of the city, especially in the poorer areas, and also one in a nearby village. These centres were visited regularly, teaching was given, a check done on those taking contraceptive pills or on treatment for tuberculosis, the under-fives were weighed and weight charts filled in, and those suffering from malnutrition given tickets for the feeding centre. An effort was also made to carry out an immunization programme using triple vaccine and BCG. Vitamins were always taken to the centres, and any who were sick were treated. It was found that, if the sick were not seen, the others also ceased to attend. Anyone needing prolonged treatment was referred to St Anne's as well as any pregnant mother. In the village centre antenatal examinations were also included in the programme.

At St Anne's the clinics continued, many coming for family planning, and others for antenatal care and general advice. More and more the pregnant women wanted to be seen when bringing their children, to obviate the need for two visits. This was made possible, and more and more the family came for checking and for treatment of any needing it. Any patients needing a doctor's advice were asked to attend on a particular day when the doctor visited. The doctors who have helped have been either young national doctors, newly qualified and doing their internship in the Medical College Hospital, or young missionaries, attending the Bengali Language School. It was found advisable to re-open a feeding centre, where between 50 and 80 children could get one good meal a day. A day centre was also opened for toddlers.

Not far from the hospital, the government built a school for the training of family welfare visitors. They asked St Anne's if they would take them in batches, to give them experience in community health and clinic work. This was arranged, and up to four at a time came for a period of a month to work with the St Anne's staff. This has proved a happy exercise in cooperation.

Since 1979, when the expatriate nurse returned to Great Britain, and is now working with Bengalis in East London, the running of St Anne's has been entirely in the hands of Bengalis.

The Golden Jubilee Medical Report of Holdsworth Memorial Hospital, Mysore, in 1956, written by Doctors Gillespie, Pierce, Charles and Robb, is quoted verbatim since it exemplifies yet another hospital in the Indian sub-continent that has adapted to change, culminating in its being recognized by the Indian Government as a hospital for postgraduate training.

'It is very interesting to read through the old reports of the hospital and note the differences and changes in the medical work through the years. It will be remembered that it was the plague epidemic in 1899 which first impressed Mrs Holdsworth with the need for a hospital for women and children, and during the early years of the hospital there were constantly recurring epidemics of plague and severe outbreaks of cholera and small-pox. In 1909 the hospital staff cooperated with the Government Medical Service in an inoculation campaign. They directed their attention mainly to persuading zenana patients and their children to submit to inoculation. At that time every fever patient seeking admission had to be carefully scrutinized to exclude plague. In 1914 tincture of iodine was used for plague patients with more success than any other treatment. These outbreaks continued until the nineteen thirties. There was severe cholera in 1908 when one of the nurses caught it and died; smallpox in 1923 and 1937; and in 1918 and until 1921 the world-wide influenza epidemic visited Mysore so that the number of in-patients in hospital doubled in a fortnight and the death rate reached great heights. A severe whooping-cough epidemic in 1927 brought high mortality among children. Today, thanks to the public health measures initiated by government these epidemics have become infrequent.

Malaria, too, was a very frequent complaint and a very high percentage of the population suffered from it. Many patients were admitted to hospital with this alone. The severe anaemias of those days were largely due to malaria, hookworm infestation, and deficiency diseases. Malaria is by no means banished; there is still much sub-clinical malaria, but while in 1932 malaria parasites were found in one in six of the blood smears examined, in 1951 it was only one in sixty, and in 1955 only one in six hundred were positive for malaria.

Yet this decrease in occurrence is not true for intestinal para-sites and the dysenteries. In 1934, 60% of examinations were positive for one or other of these diseases and the rate is still 50-60% today. Take, for example, *Ascaris* – that ubiquitous worm. Almost everybody suffers from this infestation. A woman came one day with typical gallstone colic. At operation a round worm was found in the hepatic duct, and a few days later she had another attack of colic and out along the drainage tube came yet another ten-inch round worm. A child came in with a perforated tuberculous intestine and on opening the abdomen two round worms presented at the wound. A woman came with acute appendicitis and at operation the appendix was stiff and waving about – it was rigid with a round worm. Another child had acute intestinal obstruction and hundreds of worms had to be removed at operation. One child of two years got rid of 1000 worms within a year. They simulate almost every condition including respira-tory and meningeal.

'As long ago as 1917, our hospital staff was concerned about hookworm infestation. Today various new drugs are being used and investigations of their relative value are being carried out in the hospital. Hookworm is still prevalent, and it is interesting to note the varying incidence of infestation in the men patients admitted to hospital in 1953 and 1954, from the different districts.

'Many other diseases which like hookworm are preventable and are associated with ignorance, dirt, dust and flies, still persist. At a recent preachers' meeting in Chamarajnagar the ministers and evangelists were asked to compile a list of the diseases prevalent in their villages. Here are the diseases they mentioned:

'Malaria; dysentery; typhoid; cholera; common cold; infantile paralysis; tuberculosis; syphilis; sore eyes; hookworm; round worm; tetanus; leprosy; itch; dropsy; heart failure; stomach ulcer; eczema; epilepsy; smallpox; diphtheria; measles.

'Of this list of twenty-two, all except three are to some degree preventable or controllable by public health measures, and as long ago as 1918 the importance of village dispensaries was stressed.

'Visits were made from time to time to the Mandya and Talavadi areas, but there has never been enough staff to do this work. Only the Kastur Hospital has survived through 31 years, and recently the dispensary at Hadya was re-opened and is the centre of mobile dispensary work. Now, too, transport is easier and very many of the village patients come in to hospital. The percentage of our patients who come from outside Mysore City is over fifty. But the need for public health work and preventive medicine still remains, and with this need in mind we recently started on a different venture using the visual aid material sponsored by the Christian Medical Association of India. Weekly filmstrips are being shown in the wards, and we are providing our village teachers and evangelists with visual aid material for use in their villages. But it is impossible for those doing curative work to do also the preventive side. This needs a separate team of workers.

'Much of our time in hospital, then, is spent in the treatment of preventable diseases. The other condition that brings much suffering and contributes to disease of all kinds is prolonged malnutrition. Patients come with severe protein and vitamin deficiencies. This is not surprising for one reads so often in the old reports of famine in different villages, and the story has been repeated again and again in recent years, and in 1950 malnutrition was reported to be the most serious condition of the moment.

'In 1914, the prevalent acute diseases were pneumonia, bronchitis and typhoid. Typhoid is always present in the wards today. There was a virulent form in 1950 with a high death rate. At that time chloramphenicol was so expensive that only a few could be treated with it. Now it is possible to give antibiotics to the poorest patient, thus shortening the course of the disease. The advent of these antibiotic drugs has completely altered the outlook for patients suffering from typhoid, and in our hospital we are investigating the use of two drugs in combination (chloramphenicol and tetracycline) in the treatment of this disease with promising results.

'In 1914 heart and kidney diseases were reported as the prevalent chronic diseases. Today there are more cases than ever before, and the strain of life is shown in the number of cases of hypertension and coronary thrombosis. These are increasing and are more common in men. Rheumatic carditis has always been common and is more prevalent among the women and children. Congenital heart disease of all types is quite common. In 1954 Mr Robinson, late of the Cambridge Instrument Company Ltd., obtained for us a very nice Cambridge Standard Electrocardiograph which is proving very helpful in diagnosis and prognosis. We are still hoping to start a regular heart clinic.

'I would add tuberculosis as one of the most serious menaces today. This hospital does not admit open pulmonary tuberculosis, but tuberculosis of bones and joints, intestines, pleura, glands and meninges, especially among the poorer classes, is greatly on the increase. Another condition which we see frequently is the type of thyroid defect in adults known as myxoedema.

'Osteomalacia – a disease with softening of the bones – was extremely common in the early days. It is a result of undernourishment, lack of fresh air, and childbearing, and is a form of adult rickets which responds to ultra-violet light, and calcium and vitamin D. Though we see a number of old cases, it is not often now that we see an acute new case.

'It is surprising to find what a large number of our patients have diabetes. This is of a type that seems peculiar to South India, being of a very mild nature and running a prolonged course. It is very rarely that one can get a patient to discipline himself to the dietary restrictions and the daily injections of insulin that may be required and in fact it is very difficult for them to do so when they live in remote villages.

'Diphtheria is endemic, and has been for years. It is usually of a mild type but severe cases are occasionally seen. In 1932 there were three cases requiring tracheotomy. One child's parents gave permission and the child lived. The other parents, through fear, refused and the children died. Now the people are getting their children immunized and the government are inoculating all school children with triple vaccine – diphtheria, whooping cough, and tetanus. This should bring a reduction and eventually eradicate these diseases.

'In 1927 a Venereal Disease Clinic was commenced, the first clinic to be held in the State. The clinic was held twice a week and patients were admitted to Faith Ward. Many of the patients were deserted, homeless women, and in 1938, a home was made where they could live and work in the hospital and continue treatment as required. This scheme was not successful but some of these women were rescued and now work and earn their living. When sulpha drugs and antibiotics came into use, the clinic as such was no longer necessary and was discontinued.

An ultra-violet light apparatus was first installed in 1929, and was a very useful treatment. Many children with malnutrition and rickets responded to what they called "power". Osteomalacia responded well and tuberculous glands and ulcers.

'It is impossible to give a complete survey of all the diseases we see, but mention must be made of the effects of fear and superstition on the lives of the people. In 1911 the following story appeared in the report:

"A young girl from a distant village, accompanied by her mother, was very ill, her pains being increased more than once by eating forbidden food given secretly to her. One evening, suffering more acutely than usual, she had worked herself into a state of frantic fear. In answer to my inquiry regarding her I was told . . . that the devil had taken up his abode in her stomach and was causing her much trouble. When reasoning failed the doctor suggested giving an emetic, which was followed up by the stomach pump being used. The bystanders watched the preparations with breathless interest, and, after examining the water which had been slightly coloured with colouring matter, the patient and friends were all of the opinion that the 'troubler' had been washed out, and shortly afterwards the patient was restfully sleeping. Needless to add that we have gained the wonderful power of being able to cast out devils."

Then there was the girl who told us how there had been a family quarrel which had been made up and a feast held to celebrate. She maintained that some poison had been put in the food from which she would die in three months. Nothing would persuade her that this was not true, and within the 3 months she died from fear! In very many cases the fear manifests itself in 'fits' of various types. A girl of sixteen came one day with fits. She and her friends had set off one evening to climb a hill to a shrine and were still climbing after nightfall, when they were startled by an elephant trumpeting close by. Torches were lit and the elephant scared away, and they reached the top of the hill safely. But the girl became unconscious and had fits. In her dreams she thought the gods were calling and she was afraid to go to the shrine again. She had recently lost her parents and had been left with many debts and this had been worrying her. There are endless such stories and they leave no room for doubt that the healing of the body, mind and spirit must go together. Much of one's time is spent trying to understand what is behind the illness, for perhaps half of our patients have worries and problems directly related to their illnesses. So when you reach the statistics remember that each one is an individual with cares and problems, a home and family, however humble or poor.

'There is one more task that we have to do and that is the training of staff. From the time that the hospital was opened training of staff has been carried on side by side with the treating of the sick. First in 1906 compounders and nurses in the vernacular – then nurses of the Higher Grade in English in 1934. Then laboratory technicians. From 1923 for many years Vellore medical students came for practical midwifery experience. In the year 1954 the hospital was recognized for the training of house surgeons and now in 1956 it has been recognized for training of internees under the new scheme by which this is done during their medical course.

'In connection with this training of house surgeons regular clinical meetings are held once a month and we are greatly helped by the attendance of friends from the other hospitals. There are also weekly tutorials held. A medical library has been started and is well stocked with journals and fairly well stocked with books though we need more.

'Reading through the old reports you can see, as we ourselves have seen over the years the change from fear, superstition and ignorance, to knowledge and freedom, taking place – and above all and in all the healing hand of God.'

One of the most interesting new ventures at Nixon Memorial Hospital, Segbwema, Sierra Leone, has been the establishment of the Nutritional Rehabilitation Unit aimed at persuading the mothers of malnourished children to change some of their old ideas and habits. Follow-up is done by a mobile team and post-basic students; their reports have been encouraging.

A survey of a South American Indian tribe in Paraguay (Patterson, 1980) shows that attempting to establish the pattern of disease in a remote South American Indian tribe prior to the establishment of a rural health project is in keeping with the most modern concepts of community health, while gaining access to remote rural groups such as these is very much within the missionary spirit, the essence of which has not altered over the years. Typical of the environmental conditions was the presence of *Triatoma infestans* – the vector of Chagas' disease. In 50 out of 71 houses surveyed – of 172 children, 81 had died (47%) and of these 35% had died under the age of 5 years: 24 from measles, 20 from diarrhoea, and 21 from tuberculosis.

The quality of the mission hospitals in many parts of the third world and the dedication of their staff have made them obvious venues for the training of medical students: e.g. the Wesley Guild Hospital at Ilesha for medical students of the University of Ife; Wusasa Hospital in Zaria for medical students of the Ahmadu Bello University, Nigeria.

It is to the credit of the missionary doctors that this has come about and that they are playing a substantial part in the education of doctors in the third world.

The revival of interest in indigenous medicine that has taken place in recent years and the possible use of traditional healers within the context of modern health care, including psychiatry, would certainly not have surprised Livingstone, who wrote to John Kirk:

> 'They have medical men among themselves who are generally the most observant people to be met with. It is desirable to be at all times on good terms with them. In order to do this, light cases, except among the very poor, ought to be referred to their care and severe cases should be enquired into ... and no disparaging remarks ever made in the presence of the patient.'

Although this account deals essentially with past initiatives, the missionary doctors of today are adapting to a rapidly changing and dynamic situation. As in the past they are willing and likely to be in the forefront of new initiatives, contributing to the eventual attainment of the idea of 'Health for all by the Year 2000 . . .' The same spirit of unselfish service and dedication to God and men still guides them. *I salute them.*

References

Browne, S.G. (1959) Incidence and clinical manifestations of onchocerciasis in a focus in the Oriental Province of the Belgian Congo. *Annals of Tropical Medicine and Parasitology*, 53, 421.

Browne, S.G. (1960) Onchocercal depigmentation. *Transactions of the Royal Society of Tropical Medicine and Hygiene*, 54, 325.

Browne, S.G. (1960) Onchocerciasis and leprosy. *Leprosy Review*, 31 46 Translated from *Annales de la Société belge de Médecine tropicale* (1959) 39, 257.

Browne, S.G. (1971) Comprehensive medical care delivery through a church-related rural health programme in the former Belgian Congo. Contact, No. 6. Christian Medical Commission, WCC, Geneva.

Browne, S.G. (1975) The training and deployment of medical auxiliaries in the leprosy campaign. Annals of Tropical Medicine and Parasitology. 69, 413.

Browne, S.G. (1979) The contribution of medical missionaries to tropical medicine. Transactions of the Royal Society of Tropical Medicine and Hygiene, 73, 359.

Burkitt, D. (1962) Determining the climatic limitations of a children's cancer common in Africa. British Medical Journal 2, 1019.

Burkitt, D. and Wright, D. (1960) Geögraphical and tribal distribution of the African lymphoma in Uganda. British Medical Journal, 1, 569.

Chesterman, C.C. (1922-23) Tryparsamide in sleeping sickness. Transactions of the Royal Society of Tropical Medicine and Hygiene, 16, 394.

China Mission Year Book (1910, 1913, 1931).

Faskett, R. (1964) The Zambesi doctors, Edinburgh University Press

Fisher, A.C. (1934) A study of the schistosomes of the Stanleyville district of the Belgian Congo. Transactions of the Royal Society of Tropical Medicine and Hygiene, 28, 277.

Gelfand, M. (1957) Livingstone the Doctor. Oxford: Blackwell.

Hughes, R.A. (1951) Presidential Address. Journal of the Christian Medical Association of India

Hughes, R.A. (1955) Chronic dysentery.

Keane, E. and Gilles, H.M. (1977) Lassa fever in Panguma Hospital, Sierra Leone, 1973-6. British Medical Journal, 1, 1399.

Lockhart, W. (1861) The Medical Missionary in China. London: Hurst and Blackwell.

Peaston, (1933) Preliminary note on a focus of S. mansoni infection in Sierra Leone. Annals of Tropical Medicine, 27, 497.

Patterson, M.C. (1980) A medical survey of a South American Indian tribe in the Paraguayan Chaco. Tropical Doctor, 10, 124.

CHAPTER 9

TROPICAL AND GENERAL SURGERY

P. Bewes

Surgery, it has been argued, is one of the 'luxury' disciplines that developing countries can adequately do without – an expensive way of dealing with advanced disease that could well be dealt with more economically by preventive measures. There is more than a grain of truth in this argument; yet a study of the early pioneer days of medical missionary activity shows that without the dramatic 'cures' that surgery provided, modern scientific medicine might never have gained acceptance in the societies that had, up till then, accepted only traditional healing methods.

Amudat is a tiny hospital on the border between Kenya and Uganda, unable even to boast of 75 beds, serving the largely nomadic Pokot people. Yet even here it proved necessary for the missionary doctors to practise some basic surgery, because the local populace were not ready to submit themselves to preventive measures until the doctors had 'proved themselves' by showing their ability to cope with such hitherto untreatable conditions as strangulated hernia and obstructed labour. Indeed, one missionary doctor serving in Tanzania confided that she had intended to set out with a programme of preventive medicine based on a hill hospital among the peoples of the Usambara range, only to find that first of all she had to master the elements of surgery.

Dr James Fanstone (1972) writes of the Anapolis hospital in Brazil:

'I asked myself was there no surgery in all this vast interior of a nation with all its growing towns? It was to Alarico that I put my burning question. He considered it for a moment and then answered it in the following words, "Once, some time ago, a coloured colleague and I were in consultation over a case of 'nodas tripas' (knotted bowel or volvulus, as we call it; a case of acute intestinal obstruction)." He continued, "We considered the case for operation this way and that, until finally we realized that we had neither the equipment nor the skill to operate. So we let the man die . . . In fact," concluded Dr Alarico, "in all the years of my practice in the state of Goias, I do not remember anyone having been operated on".'

Here he describes one of the problems facing the missionary doctor in the pioneer situation. Over and over again patients present themselves suffering from treatable and painful (often fatal) conditions that could be 'cured' with a comparatively simple operation requiring only a bare minimum of equipment and training. Could the doctor in all humanity dam up the springs of compassion within him and allow the patient to die, in order to release the doctor and his team for more productive work elsewhere? Fanstone's answer was to open a hospital where surgery could be performed, and the same answer has been responsible for the opening of hospitals the world over. Howard Somervell (1955) wrote from India:

'I have felt that the important thing to do is to save people from pain and crippling disability; to make people healthy and painless and able-bodied who would otherwise be disabled or suffering.'

Sir Albert Cook started medical work in Kampala, Uganda, in a little shed in 1897, later moving to a hospital of two huts with reed walls, thatched roofs and floors of mud and cowdung. Nevertheless, during his first year, in which over 17,000 patients had been seen and 189 admitted, no fewer than 454 operations had been performed (140 of them major, done under chloroform), with only 15 deaths among the inpatients (Foster, 1970). The notes of these early and historic operations have been preserved for posterity in a special library in the Makerere University Medical School, Kampala, and make extraordinary reading for anyone steeped in today's technology, brought up to believe that excellent surgery can only be done in elaborate and expensively equipped hospitals.

The work of these early pioneers led to the introduction of modern scientific medicine in country after country, and it is noteworthy that disciplines other than surgery (including preventive medicine) were encouraged to flourish. It was from Makerere Medical School itself, which owed so much to the surgical pioneering of the Cook brothers, that later came the symposium *Medical Care in Developing Countries* now recognized as one of the basic texts for those engaged in the medicine of poverty (King, 1966).

It is in a way unfortunate that much recent emphasis in surgery has been on the expensive and lavish. In many developing countries the result has been that the cost of medicine has so escalated that surgery (even at the levels that the Cook brothers practised in the 1890s) is now out of reach for many and available only to the financially elite in the larger towns and cities. Surgery has attracted much criticism to itself as a result, so that even as recently as 1979 it was fashionable to deplore the provision of surgical services and to emphasize by contrast how much more good could be done by diverting the resources to preventive medicine and community health. Happily, missionary surgeons continue to show the world that excellence in surgery can still be achieved without over-lavish expenditure and equipment (Hankins, 1980) and usually manage to do so in happy symbiosis with a programme of community outreach and preventive medicine that continues as ever to demonstrate the wide relevance of the Christian gospel.

The missionary surgeon has nearly always had to accept considerable limitations in his working conditions. Albert Cook, working in Mengo Hospital at the turn of the century, had only a mixture of compressed cow-dung and mud for the floor covering to his operating theatre. Conditions for the early pioneers were especially primitive, but what a privilege it is to be able to give crucial help under such conditions! Sir Henry Holland – pioneer of eye surgery in what is now Pakistan – writes of one of many such episodes (Holland, 1958):

' "Sahib, if you do not give our old father his sight, he will go down to his grave blind." I knew that as a Christian doctor I could not refuse, so we had the box of instruments opened, got out a Primus stove and set it up on the polo ground. We sterilized the instruments in a saucepan, put the drops in the old man's eyes, and when all was ready he was placed on his back on the polo ground and I knelt at his head and there operated on both eyes. Naturally I could not leave him without medical assistance, so I told my only surgical assistant to stay with him for ten days. He returned later with the news that both eyes had been successfully operated on.'

He also describes another operation performed in a palm grove, in which a suprapubic cystostomy was performed using a clinical thermometer case as a trocar (after it had been filed to a sharp point by a sepoy trained as an armourer's assistant). His patient made an uneventful recovery. Such tales must be legion, yet they illustrate what every missionary surgeon knows to be true: that to perform good surgery the practitioner must learn to be content with the equipment that he has, however imperfect it may seem to be, and to learn the appropriate skill and develop the necessary judgement that must accompany the use of such tools.

A few examples will illustrate how simplicity in the choice of surgical materials may still serve the missionary surgeon called upon to work in one of the poorer parts of the world. Thus, suture materials need not always be the modern pre-packaged item with the thread ready swaged into the end of the 'atraumatic' needle. The difference between the cost of fishing nylon and a sterile pre-packaged suture is of the order of thirty-five thousand per cent. Yet excellent surgery is being performed in centres all over the world using reels of nylon or cotton threaded into needles that (resharpened) are used over and over again, at a cost of less than a third of one per cent of traditional costs. I have shown that a safe abdominal closure can be performed at a cost of less than one English penny (Bewes, 1982), and one abdominal suture needle can, by resharpening, be used for over a year and still be as good as new. A hand-sharpened carbon steel surgical needle is a good match for sharpness with any needle that the instrument companies can produce at the present time.

Again, anaesthesia does not presuppose the use of the most expensive apparatus using hard-to-come-by medical gases like nitrous oxide and oxygen. Safe anaesthetics can be given using simple draw-over vaporizers costing less than a tenth of the cost of the standard Boyle's machine, and it has been shown that anaesthetics so given are no less safe than those given with more elaborate equipment. In the Kilimanjaro Christian Medical Centre in Tanzania a wide range of surgical operations was performed over an extended period using such draw-over vaporizers only, at a time when nitrous oxide was extremely difficult to get. The reason was that the carrier gas used in such vaporizers was air, which was (and still is) easily available and free. It is noteworthy that the operations in this series included several heart operations (transventricular mitral valvotomy) and chest operations on small children (division and ligation of patent ductus arteriosus). One factor contributing to the low cost of the heart and chest operations was that the anaesthetic vapour was Trilene, commonly used as a dry-cleaning agent, and costing only four English pence per hour.

Intravenous infusions – especially of blood – add considerably to the expense of surgery in developing countries. Yet it is not always realized just how much routine surgery can be performed without them. The use of the patient's own blood (taken and stored before the operation) has enabled many prostate operations to be performed without depletion of the scanty

hospital blood stores, and many abdominal operations (gastrectomy, cholecystectomy and the like) can be safely performed
using fluid maintenance therapy by the rectal route rather than
the more expensive intravenous one. Indeed, rectal saline was
the routine fluid therapy used in many centres at the very time
when the safety of such operations as gastrectomy was beginning to be shown to be of a very high order. And the cost of rectal
saline (virtually nil) makes intravenous saline (at three or four
pounds sterling a day) seem very expensive by comparison. For
emergency operations, of course, intravenous fluids are necessary, but more than one mission hospital has shown that it is
possible to make these locally at around one-twentieth of the
commercial price. Blood transfusion remains a very real problem in many developing countries. More than once I have had
to donate blood shortly before proceeding to operate. Catherine
Maddox writing from Manorom Hospital in Thailand, instances
many of the difficulties facing the introduction of blood transfusion facilities in the pioneer situation (Maddox, 1962).

It is in the realm of asepsis perhaps that the pioneer surgeon,
working often under adverse circumstances, faces some of his
greatest worries. The modern operating theatre has a plenum
ventilation system, using filtered bacterium-free air, and has a
rigid discipline that seemingly ensures that no bacterium can
enter the theatre. For certain operations, a closed system of
masks and tubes even draws the surgeon's expired air away from
the operation site while he and his assistants operate in suits that
in many ways deserve their nickname of 'space-suits'. How far
this is from the cow-dung-floored operating theatre of Mengo
Hospital at the turn of the century! How far from the polo ground
in which Sir Henry Holland had to operate! By no stretch of the
imagination can it be thought likely that within the next twenty
or thirty years such facilities will become available for the villagers of the developing nations. Happily, the experience of missionary surgeons is that such elaborate precautions can be dis-
pensed with for the vast majority of the operations they are
called upon to perform. A simple autoclave will suffice for sterilizing surgical equipment and theatre gowns and drapes, and
under really adverse circumstances operations have been performed using antiseptics alone (Dick, 1966) with acceptable
post-operative rates of infection that would put to shame some
centres boasting of far more prestigious facilities. As so often, a
clear observance of theatre discipline, a deep understanding of

the basic principles of surgery, the timely use of delayed methods of wound closure and a gentle handling of body tissues more than make up for the lack of extremely expensive theatre ventilation systems.

The author must confess to a certain preoccupation with methods of fracture treatment appropriate to the developing world. Modern methods of fracture management presuppose the use of such prohibitively expensive hardware and equipment that the missionary surgeon might be forgiven for thinking that fracture management was out of reach of all but the most advanced hospitals. Happily, this is far from true. Experience in the Kilimanjaro Christian Medical Centre, echoed also in many other centres, has shown, for instance, that most upper arm fractures can be managed without plates and screws, without plaster-of-Paris even, provided that a simple type of arm sling is properly constructed and used with appropriate exercises. A simple approach is appropriate also for a large proportion of the common fractures treated in a mission hospital in one of the poorer developing countries. Interestingly enough, the underlying philosophy common to these methods of fracture management implies that 'Nature' (Christians understand this term to mean God the Creator) has implanted within each of us a wonderful mechanism for the healing of fractures, which does not have to be 'fought against' but rather 'cooperated with' by the surgeon (and the patient) – often enabling the financial cost of fracture management to be cut by more than nine-tenths, with little or no disadvantage to the patient. I claim no originality for the methods described; it is gratifying to note that (as so often) all that is necessary is to explore existing methods that have been known for decades (if not for centuries) in the search for ways of bringing treatment within the reach of rural populations that have for so long been cut off from the benefits of the more expensive treatments (Bewes, 1982).

How often does the missionary surgeon hear envious comments from his colleagues working in the more specialized environment of the Western hospital: 'How I sometimes wish it were possible to get the kind of experience that you so clearly are getting!'

It is one of the really rewarding aspects of the missionary doctor's life that he is so much more nearly fulfilling the full life of a doctor for which his training clearly should have prepared him. Our Lord himself undertook medical work among a wide range of conditions both medical and surgical. Leprosy, blindness, mental disorder, gynaecological conditions, orthopaedic deformities, death and near death, deafness and the resulting speech impediments, medical fevers, epilepsy, and even traumatic amputation came his way. As far as we can ascertain, these were all healed. The missionary doctor, following in his Lord's footsteps, often has the (nowadays rare) privilege of a similar wide variety of medical conditions among which to work. The multiplicity of conditions to treat is not surprising when one considers the huge areas that each missionary doctor has to 'cover'. Dr Leader Stirling, who started as a UMCA missionary in Tanzania and who later became Minister of Health in that country, relates a meeting in Westminster in which he attempted to explain the vastness of the terrain to his audience (Stirling, 1977):

'Let this represent Tandahimba, a place with a big population and a boarding school, but still no dispensary even. Suppose you live here and your child is sick, the nearest dispensary is at Coulsdon (Nanyamba) or near to Hatfield (Mahuta), whichever you prefer, but nothing nearer, and to get there you must walk and carry your child; there is no public transport. Even then, there is no doctor at either. If you want to see a doctor (me!) you must walk on nearly to Cambridge (Lulindi). Even then, you will have to pay a small fee. If, as a taxpayer, you want to claim a free consultation from the nearest Government doctor, you must walk to Eastbourne (Mikindani).'

It is not surprising to find in his book, *Tanzanian Doctor*, that he had to deal with depressed skull fractures (under local anaesthesia), with open brain injuries and closed cerebral compression, with disembowellings and wild animal injuries, with obstructed labour and with major jaw surgery. All this had to be done against a background of having to supervise the building of the hospitals in which he worked, and the administration of the anaesthetics as he operated. The book is worth reading, if only for the hair-raising description of a bicycle ride across a wilderness to attend an emergency: a ride that took a full twelve hours!

Howard Somervell, writing in 1939, described the work at Neyyoor as follows (Somervell, 1955):

'On an average day we do anything from eight to sixteen operations, nearly all of them major ones, usually some five or six of them being abdominal operations . . . A visitor to Neyyoor, who was a surgeon in London for some time, spent a day watching our operations. At the end of it he said, "These big cases you do – jaws and gastrectomies – if a hospital in London does one it's posted up in various places and people come from half the hospitals to see it; and here you do three or four in a day as a matter of course!" '

This is one of the great privileges of the missionary surgeon: that of the great variety and challenge of his work. No two days seem ever the same, and it is possible to work for a year and to have to perform an operation never previously done personally in every week of that year. A surgeon will get some idea of the challenge by reading these two lists – each of them representing the operating load facing one surgeon at the Kilimanjaro Christian Medical Centre to be done in one week (in addition to whatever emergencies might turn up out of normal operating hours):

Week One (December 16-22)
    Pneumonectomy
    Transthoracic Hellers Operation
    Right inguinal hernia (child)
    Portocaval shunt
    Bilateral club-foot
    'Second-Look' operation following colectomy for cancer
    Inguinal hernia
    Diagnostic laparotomy for pain
    Pilonidal sinus excision
    Bouginage
    Inguinal hernia
    Gastrectomy for cancer
    Rib resection and drainage for empyema
    Removal of plate and screws from hip
    Gastrectomy for pyloric stenosis

Week Two (January 12-17)
    Cystoscopy
    Amputation of arm (post-snake-bite)
    Bouginage
    Cholecystectomy
    Amputation of leg (for ischaemia)
    Hernia repair
    Second stage urethroplasty for stricture
    Umbilical herniorrhaphy
    Conversion gastrectomy for stomal ulcer
    Vagotomy
    Varicose veins

Transventricular mitral valvotomy
Prostatectomy
Cautery of extensive anal warts

A surgeon from Burundi who was asked why he dared to perform difficult and technically exacting operations normally
done only by specialists answered: 'I have to – I am at times the
only person able to do this operation in a population of around a
million.' This is the extraordinary reality: that there is sometimes literally no other person able to help the patient through
his illness than the missionary surgeon himself, however weak
and relatively unqualified he may feel. It is still possible for
countries with around fifteen to twenty million inhabitants to
have no more than one or two specialists in such important
fields as orthopaedic surgery and anaesthesia, and yet to have an
almost bottomless pit of need in the very specialities where so
few specialists exist.

The missionary surgeon sometimes obtains such enormous
experience of a certain condition common in his part of the
world that he can hardly fail to become a leading figure in the
management of that condition. Such was surely the case with Sir
Henry Holland (Holland, 1958) who, working at Shikarpur
could speak from immense experience of cataract surgery when
he stated:

'It is quite unnecessary for a patient to be kept lying down after
cataract extraction – but I have had living proof of this fact over a
great many years. Cataracts have been removed from some
80,000 eyes in our clinics, and as a general rule the patient has got
up ... and I cannot remember any serious complications
resulting from this ...'

Surgeons came from all parts of the world to share in the unique
experience to be had at Shikarpur, and no wonder.

On occasion the missionary surgeon finds himself at a
moment when the surgery of the condition that is common in his
area is about to take a courageous leap forwards, and he then
finds himself privileged to be at the very spearhead of advance in
that condition. This was undoubtedly the case with Paul Brand
and the treatment of leprosy at Vellore Hospital in India. It now
seems barely credible that so much ignorance about the disease
was rife even among missionary doctors as recently as 1947, but
a reading of Paul Brand's life (Wilson, 1965) seems to show that
this was so. The cause of the mutilations of hands so often seen
in certain forms of leprosy was not known by many workers and

there was abysmal ignorance as to why fingers fell off or became
short. Dorothy Clarke Wilson's book, Ten Fingers for God, tells
the story of the early development of reconstructive surgery for
leprosy of the hand as developed by one man who 'happened' to
be in the right place at the right time, and who was prepared to
think for himself and to question the established dogmas of his
day. One may be forgiven for wondering how many other
dogmas are waiting to be challenged and exposed even today.

Many missionary doctors and surgeons, if questioned, will
humbly explain that their métier is patient care rather than
research, and indeed, when so many in the developed world are
complaining about the lack of facilities for research, it is not
surprising that the mission hospital does not immediately
spring to mind as the obvious fertile field for original research.
Yet to assume that elaborate and expensive 'facilities' are always
necessary before research can be done is to miss the point. It has
been said (cynically) that real research is that research which
was done before the receipt of the research grant. There may be
some truth in this statement. Denis Burkitt has done much to
dispel the myth that research cannot be done without huge
investment in equipment and laboratory space. His own work
in the field of the African lymphoma which bears his name
illustrates how much can be achieved by a fertile mind exposed
to an intriguing situation. By undertaking a safari in East Africa
in an ancient car and armed with some photographs of an
interesting series of jaw tumours, he proved that it was possible
to uncover a hitherto unrecognized disease entity that linked
malaria, glandular fever, a childhood lymphoma, and the newly
emerging science of immunology in a conundrum that is still
proving to be a fruitful field for research.

Burkitt was also able to enlist the help of a large number of
isolated rural doctors – many of them working in Christian missionary establishments – in yet another fruitful field of research,
namely that concerned with the possible links between the
'explosion' in recent decades of diseases associated with
Western civilization and peculiarities of Western diet (notably
the relative absence of fibre in the highly processed foods readily
obtainable today). To say that Burkitt and his many co-workers
all over the world have opened up new fields for research in
gastroenterology would be to make a blatant understatement.
Whether he is right or wrong in laying at the door of our fibre-
depleted diet such widely diverse diseases as appendicitis,

diverticulitis, varicose veins, hiatus hernia, gallstones, athero-sclerosis, diabetes mellitus and haemorrhoids remains to be seen, but the approach to many of these diseases can never be the same again in the light of the current debate. Only fifteen years ago the management of colonic diverticulosis was said to include a low-residue diet, not only to treat the disease but also to prevent it. A high-residue diet is now used (with considerable success) not only in its prevention but also in its treatment. It is happy to note that not only Burkitt himself, but also many of his co-workers are convinced and practising Christians.

One field of research which still remains, with huge areas waiting to be explored, is that concerned with the understanding of the complex interrelations between human, political, reli-gious, economic, cultural and purely 'medical' factors in the determination within any one culture of the most appropriate methods of treatment of medical and surgical conditions within that culture. Many questions of basic importance remain un-answered to this day. To mention but a few, one might ask the following:

1. Are doctors the most efficient and reliable people to deliver surgical services at village level, or should we rely more on properly trained medical assistants?
2. When does movement help fracture union by encouraging the development of healthy callus, and when does it hinder fracture union by producing pseudarthrosis? What are the rules governing movement in fracture treatment?
3. Does the routine administration of antibiotics in the manage-ment of compound fractures do any good?
4. Should medical assistants be taught to close wounds at once or after an interval of some days?
5. Are people actually taking the tablets we give them?
6. Are there any fields in which 'traditional practitioners' are doing better than we are? (If so, what are we doing about it?)
7. Are patients on the whole happier or less happy when we treat them for —————— disease?

It is encouraging to read of basic research being done, often in humble hospitals boasting of few facilities. Thus, one question that would now appear to have been resolved is: 'In the treat-ment of tetanus, has the intrathecal route of administration of anti-tetanus serum (whether of horse or human origin) a real place in reducing the mortality?' Since the work of Sanders and his co-workers at the Christian hospital in Bihar (Sanders, 1977) the answer to that question must now be a resounding 'yes', and I for one am happy to acknowledge my indebtedness to that team for this advance in the management of tetanus which has helped one patient in a ward in Birmingham towards a speedy and uncomplicated recovery from that disease while this chapter was being written.

Never has more literature abounded on the management of surgical conditions than at the present time. Yet never has the literature available been less accurately targeted towards the mass of suffering humanity than today. While more and more countries join the ranks of the 'very poor', surgical literature increasingly emphasizes the more expensive and complex ways of treating disease. One is taught that all Pott's fractures should be treated by internal fixation, and that the internal fixation used should be very rigid implants, inserted under spotlessly sterile conditions by experts of considerable experience who have had rigorous training extending over many years. Such teaching is valueless in a country that boasts of only one orthopaedic surgeon. Where is the literature that will help the isolated practitioner with only modest operating resources and only limited personal experience? Such literature was readily available fifteen years ago, but increasingly difficult to obtain now. Even the articles coming out of the universities of the developing countries themselves sometimes seem to be obsessed with the expensive and the technically sophisticated and complex.

A book was written many years ago by George Perkins (1958) which brought the management of many of the commoner fractures within the orbit of even the humblest general practitioner who had access to an X-ray machine. With this book as a guide it is possible to get excellent results with fractures of the humerus (even the difficult comminuted fractures of the lower end) with no more complicated apparatus than is present in every home. Yet this book is currently out of print, and unlikely to be reprinted at least in the West during this decade. What is true in fracture surgery is true in many other aspects of surgery today: the literature available is increasingly targeted at the affluent West, and becoming irrelevant to the needs of the majority of the people in the real world. Of what help is it to learn that skin grafts should be taken with a roller knife with replacement blades, when the truth is that the blades have been out of stock in the country in which one works for the past three years? Why are books no longer produced which teach how to take skin grafts with an open knife, and how to sharpen that knife between operations? We are in danger of losing the very skills of which we are in greatest need.

Happily there would appear to be some light on the horizon. In recent years literature has been appearing in certain fields – notably that of anaesthesia (Prior, 1976) – and work is proceeding, notably in Kenya, as a result of cooperation between that government and the German government, and as a result of the work of the African Medical and Research Foundation, on texts in surgery and related disciplines (Bewes, 1984), specifically targeted at the needs of the poorer parts of the developing world. Some of the workers involved in the production of these texts are Christians, and some have been missionary doctors experienced in the provision of medical care against a background of poverty. Some of this literature is being aimed at the medical assistant, to supplement his training. It follows in the steps of such excellent books as the *Tropical Dispensary Handbook* by Sir Clement Chesterman, himself a Christian and a missionary. Some, it is to be hoped, will be aimed at the doctor, even at the trained surgeon, called upon to work against a background of poverty.

References
Bewes, P.C. (1982) *Medicine Digest, 8,* 11, P.5-13
Bewes, P.C. (1982) *World Health Forum* 3(1): 58-61.
Bewes, P.C. (1984) *Surgery – a Manual for Rural Health Workers.* Nairobi: African Medical & Research Foundation.
Clarke Wilson, Dorothy (1965) *Ten Fingers for God* London: Hodder & Stoughton.
Dick, J.F. (1966) *Lancet,* ii. 900-901.
Fanstone, James (1972) *Missionary Adventures in Brazil* London: Evangelical Union of South America.
Foster, W.D. (1970) *The Early History of Scientific Medicine in Uganda.* Kampala: East Africa Literature Bureau.
Hankins, G.W. (1980) *Surgery in a Mission Hospital. Annals of the Royal College of Surgeons, 62,* 439-444.
Holland, Sir Henry (1958) *Frontier Doctor* London: Hodder and Stoughton.
King, Maurice (Ed.) (1966) *Medical Care in Developing Countries* Nairobi: Oxford University Press.
Maddox, Catherine (1962) *Paddy Field Hospital* London: China Inland Mission.

Perkins, G. (1958) *Fractures and Dislocations* London: Athlone Press.

Prior, F.N. (1976) *A Manual of Anaesthesia for the Smaller Hospital* New Delhi Emmanuel Hospital Association Publishers.

Sanders, R.K.M. (1977) *Tropical Doctor 73*, 99-104.

Somervell, T. Howard (1955) *Knife and Life in India* London: Livingstone Press.

Stirling, L. (1977) *Tanzanian Doctor* Heinemann (East Africa) Ltd.

CHAPTER 10

THE CHRISTIAN CONTRIBUTION TO LEPROSY AND TUBERCULOSIS

Stanley G. Browne

The Christians of the apostolic period do not appear to have carried out literally their Lord's command to 'cleanse the lepers' (Mt.10.8), since there is no reference to leprosy in the Acts or the Epistles, or indeed in the records of the apostolic church (Browne, 1979). The earliest mention of leprosy in ecclesiastical literature comes in the 4th century when, during the reign of Constantine, a hospital destined especially for the care of leprosy sufferers was built in Rome (Browne, 1975). Later in the same century, around AD 372, St Basil is reported to have built such a hospital in Caesarea, and St Gregory Nazianzus is said to have concerned himself with sufferers from leprosy. Thereafter the records are silent. We know from other sources that leprosy was gradually spreading throughout the Western world, being carried probably by soldiers, sailors, merchants and administrators, but its impact was not sufficiently obvious or important to evoke a widespread compassionate concern among ordinary Christian people.

The situation changed when the insidiously spreading endemic claimed an increasing number of victims suffering from the chronic ulcerating extremities and other stigmata of advanced leprosy. Incapable of fending for themselves, they drifted as beggars to the almshouses and hospices endowed by Christian charity and served by generations of devoted nuns and monks. The motivation of many of these Christians was undoubtedly mixed: they were ministering to 'Christ's poor'; they were helping to meet an obvious need; they were following their Master; and they were serving in his name a section of humanity thought to be specially sinful and specifically punished by a mysterious condition that did not respond to ordinary medication.

The outstanding name associated with leprosy in medieval literature is that of St Francis of Assisi, who established a Company of Brothers especially concerned to care for leprosy sufferers housed in hospices of the Crucifier – another Order. Thanks to the reputation and influence of St Francis in 12th century Italy and beyond, a wave of rather sentimental interest swept over Christendom. The Pope gave a special blessing to the Knights of the Order of St Lazarus late in the 12th century. Hospices and lazar-houses sprang up in many countries in Western Europe. Actually, it was the Orders of Chivalry (Malta, St Lazarus and St John) that were the first to bring Christian compassion in an organized way to sufferers from leprosy (Browne, 1980).

The Christians of medieval Europe were the only people who cared, and they housed and fed the dirty and verminous beggars, dressed their repulsive ulcers, and showed them kindness and compassion. The concurrent ambivalent attitude is indicated by the 'Leper's Mass', observed mainly in continental Christendom, in which the hooded leprosy sufferer heard the solemn cadences of the Burial Service read over him before he was banished for ever from the community of healthy godfearing citizens.

For reasons still obscure, but probably associated with the improvement in socio-economic conditions, leprosy began to die out during the 14th and 15th centuries in Western Europe, and the hospices and lazarets saw their population of the leprous and ne'er-do-wells dwindling. At this time, the connotation of the world 'leprosy' became extended to include not only the sense of plague or visitation, but also the mildew of stored grain, the blight of growing crops and the mange of cats and horses. The human disease was a hotch-potch of skin abnormalities, venery and indigence, vague and ill-defined.

Christian physicians shared the general ignorance and lack of interest. Later, leprosy became a problem of public health importance in Norway, and as such attracted the attention of Norwegian dermatologists (Irgens, 1973). In 1872 Dr G.H.A. Hansen, working in Bergen, discovered the cause of the disease, subsequently named *Mycobacterium leprae*.

In the early 1870s, two other events of the utmost importance to leprosy occurred. A Belgian priest, Father Damien, with a family history impeccably free from leprosy, actually caught the disease while ministering to leprosy sufferers in Molokai, an island in the Hawaii group (Neimark, 1980). Father Damien (Joseph de Veuster) was born in Belgium in 1840, and trained for the Roman Catholic priesthood under the aegis of the Picpus

Fathers. He volunteered to serve in the Hawaiian Islands, and while there saw the misery of those afflicted by leprosy who were forcibly torn from their families and exiled to the neighbouring island of Molokai. When the opportunity unexpectedly came to him to go to Molokai as resident priest, he eagerly took it, landing on the island on May 10 1873, knowing that for him this would mean permanent exile. He found Molokai a place of indescribable filth and moral degradation, and set about cleaning it up. He began by himself burying the rotting corpses littered about the island, and then brought order and cleanliness and compassion into the lives of his parishioners. The story of his contracting leprosy and announcing the fact to the hushed congregation at worship one June Sunday morning in the church he built – 'We lepers . . .' – has echoed round the world. After he had passed away on 19 April 1889, his influence grew. A committee was formed in far-away England under the patronage of the Prince of Wales, who said: 'The heroic life and death of Father Damien has not only aroused the sympathy of the United Kingdom, but it has gone deeper – it has brought home to us that the circumstances of a vast Indian and Colonial Empire oblige us, in a measure at least, to follow his example.'

An outcome of the meeting of the committee was the appointment of a Leprosy Commission on India, whose Report (published in 1891) inaugurated an era of governmental interest in, and concern for, leprosy sufferers in India.

The other event, destined to rouse Christendom to face its responsibility towards sufferers from leprosy, was the founding in 1873 of the Mission to Lepers in India by one Wellesley Bailey (Miller, 1964), who as a missionary in the garrison town of Ambala in the Punjab had seen the plight of leprosy beggars neglected and ostracized by their healthy fellows.

Interest in sufferers from leprosy in that vast and populous subcontinent had already been stirred by William Carey (Drewery, 1978), the 'Father of modern missions' who had been moved by the sight of the inhuman treatment meted out to leprosy victims who were often buried or burned alive. He wrote in 1812 from Katwa; 'Last week I saw the burning of a poor leprous man'. In 1818 he founded an influential journal The Friend of India which provided in its pages a forum for informed discussion of this and other social evils. Helped by soldiers and administrators, Carey and some Christian laymen established an asylum for leprosy sufferers in Calcutta and another in Allahabad.

Wellesley Bailey as a young teacher-missionary with the American Presbyterian Mission was taken in November 1869 to visit 'on the other side of the road from his house, a group of huts' where sufferers from advanced leprosy were living (Miller, 1964). The visit made an ineffaceable impression on him. He was convinced that 'their first and greatest need was the Gospel', but the next year wrote: 'In taking them the Gospel it soon became evident that a good deal more was needed, e.g. good living rooms, good food, clothing, medical attendance, sanitary regulations, etc., and that much could be done for them along these lines.'

Three years later, he was instrumental in founding in Dublin, 'The Mission to Lepers in India', a small and unpretentious group of concerned Christians. Against all medical opinion, Bailey (in 1875) considered that eventually leprosy might prove to be a treatable disease; this opinion was actually endorsed at the next (the second) Leprosy Congress, held in Bergen (Norway) on August 15-20 1909, under the Presidency of the great Dr Hansen himself, at which Bailey as an invited guest, was permitted to take an active part in all the sessions. He was acknowledged to have had a wider experience in leprosy in the world than any of the distinguished leprologists present.

These two events, mutually reinforcing each other and following the discovery of the causative organism, were to play a determinative role in the fight against leprosy and to emphasize Christian concern for leprosy sufferers. The conscience of Christendom was beginning to stir. The Christian public was becoming aware that a forgotten problem which had largely disappeared from the Western world was a cause of tremendous amount of personal suffering and social ill in most of the lands of Africa, Asia and America. At the time there was no thought of treatment, for leprosy was scarcely regarded as a disease, but rather as a mysterious condition associated with sin and divine punishment, and demanding the exhibition of compassionate caring in a setting of custodial segregation. The Mission to Lepers in India published a little booklet written by Wellesley Bailey and entitled Lepers in India which bore on its title page the quotation from Leviticus 13.44: 'He is a leprous man – he is unclean.' This most successful 'Penny Beggar' went through numerous editions, bringing in thousands of pounds to the Mission and stimulating enormous interest in leprosy.

The plight of leprosy sufferers, described in emotional terms and reproduced photographically in all its stark hideousness, made its impact on the Christian public, first in the British Isles and subsequently in the United States and the countries of the Commonwealth. Christian Missions in many lands began to receive grants from the Mission to Lepers, doctors devoted themselves to the care of leprosy sufferers, nurses bound up filthy ulcers, and the Gospel was commended by more and more Christian workers who saw themselves as obeying in a special way their Lord's command. In so doing they were in fact repaying a debt incurred by their Christian forebears in regarding the victim of leprosy as especially sinful or especially unhygienic, and thus meriting this signal mark of divine disfavour.

Meanwhile, a few Christian doctors – some of them assisted financially by the Mission to Lepers in India and the East – were helping leprosy sufferers and using medicines and surgery to alleviate their lot. Such a one was Dr Neve who admitted leprosy patients to the general wards of his mission hospital in Kashmir, operated to relieve tension in peripheral nerves, and wrote (in 1883): 'I am inclined to believe in the contagiousness of the disease.' At about the same time in Calcutta a few missionaries began to care for victims of leprosy. Whatever the motives, it is an undeniable fact that Christian medical men and women and Christian missionaries were the pioneers in caring for this despised and neglected section of the community.

The actual proportion of leprosy sufferers who were helped in this way was admittedly small, but the exemplary impact of the effort was not lost on Governmental authorities. They had to take notice that 'foreigners' were doing something that was really their responsibility. The lay (non-medical) founder of the Mission to Lepers in India, Wellesley Bailey, in his insistence on the creation of a leprosy hospital in every Indian State, openly stated that he hoped officialdom would be thereby stimulated to fulfil its duty towards leprosy sufferers.

Another influential boost to interest in leprosy came from the publicity surrounding the person of Mary Reed. As a young American missionary, she visited a group of leprosy sufferers segregated in remote hill-country in India (Miller, 1964). On her first leave in 1891, she thought that she had contracted leprosy, and returned to India to work among the sufferers she had seen at Chandag. The signs of leprosy in her body disappeared after nine years, but she continued to devote herself unstintedly to the welfare of her patients. At the ripe old age of 86, nearly blind, she was still on the job – a remarkable example of service.

Meanwhile, stimulated by the example of people like Mary Reed and Wellesley Bailey, the government of India took the best advice then available, and passed (in 1895 and 1898), the so called Lepers' Acts, which advocated compulsory segregation for 'lepers' as the only procedure likely to contain the growing problem. The First International Leprosy Congress, which had been held in Berlin in October 1897, had recommended this policy, but the Mission to Lepers in its quarterly magazine, *Without the Camp*, commented: 'All this argues very strongly in favour of Voluntary Asylums, such as ours', and strengthened the case for the establishment of homes 'for the untainted children of leprous parents.'

In China the first hospital for leprosy sufferers was established at Pakhoi (near Canton) in 1890 in connection with the Church Missionary Society, Dr T.G. Horder being the doctor in charge. At the annual meeting of the Mission to Lepers in India in 1891, an appeal for help from China was received, and in 1893 (March 30) the name of the mission was changed to The Mission to Lepers in India and the East.

Grants were made to Pakhoi, to Hangchow, and to Swatow. A few leprosy sufferers had been helped in the first year of the Swatow hospital's existence (in 1863), Dr Wm. Gauld being in charge, and in 1875 153 leprosy patients were treated. In Hangchow Dr Duncan Main, working at the General Hospital of the CMS, appealed to the Mission for help in erecting a building for men suffering from leprosy and then another for women. By the turn of the century, the Mission was helping to support seven leprosy institutions in China. In 1907, Broomhall writes with great appreciation of the demonstrative value of such expressions of Christian compassion in a country 'which sometimes seems like a vast wilderness of unalleviated sorrow and suffering.' Outstanding Christian doctors in China, like Duncan Main, Henry Fowler and James Maxwell, overcoming considerable local opposition and hostility, set themselves out to care for leprosy sufferers, providing asylums for them in quiet and peaceful surroundings. Enlisting the help of Chinese Christian doctors and interested laymen, and stimulated by the visit of the secretary of the American Mission to Lepers (an independent offshoot of the parent British body), they founded in 1926 the Chinese Mission to Lepers. From 1927 to 1941 this Shanghai-based organization published *The Leper Quarterly* which, providing a forum for serious scientific articles, exerted a great influence on medical and official thinking on leprosy in China and beyond. An indication of the extent of the Christian contribution to the control of leprosy in China is the fact that at 'liberation' in 1947, 39 of the 40 institutions caring for leprosy sufferers were run by 'foreigners', i.e. Christian missionaries, most of them Protestant.

In Japan the first real attempt to help leprosy sufferers dates from 1893, and here again it was the CMS that was concerned. The sterling work of this modest institution so impressed Japanese officialdom that it became the inspiration of government policy towards leprosy and its victims, and members of the Imperial family became personally concerned in the venture. Hospitals and settlements were subsequently created by the authorities to care for the most needy of the 28,000 known leprosy sufferers. Within twenty years, the Christian initiative had made a tremendous impact on the leprosy problem in Japan. In the Japan Year Book for 1913, it was stated that 'all the private asylums and hospitals for lepers' in Japan had been founded by 'foreign missionaries'.

The American filial of the old Mission to Lepers and the East, having amicably achieved its independence, assumed responsibility for initiating work for leprosy sufferers in the Americas, the Philippines, Thailand and elsewhere. Successful representations by the Mission led to the creation of the National Hospital in Carville, Louisiana. The secretary of the Mission in USA gave valuable information to the Congress Committee enquiring into the needs of leprosy sufferers in that great country, and organized support for the Bill which was passed by the Senate in 1917. The Daughters of Charity of Saint Vincent de Paul had begun to succour leprosy sufferers in 1896 at Indian camp (later known as Carville). The institution was taken over by the Federal Government in 1921.

The parent body, The Mission to Lepers, also pioneered help for leprosy sufferers in Indonesia and Korea.

For many years, treatment was with chaulmoogra oil, extracted from the seeds of *Hydnocarpus wightiana*, long used in China, and in India and Burma. The pure oil was given by intramuscular and intradermal (intralesional) injection, and also by the mouth – giving rise to the despairing comment 'internally, externally and eternally.'

Christian doctors like Sir Leonard Rogers (of the Indian

Medical Service), Ernest Muir and Robert Cochrane all made significant contributions on the subject in scientific journals, but it was left to Wellesley Bailey, a Christian layman, to state categorically at the 1909 International Leprosy Congress held in Bergen that an effective treatment for such a transmissible disease as leprosy must be forthcoming sooner or later. Little did any participant then realize that a few months before, two German chemists had synthesized diaminodiphenyl sulphone, a compound destined to revolutionize the treatment of leprosy. Before this was recognized as effective (in 1943) in Carville, Louisiana, Christian doctors were elucidating some of the mysteries surrounding leprosy by their painstaking research.

Ernest Muir was an outstanding leprosy research worker and teacher, based on the Calcutta School and Hospital, and a quiet Christian gentleman. A leading Hindu professor was heard to remark: 'Dr Muir is the man most like Jesus Christ that I know.' His example inspired many – among them John Lowe and James Ross Innes – both of whom were to leave their mark on leprosy. Robert Cochrane is another outstanding Christian leprologist, who has done more than any other man to put leprosy on the scientific map. By his researches and tireless and aggressive advocacy, he has made medical men realize that leprosy constitutes a scientific challenge as well as a social tragedy of enormous dimensions, and has stimulated doctors and others to undertake research into many aspects of leprosy. In 1923, the Mission to Lepers helped to establish the Lady Willingdon Leprosy Hospital in Chingleput, which after independence, became the Central Leprosy Teaching and Research Institute, under the Indian government. It was here that Dr Robert Cochrane was introduced to leprosy, and it was on patients at Chingleput that he investigated the use of dapsone (the parent sulphone) in leprosy treatment.

In 1924, a significant step forward was taken by a group of three Christian men, which resulted in the founding of BELRA (the British Empire Leprosy Relief Association). The three were Sir Frank Carter, a Calcutta businessman and philanthropist, Dr (afterwards Sir) Leonard Rogers, a distinguished medical research worker, and the Rev Frank Oldrieve, a Baptist minister and secretary for India of the Mission to Lepers. A meeting was called by the Lord Mayor of London at the Mansion House on January 31 1924, but the appeal then launched met with a disappointing response. Nothing daunted, the three persuaded the

Viceroy of India to inaugurate an appeal: this resulted in the formation in 1924 of the Indian counterpart of BELRA, the Hind Kusht Navaran Sangh, which awakened interest in leprosy throughout India. BELRA continues today under the title of LEPRA. One of its activities is the publication of the valuable periodical, *Leprosy Review*.

Mahatma Gandhi's interest in leprosy is almost proverbial. At one stage, he wanted to make an individual's attitude to leprosy sufferers the criterion for his suitability to be a member of his political party. Gandhi himself 'had a Christ-like compassion for leprosy sufferers', remarked Professor Jagadison and Gandhi himself said: 'It is largely the missionary who, to his credit, bestows care on the leprosy sufferer. All honour to them,' he added, 'but what of ourselves?' Gandhi encouraged Dr Cochrane to draw up a statement, which was signed by a score of leading Indian doctors in 1946. This statement included the following words: 'There is no short cut to the control of leprosy. Only patient study, real devotion on the part of doctors and lay workers, and intelligent and sympathetic understanding on the part of the leaders and the public will result in the desired end – the elimination of leprosy from our beloved land.'

When 'India secured her freedom from British rule, there were 231 colonies accommodating just about 28,000 patients in India – most of them run by Christian missions and Christian missionaries,' wrote a distinguished Indian leprologist, Dr K.V. Desikan, in 1981.

Little in the way of helping leprosy sufferers in the great continent of Africa had been done until the years immediately preceding World War I. The Mission to Lepers responded to an appeal (1913) from the London Missionary Society for help at M'bereshi in Northern Rhodesia. Soon afterwards, a grant was sent to the Government Leprosy Settlement at Westfort, Pretoria, in South Africa. In 1926, in Nigeria, a fine Scots doctor aided by his equally devoted wife founded a colony for leprosy sufferers at Itu in Eastern Nigeria. This modest beginning developed into a huge and well-organized community of 4000 leprosy sufferers, marshalled by Dr A.B. Macdonald and ticking over with clockwork efficiency. It was all there: palm-oil plantation, rice-fields, peanut farm, livestock, Scouts and Guides, brass band, a huge church seating 3000 worshippers, hospital, ulcer ward, and patients working everywhere – in the hospital, on the roads and the canal, in the plantations and gardens. Chaulmoogra oil injections by the thousand; uniforms, bed-linen and dressings; a Christian community that cared and helped: all were features of an outstanding scene for the alleviation of leprosy sufferers. Later on, in 1935, in another part of Eastern Nigeria, the Iyi Enu Hospital of the Church Missionary Society was seeking new lands to conquer. The CMS, with help from BELRA and the Mission to Lepers, co-operated with the native administration in founding a leprosy settlement at Oji River, destined to play a decisive role in leprosy control in that country.

A hundred miles away, things were happening at Uzuakoli where Dr James Kinnear Brown had begun work under the Methodist Missionary Society to found an agricultural settlement for leprosy sufferers. He was joined in 1936 by Dr T. Frank Davey, who was to leave his mark on Nigeria and the world. The original 'settlers' in unclaimed forest land under the curse of local medicine-men were leprosy sufferers ejected from Port Harcourt and abandoned ninety miles from 'home'. They refused to die, however, made themselves gardens and plantations, sang their gospel songs under the inspiring leadership of one, Harcourt Whyte, and eventually became the nucleus of a thriving Christian community. When Davey arrived in 1936, there were 820 patients at Uzuakoli, lodged in mud huts.

Frank Davey realized that leprosy was a huge problem throughout the whole of Eastern Nigeria, and with the blessing of the government and the active co-operation of the native administration, he set to work making pilot surveys, identifying areas of high prevalence of leprosy, training leprosy control officers, and (in the pre-sulphone era) organizing 'segregation villages' where leprosy sufferers could lead a more or less normal life, grow their own food on the adequate land which was made available and readily placed at their disposal by the local paramount chiefs. The 'segregation' was voluntary and far from complete, and depended on the willing co-operation of patients and their families. A resident paramedical worker, in some cases a leprosy patient who had been trained at Uzuakoli, provided medical and nursing care, and Frank Davey gave professional oversight. The idea caught on, and soon neighbouring chiefs from other parts of Eastern Nigeria were clamouring for the creation of villages in their territories: they had a great fear of leprosy and were only too willing to get rid of these embarrassing people. Davey aimed at interrupting the cycle of transmission of the leprosy organism and thus reduce the incidence of

new cases. His colleague, Dr Kinnear Brown, later reproduced
the same pattern in Uganda.

Then came the sulphones. By this time, Dr John Lowe had
joined Frank Davey. Lowe had been trained in the School of
Tropical Medicine in Calcutta under Ernest Muir, and was fully
equipped to undertake leprosy research work. It was a wonderful team, soon to be joined by a competent biochemist. Together
they pursued researches into the action of the complex (and
expensive) derivatives of dapsone that led to a fundamental
breakthrough, the prelude to the abandonment of expensive
derivatives and the administration of dapsone in lower doses.
They inaugurated mass treatment through the 111 district
clinics and in all the segregation villages under their control.
Uzuakoli became the foremost leprosy research centre in Africa
– perhaps at that time in the world. The population of the segregation villages declined dramatically with the reduction in
numbers of new infections. By the early 1960s, no fewer than
21,000 leprosy patients had been discharged symptom-free and
leprosy was considered as being under control throughout
Eastern Nigeria.

The government had assumed responsibility for the mission
leprosaria run by the Protestant Missions (the Church Missionary
Society at Oji River, the Methodists at Uzuakoli, the Church of
Scotland at Itu and Uburu, the Qua Iboe Mission at Ekpene
Obom), and the Medical Missionaries of Mary at Abakaliki and
Ogoja. By a happy arrangement, Frank Davey, the director of the
Leprosy Research Unit at Uzuakoli was senior specialist lepro-
logist to the government of Eastern Nigeria and adviser to the
federal government. He was also associate lecturer in leprosy at
the medical school at Ibadan.

Christian doctors were also at work in other parts of Africa.
After serving in India, James Ross Innes set an example of whole
population surveys for leprosy in East Africa. Stanley Browne
who, with Trevor Knights, was the first to use the sulphones in
the then Belgian Congo, pioneered in the integration of leprosy
in a community health programme covering the whole population in a medical sector in that country. Later, in Uzuakoli, he
was the first to investigate the antileprotic and anti-inflammatory
activity of clofazimine.

The training of medical colleagues and auxiliaries has traditionally been the prerogative of Christian doctors working in
leprosy. Born of necessity, this task has been an integral feature

of the Christian leprosy service in many countries. The level of trustworthiness and dependability shown by these men has been matched by their professional competence. Having been the principal of a government-recognized school for medical auxiliaries in Zaire (the former Belgian Congo) for over twenty years, I can pay a sincere tribute to successive generations of Christian students. Recommended for entry by protestant missions of several denominations in the east and south of Zaire, they all followed a three-year course of theoretical and practical training to fit them for service in a mission, commercial company, or government health programme. In addition to general instructions, they became competent in the clinical diagnosis of the various types of leprosy; the taking, staining and reading of smears from skin, nasal mucosa and nasal mucus; and the treatment of leprosy and its complications and sequelae. Special attention was paid to the differential diagnosis of early lesions. With a total coverage of the whole population through a network of 18 health centres and 35 dispensaries, and regular whole-population surveys, the deformity rate among newly diagnosed leprosy sufferers was zero, and early treatment ensured that deformity did not develop subsequently in most cases. The genuine interest of these Christian auxiliaries in the individual patients on their books made for an unheard-of regularity of attendance at the clinics, and their Christian character showed itself in an excellent rapport with the villagers that resulted in the presentation of very early abnormalities of the skin that might be leprosy.

The most outstanding of this excellent team of Christian auxiliaries specializing in leprosy was undoubtedly a man named Dickie Likoso. Highly intelligent, fluent in ten languages, and an extremely competent leprosy diagnostician and microscopist, he developed suspicious neurological symptoms and was eventually found to have early lepromatous leprosy. He volunteered to be transferred from a distant dispensary to the Yalisombo Leprosy Hospital, where he became my righthand man in painstaking research projects. He was utterly dependable and trustworthy. Unfortunately, in those presulphone days, his disease progressed and early nerve damage manifested itself. He showed an utter selflessness in volunteering to care for other leprosy sufferers worse than himself. When the first delivery of the sulphone drugs arrived, he was the only one to volunteer to take the drugs for a disease that, in the eyes of everybody, and in the words of proverbs in every local language, could not be cured. The clinical signs of leprosy in his skin gradually disappeared, and the leprosy bacilli disintegrated under the action of the new drug. The population at Yalisombo jumped from 118 to 1025 in two years, as the news of dramatic cures spread, and eventually we had sufficient supplies of the drugs to bring under controlled treatment all the registered sufferers from leprosy in the medical district for which we were responsible. Dickie, now cured and radiant, acted as controller and adviser for the treatment of the 5000 cases of leprosy in the district, helping the local medical auxiliaries with their problems of diagnosis and therapy. After the disastrous Simba Rebellion, in which the Yalisombo Leprosy Hospital actually became the rebel headquarters, Dickie was asked by the government to become adviser in leprosy for the whole of the east of Zaire: a remarkable Christian gentleman by any standards, and a faithful follower of his Master. Many Christian doctors working in leprosy in Zaire have been privileged to be helped by such men as Dickie.

In another African country Dr Dale du Toit tells how Dr John Helm (who had been a classmate of J.C. Smuts and D.R. Malan in Cape Province, South Africa) rescued a leprosy sufferer (in 1899) who was being buried alive in a cleft in granite rocks; the victim recovered and later found faith in Christ. In 1907 four leprosy sufferers sought refuge under Helm's care – and thus the first leprosy hospital in Rhodesia came into being, with government approval.

Until the mid-1960s, there was no centre in the whole of Africa where training in leprosy was available, apart from isolated, uncoordinated and piecemeal programmes in such places as Uzuakoli (Nigeria), Bamako (Mali), Dakar (Senegal), Alupe (Kenya) and Kumi (Uganda). The Leprosy Committee of the International Society for Rehabilitation of the Disabled organized a meeting at Carville, Louisiana, in 1963 to discuss this lack of training facilities in Africa and to make recommendations. Under the chairmanship of Dr Paul Brand (who had been responsible for developing Karigiri leprosy centre in South India and the orthopaedic department of the Christian Medical College, Vellore, as a centre for training all grades of leprosy workers), the ad hoc meeting strongly recommended that a similar centre should be created in Africa, and commissioned me to submit proposals. The desiderata were: a country with a high prevalence of leprosy; a medical school attached to a

university; a sympathetic government; the prospect of political
stability for the next ten years. Ethiopia was the only country fulfilling these conditions, and Addis Ababa was chosen as the site
of the centre. At the inauguration of the project in 1966 the
founding members were: the imperial government of Ethiopia,
the Haile Selassie I University, the Leprosy Mission, the
American Leprosy Missions Inc. and the International Society
for Rehabilitation of the Disabled. The project, to be named
ALERT (All-Africa Leprosy Rehabilitation and Training Centre),
was installed at an existing mission hospital just outside Addis
Ababa. With government co-operation and subsidy, plans were
soon afoot for the attachment of a large rural area to the Centre for
purposes of leprosy control, and the original concept was modified to make the prevention of deformity assume a larger place in
the programme. Other deforming conditions e.g. infections,
trauma and tuberculosis were included in their interests.
A strong staff was enlisted and teaching programmes in leprosy
were organized for English-speaking African countries. The
World Health Organization, Christian missions and governments sponsored candidates for the various courses offered:
physicians, orthopaedic surgeons, leprosy control officers,
laboratory technicians, administrators of leprosy programmes.
Increased financial support came from several countries and
many national and international health agencies.

When the Armauer Hansen Research Institute was founded
and opened its laboratories near the hospital, the first-class
investigative work done by its staff soon gained world acclaim.
In particular, the research into subclinical infections, drug resistance and immunology has made a tremendous impact on
leprosy control programmes throughout the world. A work that
began as a Christian initiative subsequently expanded: the
Christian spirit still permeates the activities of the institution
and the staff members seconded by the founder members and by
Christian missions help to maintain the distinctive ethos of the
place.

The era of treatment and training, ushered in mainly by
Christian doctors and following the era of compassionate caring
in a custodial setting, has been succeeded by an era in which
Christian doctors have again fulfilled an initiating and pioneering rule. The outstanding name in this connection is that of Paul
Brand, whose work in applying the principles of reconstructive
surgery to the deformities occasioned by peripheral nerve

damage in leprosy has earned worldwide acclaim (see Chapter 15). He has also made noteworthy contributions to the understanding of neuropathic ulceration and the influence of temperature on tissue damage in leprosy. He has inspired many Christian surgeons to develop their operative skills to help sufferers from the results of neglected leprosy. His wife, Margaret Brand, is by way of being the world's most knowledgeable ophthalmologist in the matter of eye damage caused by leprosy. Reconstructive and plastic surgery owes much to the pioneering work of Harry Williams in Nagercoil (South India). His fame spread far and wide, and the department he organized trained a succession of competent Indian surgeons in this speciality.

Now that reconstructive and plastic surgery, pioneered by Christian doctors, is firmly accepted by leprologists and governments, together with the necessary activities of nurses and physiotherapists (again, many of them Christians), a new era of rehabilitation and social integration is dawning. Hitherto, most governments have left initiatives in this field to concerned voluntary organizations, since these activities have a low priority in the context of the control of transmissible disease and are costly in terms of personnel and finance. Christian missions, and Christian-related institutions, emphasizing as they do the crucial importance of the individual in the setting of family and community, have been able to blaze a trail in matters like vocational training, farming and smallholding, the raising of chickens, rabbits, goats and pigs, the sale of eggs, market gardening; training in saleable skills, such as weaving, basketry, embroidery; repair of motor-cars, bicycles, radios, watches; sheltered workshops. It is now generally recognized that it is far better from all points of view, and less costly and less disruptive, if social dislocation is avoided by a domiciliary treatment programme integrated into a multipurpose health service. Christian doctors and health workers are showing how this can be done effectively and inexpensively.

In the matter of research in leprosy, particularly drug trials, the genuine mutual trust and confidence between patients and investigators are precisely those qualities that should be the hallmark of the Christian doctor.

Of recent years, since leprosy has become academically respectable, the Christian contribution in research has declined relatively, and government institutions are undertaking an increasing share in providing costly equipment and facilities.

It is still true, however, that many concerned Christians are to be found working alongside their non-Christian colleagues and contributing their qualities of reverent enquiry, scientific integrity and motivated persistence to the ongoing programmes. Similarly in the field, with governments in increasing measure assuming the health care of their citizens, the relative importance of the Christian voluntary agencies is becoming reduced. Here again, it is true that the best programmes rely on adequately motivated staff for the implementation of disease-control programmes. When it comes to leprosy, a chronic disease requiring the prolonged following of a treatment regimen, the honesty and integrity of well-motivated auxiliaries are obviously necessary qualities if eventual success in the control of leprosy is to be achieved. Christian character and dependability will make for success in any programme for the control of a chronic transmissible disease – and their absence will mar any programme. In the wider world of co-operation between Christian missions and governments, and between individual Christians and fellow-workers in leprosy, and between Christian and secular organizations interested in some aspect of leprosy, Christian doctors and paramedical workers have played a significant role out of all proportion to their numbers.

It is interesting to note that at the Consultation called by the Leonard Wood Memorial Foundation in Manila in 1931, which resulted in the formation of the International Leprosy Association, the majority of the participants were Christians, and their interest in leprosy was a direct consequence of their Christian faith.

Many office-bearers of the Association, presidents, councillors and secretaries, have been men of deep Christian faith and conviction. At the quinquennial congresses of the Association, notable contributions have been made by Christian leprologists, and important and valuable scientific articles are contributed by Christian research workers to such specialized periodicals as *The International Journal of Leprosy*. The presence and influence of Christians in the workshops that are held in connection with the Congresses, and the emphases made by Christian doctors, ensure that leprosy avoids the risk of isolation from the real world of human suffering. In the same way, Christian doctors have ever been to the fore in applying conscientiously to the individual leprosy sufferer the best results of modern therapeutic research. Christian missions are not slow to allocate from their resources funds for the purchase of expensive drugs for multidrug therapy where indicated. Although some voluntary agencies are non-religious and non-sectarian in their basis and appeal, many of their organizational and fund-raising staff are Christians and undertake their tasks because they are motivated by the ideals of Christian compassion.

It is worth recalling, too, that the present avenues of cooperation between voluntary agencies interested in leprosy, have their origin in the enthusiasm of an outstanding French (Roman Catholic) Christian, Count Raoul Follereau, who, not content with having created World Leprosy Day in 1931, goaded several national and international bodies (in 1966) to meet and agree to work together. This organization, originally called ELEP (European Leprosy), now embracing voluntary agencies in USA, Canada, New Zealand and Japan, is known under the title ILEP (International Leprosy). The initial stimulus was Christian, but there is no confessional basis in its constitution, and Christian and non-Christian, catholic and protestant, work happily together and share in various cooperative activities.

Another area of leprosy in which the influence of Christian leprologists is very evident is the Expert Panel of the World Health Organization and the Expert Committee on Leprosy (drawn from the Panel). Selected because of their knowledge and expertise, the latter group has usually included more than one Christian in its limited membership. In this way balanced judgements and recommendations are brought to bear on a world-wide scourge once the Expert Committee Report has been accepted by the General Assembly of the WHO.

Because of its influence on the world of leprosy, mention must be made of a facility initiated by Dr Robert Cochrane in 1951. Convinced of the need to bring leprosy into the mainstream of medical thought and medical education, and not content with what he had already achieved in this sphere, Dr Cochrane founded the Leprosy Research Fund to act as a co-ordinating centre for leprosy research, a histopathological reference centre, and a place where teaching on any aspect of leprosy could be provided. Before this organization, which was renamed The Leprosy Study Centre in 1965, had to close down in 1980, it had served the world of leprosy in a unique way. Its histopathological service had given detailed reports on upwards of 16,000 biopsies that had been sent from many countries overseas for processing and examination; it had provided courses of instruction to many students and postgraduates; it had organized seminars, and acted as a clearing-house for anything to do with leprosy in the world. The unique collection of catalogued histopathological sections, now housed in the Hospital for Tropical Diseases in London, is available for study and research. The extending influence of Christian teachers (like the reconstructive surgeon, Dr Grace Warren, and the physiotherapist, Miss Jean Watson) working under the aegis of the Leprosy Mission International brings the best of modern insights and knowledge into many countries deeply appreciative of this help in their leprosy problem.

A name that springs readily to the minds of most people when medical missionary work or leprosy is mentioned is that of Dr Albert Schweitzer of Lambarene. Everybody has heard of his distinction in several fields – philosophy, theology and music – and many know that he devoted a large part of his Nobel Peace Prize to the amelioration of 'Le Village de Lumière' – the Village of Light – where leprosy sufferers were cared for in a Christian setting by a devoted team of doctors and nurses.

Another name associated with leprosy (as well as with other activities such as the rescue of abandoned babies and care of the friendless dying found on the streets of Calcutta) which cannot be omitted, is that of Mother Teresa.

Many are the doctors and nurses, unknown and unsung for the most part, who have devoted their lives amid obscurity and ingratitude to bring health and healing in the name of Christ to the despised and ostracized, the neglected and forgotten victims of this age-old scourge. The motive and mainspring of their selfless devotion has been their Christian faith. On their part, they have the joy of an inward happiness, 'job satisfaction' of undreamed dimensions, and rich rewards of spiritual blessings that have come unexpectedly from grateful patients.

Robert Cochrane joins with Ernest Muir and Frank Davey and hosts of others in affirming 'You couldn't go through these experiences year after year unless you had a Christian faith,' and 'I can't imagine any sphere of medicine in which I could have found the fulfilment that I have found in leprosy.'

Tuberculosis

Although the causative organisms of tuberculosis and leprosy are similar in appearance when stained by standard techniques, they show considerable differences in many other respects, notably cultivability, physiological requirements, pathogenicity and susceptibility to drugs. *Mycobacterium tuberculosis* attacks the lungs and bones predominantly, whereas *Mycobacterium leprae* prefers the skin, peripheral nerves and the lining of the upper respiratory tract. *M. leprae* was one of the first organisms to be identified and associated with human disease (1872-74); *M. tuberculosis* was isolated by Robert Koch in 1882.

There were said to be 4000 cases of tuberculosis per million in England and Wales in 1838; in 1960 the figure had fallen to 100. The disease is under control in the Western world but elsewhere it constitutes a major public health problem.

Tuberculosis has never figured among the interests of Christian doctors to the same extent as leprosy. Because of the frequent mention in many versions of the Scriptures, and its linguistic and cultural association with sin and punishment, leprosy has appealed to Christian medical workers in a way that tuberculosis never has, and the latter makes little appeal to donors and fund-raisers. The stigma that used to attach to 'consumptive' has almost disappeared (since treatment has been seen to be effective), but the world 'leper' persists as a journalistic pejorative, despite its being outlawed by the World Health Organization.

It is not that tuberculosis was unknown in mission hospitals (SAIMR, 1932) or that Christian doctors were unaware of the ravages of the 'captain of the men of death', but because it was unromantic and untreatable it failed to stimulate Christian initiatives (Wilcocks, 1962). Doctors in mission hospitals with a surgical bent performed various heroic operations on the victims of advanced tuberculosis, but little was done – or could be done – in the way of treatment.

One of the pioneer missionaries in the field of tuberculosis was Dr Arthur Lankester, who served with the CMS in Peshawar. He was secretary of the Indian Medical Missionary Association. Just before World War I he was invited by the Indian government to take part in the All-India Sanitary Conference at which an important topic was the control of tuberculosis in India. His contributions to the discussions were regarded by the officials present as so practical that the government invited him to help in the implementation of his suggestions (CMS, 1914). The Home Committee of CMS readily agreed to his secondment to government service, considering that the opportunity should not be ignored.

Another missionary doctor who left his mark on the control of tuberculosis was Neil Macvicar. Based on the Victoria Hospital in Lovedale, he pioneered in health education as a means of control of this increasing problem, paying particular attention to publishing suitable material in several of the languages of southern Africa, and enlisting the help of teachers and community leaders.

In Nigeria Christian doctors were often consulted by patients whose cervical adenitis had been treated by indigenous practitioners by needling or crude surgery, with predictable results – chronic sinuses, secondary infection, sometimes with a fatal ending. The standards of clinical care shown by Christian doctors to patients with progressive tuberculosis were often in stark contrast to the prevailing neglect and despair. By good nursing and good food, by inculcating hygienic practices, they did something to control the disease in the absence of specific therapy. Some doctors paid with their lives from this exposure to M. tuberculosis. In one report (CMS, 1919) we read of three doctors out of four in one institution succumbing to pulmonary tuberculosis.

An outstanding pioneer in the control of tuberculosis is a Danish missionary doctor, Johannes Fridmodt-Moller, whose father had set up a sanatorium in Madanapalle in south India. After he succeeded his father as director, he quietly pursued studies on several aspects of tuberculosis, and during thirty years published a series of reports of high scientific value (Fridmodt-Moller, 1964; 1973; 1981). These included detailed prevalence surveys, the protective value of BCG vaccination in a rural community, tuberculin sensitivity modified by atypical mycobacteria, and controlled drug trials using different treatment regimens. He was highly regarded in India, and was appointed by the government as its first tuberculosis adviser.

In several Salvation Army hospitals in India, treatment for tuberculosis was a feature, and a Canadian missionary, Dr. Wanless, was knighted for his outstanding work at the American Presbyterian Mission Sanatorium in Maharashtra. In Hong Kong Sister Doctor Mary Aquinas, working at the Ruttonjee Sanatorium has for several years been carrying out very successful research programmes in tuberculosis, both independently and in association with colleagues.

Some Christian doctors made important contributions to chest surgery for tuberculosis. Professor Reese Betts was the first thoracic surgeon in India when he was appointed to the chair at the Christian Medical College, Vellore, while Dr John Thompson-Wells left an indelible impression of extremely competent chest surgery from his base at the Madas Sanatorium in Rajasthan.

Individual Christian doctors have provided governments with examples of good treatment programmes, and have shown how these can be implemented efficiently and economically. Among these was Dr Joshi, of the Methodist Hospital near Patna in Bihar. With real administrative flair, he organized a large out-patient department dealing with 150 patients daily, keeping hospital admissions to a minimum.

An enthusiastic Christian in this field is Norburu Iwamura, a Japanese working with the United Mission to Nepal (Lindell, 1979). By his charismatic personality he has popularized an anti-tuberculosis programme that has been very successful. He uses a mobile X-ray screening machine, and includes the diagnosis and treatment of tuberculosis in the primary health care project now being implemented by the government in co-operation with the United Mission. He teaches and trains, he controls and he inspires.

Dr Denis Roche also worked in Nepal (Lindell, 1979). After gaining the Cardiff Diploma in Tuberculosis and Chest Diseases, he concentrated on the treatment of patients with tuberculosis who had been referred to him at Bhadgaon from the Shanta Bhawan mission hospital in Kathmandu. His special contribution to the control of this disease has been the training of tuberculosis visitors who follow up discharged patients and supervise treatment. Tracing contacts is a formidable task in the mountainous terrain of Nepal.

While today most of the initiatives in tuberculosis and most of the research work has passed to Governments and secular organizations, the Christian input in some of these bodies is by no means negligible. For instance, work of a very high scientific quality has been done under the aegis of the (British) Medical Research Council, by Dr P.R.M. Pattisson, a Christian, at Masan, South Korea. He is concerned with extra-pulmonary tuberculosis, mainly of bones and joints. Such conditions have traditionally been regarded as being within the province of the orthopaedic surgeon, but recent advances in chemotherapy called for a controlled trial. Dr Pattisson was the man for the job: his characteristic Christian qualities of compassion and empathy have ensured the deep trust and mutual confidence necessary in investigations of this kind. He understands the social, emotional and financial pressures to which his patients and their families are exposed. His reports in the appropriate professional journals testify to the standard of his work.

Now that chemotherapy for both pulmonary and extrapulmonary tuberculosis is available, more and more Christian hospitals in Third World countries are reaching out through primary health care programmes to the local communities, and the treatment and prevention of tuberculosis are integral parts of this policy.

A recent example of a pioneering Christian initiative in controlling tuberculosis comes from Mindanao in the Philippines (OMF, 1979). The disease was extremely prevalent among the aboriginal population. Integrated into the primary health care programme being introduced by CMF missionaries, the activities of case-finding and multi-drug therapy for tuberculosis made a real impact on the disease. Because of bacillary resistance to streptomycin and INH, more expensive drugs had to be used.

In South America, tuberculosis is a growing problem, as Dr M.C. Patterson found when he arrived in Northern Argentina in 1963 (Patterson, 1980). By 1970, he had 150 patients under treatment, but in the next five years the new drugs had so reduced the patient load that fewer than 50 needed treatment.

Another area in which Christian doctors are leading the way is through combined tuberculosis and leprosy programmes in countries like Sierra Leone, Zambia and Tanzania. Both these chronic diseases necessitate treatment over a period of months or years; both require a similar kind of laboratory cover; both have a social component, and both need conscientious follow-up and contact examination for the diagnosis of early infections. The duplication of control programmes for each disease separately is obviously uneconomic. Christian medical auxiliaries, adequately trained and adequately supervised, play a leading role in the implementation of official policy.

Although tuberculosis, a disease once dreaded by our Victorian forebears, is now under control in the West, largely as the result of chemotherapy and the concurrent raising of the socio-economic standards, it is still a major health problem in countries of the Third World, and continues to call forth the qualities of competent medical care and Christian compassion.

References   Leprosy

Broomhall, M. (1907) *The Chinese Empire. A general and missionary survey.* London: China Inland Mission.

Browne, S.G. (1971) Comprehensive medical care delivery through a Church-related rural health programme in the former Belgian Congo. Contact No. 6. Christian Medical Commission, Geneva. 1971.

Browne, S.G. (1975) Some aspects of the history of leprosy. The leprosie of yesterday. *Proc. R. Soc. Med.* 68, 485.

Browne, S.G. (1975) The training and deployment of medical auxilaries in the leprosy campaign. *Ann. trop. Med. & Parasit.* 69, 413.

Browne, S.G. (1979) *Leprosy in the Bible,* 3rd Edn. London: Christian Medical Fellowship.

Browne, S.G. (1980) *Leprosy in England.* London: Leprosy Study Centre.

Browne, S.G. (1980) In *Health in Tropical Africa during the Colonial period.* (Ed. Sabben-Clare, E.E., Bradley, D.J. and Kirkwood, K.) Oxford: Clarendon Press.

Drewery, M. (1978) *William Carey.* London: Hodder & Stoughton.

Duncan, P. and Duncan, S. (1958) *Bonganga.* London: Odhams Press.

Feeny, P. (1964) *The Fight against Leprosy.* London: Elek Books.

Fox, G.N. (1972) *God the Builder.* London: The Leprosy Mission.

Irgens, L.M. (1973) *Leprosy in Norway. Internat. J. Epidemiol.* 2, 81.

Jagadisan, T.N. (1965) *Mahatma Gandhi Answers the Challenge of Leprosy.* Madras: 53B Edward Elliot Road.

Leprosy Mission (1974) *This Spreading Tree.* London: The Leprosy Mission.

Macdonald, A.B. (1957) *Can Ghosts Arise?* 5th Edn. Edinburgh: Church of Scotland.

Miller, A.D. (1964) *An Inn called Welcome.* London: Mission to Lepers.

Neimark, A.E. (1980) *Damien, the Leper Priest.* New York: Wm. Morrow & Co.

Schweitzer, A. (1934) *On the Edge of the Primeval Forest.* London: A. & C. Black Ltd.

Thompson, P. (1980) *Mister Leprosy.* London: Hodder & Stoughton.

du Toit, D. (1975/76) John Helm Memorial Hospital, Morgenstern Annual Report.

Wilson, D.C. (1965) *Ten Fingers for God.* New York: McGraw-Hill Book Co.

Tuberculosis

CMS (1914) Annual Report. London: Church Missionary Society.

CMS (1919) Annual Report. London: Church Missionary Society.

Frimodt-Moller, J., Thomas, J. and Parthasarathy, R. (1964) Observations on the protective effect of BCG vaccination in a south Indian rural population – Second Report. *Bull. WHO,* 30, 545.

Frimodt-Moller, J., Acharyulu, G.S. and Kesara Pillai, K. (1973)
    Observations on the protective effect of BCG vaccination in a
    south Indian rural population – Fourth Report. *Bull. Int. Union
    Tuberc. 48,* 40.
Frimodt-Moller, J. (1981) A controlled study of the effect of a domi-
    cilary tuberculosis chemotherapy programme in a rural
    community in south India. *Indian J. med. Res. 73,* 1.
Lindell, J. (1979) *Nepal and the Gospel of God.* United Mission to
    Nepal.
OMF (1979) Annual Report. Singapore: Overseas Missionary
    Fellowship.
Patterson, M.C. (1980) A medical survey of a South American Indian
    tribe in the Paraguayan Chaco. *Tropical Doctor 10,* 124.
Richards, M. (1979) *It Began with Andrews.* London: Salvationist
    Publishing and Supplies Ltd.
Shepherd, R.H.W. (1941) *The Story of a Century, 1841-1941.*
    Lovedale: The Lovedale Press.
SAIMR (1932) South Africa Institute for Medical Research. Report
    on Tuberculosis.
Wilcocks, C. (1962) *Aspects of Medical Investigation in Africa.*
    Oxford University Press.

CHAPTER 11

DISEASES OF THE EYE

W.A.R. THOMSON

Traditionally the blind beggar with his plaintive cry was for long one of the permanent, if pathetic, features of the non-Christian countries of the world. His compatriots might pity him, but the pity was seldom accompanied by active measures to ameliorate his lot, rather the reverse in fact. Around the turn of the century, according to *the Encyclopedia of Missions* (Dwight *et al*, 1904),

> 'schemers for easy gain take advantage of the calamity in some of the Asiatic Countries. A blind child is taken in hand and cared for, as a business investment by men who clutch as their due the proceeds of the beggar's appeal to the pitiful. In Turkey, men make it their profession to scour the country in search of such impotent folk in order to hire or buy them from their relatives, and then to exploit their miserable condition on the streets of the cities. In China, it was in past years generally the custom of similar harpies to gather up blind girls and house and feed and clothe them in order to make money by thrusting them into a life of debauchery . . . Filthy and immoral habits, and the brutality of parents who wilfully blind their children through greed of gain, are also causes of blindness in China'.

In fairness, it should be said that the commercial exploitation of the blind was not the prerogative of Asia or Africa, as any student of Dickens will recall. The fundamental difference, however, between East and West – or non-Christian and Christian – was that the former looked upon blindness as a natural calamity for which there was no relief, while the latter, inspired by the example of Christ himself, felt called upon to do everything possible to alleviate the lot of the blind. It might not be possible to restore sight to them all but at least they could be given help to read, earn a living and live in comfort in an atmosphere permeated by the love of Christ for the outcast. This, of course, was a much more positive approach than that laid down in the Mosaic Law, according to which: 'You shall not put a stumbling block before the blind' (Lev. 19.14) and 'Cursed be he that makes the blind to wander out of the way' (Dt. 27.18).

179

Initially little could be done to 'cure' blindness except in the case of cataract, but no surgical operation has produced more recruits to the church of Christ throughout Asia, Africa and South America than that for cataract. To make the blind see was indeed a miracle, and the reaction was as enthusiastic as that of the two blind men, to whom Christ restored their sight, who, in spite of Christ's injunction 'See that no man know it', 'spread abroad his fame in all that country' (Mt. 9. 27-31).

In the early days little could be done to prevent blindness, and it was not until the common causes were discovered, such as trachoma, leprosy, onchocerciasis and malnutrition (particularly lack of vitamin A), and their treatment evolved, that active measures could be taken to save a toll of human vision that was devastating in its extent. Today prevention or cure are possible in most of these cases, and the contribution of Christian missions to this amelioration of the lot of the blind can best be illustrated by a round-up of the course of events in Asia and Africa.

In China, according to Dr H.T. Pi (1929), of the Department of Ophthalmology, Union Medical College, Peking, 'ophthalmology had its beginnings in the beginning of the nation, over 4000 years ago . . . and it was around 2679 BC that the most important of all treatments of eye diseases, the needling method, originated, and books on medicine in general, including eye diseases and their treatment, were also written for the first time'. All down the millenia textbooks dealing with eye diseases continued to appear and, according to Dr Pi, 'almost all native physicians of ophthalmology today look to *The Most Complete Eye Book*, written in 1628 AD, in six volumes, dealing with 106 kinds of eye diseases, for guidance'.

To remove the cataractous lens a golden needle, 10 cm long was used. When not in use, it was kept in a special box protected by a quilt of goose feathers. Before use it was laid before Buddha on the altar.

> 'The operation', it was decreed, 'must be done at the middle of the month with prayers to Buddha, recitation of incantations seven times and wrapping up the needle in a charm before performance of the operation. Before the needle is used the physician should fast, burn incense, write another charm, so as to transfer the sun's light to the eye for restoration of eyesight, and call out loudly the name of the God of Mercy to save him from bitterness and suffering. The physician who uses the needle

will also be strengthened mentally by reciting a certain kind of incantation'.

The advice given was a curious mixture of what might be described as the ridiculous and the sublime. Thus (Pi, 1920), according to a textbook written in 1368 AD, cataract is often seen in people with bad tempers. There is no pain or itching, but occasionally double vision. It is usually confined to one eye. Needling with a gold needle is recommended, and a day for the operation selected by a fortune teller. Stormy days, rainy days, cloudy days, hot and cold days are all considered unfavourable for the operation. The beginner is recommended to practise on sheeps' eyes 'until he becomes an expert before he attempts to operate on the human eye'. One wonders how many of the Chinese oculists took note of the observation of Dr Pi that 'another method of treating diseases of the eye is by offering prayers to the gods. During the Tang dynasty, circa 620 AD, this method of treatment was used'.

If such was the basis for the Chinese practice of ophthalmology, it is not surprising that diseases of the eye were among the first medical problems tackled by the pioneer missionaries. The initiative was taken by Dr Thomas Richardson Colledge, who was trained at St Thomas's Hospital and went out to China under the aegis of the East India Company. He was posted to Macao where in 1827 he founded what has been described as 'the first institution ever opened in China for the purpose of bringing the benefits of Western medicine to the suffering Chinese – the Macao Ophthalmic Hospital' (Balme, 1921).

Although, as Balme points out, 'Colledge was not a medical missionary in the ordinary sense of the term', Joseph Thomson (1888), the American historian of medical work in China, regards him as 'the originator of medical missions in that country'. This is a view supported by Balme, according to whom, 'he was a man of great devotion and piety, eager to employ his talents in the service of humanity and in the extension of the Kingdom of God'.

'Thus it was', he adds, 'that when, in the October of 1834, there landed in Canton the first medical missionary ever appointed as such by a Missionary Board – Peter Parker, of the American Board of Commissioners for Foreign Missions — Colledge extended to him the warmest welcome, and the two became fast friends'.

Parker, who, it has been said, 'opened the gates of China with a lancet when European cannon could not heave a single bar', used his lancet to good effect in the eye hospital which he opened in Canton in 1835.

Thus the good work began and duly spread as medical missionaries penetrated the bamboo curtain, but, of course, their work only touched the fringe of the problem. The magnitude of the task is indicated by the fact that in the English Presbyterian Mission hospital opened in Swatow in 1863 by Dr William Gauld, one-fourth of the patients were eye cases. That the shrewd Chinese appreciated the value of these Christian ophthalmologists is indicated by the somewhat bizarre episode reported by Dr Gauld in 1875, when one patient suffering from an eye disease sold his daughter for 3 dollars so as to get the wherewithal to pay for the treatment of his eye trouble at the Swatow hospital.

The persisting immensity of the problem is well illustrated by the following extract from the Eye Department report in the 1935 annual report of the Methodist General Hospital in Hankow.

'During the year, 1358 new cases have been treated. Of these, about 200 were admitted to hospital and the rest treated as outpatients. In China, eye work tends to be overshadowed by the one disease – trachoma . . . In order that the doctor in charge should not spend so large a part of his time doing treatments for this one condition, at the end of the year we began to pass these patients through to a graduate nurse whom we had trained to do this work. He performed 495 treatments for trachoma in the last six weeks of the year'.

Almost half a century later, a medical missionary who made a tour of inspection of China reported: 'trachoma has been eliminated by treating every case discovered in whole-population surveys in endemic areas' (Browne, 1982). The same observer noted that 'standards of nutrition have been generally and noticeably raised. We saw no undernourished adults or children anywhere'. This is in striking contrast to what the China Mission Year Book was reporting in 1933: 'Serious eye conditions due to lack of essential elements of food are found everywhere and an appreciable amount of the blindness in China is due to this cause'.

Comparisons tend to be invidious, but these apparently striking ameliorations in the health of the Chinese inevitably raise issues that medical missions of today cannot afford to ignore. Stanley Browne certainly does not when he writes: 'These, then, are the major and more obvious benefits that have accrued to China's millions since the communists came to power and initiated their colossal political and medical experiment'. And he adds: 'It would take a very wise man, very knowledgeable and very percipient, to weigh the costs and benefits. History alone will be able to judge'.

But until recent times the masses of blind people for whom nothing medical or surgical could be done to restore sight presented a tremendous social problem. In 1915 it was estimated that the total number of blind in the country was around a million, with a proportion of blind to seeing of 1 in 400, compared with 1 in 1500 in Europe. From an early stage the various missionary societies did what they could to cope with the problem. Thus, as early as 1857 the US Protestant Episcopal Church Mission established a school for the blind in Shanghai. Some twenty years later another was opened in Peking which taught blind beggars to read and write and to work for their own support. By the turn of the century there were around a dozen institutions for the blind, and this number gradually increased until finally practically all the major societies were running one or more such institutions. A report from Fukien province in 1907 comments: 'Our hospitals are usually crowded with patients; sightless children of both sexes are gladly handed over to us to be taught useful trades' (Broomhall, 1907).

An even more interesting development was the early introduction of braille. For this the credit goes to William Hill Murray, a colporteur of the Bible Society of Scotland. So effective was his adaptation of Chinese to braille that even Chinese with perfectly normal sight found it easier to master and use braille rather than the ancient scripts, Mandarin and otherwise, that were still the only reading material in many parts of the country. In the school for the blind which Murray opened in Peking, to which reference has already been made, he not only taught the blind to read by braille, he 'transformed some of these hopelessly dependent creatures into active missionary agents, as Scripture readers, singers of sacred songs, and organists in Christian chapels. The amazement of the natives on seeing a blind child read with his fingers arouses the deepest interest and becomes a means of turning men's minds to study the reason for the intelligent humanity of the followers of Christ' (Dwight et al, 1904).

The value of braille was rapidly appreciated, and by the turn of the century large portions of the Gospels were available in

Armenian, Turkish, Arabic, seven of the languages of India, and in Burma, Ceylon, Sumatra and Uganda. Today it is being used in all mission fields, one of the most active agents being the John Milton Society, founded in New York in 1928. Supported by protestant churches in USA and Canada, it is providing literature in braille to Christian institutions serving the blind in many countries.

In India, too, the dramatic effect of surgery in restoring sight to the cataractous patient played an important part in the propagation of the Gospel. This was particularly the case in the northern provinces where cataract was especially rife. In this sphere two names are pre-eminent: Dr J.M. Macphail of the United Presbyterian Mission, and Sir Henry Holland of the Church Missionary Society.

Blessed with a sense of humour as well as a sense of duty, Dr Macphail who arrived in the Santal Mission in Bihar in 1890, had no difficulty in adjusting himself to the novel conditions he had to face as a medical missionary, such as discovering that the medicines he had carefully given out were taken by the nervous patients to their minister for his approval and sanction. That this in no way curtailed the popularity of the medicines he prescribed is indicated by an entry in his diary in 1893: 'If my work is going to increase as rapidly during the coming years as it has done in the past, some new machine on the principle of the Maxim gun must be invented for dispensing medicines wholesale'.

Equally novel was his introduction to cataract surgery, in which he achieved such fame that he became known as 'the eye-maker'. He had to pay 5 rupees to the patient before he was allowed to perform his first cataract operation. But he never had any doubt as to the promise of cataract surgery in the mission field. 'There is probably no line', he wrote, 'in which we can do so much good, so cheaply and so easily, as in the treatment of eye disease'. By 1895 he was performing 95 cataract operations in a year, and this was just the beginning of a great work carried on by his son, Dr R.M. Macphail. In the original hospital alone, at Bamdah, 501 such operations were performed; by 1946 they had grown to 2414. The comparable figures for the whole of the Santal Mission were 1111 eye operations in 1905, and 5980 in 1947.

Dr Holland, as he then was, arrived in Quetta in Baluchistan in 1900. From its foundation in 1889 by Dr S.W. Sutton, 'Quetta had been an "eye" hospital' (Holland, 1958). 'Its founder, Dr Sutton', he notes, 'was a Moorfields man, he started eye treatment in response to the very great need, and became well known as an ophthalmologist. Dr Summerhayes [whom Dr Holland succeeded] continued the work and performed many operations for cataract'. To which he adds: 'There is said to be more cataract in the Indus region from Peshawar to Karachi than in any other part of the sub-continent'.

Equally cogent is his comment:

'From my early experiences in wards and outpatients I quickly sensed that, while the atmosphere was distinctly hostile towards the Christian message, our small hospital at Quetta was already beginning to win a measure of confidence among the people of this isolated countryside. There it stood in Quetta city, on the border of the cantonment, a brave gesture of Christian care and compassion in the heart of a Muslim area. Now that I was actually seeing it for myself in its frontier setting, it was easier to grasp something of the vision which had planned this hospital as the southern bastion of a chain of mission hospitals along the North-West Frontier – Peshawar, Bannu, Dera Ismail Khan, Quetta. It has been said that each of these hospitals linked with the chief mountain passes was worth three battalions of troops in keeping peace on the Frontier'.

Such was the fame achieved by Quetta as an 'eye' hospital that in 1911, largely at the instigation of a Hindu banker, and entirely financed by him, an eye clinic was opened at Shikarpur, 200 miles southeast of Quetta. Here the Quetta medical team spent two months (January and February) every year. In its first two-month spell (1911) they operated on 563 patients with cataract. In his autobiography Sir Henry records that

'the Shikarpur venture became one of the largest eye clinics in the world, able to care for as many as 600 patients at a time. With practically half a century of experience behind it, the hospital can record more than 150,000 eye operations, including over 80,000 cataract operations . . . out of the thousands of cataract operations performed over the years ninety-seven per cent proved successful – in spite of what we at home should consider primitive and altogether inadequate conditions of work'.

He himself thought nothing of performing up to seventy cataract operations a day, and is said to have performed 60,000 cataract operations in his time in India.

Such was the world fame it achieved that it became a meeting place for eye surgeons from all over the world – from USA, Britain and Europe as well as India and Pakistan. In his time alone, around 150 had visited and worked in the clinic, some of them returning for more than one season. Equally significant, however, is what might be described as his *religio medici*.

'At Shikarpur we always pray before we operate and thus witness to Him in whose name we work. To me, prayer, preaching, and healing all go together, I feel I am expressing the Gospel of God's healing love with my hands, as a surgeon, working with Him. Our Lord Himself undertook the work of healing without waiting first for a man to listen to Him, and I feel that I am expressing Christ just as much in performing an operation as in preaching in the ward'.

Age could not hold his hand, and year after year following his official retirement, he went back to Shikarpur for the two-month operating season. In 1955, when he was 80, he wrote home from Shikarpur:

'We have had a very busy season, the busiest since the transfer of power. We have seen nearly 1000 more new cases than last year and have done 2200 operations, including 1125 cataracts and the innings is "not out" as we have three more days to go here. I have myself done about 250 operations, including 180 cataracts'. To which he adds the characteristic comment: 'I'm very lucky at my age to be able to help. I'm just a tough guy, and I'll go on as long as I can'. Which he did till shortly before his death in 1965 at the age of 90.

The problems faced by these pioneers is admirably exemplified in the following extract from a Church Missionary Society report from Kashmir in 1883.

'Dr A. Neve, a young doctor, went through Ladak, a tedious march of 250 miles through exceedingly mountainous country. At every stage in the journey the sick from neighbouring villages were collected in camp and treated as well as a passing visit permitted. A week was spent at Leh . . . Here 30 cases of cataract were operated on . . . *One boy walked more than 100 miles to have his eyes seen by the doctor*'. (The italics are ours).

The other outstanding contribution of Dr Holland was the establishment of 'eye camps'. In retrospect this may seem the obvious solution to the problem of how to bring maximum relief to the maximum number of victims of eye diseases in an area where distances were such that it was impossible for more than a small number of them to reach the few hospitals in the area. At the time, however, it was an original idea, based on the initiative of Dr Holland in deciding to take the doctor to the patients, rather than the reverse.

Eye camps have now been developed in a big way, as exemplified, for example, by the Canadian organization with the imaginative title of Operation Eyesight Universal. This dates back to 1911 when, under the aegis of the Canadian Baptist Foreign Missionary Board, Dr Zella Clark was posted to Sompeta, a village on the east coast of India, about halfway between Calcutta and Madras. In 1936 she was succeeded by Dr R. Ben Gullison who was responsible for the building of a hospital. Originally a general hospital, it gradually developed into an eye hospital as Dr Gullison realized the high prevalence of eye diseases, estimating that some 200,000 curable blind people lived within easy travelling distance of the hospital.

In 1949 he was joined by an Indian ophthalmologist, Dr John Coapullai. In 1967, in view of the increasing amount of eye work, the Arogyavaram ('The Divine Gift of Healing') Hospital, as it was known, became the Arogyavaram Eye Hospital. One of the arguments advanced by Dr Coapullai for this switch was that, in his opinion, Mission Board-sponsored hospitals could only survive if they went into speciality work. So many secular and state hospitals had been introduced in India that mission hospitals could only attract patients if they were superior in skills, services and specialties.

In due course it became known as one of the best equipped eye hospitals in India, with 125 beds. By 1976 Dr Coapullai had performed over 100,000 eye operations – with no failures – in the previous twelve years. The daily average of eye operations, including those in the eye camps, was 42, rising to as many as 80 on some days. By the 1960s the cost had become more than the Canadian Baptist Foreign Missionary Board could provide, and in 1963 was founded Operation Eyesight which, in 1969, became Operation Eyesight Universal (OEU) and assumed full financial support of the hospital.

In collaboration with the Royal Commonwealth Society for the Blind OEU steadily expanded its interests. It put its first mobile eye unit on the road in Kenya in 1970. This was followed by one in Bangladesh. Today it has more than 30 mobile units in action. It also assists the Lions' Eye Hospital in Chittagong, the Christian Hospital in Chandraghona and an eye hospital in Khulna. It now has seven mobile eye units operating in Kenya, as well as a Children's Eye Care Programme.

Its work is steadily expanding. It is currently involved in projects in Nepal, Pakistan, Haiti, Peru, Tanzania, Uganda and Liberia. 'These', it is recorded, 'range all the way from highly

sophisticated surgery in up-to-date hospitals to sending ophthalmic paramedics out into the Andean jungles on horseback'.
OEU is also involved in training. At Manipal on the west coast of
India there is an OEU Institute of Ophthalmology, part of the
Kasturba Medical College. Overall, there are now over 50 OEU
projects in more than a dozen countries, treating more than
500,000 people for the prevention of blindness and performing
over 45,000 eye operations a year.

While much of this noble work can almost be described as
routine and can therefore be planned in advance, emergencies
must always be allowed for. Thus, from April to June, 1981, an
epidemic of viral conjunctivitis swept across India, leaving in its
trail many blinded by corneal opacities. During May and June
the Arogyavaram Eye Hospital dealt with over 6000 cases.

Eye diseases are still a major problem in India, and that medical missionary societies are still rising to the occasion is admirably exemplified by St Luke's Hospital at Hiranpur in Bihar. It
originated as a 12-bed hospital, the parting gift of a judge of the
Indian Civil Service to the province in which he had served.
When it celebrated its golden jubilee in 1979 it had 150 beds.
Ecumenical in the best sense of the term, it attracts support from
all denominations, notably, of course, the Church of North India.

Such was the high incidence of cataract in the area that during
the cold season, when other demands were at a minimum, three
small wards were given over to cataract patients. Gradually,
however, it was found that these wards could not be spared for
these patients – even in the cold season. In 1976, therefore, with
money from Germany channelled through the local Roman
Catholic Bishop, a new two-storey eye block was built which
houses eye patients in the winter.

Another major cause of blindness in India in the past, as in so
many other Asiatic countries, is vitamin A deficiency. For long
this was endemic in South India, assuming almost epidemic
proportions during the famines which all too often swept
through the country. Today such deficiency is still common all
over India, and it is of interest that in the Golden Jubilee History
of St Luke's Hospital, Dr S.N. Chauduri, of the Child in Need
Institute, Calcutta, draws particular attention to the regular
administration of oral vitamin A supplements 'to prevent
malnutrition blindness in children aged 1 to 6 years.'

Diseases of the eye, of course, are rampant throughout the
whole of Asia, and there are few, if any, of the Asiatic countries

in which Christian medical missions are not found, often playing a vital role in the health services of the countries concerned. Typical of this continuing and updating service is the Manorom Christian Hospital in Central Thailand. Opened in 1956, it has a well-equipped eye unit, complete with slit lamp microscope and other apparatus. Its eye work is supported by the Christoffel Blindemission, and provides virtually the only facility for ophthalmology available in Central Thailand.

In Africa the specific problems of eye disease may vary from those in Asia, but they are just as serious, and just as liable to lead to blindness. The developing nations of this vast continent are gradually introducing public health measures to counteract the evils of so many traditional medical practices, such as the use of mother's urine for the treatment of measles conjunctivitis in their children – a common cause of blindness in East Africa. There still remains much to be done, however, such as the control of trachoma north of the Sahara and of onchocerciasis in West Africa.

Throughout the Continent medical missions are contributing much in this field, as is well exemplified in the following extract from the autobiography of Bishop Leslie Brown (1981), who was Archbishop of Uganda before returning to England in 1966 to become Bishop of St Edmundsbury and Ipswich. He writes:

'We noticed in Busoga that at every confirmation there were two or three blind children, and adults, who, while not blind, had great difficulty in seeing. We were concerned at this and through our hospital at Mengo Winifred [his wife] contacted an association of doctors in America who were accustomed to give a tenth of their income and their time to specifically Christian work. These doctors set up an eye project in Busoga. A highly qualified ophthalmologist spent six months touring the area, inspecting the children in the school and stopping passers-by so that he could prepare a proper report on the incidence of the disease. Their Society found and supported an American nurse with experience in this field to work in Busoga and provided a van equipped as a travelling dispensary. The result was that by the time we left, cases of eye disease, trachoma and onchocerciasis, were comparatively rare in the district. Many people who had been losing their sight had it restored.'

An even more vivid account of the eye problems still rampant in Africa is provided by Dr Stella Bowcock (1981), who spent her 'student elective' period at a hospital at Ler in the Southern Sudan. During her stay, she writes, 'an eye safari team, led by a British ophthalmologist, flew in to operate for three days. They worked almost without stopping, completing about 70 operations – mainly cataract removals and entropion repairs. Their visit, although exhausting, together with the problems of feeding everyone in such a barren, isolated area, was well rewarded when the bandages were removed and glasses were handed out: in this country blindness commands so little support. Following their visit I was able to do some entropion repairs myself on the unfortunate people who had arrived too late.'

In combating blindness in Africa a leading part is played by the Royal Commonwealth Society for the Blind under the distinguished leadership of Sir John Wilson, its blind founder and first director. In Africa, as well as elsewhere in the Commonwealth, the Society works in close association with the medical missionaries in the field. A typical example of this collaboration comes from Sierra Leone, where ophthalmic surgery was introduced by Dr Wilkinson of the Methodist Mission.

The Society arranged for an ophthalmic surgeon, Dr A.V. Kerur, to visit Sierra Leone from March to May 1977 and to work in all mission hospitals. He rapidly realized the need for a rural ophthalmic service. In addition, the Society agreed to found an eye ward in the Nixon Memorial Hospital at Segbwema. It provided the surgical and diagnostic equipment, as well as a Landrover for the rural work. The aim of the Society was 'to give a mobile medical and surgical service to the people in the village situation'. 'In developing countries', it notes, 'eye diseases are common and therefore important, and cause much suffering and loss of valuable manpower'. 'Often very simple measures', it adds, 'can provide immense benefit at little cost. This type of service also prevents a blind man and his relatives making an expensive journey to a big city, where he is a complete stranger, to seek help about his blindness'.

The visiting team consisted of an ophthalmic surgeon and sister, four qualified nurses, four nurse aids and one student nurse in training. The response to the initial publicity campaign, mediated, among other means, through church notices, is described as 'most rewarding'. Their modus operandi is described as follows. 'We are in the village at 7.30 am, driving as far as possible and then walking the rest of the distance with our essential equipment in our shoulder bags. For these village clinics we work closely with the public health nurses living in the villages and the village health committee. The whole village is screened and patients requiring operative treatment are given transport facilities'.

Between March 1979, when the campaign began, and April 1980 10,689 people were seen and 3910 were treated. The number of operations performed was 398: 270 for cataract, 95 for glaucoma, entropion and pterygium, and 33 for eye removal and conjunctivoplasty. In other words, what are described as 270 'sight-restoring' operations and 95 'sight-saving' operations. On all of which the comment is made: 'There is no greater thrill for surgeon and staff when a delightful smile lights up a patient's face, and a hand is offered in thanks when he can see again'.

Such a rural ophthalmic service, based predominantly on village health committees, is an admirable example of how health services, missionary and otherwise, must develop in the future. In the words of Sir John Wilson:

'The concept of primary health care, though obviously not a universal panacea to all the health needs of the developing world, has, since its enunciation in the Alma-Ata Declaration, been broadened to the point where I believe it has a significant relevance to many causes of disablement, and certainly is the basis of any attack on avoidable blindness . . . Of the four priority causes of blindness which are now the main thrust of our prevention of blindness programme, two – trachoma and xerophthalmia – can certainly be tackled at the level of primary health. The other two causes – cataract and onchocerciasis – do require secondary or tertiary care and, in the case of onchocerciasis, environmental control'.

His overall conclusion is that

'it is this basic ability of a competent primary health system to know its community, identify what it can do and refer what it cannot, which is generally regarded as its most important characteristic. Encouraged by the attention which has been brought to bear on disablement by the recent International Year of Disabled Persons, and by support from the World Health Organization, the important thing now is to get long-term action, and the centre of that strategy must be an effort of *prevention* of the major causes of disablement'.

John of Wurzburg in 1160 wrote:

'Over against the Church of the Holy Sepulchre, on the opposite side of the way towards the south, is a beautiful church built in honour of John the Baptist, and a hospital, where in various rooms is collected together an enormous multitude of sick people, both men and women, who are tended and restored to health daily at very great expense'.

The hospital he thus describes is now the St John Ophthalmic Hospital, Jerusalem. It can trace its ancestry back to a Hospital for Pilgrims founded by Pope Gregory circa 600. After many vicissitudes, during which it had become associated with a Benedictine monastery, the hospital was granted the status of an independent Order in 1113 as 'The Order of the Hospital of St John of Jerusalem'. The patron at this time was St John the Almoner, Patriarch of Alexandria, who was the founder of many hospitals, and died in 619. In due course the Order annexed the ancient Orthodox Monastery of St John the Baptist, who thus became its patron. In 1291 the Knights Hospitaller had to leave the Holy Land, and moved to Cyprus and then to Rhodes where they established a sovereign state. In 1522 they had to move again, this time to Malta.

The Order was now primarily a naval power but it always maintained its hospital, which had the reputation of being one of the most advanced institutions of its kind in the world. One of its many proud boasts in this context is that the first Professor of Ophthalmology in the world, Guiseppe Barth, appointed to the Chair in the University of Vienna in 1773, was trained at the Hospital of St John in Malta.

In England the Order was established in the priory of Clerkenwell around 1145, where it functioned actively until it was deprived of all its properties and assets at the time of the dissolution of the monasteries by Henry VIII in 1540. Some three centuries later – in 1831 – it was revived as the Grand Priory in the British Realm of the Most Venerable Order of the Hospital of St John of Jerusalem. In 1888 Queen Victoria became Sovereign Head of the Order, a precedent followed by each of her successors.

In 1882 the British Grand Priory, which is ecumenical and today has around 19,000 members including 700 Knights, decided to refound the hospital in Jerusalem. This decision was based on the realization of the terrible prevalence of blindness and eye diseases amid the poverty and political unrest of the Middle East, with little, if anything, being done to relieve it. The only hospital in the area specializing in ophthalmology, it passed through the traditional vicissitudes which have beset the Order from its earliest days. The original hospital was so badly damaged in the fighting that followed the termination of the British mandate in 1948 that it became unusable.

After an interregnum, in which the work was carried on with difficulty, the present hospital was opened in 1960. Here the

Order applies the same principles as it has applied to all its hospices and places of healing from its foundation: 'For the Faith', 'In the service of Mankind', and 'to bring relief to the sick and suffering without distinction of race, class, or creed'.

The hospital, with 80 beds, has a staff of seven doctors from various countries and some 50 nurses. It has two operating theatres and an eye bank. The work load is heavy and varied, with the surgical emphasis on cataracts and squints. Glaucoma is still a problem, as is trachoma which, in spite of modern treatment, is still the most common cause of blindness in the Middle East. Statistics never tell the whole story, but those for 1980 give some idea of what is being achieved. There were 15,091 new outpatients, 34,470 total outpatient attendances, 2274 inpatients, 4464 operations, and 4109 spectacles were ordered. Over 99% of the patients are Arabs. Needless to say, annual costs have risen – from £100,000 in 1970 to £500,000 in 1980. To mark its centenary an appeal was launched for £5 million and the occasion was commemorated by a special service of thanksgiving in St George's Cathedral, Jerusalem, for what has been described as this 'spiritual lighthouse' at which the preacher was Lord Coggan, Prelate of the Order.

It has been described as 'one of the finest and busiest ophthalmic hospitals in the world', and its activities are gradually spreading outside its walls, notably in research which is carried out in conjunction with the Medical Research Council and the London University Institute of Ophthalmology. This work began in 1954 in research laboratories in the temporary hospital, and was concentrated primarily on trachoma. Two years later the research programme was transferred to Iran and the Sudan. In Iran political unrest has sadly interfered with the programme, but in the Sudan it is being actively pursued in collaboration with the University of Khartoum and the Communicable Eye Diseases and Filariasis Division of the Sudanese Ministry of Health. The emphasis is on trachoma in North Sudan and onchocerciasis in the South, and a national programme is being evolved for the prevention of blindness from these two diseases. To carry this programme into effect, training programmes are maintained for graduates and technicians involved in studies on blinding eye diseases, the prevention of blindness and other external eye diseases, including laboratory techniques. The Order is also participating in the prevention of blindness project in Burma, with the emphasis on trachoma and corneal ulcers.

Of equal significance is what the Order itself describes as 'an exciting new Sight Project'. This has been made possible by a grant of $7,000 from the United States Presiding Bishop's Fund for World Relief, the Presiding Bishop at the moment being the Rev John Maury Allin, who is Presiding Bishop of the Episcopal Church and a Sub-Prelate of the Order. The purpose is to set up a training programme in preventive ophthalmology and primary health care for a hundred Arabic-speaking nurses. They will work in the villages and camps of the West Bank and beyond, providing a network of basic health education with emphasis on the eyes, and initiating self-help programmes for the people concerned. As the project is to be based on the hospital, the benefits for the local people and those living beyond will be a godsend.

The training for these nurses will fit in with the nurses training school in the Hospital. Unfortunately, due to lack of funds and tutors, this had to be closed in 1973, but it was re-opened in 1979 under the supervision of Miss Ena Burke who had served for twenty years under the Church Missionary Society as sister tutor in the refugee camps of Jordan and then Director of Nursing Training in Isfahan in Iran. Under her supervision an 18-months' course of instruction in ophthalmic nursing has been instituted for local Arabs, both men and women.

Such is a brief outline of the work of the Order, of which its members have every reason to be proud. As the Order itself stresses, 'the St John Ophthalmic Hospital is far more than just a centre of healing. It is a place where compassion, understanding and cooperation are fostered among all peoples. It is truly a place of goodwill'.

The same view is expressed, perhaps rather more picturesquely, by Dr Henry Backhouse, the senior eye physician:

'The Hospital has retained an enviable reputation for good treatment and faithfulness . . . Patients come from all over the country because they trust the advice we give. The season is almost upon us when Palestinians from all over the Middle East come home and consult us for themselves and their children, even though today there are excellently equipped hospitals in every Middle Eastern country. They do not return to us because we have a laser or an ocutome amongst our modern equipment but because generations have learnt to trust our word and expertise. We are *their Hospital, the people's Hospital*. So, when we say to Abdullah [one of the child patients he has been writing about] "let us have a look at your eyes", behind these words is a history of excellence; a history of caring and history itself of which, by God's grace, we shall remain a part'.

The service of blind Arab girls was pioneered around 1896 by Miss Mary Lovell, a trainee teacher with experience of the blind who went to Palestine, first as a companion to the wife of a British consular officer and later as a freelance missionary. In time, with the help of British friends, she secured rented premises in Bethlehem, and in due course was responsible for the care of some 40 blind children whose ages ranged from infancy to adolescence. This work lapsed in the 1920s following the illness and death of Miss Lovell, but was restarted around 1935 by two former students, Miss Adele Dafesh, a totally blind Arab who opened a home-school in Bethlehem, and Miss Sirranoosh Ketchejian, an Armenian, who began work in various rented properties in Jerusalem. In both cases a strong evangelical Christian atmosphere prevailed.

During World War II financial support sadly fell but the Bethlehem home in particular was discovered by British Service personnel who organized regular financial support. Then after the war the leaders of this group were responsible for the foundation of the Bible Lands Society, which is officially defined as:

'A Fellowship of Christians united in the common aim of helping Christian Missions in the lands of the Bible, especially the Holy Land, in the work of carrying the Gospel to the land of its birth and in the work of comforting and healing the sick, blind, poor and homeless'.

Much good work is now being done on its own or in conjunction with the Order of St John, the Lutheran Mission, a Roman Catholic Order in Nazareth and the Arab National Society for the Visually Handicapped.

In these latter decades of the 20th century, the preservation and the restoration of sight play an increasing role in the service of mankind. It is a mission that is growing in scope and efficiency, and the aim of Christian churches throughout the world is to ensure that everything possible should be done in this example set for us by Christ himself.

Typical of the scope of Christian concern in this field overseas is this selection of grants being made currently by the British National Committee for the Prevention of Blindness. *Bangladesh*: Training medical auxiliaries in performing sight-restoring operations. *Burma*: Purchase of equipment for blindness prevention in Rangoon. *India*: Equipment for a mobile eye clinic. Establishment of a Malnutrition Unit for mothers and children, to combat blindness in children due to deficiency of vitamin A. *Sudan:* Plan for the prevention of blindness. *Jerusalem:* Grant to the Outreach Project to assess the prevalence of trachoma and other infectious eye diseases on the West Bank of the Jordan, to initiate early treatment, do prevention work and educate the community.

The initiative of the Church Missionary Society in the care of the blind played a leading part following its introduction to Cairo with the arrival in March 1889 of Dr Frank K. Harpur. He rapidly founded the Old Cairo Hospital, which soon became the strong centre of the CMS in Egypt. Inevitably it became involved with what all down the ages had been a major problem in Egypt – that of blindness. Some idea of the scope of the problem was the statement made in 1931 that there were no less than half-a-million blind and partially blind people in Egypt. Among the notable work done was that of Miss Adeney and Miss Liesching among blind women and girls, while Gindi Effendi Ibrahim, himself blind, worked among students. Characteristic of his work was the blind school he opened in March 1925 in a rented house near Al Azhar University, the famous Cairo University founded in 970, which has been described as 'the Sorbonne and Cathedral of Moslems all over the world'. Here he taught braille reading and writing as well as handicraft. By 1929, a hundred and fifty or so students were attending his classes.

Today, almost two millenia since Christ performed his miracles to the crippled and blind in what to Christians will always be the Holy Land, the medical missionary prays to Almighty God that the appeal for the prevention of blindness will increasingly ensure that those among whom we work will retain, or regain, the light of the world whïch still floods out over the world, and for the preservation of which so many of us are doing so much.

References

Balme, Harold (1921) *China and Modern Medicine,* London: United Council for Missionary Education.

Bowcock, Stella J. (1981) *British Medical Journal, 282,* 130.

Broomhall, Marshall (Ed.) (1907) *The Chinese Empire. A General Missionary Survey.* China Inland Mission.

Brown, Leslie (1981) *Three Worlds: One Word,* London: Rex Collings.

Browne, Stanley (1982) *In the Service of Medicine, 28,* 8.

Dwight, H.O., Tupper, H.A., and Bliss, E.M.M. (1904) *The Encyclopaedia of Missions*, (2nd ed.) New York: Funk & Wagnalls.

Holland, Henry (1958) *Frontier Doctor*, London: Hodder & Stoughton.

Jones, W.H. (1977) *The Eye Openers*, Calgary, Operation Eyesight Universal.

Pi, H.T. (1920) *National Medical Journal of China*, 6, 188.

Pi, H.T. (1929) *ibid* 15, 604.

Thomson, Joseph (1888) *China Medical Journal*, p.41.

CHAPTER 12

MENTAL HEALTH

J. Bavington

Psychiatry raises special questions for us because it lies in a border country between physical medicine and various non-medical disciplines such as sociology, psychology, education, theology and anthropology. It is perhaps partly an accident of history that a group of conditions and states, in which there are certain kinds of abnormality of behaviour, thought and emotion have, in the West, come to be termed 'mental illness'. Help for them is considered to be largely the sphere and responsibility of medical science, admittedly with substantial support from other professions where social and spiritual issues are involved.

In pre-scientific times help and healing for people we would nowadays recognize as suffering from some form of emotional disorder came mainly through 'spiritual means' as, for example, the experiences of saints and mystics bear witness. On the other hand, and perhaps as a general rule, the attitude in 'Christendom' towards the mentally disturbed was harsh and often utterly cruel, such as the burning of witches. There have, however, been a few notable examples of Christian initiatives in the history of the evolution of psychiatry as a medical specialty in the West, in particular, the founding in 1792 of The Retreat at York by the Quakers at the instigation of a layman, William Tuke. He advocated what he called 'moral treatment' based on a blend of humanitarianism and Christianity at a time when existing medical methods were generally repressive and sadistic.

In the story of medical missionary work in the developing world, it is noteworthy that, as compared with the tremendous contributions in other medical and surgical fields (as documented in this book), relatively scant concern has been expressed for that vast group of suffering humanity whom we now call the mentally ill. One reason for this may be the belief, still encountered, that mental illness is much less common in the Third World. Although in most of these developing countries it has not been possible to study the prevalence accurately, there is now plenty of evidence to show that most of the broad categories of mental disturbance, such as depression, schizophrenia and anxiety states, can be clearly identified and are quite common – although with culturally influenced modifications in their presentation and in their relative frequency. The less obvious, and less dramatic or bizarre conditions, such as anxiety and depression, tend to be more hidden because of the well-established finding of a greater tendency to 'somatize' emotional distress. This has led earlier European observers to express the rather ethnocentric opinion that such neuroses were rare in 'primitive societies' because they were related to more 'sophisticated' stages of social development and 'civilization'.

A second reason arises out of the uncertainty that Christians have felt about the whole subject of psychiatry in relation to Christian faith and experience. It is often difficult to know where to draw the line between 'mental illness' and 'spiritual problems', and indeed there is no clear line to be drawn since there is much overlap. (A similar type of problem in cross-cultural psychiatry is that of defining what is 'mental illness' in various cultural settings). Attitudes to psychiatry have ranged from a dogmatic condemnation of the subject as 'of the Devil' to a rather cautious and reserved acknowledgement of its place and value. These attitudes have perhaps been particularly strong among missionaries influenced more by the prevailing local view of mental disturbance as 'evil' or 'satanic'. It is often stated that cases of demon possession are more common on the mission field because, it is held, of the more immediate and powerful presence of 'evil' and 'heathen darkness' – a blatantly ethnocentric view. While not wishing to deny the possibility of spirit possession, from my experience of many years in Pakistan I can hardly think of a single case of alleged possession which could not, at the same time, and from a psychiatric perspective, be recognized as either epilepsy, hysteria, schizophrenia or, more rarely, some other diagnostic category. Making such a diagnosis does not, of course, exclude other possible levels of aetiology.

In most Third World countries much mental illness, even if locally given the label 'madness', is usually believed to be the result of evil spirits or the influence of magic, perhaps arranged by someone wishing evil on the victim. Also, indigenous forms of help for the sufferer are traditionally nonmedical, such as various exorcism practices or ritual measures to counteract magical or spiritual forces. It is understandable then that Christian missionaries have felt some reluctance to enter this arena from the medical angle. Some have preferred to try 'spiritual' methods of healing when they have encountered problems or perhaps responded in ways similar to that of Dr McVicar, who was the Medical Superintendent of the Victoria Hospital, South Africa, from 1902 to 1937 (Shepherd, 1941):

> 'They (the non-Christian Bantus) often attributed illness to the evil machinations of their neighbours acting by means of evil spirits or other occult sciences ... Dr McVicar held that it was one of the special duties of Medical Missions in Africa to enlighten the Bantu mind as to the real nature and causes of disease and to seize every opportunity of combating these superstitious beliefs which hindered so seriously the progress of Christian thought – by talks with outpatients something could be done in that direction. Towards the combating of such an evil and the positive enrichment of spiritual life, all the religious work of the hospital was directed ... a hospital ought to be a living gospel. It was the most notable concrete expression in modern life of the teaching "Let us not love in word, neither in tongue, but in deed and truth". Hospital work was love expressed.'

However, in spite of such sentiments, which could be considered representative of the philosophy of much medical missionary work of that era, there seem to have been no endeavours, particularly on the African Continent, comparable to those in Asia to deal with 'the real nature and causes' of mental disorders – perhaps because of ignorance about them and about appropriate forms of help. As Dr Frank Davey (personal communication) has written:

> 'Demon possession was important when I was in Nigeria ... My colleagues in general medicine were unable to cope with the problems of people convinced they were demon possessed and dying of fear.'

Similarly Terence O. Ranger (1981) discusses the ambiguity felt over the problem of madness in East Africa:

> 'This was a problem which, before the introduction of tranquilliser drugs, the mission doctors had little idea how best to treat. As Leader Stirling writes: "Until quite recently, the problem of mental illness was largely ignored in Tanzania ... In the whole country there was only one general mental hospital for all types of insanity ... None of the ordinary hospitals, either government or mission, had any facilities for dealing with such cases, and were naturally reluctant to admit them. Consequently, the 'harmless' kind were simply left to roam the roads and villages ... Only when they became violent was any action taken. First they would be tied up with rope in the village. Then, if they could not be controlled, they would be handed to the police, whose duty was to dump them handcuffed in the nearest

gaol" (Lucas, 1914). Yet it was not a problem which the mission could ignore. Their own African clergy and teachers, placed as they were in a position of intolerable tension between two sets of values, were peculiarly vulnerable to mental breakdown. In such cases the mission had to try whatever medical remedy might be at hand. Sometimes the clergy even attempted spiritual remedy.'

By contrast, Dr Hughes, working in Shillong, N.E. India, had spotted one effective medical response to an apparently 'spiritual problem' in the 1960s.

'I recognized hyperventilation tetany as the basis for lay-diagnosis of spirit possession. Fancy lecturing ministers and elders in a general assembly on the recognition of tetany and giving them grounds to believe that they were not enchaining the spirit by refusing to accept the evidence presented by the posses-sed. A shot of calcium gluconate could exorcise the most persis-tent "spirits".'

In some ways China, the Middle East and the Indian sub-continent demonstrate particular initiatives in this sphere and these will be dealt with first. Subsequently the attitude in Africa will be dealt with by Dr Dorothy Lowe based on her experience in Uganda.

In China an awareness of need appears on record towards the end of the 19th century, and eventually resulted in the opening of 'The Asylum for the Insane' at Canton in 1898 by Dr J.G. Kerr of the American Presbyterian Church (North) (Balme, 1921). Dr Kerr was director for nearly half-a-century of a mission hos-pital in Canton and first advocated the Asylum in 1872 – it appears to have been the first of its kind in China. Latourette notes that 'by 1909 [he] had treated 1,198 patients'. But we have no information as to what form the treatment took – whether it was along the custodial and rather harsh lines then current in the West, or included less orthodox approaches such as might be the outcome of applied Christian compassion. Referring to the John G. Kerr's 'Home for the Insane' under Dr Sheldon and a school for the Deaf and Dumb in Shantung, the China Mission Year Book (1910) comments 'The powers of such institutions are object lessons in a country like China, which sometimes seems a vast wilderness of unalleviated sorrow and suffering.'

The need to develop such special institutions was strongly felt and the 1913 China Mission Year Book of the Church Missionary Society states: 'We should encourage and help the Chinese to establish institutions for the care of the insane, the blind, the incurable and also sanatoria for TB and leprosy

patients'. Yet no specific further initiatives as regards mental illness appear to have been taken thereafter, and there is no information as to what eventually became of the venture in Canton.

It seems probable that many psychiatric problems were seen
and helped in the context of busy 'general' mission hospitals. An
example of this is a report on the Fatshan Hospital (South China)
for 1941, which apparently continued to function under
Japanese occupation and which, under the heading 'Department
of Neurology and Psychiatry' reports:

'The number of patients suffering from nervous or mental diseases admitted during 1941 represented 2.2% of the total admissions, if cases of the nervous type of beri-beri be excluded. Of this
number (69), 14 were cases of cerebro-spinal meningitis, 14 were
opium addicts, 18 were hysteria, 5 of tabes dorsalis and 3 each of
myelitis and encephalitis.'

Some impression of the kind of treatment attempted and the
problems encountered can be gained from a later paragraph:

'There are many difficulties in the treatment of nervous and
mental cases here, both patient and his family are usually too
impatient to endure long treatment. When cure is not rapid they
generally leave the hospital, probably to go to another doctor; for
this reason it is seldom possible to treat syphilis adequately. Still
more difficulties arise in dealing with mental neurotic cases. The
language forms, for the European, a serious handicap in the
thorough exploration of the mental state of the patient. A language should be perfectly spoken and understood when psycho-
therapeutic measures are to be used. Another point is that the
Chinese nurses have not, as a rule, sufficient experience in
dealing with these patients and if they are afraid of them, or laugh
at them, they will hinder rather than help, especially when the
patient is not "crazy" but only suffering from some slighter and
often temporary disturbance of his mental equilibrium. The
patient's family is frequently another source of hindrance,
because it is often most difficult to separate the patient from his
relatives – a condition essential for success. The State gives the
doctor or hospital no authority to act in these cases against the
wishes of the family, as in Europe, where such powers may be
given in the interests of the patient or of society in general.'

These comments indicate some attempt to tackle and wrestle
with attitudes in staff, relatives, society and patients which are
commonly encountered in the field of psychiatry, especially
when differences of culture are involved.

Another area of great need in China was the very common
problem of opium addiction, to which there are frequent references in missionary writings of the last century. The concern and

the compassion generally expressed by Christian missionaries are in striking contrast to the disgraceful story of the opium trade between India and China, built up by the East India Company with the support of the British government in the late 1830s, leading eventually to the Opium Wars of 1840-42. There is reference to the 'Reopening of the Opium Refuge at Ning Po' (? 1870) and of the permission granted by the donors of the Opium Refuge Fund to use a portion of the principal of the fund in carrying on the refuge. At this time, also, a request was made to the Edinburgh Medical Missionary Society for a medical missionary who could help meet the need for proper medical aid at the Refuge, which was presumably functioning at that time without a doctor.

Dr Galt and his wife, who had been working at the Ning Po Refuge in 1872 were moved to open an Opium Hospital in Hangchow in 1873. It is recorded (CMS Medical Documents 1875-1899):

'It had accommodation for 20 patients. Six inmates were soon admitted. A valuable native assistant was obtained from the American Mission, who dispenses medicine and gives religious instruction. [This hospital] had been built largely through the gift of a British Customs Official at Malawa in India, who had become conscience-smitten at the accounts which were reaching the outside world . . . of the Indian opium trade with China . . . Two years after his transfer to Hangchow, Dr Galt was treating about 250 addicts in the year.'

The methods used and problems encountered sound similar to those of a modern day Narcotic Addiction Unit – with perhaps better results.

Dr Galt writes: 'Reports come from every quarter of the unsatisfactoriness of the cure of opium smokers; very few being permanently rescued.' In 1874 he reported:

'Up to the end of September, 120 opium patients had been cured . . . The work has been very harassing from their outrageousness and the difficulty of having the rules of the hospital enforced. From time to time we have had to expel the worst ones . . . Our plan has been to stop the smoking and give gradually diminishing doses of opium internally, accompanied by other stimulants. This plan seems to mitigate their sufferings to a certain extent.'

A Society for the Propagation of the Gospel report (SPG, 1901) concerning Yung Ching records:

'The opening of a dispensary in 1896 naturally helped to strengthen the position of the mission. A rumour got abroad that

Mr Norman (who had acquired medical knowledge at Salisbury Infirmary) could break the habit of opium smoking and in response to many pitiful entreaties he took in several patients and eventually sent them home cured of the habit.'

Medical missionaries working in China must have accumulated a wealth of experience and skill in handling the problems of opium addiction. An item from the English Presbyterian Mission (Band, 1948) suggests that this ministry was at times very widespread in the country.

'The anti-opium edicts of September 1906 had declared that the growth, sale and the consumption of opium must cease within 10 years and officials were called upon to set an example. They were threatened with dismissal if they did not break off the habit within a given time. Consequently, all over China, mission hospitals were suddenly crowded with officials and teachers, scholars and soldiers, and other opium sots, all clamouring to be cured. It was an opportunity not to be missed and all our mission doctors rendered useful service. At Yung Ching, during 1906, Maxwell took in 115 opium addicts, of whom 98 were cured.'

A mention from the same source of opium addiction in a member of the medical staff (always an 'at risk' group in our own times) is of interest as throwing some light on the method used to provide emotional support during the period of distressing withdrawal symptoms:

'No account of the Chuanchow medical work would be complete without the mention of Dr Lewis Paton's Senior Assistant, Yap Sin-hun, who was so capable that Paton left him in charge of the hospital when he went on furlough in 1911. He was an elder in the South Street Church with a remarkable history.

He finished his medical course under Dr Paton in 1900 and went into practice in the city. By and by he became an opium addict and for a long time all efforts for his rescue failed. In 1906, Dr Paton and his students went in a body to his house to plead with him to given up the opium habit. He kept to his bed for a week, the students in turn sitting beside him to help and cheer him. From that time he did not touch the drug. He returned to the hospital as an assistant and continued to render faithful service.'

Rather nearer to home but, remarkably, in the same year as the establishment of the asylum in Canton, was the opening of the Lebanon Hospital for the Insane, on the western slopes of Mount Lebanon, 3 miles from Beirut. Behind this venture, of which we have more details, lies the vision and deep concern of one, Theophilus Waldmeier (Hobhouse, 1925), a Swiss missionary (born 1832) who laboured in the Middle East from the age of 22 for about 40 years, at first in Abyssinia, before moving to Beirut in 1869 as a worker with the British Syrian Schools Mission. Later, in 1875, after becoming a Quaker, he started on his own initiative the Mount Lebanon Mission which was, in due course, adopted and supported by the Society of Friends.

The idea of the Hospital for the Insane was conceived late in his career, as he recounts:

'On my return from England in October 1894, I felt my work here was drawing to its close – there were capable fellow-workers who could carry it on. A burning concern began to take hold of my heart for the establishing of an asylum for the mentally afflicted. Though I was getting on in years, yet I longed to plead the cause of these poor suffering ones in Europe and America. I trusted Friends would follow me with their prayerful interest and Christian sympathy.'

His idea received the approval of the Friends Foreign Missions Association, and on April 17 1896 an executive committee of ten was set up in Beirut. This was attended and supported by the then director of the Morningside Asylum (Edinburgh), Sir Thomas Smith Clouston, who is reported as saying at the meeting:

'I have travelled in Palestine and Syria, and seen the cruelties and atrocities practised on the insane, who often, in consequence, have lost their lives and it is a sin that the missionaries, doctors and ministers have not yet cared for the most unfortunate sufferers in this country; it is also a shame to Europe and America that they have neglected them for all these centuries, but I am now comforted to see that you are awake to the urgent need of doing something for them and that Mr Waldmeier is going to plead their cause in Europe and America. When he comes to Edinburgh I shall help him and now I put down £10 for this most urgent undertaking.'

A committee of nineteen was organized in London and the initiative of Waldmeier resulted in support from doctors in Europe, including Dr David Yellowlees of Glasgow, and Sir Robert Armstrong-Jones, HM Visitor in Lunacy, who is recorded as having been the collector of the first £100 raised in England for the hospital.

'On Monday August 6 1898', it is recorded, 'the first asylum in a Bible Land was officially opened for the mentally afflicted sufferers of Syria and Palestine. The first insane patient was taken in on August 8, a girl of 16 years of age'. During the first 21 years 1193 men and 707 women passed through the hospital, of whom 511 were reported 'cured'. By 1924 there was accommodation for 150 patients, but by Christmas 1935 this had grown to 350,

with plans to expand to 400, and the capacity was noted to be
410 by 1936. From these numbers it can be deduced that the
length of stay of many patients must have been in terms of years
and that the institution followed the pattern of Western asylums
of the day, in acquiring large numbers of long-stay residents.
Dr Sidney Coupland, one of HM Commissioners in Lunacy, had
recently testified: 'I do not know any hospital for mental patients
of the same character, in any other part of the world. One can see
from the results how admirably the hospital must be carried on.'

The annual reports make fascinating reading, with many
quoted tributes to the uniqueness and value of the ministry and
the distressing plight and needs of those being served; for
example,

1907   Dr John Fraser of Edinburgh, HM Commissioner in
         Lunacy wrote – 'The good work of the Lebanon Asylum
         has only to be known to command support.'
1919   There is no hospital for the insane between Cairo and
         Constantinople except the Lebanon Hospital.
1922-23 A policeman would just as soon think of withholding
         his riding whip from a troublesome maniac as he
         would from applying it to a donkey. Some patients
         have been so badly handled before admission that after
         a hot bath and a hot drink it is astonishing how they
         will lie down quietly in a clean, comfortable bed, as if
         glad to rest their weary bodies.'
1925-26 Although this hospital has been open for the reception
         of patients for over 25 years and is known all over the
         country, elsewhere primitive methods of treatment in
         the form of exorcism are still much in use; spells are
         still believed in; chaining naked people in damp caves
         and beating them with shoes to trample out the demons
         are still practised, and we still continue to receive
         patients who have had crosses and other devices
         cauterised on their heads by means of red-hot irons.
         Bleeding is commonly resorted to as a means of
         treatment.

A report on the opening of the Beirut Neuropsychiatric Clinic
in 1947 indicates that perhaps not much had changed in 20
years: 'There is still, in Lebanon and other Middle Eastern
countries, a vast barrier of prejudice and ignorance concerning
mental disease.' Similar comments and descriptions would still
be true for many parts of the developing world in the 1980s.

1926-27 Asfuriyeh (Lebanon Hospital) still stands unique, not
         as a government hospital, but as a purely philanthro-
         pic institution and the direct outcome of practical

Christianity in a country where the principle of 'do to others as you would have them do to you' is but a vague conception . . . A rather remarkable event occurred this year in the admission to the hospital of a prominent Muslim Sayed, a man of noble family from Mecca. When I asked his relatives why they did not take him to the Asylum at Cairo, or to the one at Bethlehem they told me that after enquiry they had come to the conclusion that this hospital was the best. The patient got better. No provision whatever is made in this country for idiots, the feeble-minded, epileptics or the infirm insane.

Although it was a characteristic attitude of the times to be somewhat excessively dismissive and disparaging of local methods and practices, which today we would feel deserved more consideration for their possible value, this was understandable given the overwhelming impression of need and suffering – as Sir Maurice Craig, Consultant Physician, Guy's Hospital, stated in 1927-28 – 'This hospital is doing pioneer work, if it were not doing it the work would not be done, the suffering would be unrelieved.'

Similarly, Sir Robert Armstrong Jones commented: 'This small hospital (297 patients under treatment throughout the year) still remains the only one in the country . . . The hospital has always been regarded as an object lesson in Syria, as to how the insane can be cared for.'

Clearly, the original burden and vision of Waldmeier continued to be felt by Christians long after his death, although without his inspired initiative the suffering would probably have remained unrelieved, as was the case in many other countries of the world where similar pictures of distress have been described.

In addition to clinical work, the hospital contributed to training in the field of psychiatry; for example in 1921-22: 'Arrangements have been made whereby the director of the hospital gives a course of lectures and clinical demonstrations on mental disease to the 5th year medical students of the American University of Beirut'.

Several years later the director and medical superintendent, Dr H. Watson Smith, OBE was appointed Clinical Professor in Psychiatry at this University. In 1938 the institution was renamed the Lebanon Hospital for Nervous and Mental Disorders, and in 1939 was recognized by the Royal Medical/Psychological

Association as a Training Centre for the Mental Nursing Certificate. During the 1939-45 War, the hospital continued to function and grow in its international reputation. According to Professor Alex Kennedy, Professor of Psychological Medicine at Durham University, 'It is regarded with one other hospital in Egypt as technically the best of its kind in the Middle East, and its example of patient work, technical skill and kindliness has had a widespread influence.' The 1949 report records that 14,000 patients had been treated in the 50 years since the opening of the hospital.

Thus, what started as a pioneer expression of Christian love and compassion, the moving burden of one man touched by the love of Christ, developed into a leading professional centre for an important area of the world.

It was much later before any special initiative in the field of mental health emerged in India. This time, again as in the case of Lebanon, it arose out of the dream of a particular servant of Christ who had been ministering in India for about 50 years – Dr E. Stanley Jones (1884-1973), spiritual counsellor, founder of the Ashram Movement (the Christian application of the tradition of Hindu religious communities) and writer of many devotional books. 'As he counselled people, he met many who had mental and emotional problems and he began to dream of a Christian psychiatric centre, which would combine professional efficiency with care for the whole person.'

So, 'On December 13th, 1950 the first patient, a Muslim gentleman, registered at Nur Manzil Psychiatric Centre, [Lucknow]. Nothing more is known about him today, for the official case records begin at No. 2, a Hindu lady. Certainly however, these first patients need to be congratulated for they must have come with some trepidation to the Centre.'

The psychiatrist who opened the doors of Nur Manzil was Dr Dagmar Norell of Sweden, who heard God's call to this work on meeting Stanley Jones while she was studying in the USA. The 1975 Silver Jubilee Book (Nur Manzil, 1975) reports that 'From the first, the keynote has been individual care. High professional standards combined with time to listen, integrity and loving concern has been the aim.' Over the 25 years to 1975, 9000 patients have been seen, of whom 2800 have been admitted. 'Persons from many different places have come for treatment: Uttar Pradesh, Bihar, Rajasthan, Bengal, Bangladesh, Punjab, Germany, Norway, U.S.A., U.K., Australia, New Zealand, Tibet,

Nepal, Tamilnadu, Kerala . . . Professionally, anyone from villagers to professors and politicians has come.'

The staff, too, have been drawn from many nationalities. Following Dr Norell came Dr Erna Hoch of Switzerland, and Dr James Stringham from USA served as director from 1962-72, with close support from his wife Charlotte, a qualified social worker. They were succeeded by Dr Ernest Chander, the first Indian director, 'who fulfilled the long awaited desire for Indian leadership.' He left in 1973 to take up a senior position in psychiatry at the Christian Medical College, Ludhiana, to be succeeded by Dr Marjorie Foyle (1973-81) from Britain, who had earlier been a medical missionary in the initial stages of the United Mission to Nepal. Since her retirement the Unit has been under the clinical charge of an Australian psychiatrist. In its 25 years at least 24 Doctors, 25 Nursing Sisters, 9 Administrative and Office Staff, 5 Occupational Therapists, 3 Clinical Psychologists, 6 Housekeepers and many faithful servants have served Nur Manzil.

The Centre is a charitable institution vested in the Methodist Church of South Asia and much of its financial and administrative support has come from US Methodist Mission sources. In 1975 the financial position was that:

The patients pay what they can, the rest is made up by loving donations. Currently, only 47% are fully paying, 44% are on part concession and 9% are totally free. Each year the Centre gives away about rupees 60,000 free treatment and at least another rupees 50,000 free drugs . . . This is a heavy drain on a 4½ Lakh budget (= rupees 450,000). The question asked on the ward round is not 'can he afford milk . . . eggs . . . a visit to the cinema . . . an expensive injection . . .' but 'does he need it?' If he does he gets it whether he can pay or not – no wonder the Finance Committee has grey hairs!

The chairman of the Board at the time of the Jubilee celebrations was Bishop Joseph R. Lance, of the Methodist Church of UP and Bengal. He added his tribute with these words:

'The Silver Jubilee celebration of Nur Manzil Psychiatric Centre is a reminder to us that Dr E. Stanley Jones, through the vision given to him by God to establish such an institution, was concerned for the development of the whole person in and through Jesus Christ, this wholeness includes mental health . . . No divine action of love for men can escape the agony and pangs of human society. The efforts of those who labour in this unique institution are no exception. We bow in reverence before God when we think of devoted and selfless people like Dr E. Stanley

Jones, Dr Norell, Dr Hoch, Dr and Mrs Stringham, Dr Ernest Chander and the present staff. They have not sought any laurels for themselves but for their Lord.'

The institution conforms more to the model of a modern psychiatric unit, with the usual professional categories of doctor, nurse, psychologist, social worker, occupational therapist, etc. It has a small number of beds (35 plus) and a fairly short length of stay, with rapid turnover and an emphasis on active treatment which is thoughtfully planned for each individual, for example:

'Once a week the Director and the Occupational Therapist sit in conference for an hour, each patient is discussed and an effort is made to fit the task to the needs of the person. Timid patients are encouraged to mix with a friendly group of patients. Aggressive persons are directed to the punch ball in the corner of the room and encouraged to take it out on that! Patients with a particular type of relationship problem are put into the type of group activity that will help them to overcome it . . . Many problems are exposed in the O.T. Department and it is rewarding work. There is no thrill like seeing a patient get up at the monthly party and sing a song, when only a week before he was unable even to talk.'

To a casual visitor the ethos of the Unit appears quite strongly within the orthodox medical tradition, with an emphasis on hierarchy, separate professions, nurses in uniform, ward rounds, some locking of wards and the use of drugs and electro-convulsive therapy. Yet, on more detailed acquaintance, many features are apparent which make Nur Manzil unique and distinct from any other psychiatric work in India. The emphasis on counselling and psychotherapy, which was, in particular, established by Dr and Mrs Stringham and further fostered by Dr Foyle, is surely unequalled anywhere in the subcontinent, in contrast with the popular tendency to question the applicability of such psychological methods of help for any but the more sophisticated élite. Each patient's initial interview and assessment session takes 2½ hours and includes time for the family. Suitable patients have 2 hours individual counselling per week, in addition to various kinds of group work as appropriate, such as drama therapy or family therapy.

Importance is also given to 'teaching', not only or primarily of the academic type. The tradition of a weekly lecture for patients and relatives, pioneered by Dr Stringham in 1963, has continued ever since and is an approach to public education which could well be applied in the West. The staff take it in turns: topics on relevant subjects are chosen, such as 'Family Relationships',

'How to Stay Well after Discharge', the 'Reasons for Giving Medicines', 'How to Handle Fears', 'How the Mind Works', 'What is Mental Health?'

More formal teaching and training for new staff have been a growth area and Dr Foyle has latterly gained a wider reputation also for her Counselling Courses at the YMCA, Delhi, and has been in considerable demand further afield. The Centre is now recognized as a training post for psychiatrists for the Indian MD (Psych.) and for the British MRC Psych. Dr Foyle has felt this professional academic contribution important to bring the Centre into line with orthodox psychiatric practice in India, in order, among other things, to attract good staff.

1973 saw the opening of a modern three-storey building, Windecker Hall, which has further enriched the facilities of Nur Manzil. 'At present the ground floor is the new half-way house. Some persons are admitted there directly but the real use is half-way between hospital and home, a stepping stone. Sometimes men live there while getting readjusted to their work in the city; families may move in together while their problems are sorted out . . .' One such group are missionaries with emotional problems, who have come often from long distances to receive concentrated in-depth help – a service which has saved many from having to return to their countries of origin with the usual consequences of loss to the missionary cause and the distress of feeling permanent 'failures' in their calling.

The Half-Way House has 8 beds and only got going fully in about 1980, with the appointment of trained staff. The achievement of introducing the modern practice of rehabilitation in a therapeutic community setting is surely another 'first' for Nur Manzil.

But what ultimately defines and characterizes an institution is its total atmosphere which depends more upon such important matters as staff morale and relations, attitudes and motivation. It is at this level that Nur Manzil has made its uniquely Christian contribution along the lines foreseen by its founder. 'A Psychiatric Centre is usually only as good as its staff. Staff relationships are cared for as far as possible. One way of doing this is by praying together daily in the Chapel; another way is by monthly tea-parties and celebrations of "family affairs".'

In this area Christian institutions can call upon reserves of love and grace and forgiveness not available in the secular world.

'Some people say to us "you have a wonderful spirit." This, of
course, is not always true, we have our quarrels and problems
like anyone else but there is a basic underlying motivation of all
our work – the Service of Our Lord Jesus Christ – this is what
constantly reunites us as a staff group. Central to all our work is
the Stanley Jones Chapel. Every morning we pray together and
any patient who wishes to join us is free to attend. At Easter time
each year we observe a 24-hour vigil, the staff succeeding each
other for half-hour periods of prayer. From time to time patients
ask us to pray for them, so on Tuesday evening, any who wish can
come to the Chapel for individual prayer. In this way they can
experience the strength and healing which God alone can give, as
they struggle back to mental health.'

Nur Manzil is not the only Christian venture in psychiatry to
be found in India. The famous Vellore Christian Medical College
has had a Mental Health Centre and Department of Psychiatry for
many years, of which the present head is Professor Abraham
Verghese. One of his special emphases has been 'Family Participation in Mental Health Care', arising out of an appreciation of
the therapeutic value of this perspective and a 'recognition of the
importance of the traditional Indian family ties'. Hence out of
about 3000 new consultations each year 25% are admitted to the
Mental Health Centre, with an average length of stay of seven
weeks. During this time one or two family members stay with the
patient in 'small self-contained living units'. In this way they are
able to participate in various ways in the treatment programme.

'They thus get an insight into the treatment techniques and
also a chance to dispel many wrong notions and attitudes about
mental disease which they have been entertaining. Through
spread of this knowledge into wider circles of the public, a
general education in matters of mental disease is effected. . .
A therapist interviews the relatives regularly to know more about
the family dynamics. . . Thus an attempt is made to restore the
family homeostasis.'

This is one development in which much subcontinental
psychiatry is well ahead of the West, where it is extremely rare to
have relatives admitted and so closely involved. It has, of course,
been made possible because of the widespread general medical
practice, born out of necessity, of using relatives to supplement
the very limited nursing care available. A similar approach has
been established at the Mental Health Centre, Peshawar, except
that on some occasions it has been found important to exclude a
certain 'smothering' relative – the only times when doors have
had to be locked.

Other examples of Indian Christian Hospitals which have started psychiatric departments are: (1) Mandiram Hospital, Kottayam, Kerala; (2) Miraj Medical Centre, Miraj, Maharashtra; (3) The Orthodox Syrian Christian Hospital, Kolencherry, Kerala; (4) Ludhiana Christian Medical College, Punjab, which, like Vellore, has an academic Department of Psychiatry involved in teaching medical students.

Even more recent than developments in India, has been the birth of the Mental Health Centre, Peshawar, which I described in an article in *Saving Health* (Bavington, 1978) on which the following paragraphs are based. Some early inspiration came from the efforts of Dr J Karcher, an American physician working at the United Christian Hospital, Lahore, who in 1961-62 included counselling and other psychiatric treatment as part of his busy general medical work. During the later 1960s I began to 'try out' something of what had been learnt during 1½ years furlough, spent mainly in junior posts at a British psychiatric hospital, until it eventually became clear that I was being called to a full commitment to psychiatric work in Pakistan. A visit to Nur Manzil provided further inspiration and many concrete ideas, so that much of the original conception of the Mental Health Centre was actually modelled on the Lucknow Unit, with notable modifications which became more evident as the Centre grew.

Typical of the several thousand patients who have been to the Mental Health Centre since it was started in 1971 is a young man we were asked to visit.

After the preliminary tea-drinking and introductions I was taken to a small dark hut where the patient, Ishmael, was sitting on a pile of stinking straw. When I tried to shake hands with him, I discovered that his arm was held by a chain to a stake in the ground. We learned that he had been in this schizophrenic state for the past five years and periodically broke his chain and ran off violently. He looked very frightened and indicated his reluctance to come with us. When, two visits later, he did finally agree to be admitted, he insisted on bringing his chain with him and it took quite some time before we were able to wean him from it.

In our North West Frontier Province the only existing psychiatric facilities for a population of ten million was a small 'mental hospital' – a modified part of the Peshawar Jail – and one qualified government psychiatrist. Towards the end of the sixties the plan slowly evolved to set up a Christian Centre for Mental

Health Care, by adapting a portion of the mission hospital and creating a small unit which would provide modern psychiatric facilities of a good standard, adapted as necessary to the cultural situation. The initial six-and-a-half years saw a steady growth from those early beginnings. We are grateful for generous help from 'Bread for the World', CMS and the Dutch Presbyterian Church which has made it possible, by remodelling old buildings, to create a separate area for up to 35 inpatients, and a sparkling modern building housing outpatient offices, a kitchen, and dining room-cum-lounge; plus all the furniture and other equipment.

In general there is a surprising degree of similarity with Western psychiatric practice. A recent analysis of our records shows comparable percentages of the major diagnosis categories especially of depression and schizophrenia. Hysterical conditions are rather more common – more so in women – and sexual problems in men account for about 10% of our patients. As would be expected in the extended family structure there is hardly any geriatric problem. Drug addiction is rare, although we often see the effects of the locally common habit of 'charas' (marijuana) smoking. The effect of culture is more obviously seen in the detailed symptomatology of conditions. For example, suicide and severe pathological guilt are rare but religious delusions are more common.

From the outset I have aimed at creating a 'Therapeutic Community' – an approach learned in Britain, but again acceptable, with modifications, to our Pakistani situation. This method is based on the realization that the total 'atmosphere' of an institution powerfully influences other treatment measures, not only for the emotionally ill. Out of this has come the idea of creating a type of staff and patient community based on a different style of relations. In a therapeutic community every effort is made to encourage a spirit of acceptance, toleration and understanding in which there is the fullest possible communication of thought and feeling at all levels between all members. Much time is spent in patient and staff meetings where all problems of relations and management are freely, honestly and democratically worked out. In the Mental Health Centre we begin our day with a simple time of worship followed by a community meeting in which we all sit in a circle on one of the carpeted office floors, thus minimizing any hierarchical presuppositions. This meeting is conducted along the lines of group therapy – with the group encouraging patients to share their deepest concerns in the supportive family environment of our meeting. We have found the richer concept of 'the family' a useful way to evoke caring responses in the group.

As a Christian I have felt a compelling challenge in this way of working and something of particular relevance to our calling and commitment to making real God's healing grace in Christ. For in creating such a concerned, caring community, the essence of the Gospel communicates itself at levels deeper and more effective than the verbal. As the work has grown a number of 'sub-projects' has begun to emerge. A small school for subnormal children is slowly growing, having been started with the help of a CMS 'short-termer' and again because of the total inadequacy of facilities in this field. We are sure it will continue to grow for the need is great.

We have increasingly come to see our main role as a teaching one and have recently devised a fuller scheme for training mental health workers and for their use in the community. Six months ago we placed one of them in a rural area giving him the supervised task of seeking to provide, in collaboration with other health workers in the area, a basic level of psychiatric care both by treatment and education. It is hoped that this may be a model for the government health authorities eventually to copy and that the whole area could thus be covered with mental health workers and a supporting structure. We have, in fact, been increasingly looking outwards, and hope the Mental Health Centre will not hinder effective outreach, but rather act as a vital base for future efforts. There is often need for an 'open door' policy for staff as well as patients.

For me these years of pioneering have been exciting and satisfying, and I have often thanked God for calling me to this ministry.

It should be added that government and some private psychiatric services grew and improved during the 1970s but provisions still remain minute and very limited in scope. The Mental Health Centre represents an initiative mainly by virtue of having introduced approaches and a 'philosophy' practically unknown anywhere in Pakistan: a way of working which owes its inspiration largely to a Christian view of human nature and mankind's deepest needs.

Although there are now government plans to incorporate some form of psychiatry into the primary health care structure, the training of mental health workers and the pilot Community Mental Health Scheme is the only instance to date of any substantial attempt to demonstrate and evaluate this approach in Pakistan. Yet it is unlikely that even the simplest forms of psychiatric help will ever reach the millions of the subcontinent unless something of this kind is widely applied. There is still vast scope for pioneering in this field.

Since 1978 there have been further changes. The School for the Mentally Handicapped has grown and flourished under the leadership of Mike and Christine Miles of CMS, and this has now sprouted a number of branches and become recognized throughout Pakistan as one of the main centres for teaching and training of the handicapped and the education of the public; the production of educational materials (in English and Urdu); and community surveys and innovative ideas on appropriate facilities for this greatly neglected area of need. The latest piece of pioneering has been the work of a Community Rehabilitation Development Project, with support from UNICEF and the Frontier Association for the Mentally Handicapped (an earlier child of the Mental Health Centre) which has been facilitating the creation of parents' and professional associations for handicapped children in the cities of the North West Frontier Province, with an emphasis on local initiative and self-help in creating local services. So far there has been an enthusiastic response.

Looking back it is surprising how slow we have been to see psychiatry as a legitimate sphere for Christian and missionary involvement. Yet as we deal with man at the level of his psyche we are touching the tender places of his guilts and fears; his moral anguish and conflicts; his emotional bondage and deepest longings. What better resources can we have for him than the sure knowledge of God's unconditional love and forgiveness which frees men and makes them whole.

PSYCHIATRY IN UGANDA

Dorothy I. Lowe

Student health
Modern scientific medicine places great emphasis on the physical basis of illness and the prescribing of appropriate treatments, but the patient's feelings about his illness may receive scant attention. Evidence abounds, however, that a patient's attitude may play a part in the original pathology and also affect the

prognosis. What tends to be forgotten is that attention to the 'psychiatric' element of medical care is an important part of medical mission – health in body, mind and spirit. In a student population in Uganda gross psychiatric illness was rare, but anxiety states, hysterical conversion phenomena, and depression described as 'weakness' were common, but presented most often in the form of physical symptoms related to eye strain, headaches, stomach and chest pain.

It was not long before I began to question the meaning to the student of the succession of symptoms with which I was being presented. One student had a total of 13 symptoms on one occasion. Clear clinical diagnoses of malaria, infections, broken bones, and the like responded well to conventional treatment, but there were some students who never seemed to be without a burden of illness. Cure one symptom and another presented itself. At times I felt irritated and dismissive, at times compassionate. Three changes of approach occurred to me. Each student on entrance was given a full medical examination and treatment given for any condition diagnosed. All was fully recorded. No student needed to present with a symptom as the only way of having a medical check-up. Many fears of serious illness were allayed in this way and some long-term ill health became a thing of the past. All subsequent visits were also recorded and when a series of apparently trivial complaints was made I offered a long session to allow the student time to talk about his fears and anxieties and symptoms. Sometimes the trouble had its origin in financial worries. Offering for ordination could mean a serious reduction in salary, deplored or little understood by dependent and poor relatives. At other times fear of failing intellectually was relieved if poor health could be pleaded. These long sessions were valuable and often marked a turning point from which a 'sickly' student became and remained well.

It was easy to become dependent on readily available help while in college and this could impair a student's ability to cope in remote places. 'Sickly' students requested that their bishops place them in parishes near hospitals for constant medical attention for themselves and their families. Illness in Uganda was often quite frightening. Children quickly became dehydrated and died as a result of gut infections and malaria. Teaching on hygiene and simple initial treatments and the provision of basic medical kits and instructions led to a greater ability to take appropriate action which was often life-saving. Fear and anxiety diminished as confidence grew, and all of this was in the context of lively faith and trust in God.

These three measures of medical examinations (and appropriate treatment where needed), longer sessions when successions of symptoms were presented, and self-help kits led to a marked reduction in the attendance at the health service and to increased confidence and physical and emotional health. These simple and cost-effective methods could have equal relevance in more sophisticated societies.

Butabika psychiatric hospital

Although this hospital was not part of a missionary organization, a high proportion of the staff were actively Christian. Careful consideration was given to a patient's religious belief and its relevance in treatment and aftercare. Theological students and their tutors worked there each week and there was a full-time chaplain. On some wards charge nurses held regular times of worship and prayer with their patients. The whole concept of caring for the weak, the confused and the mad followed the teaching of Christ and was a direct response to the coming of the Gospel to Uganda. In contrast the traditional treatment for the mentally ill was often derived from a belief that the derangement had its origins in spirit possession and bewitchment, and for this harsh custodial care and mutilation and incantation were prescribed.

When I told my UK friends that I had started to work with mentally ill people in Uganda, many of them expressed surprise. 'Oh, do they have that there too?', they asked. To which I replied, 'Of course, it is part of being human.' Rousseau expounded a primitive society, free from stress and therefore free from mental illness. It used to be fashionable to accept this; to blame those whose coming had disrupted the idyllic state. But it is obvious that there are in Africa, as everywhere else in the world, plenty of mentally disturbed people, and that African society is by no means free of stress. There are worries relating to physical dangers; high infant mortality rates, infertility, crop failures. There is the very important and ever-present fear of bewitchment or of other evils caused by the constantly present world of malevolent and hostile spirits. In more modern times schoolboys having their fees paid by relatives are in constant anxiety to do well and succeed to a well paid job so that they in turn can pay the fees for the next generation. It is easier to rationalize failure on the basis of headaches and ill health than to face up to possibly limited ability. Failure to work hard at studies is almost unknown. There is no shortage of stress.

To meet the need for psychiatric help the Uganda government opened one large mental hospital and a mental health clinic at Mulago in Kampala for outpatients. Mental health units were also opened at several of the general hospitals, staffed by mental nurses and visited by psychiatric consultants on a regular basis. Seven such units were established throughout the country.

Butabika hospital, built between 1958 and 1962, consisted of 700 beds for civil and 300 for criminally insane patients, formerly called Broadmoor but renamed the Kirinyl Unit. Long low bungalows each contained two 30-bed dormitories with consulting rooms and nursing offices. Patients spent a lot of their time out of doors on the verandahs and under the trees. The grounds were well kept and spacious with lawns and flower beds and a lovely view of Lake Victoria. Only two admission wards have locked doors, so patients are free to wander all over the grounds. Men are in wards on one side and women on the other but they are not restricted from meeting each other in the course of the day.

The Psychiatrist's work

The psychiatrist sees patients regularly and assesses them with the help of the nursing staff. Language can be a great problem. None of the staff could know all of the 15 or so languages needed to communicate with the patients, but as nurses were recruited from all areas of Uganda it was always possible to have the help of a nurse who knew the patient's language and local culture. The range of treatment included drugs, electroconvulsive therapy (ECT), group therapy and occupational therapy.

Patients were admitted directly from the mental health clinics at the general hospitals and more often through the police on urgency orders. Seriously disturbed patients were commonly committed to Butabika when their behaviour was beyond the toleration of their relatives. The worst things were 'destroying crops' and 'breaking cups'. In 1972 there were 14,000 outpatient attendances at the mental health clinic at Mulago Hospital, Kampala.

The incidence of mental illness is much the same all over the world, though the illness may present in different ways in different cultures. Many patients had been taken to a traditional healer before being brought to Butabika. This was perfectly consistent with the cultural understanding of mental illness as a manifestation of disturbance in interpersonal or intertribal relations and the spirit life of the tribe.

In Uganda many patients were confused or violent on admission — more than half of these because of physical illness such as pneumonia or malaria or pelvic infections following childbirth. Such patients recover quickly on getting the appropriate medical treatment. Forty per cent of male admissions are due to alcohol, often home distilled and contaminated. Unlike the pattern of alcohol dependence in the West, a number of these patients were able to stop drinking alcohol altogether in response to being told of its effects on their liver and brain. It was a sad fact that many in high professional jobs took to alcohol as a sedative in the strain of their high office and became dependent on it. In this way their essential contribution to their country was destroyed.

The incidence of schizophrenia is similar to that in the West but the illness is often more transient and the prognosis for schizophrenia in Africa is much better than for similarly diagnosed patients in the UK. This is thought to be related to the greater readiness of society to accept a wider range of behaviour as being within normal limits. It is also related to the physical element in the disturbance which responds to medical treatment.

There were twice as many male admissions as female. The high admission rate for alcoholic confusional states in men accounted for 40% of male admissions. Men who are disturbed are more violent and difficult to control and brought for admission much sooner than women who can more easily be tied up and kept where they can do no damage.

Depressive illness was responsible for much complaining of 'weakness', stomach and chest pain and headache at general medical outpatients all over the country. Many of these patients spent a lot of time and effort and money on attending hospitals, private doctors and traditional healers. Relatively few of them found their way to the mental health clinics but those who did responded well to antidepressant treatment and were most grateful.

Training for both State Registered Nurses and Enrolled Nurses took place at Butabika. Senior nursing staff had received their training at hospitals in the UK, but with the development of the nurse training school at Butabika subsequent training took place within Uganda. Many of these nurses were excellent, calm and consistent and endlessly patient.

Much of the work of the hospital – peeling vegetables in the kitchens, ward cleaning, laundry work, gardening, growing of food crops and the like – was done by the patients themselves as a most appropriate form of occupational therapy, preparing them to take their place once more in their families and home communities on their discharge. In addition there were workshops and articles made were sold to get money for new materials. Sisal mats, stools, copper work, fabric printing and piece work for local industry were among the activities.

Social workers were engaged in occasional home visits and in interviewing patients and their relatives to get a social history and family details, but most of all for helping with the details of the discharge of patients from Butabika. Many of the more violent patients were admitted in the torn remnants of their clothes or even naked. Clothes had to be found so that when they returned to their villages they were seen to be 'clothed and in their right minds'. The other big problem was to find where patients had come from, especially when they had been brought by the police and had perhaps wandered in confusion many miles from their original homes. Police forms accompanying patients often had useful information but I well remember one deposition which read: 'Into the station and hands in one unknown female. This happened at unknown time in unknown place'. In due time this patient made a good recovery but, as she had never left her village in her life, it was quite a job to discover where it was. The social worker went to the referring police station 50 miles from Kampala, and eventually her home was traced. Later we had a delighted letter from the patient's father. 'I had long since considered that this my daughter must be dead', he wrote.

For the mentally ill, difficulties with transport have resulted in fewer admissions to Butabika and fewer attendances for maintenance drugs at the mental health clinics. For the majority the age-old pattern of turning to traditional healers and exorcists will continue and will sometimes be effective as has been the case in the past. Some patients will suffer a great deal; some will die. But a few will benefit from being with their families and on recovery will not have the problems of rehabilitation so difficult

after a prolonged absence from home and community. I recall
one patient, the mother of 12 children, the youngest only two
years old, who was admitted for treatment. By the time she was
discharged three weeks later her husband had taken a new
younger wife. On her next visit she told me of this. The children,
being her husband's property, would remain with him and the
new consort. She had resigned herself to spending the rest of her
life living with her mother. Perhaps if she had not had Butabika
to go to, her situation would have been better.

References

Balme, H. (1921) *China and Modern Medicine.* London: The Carey
    Press.
Band, E. (1948) *Working His Purpose Out. The History of the
    English Presbyterian Mission.* London: Presbyterian Church of
    England Publishing House.
Bavington, J. (1978) Pioneering in psychiatry. *Saving Health,* 17, 7
China Mission Handbook (1910) London: Church Missionary
    Society.
CMS Medical Documents (1875-1899) London: Church Missionary
    Society
Hobhouse, S. (Ed.) (1925) *The Autobiography of Theophilus
    Waldmeier.* London: The Friends Bookshop.
Lucas, V. (1914) That we may never forget *Centr. Afr.,* 32, 238
Nur Manzil (1975) *Silver Jubilee Book, 1950-1975.* Lucknow: Nur
    Manzil Psychiatric Centre.
Ranger, T.O. (1981) *Soc. Sci. Med.,* 15B, 268.
Shepherd, R.H.W. (1941) *The story of a Century, 1841-1941.*
    Lovedale: The Lovedale Press.
SPG (1901) *100 Years of the SPG,* vol. 2. London: Society for the
    Propagation of the Gospel.
Verghese, A. (1978) Involvement of families in mental health care.
    Christian Medical College, Vellore, Alumni Journal, Vol. 12.

CHAPTER 13

NURSING SERVICES

Jean M. McLellan

The early days of what we now know as nursing are lost in the mists of time. The Greeks had no concept of nursing as such, though there were midwives. Primarily, the development of nursing lay in a combination of religious practice and specific medical skills. There is no mention of the actual name 'nurse' in those times, though midwives are mentioned. Homer wrote of 'wet' nurses, while Plato mentions the practice of midwifery as being restricted to elderly and experienced matrons.

With the dawning of the Christian era, the example of caring with compassion as exemplified by Christ, was continued by his followers. While there was no concept of educated nursing, the deaconesses of Rome were not unlike the nurses of today. There was a sense of caring for one's neighbour, or being the 'good Samaritan', of following the example of Christ in his healing ministry.

The Empress Helena, mother of Constantine, was converted to Christianity at the age of 64. She made a pilgrimage to Jerusalem, and is remembered for the founding of the first Christian hospital there. She died in Palestine on her second pilgrimage in 328, aged 80 years.

Fabiola was another genuine nurse. She was a wealthy woman who founded a *nosocomium,* or hospital, for the poor sick in 390, giving up her rank and wealth and freely devoting her whole life as a Christian to tending to the needs of the sick. Her influence spread all over Europe, eliciting, among others, the high praises of St Jerome.

Modern nursing owes its origin to Florence Nightingale (1820-1910). Other well-known personalities, such as Mrs Bedford Fenwick, must not be overlooked, but it is to Miss Nightingale that the prime honour must be attributed. Her *Notes on Nursing* are a revelation to any layman or nurse today. God gives to each one of us a vision if we truly open our eyes to see it but, if we do not respond, he will pass it on to someone else. Modern nursing came into being through the response given to God by Florence Nightingale when she heard him clearly speaking to her when she was 17 years old. Her call to nursing came during a visit to the Continent when she visited the famous Kaiserswerth Institute in Germany, pioneered by Pastor Fliedner. Here she was deeply impressed by the devotion of the deaconesses, a religious order in which high standards of nursing were combined with care for the spiritual needs of patients. From this time she never looked back. On June 24 1860 was opened the Nightingale Training School for Nurses at St Thomas's Hospital in London. Starting with only fifteen probationers, it set a standard and an example which were soon followed by schools for nurses and midwives throughout the country and overseas. Thus was initiated a tradition which was to inspire the Christian church to bring the great assets and principles of a noble profession to the succour of the sick, thus summarized in her own words:

> 'The Kingdom of God is within and we must also make it so without. God meant man to work for man's own improvement; the spiritual and the material are one. To be a good nurse one must be a *good woman*, or one is nothing but a tinkling bell.'

As late as the turn of the present century it was still difficult to convince many Mission Home Boards that medical work was not secondary to evangelistic work, and that was nearly a century after the skill of Dr John Thomas (1757-1801), the erratic pioneer Baptist doctor, had opened the way for William Carey to make his first convert – that of the high caste Brahmin Krishna Pal. There was a failure to recognize that the explicit command of Christ was to teach and heal, so well exemplified by his own life on this earth. The one was an integral part of the other especially in the primitive missionary situation faced by the early pioneers. They could not be separated. Even when doctors went out to exercise their healing ministry it was still felt at home that too great an emphasis was placed on the healing of the sick. Nor was the need recognized for hospitals and nurses.

So we trace a few of the early nursing pioneers, with apologies to the very many of whom space does not permit mention in this chapter. There was a certain quality of life about the early pioneers. They were undaunted in the face of difficulty and did not give in easily. In this modern age we can thank God for them and the way in which they blazed the trail in so many pioneer situations. Often they were alone, or perhaps with a woman evangelist, but they had no doctor to look to for guidance, and one realizes all that was involved in caring for the sick, ordering their medicines and many other matters which were far beyond the sphere for which their training fitted them.

One of the earliest pioneers, almost totally unheard of, was Miss Greenfield, a qualified teacher who went out in 1881 to the American Presbyterian School in Ludhiana in the Punjab. She came from Edinburgh and it was not long before she was over-whelmed with the need for medical help which she could not meet. Nevertheless she opened a small dispensary, and immediately sent home for her sister who was a qualified nurse and a Sister at the Great Ormond Street Hospital for Children in London. With her sister she eventually obtained the use of a little old church building, and put in a few beds. Such were the early beginnings of the Brown Memorial Hospital and the Christian Medical College, Ludhiana. Their brother, a wealthy businessman in Edinburgh, gave his financial backing to the whole project. It was to this setting that Dame Edith Brown came when released from the Baptist Missionary Society hospital at Palwal in 1894 (See p.234).

Miss Katharine Timpson, later Lady Cook, an early pioneer nurse of the Church Missionary Society, went out to Uganda with a group of missionaries in 1897. She had been trained at Guy's Hospital, London, and is described by Dr Foster (1978) as 'a woman of formidable character and of handsome if somewhat forbidding appearance'. Dr Albert Cook, another member of the party, was ahead of his time in his vision to establish medical work. He started seeing patients in 1897 in a shed which had been a smithy. The first hospital was of reed walls and grass roof. Ten years later one of wattle and daub was built in the form of a Maltese Cross, and was opened by Sir Harry Johnston. Two years later the 120 tons of grass in the roof was set on fire by lightning and the entire hospital burned to the ground. A new hospital arose out of the ashes, and the slopes of the hills below the great Cathedral are now dotted with permanent buildings, including the first X-ray plant ever erected in Central Africa. Although hindered initially on every side, particularly by theological colleagues, Cook fully realized the necessity of having well-trained nurses to help him. In Katharine, whom he married in 1900, he found the ideal nurse. Tact may not have been her strong point, but she was a woman of indomitable strength of will, and with her vigour, strong personality and nursing ability she will go down in history as one who made a splendid cont-ribution to nursing in Uganda and who shared with her husband and their colleagues the credit for founding the most outstanding medical work in tropical Africa – the Mengo Hospital, Kampala.

In the early years of the 1920s a mass movement to Christianity was in progress among the people in the Delta region of Western Nigeria, bordered by the River Niger and creeks on three sides. Communication was by bush paths, swamped for several months each year as the Niger rose and overflowed its banks. The movement came about as a result of the murder of twins born to a young woman who lived in the village of Igbide. Multiple births were feared, as it was believed that the woman had conceived through the work of an evil spirit. In accordance with tribal tradition therefore the twins were drowned in a neighbouring lake, and the woman, Bribina by name, was driven from home, put in a canoe and sent off to drift away through the lake. Eventually she reached the town of Patani on the Niger, where she landed and was given shelter.

One morning, in her distress and loneliness, she wandered into the little village church, where a service was being conducted by the CMS missionary, the Rev. H. Proctor. She listened to the prayers and became interested in the teaching and in due course was baptized into the Christian Church, taking the name of Rachael. She found peace in the love and friendship of her fellow Christians, eventually feeling impelled to tell her husband and non-Christian friends about the love of God and his goodness to her, and offering it to her own people. Her husband welcomed her home (surely the work of the Holy Spirit) and he and his family and friends accepted her new-found faith. A little church was built on the banks of the lake from which she had been exiled and, as more and more people became Christians, a new village grew up around the church and was named Owodokpokpo, meaning the New Town. Rachael became a leader among the women, persuading them to get rid of their idols.

The thrilling part of this story, told so ably by Doris Rose, is that later the women became quite desperate to have help while in childbirth, and for their children. An appeal was made to the CMS, and in 1929 Doris Rose, a nursing sister, and Margaret Sheath, an evangelist, were sent out. They lived in mud huts, under primitive pioneering conditions in an almost inaccessible area. They were faced with many difficulties, and the District Officer, living some ten miles away, was fearful for their safety, and kept a close watch on their comings and goings, but they were received warmly by the people. They were faced, however, with a quite terrifying prospect: many maternal deaths, a high mortality among the babies, rampant tetanus and sepsis, wrong feeding, children with kwashiorkor, hookworm, and other intestinal troubles, women with fevers and yaws. A daunting task, but one carried out with great faith and loving compassion.

Eventually a school was built, women were taught simple, safe and clean midwifery, and the mortality rate among the babies was greatly reduced. The Church grew and thrived. Under the tuition of Miss Rose and Miss Sheath, the women learned to read the Gospels, to knit and sew and keep their houses clean. They themselves carried out antenatal care, and brought difficult cases for professional help. The first child born at Bethel, one of the three villages covered by the gallant pair, is now an influential member of the Nigerian Government. A girl born there at about the same time is now an SRN, midwife and tutor at the Harcourt Hospital, and married to a Nigerian judge.

In Zaire, formerly the Belgian Congo, wonderful pioneering work was carried out by nurses in remote areas. As early as 1908 a hospital was founded at Bolobo; and later others at Tondo, Pimu and Yakusu, pioneered by the BMS. One of the early pioneers was Nurse Petrie from Aberdeen. In those days evil and superstition had to be overcome as well as many practical difficulties. The hospital at Yakusu was an outstanding centre for the training of *infirmiers*, young African men who became medical auxiliaries, and carried out marvellous work in holding clinics and supervising dispensaries in outlying villages. Although there are no nursing training schools equivalent to those set up in West Africa and India, there is a two year training course for female nurses which is supplementary to the *infirmier* training.

Tribute must be paid to the many nurses who carried on alone after the recent troubles there, when European doctors were unavailable. Left alone to carry the entire burden of the clinics and all the administrative work, they continued to bear witness to the excellence of their service. One who carried on in this situation was Miss Fagg, who finally came home to retire in 1974. A new hospital was built at Bolobo but, because of lack of doctors, it had to be handed over to a government agency, though missionary nursing sisters continued to serve under the new regime. The hospital has now come back into BMS hands, and Dr David Masters and the nursing personnel are labouring in Christ's name to build up the hospital's contacts and reputation.

Equally typical of the pioneer work of missionary nurses is

the following extract from the report of Sister F.G. Butlin in *The Mission Hospital* in 1929, based on her experience in visiting around thirty unevangelized villages in Jordan within the course of a year:

'Houses are difficult to secure, so I opened a school in my house in the dispensary room. This was rapidly filled with twenty pupils, and I saw patients in the passage where I sleep. The Bible woman also used the dispensary for her bedroom. No extravagance here . . .

The dispensary work is heavy and I think every child in Garish has had measles. As the doctor is away on the district, the sick have to depend on me. How splendid it would be if we had a hospital at Ajlun, instead of being obliged to send serious cases to Amman by car, which takes two-and-a-half-hours. It requires courage to work on at Gerash, but, thank God, there is improvement in the children, and we must sow the seed, trusting God to give the increase.'

The long established Church of Scotland hospital in Nazareth is another centre where many nurses have played an important part in helping to cope with the ever-recurring problems of this disturbed part of the world.

The missionary personnel in Papua New Guinea came from many countries: Continental Europe, the United Kingdom, Australia, New Zealand, Ireland and Canada. One of the pioneers was Mary Woolnough, a Methodist who had only taken a St John's Ambulance Brigade course. At that time the Methodists, like other missionary societies, were not particularly calling for trained nurses. The shortage of equipment she had to endure is admirably exemplified in her report in 1921 of having to suture with an ordinary needle and hair out of the Mission horse's tail. Rosette Keppler, a Swiss member of the Lutheran Church, who arrived in New Guinea in 1904, was another pioneer nurse. Besides doing general nursing, she served as field midwife to the Mission wives along the coast, delivering the babies and caring for the families at the same time. In thirty-eight years of midwifery she never lost either a mother or a baby, claiming that much of her success was due to having learned to wait patiently for Nature to do its part in delivery. As a kind understanding midwife she had confidence and helped the mothers to relax, a factor which greatly reduced complications. By 1954 the Church missions jointly had 96 centres providing maternal and child health services.

A small building in the centre of the busy Indian bazaar in

Ludhiana in the Punjab, North India, marked the beginning in 1881 of the Brown Memorial Hospital, named after its founder, Dame Edith Brown. As has been said, the hospital just grew and grew like Topsy, with wards and departments being added to meet the ever-increasing demands made on it by patients. Miss Henderson was the first nursing superintendent, followed by Miss Mason, a tall, gracious, able lady with a military bearing, who made an outstanding contribution to nursing, not only in Ludhiana, but all over the Punjab. For many years the work of the maternity unit and domiciliary midwifery was carried out by trained nurse *dais* under the guidance of European midwives.

Upgrading of Nursing

I was first introduced to Ludhiana, in which I spent many happy years, during the days of partition, when the hospital staff performed a gigantic task caring for the wounded of all communities. Previously, nurse training had only been of B grade, the nurses having to complete six months in a government hospital in order to gain the grade A certificate. When it became a general hospital in 1948, Ludhiana was immediately recognized for grade A training, and nurses from Christian hospitals all over the Punjab, and farther afield, and the many zenana hospitals, came to gain the top A grading. The upgrading of both the hospital and the nurses' training, achieved in spite of the sorrow and suffering involved in the loss of a million lives at partition, was a major step in raising the status of nursing in India.

The Holdsworth Memorial Hospital in Mysore is one of the outstanding nurse training schools in South India. Miss Campbell, appointed in 1909, was the earliest nursing superintendent. Typical of the difficulties facing these early pioneers is the case of one patient who was in the hospital for three years. Admitted in a desperate condition, she was so cared for that she was able to do many things in the ward and help in many ways. She did so well that a scholarship was provided and she was trained as far as possible in a practical way, though she was unable to read or write. Throughout the years nurse training progressed, but it was not until the 1950s that suitable candidates began to come forward in any number.

In 1945 there was only one suitable candidate for ten places, and the missionary personnel had to accept as nurse *dais* girls whose qualifications were below the accepted educational standard. The staff were faced with continual problems, not the least of which was that these early accepted candidates left one by one until finally only one remained. In 1955, the Jubilee year, however, 150 girls from all over South India applied for only twenty-two places. All had a good standard of education but spoke many languages. To overcome this multiplicity of languages, all teaching is now in English. In the hospital at Mysore, the latest step has been the opening of a men's department in 1951. This immediately raised the standard of the hospital and the training school to that of a general training school, and the granting of the grade A2 certificate, which has reciprocity with equivalent certificates of the General Nursing Council for England and Wales.

In 1908 the Trained Nurses Association of India was formed, but was not affiliated with the International Nursing Council until 1924. In 1931 the Nursing Auxiliary was formed which, together with the state government, recognized training schools. The Indian Nursing Council, established in 1947, is responsible to the central government for all nursing legislation, and works towards uniformity.

After the partition of the Indian subcontinent, with many English nurses leaving India, the Indian government, as already noted, set up an Indian Nursing Council which proposed to appoint a superintendent of nursing services in each state. Initially there were not sufficient candidates with the requisite experience to fill these offices. To cope with the situation in Assam, Colonel Bhatia, the inspector general of civil hospitals in Assam proposed that Miss Amy Bullock, a missionary nursing sister with the Welsh Mission, should take up this post. Although the Mission was short of nursing sisters, the Welsh Mission gallantly released her for the greater benefit of the state and she took over this crucial appointment in 1947.

One of the major practical problems in Assam was its division into districts, each with different tribes and languages. Miss Bullock therefore set out to establish a training school in each district. She visited all the civil hospitals, making many perilous mountain journeys, and succeeded in placing trained Christian staff from four of them as a nucleus in different training schools. One of the major problems was that it was against the Hindu religion for a woman to do such work. It was easy to get tribal girls, but these were lacking in education. At first therefore the authorities had to be content with a low standard, but once the tribal girls began their training they learned quickly and became quite fluent in English. Nurses were examined in ten languages, and Miss Bullock travelled the length and breadth of the state, advising, encouraging, helping to solve local problems, and carrying out the practical and oral examinations with a doctor.

Bangladesh, formerly West Bengal, the stronghold of the early pioneer work of William Carey, has its main hospital at Chandraghona, which is also a training school for nurses. During the birth of the new country the hospital staff were taxed to the utmost. The river behind the BMS hospital was all too often turned into a river of blood. Miss Jean Westlake did a magnificent job with her colleagues. One of the nursing sisters, Christine Preston, was released to work with the Christian Medical Association to visit the many government hospitals and provide encouragement for the staff in India and Bangladesh.

In Kathmandu, the capital of Nepal, there is a new hospital, which includes an excellent nurse training school, staffed by graduate nurses trained at Ludhiana and Delhi. In this and other smaller hospitals, as well as dispensaries and clinics, nurses from different countries and different denominations are serving together, many under the United Mission to Nepal. There is close liaison with the government senior nursing personnel, and it is most impressive that Nepali girls are being trained to serve their own people in a Christian environment.

Perhaps my most vivid memory of a visit I had the privilege of paying to this fascinating country was of a small village leprosy hospital, where a Scottish nurse was carrying on alone with great courage and fortitude and not a complaint – the quintessence of Christian service.

A school for practical nurses was started from small beginnings after the opening of the Manorom Christian Hospital in Thailand. Two of the original group of nurses are still giving loyal service. Every year an increasing number of students from all over the country apply for training. In 1976 400 sat the entrance examination for 25 places. There were 60 students in the 3-year programme and another 70 graduates staffing the hospital. A number have come to know Christ while at the hospital, while others have been strengthened and built up in their Christian faith. Many graduates are now working in hospitals throughout the country. By 1978 government policy on the training of practical nurses changed and it was no longer possible to train nurses to this standard, but the training of a lower grade of nurse was permitted. Several practical nurses went to England for further training, and have returned to strengthen the nursing team in the hospital. Some years ago three girls were able to take advantage of a scholarship provided by the Danish government, and received full nurse training in Copenhagen. They returned to work at Manorom where they made an excellent contribution, one of them still being on the staff.

In West Africa nursing was an honourable profession from the start, and in earlier years attracted more young men than women. At first it fell to individual sisters and doctors to train the assistants they needed, and in those days, when standard VI was the highest level of education available, training had to be simple, direct and practical. Nothing could be taken for granted. It used to be part of the routine to demonstrate to each successive fresh class of students what boiling water actually was; so many of them had no clear idea of what this meant. So we solemnly sat there while a saucepan of water was boiled on a primus stove, and each student was asked to indicate when he or she thought the water was boiling. The results were surprising, but Africans make apt students. Lessons were quickly learned, and there was a thirst for knowledge, which made teaching a pleasure. It was astonishing how much semi-literate helpers could absorb, and there is more than one hospital labourer who, on occasion, has proved a valuable surgical assistant.

As hospitals developed, the demand for nurses grew, and with it the need for more standardized training and duties. For a number of years the responsibility for training remained local. With the introduction of state registration, standards have continually been raised. The high standard of training at Christian hospitals encouraged cooperation between the government and the National Christian Council of Nigeria. The resultant uniform standards of professional ability have given nursing in that country its present high status. There is now abundant evidence in Britain that West Africans, like West Indians, make extremely good nurses. As in India, training in a Christian setting has given the two-fold emphasis: science and skill on the one hand, and integrity and humanity on the other. In West Africa today some of the best nurse training schools with highly qualified African staff holding degrees are equal to anything to be found in the United Kingdom.

Throughout Sierra Leone, from the capital to the smallest villages, in all sorts of hospitals and clinics, are Christian nurses and midwives who were trained at the Nixon Memorial Hospital. Most of them are highly respected and well liked by employers and patients, especially for their caring attitude to patients of whatever tribe or language. The nursing school at the Nixon Hospital was pioneered by Elsie Fielding, SRN, SCM, backed by Dr John R. Ross. Its aim has always been 'to train Christian nurses and midwives', and its motto is Florence Nightingale's 'Enter in to learn, go out to serve'.

One of the most fascinating accounts of missionary endeavour is to be found in the book by Dr James Fanstone, which tells the amazing story of the Anapolis Hospital in Brazil. Notable in this record is the pioneer work done by British nurses. The first of these was Dr Fanstone's wife, Baird. She was shortly joined by Mary Hamilton and Alice Callear, and this gallant quartet, starting in a simple primitive set-up, laid the basis of what is now one of the best hospitals in Brazil. From the onset they encouraged educated Brazilian girls to take up nursing as a career.

It was later, when Isa MacIntyre, who had trained at the Western Infirmary, Glasgow, joined them that the training of nurses began in earnest. Isa, the eldest daughter of the pioneer missionaries, the Rev. and Mrs Archibald MacIntyre, had been born in Brazil. Working under the auspices of the Evangelical Union of South America, she established the Florence Nightingale Nursing School. This was recognized by the federal government, and such was its standard that, on completion of their training, the nurses were in demand all over the country. For long it was one of only three nursing schools in the whole of South America.

So successful was she that the government asked the Anapolis Hospital to release her to set up nursing schools in more rural areas throughout Northern Brazil. In these, Christian witness and evangelical efforts were an integral part of training, and many of these Brazilian trained nurses maintain their Christian witness wherever they serve.

When her elderly parents returned to Scotland after a lifetime of service for Christ in Brazil, Isa returned home to join her sister Mamie, who had been a BMS missionary nurse in Zaire, in looking after their parents. When her father died in 1982, a few months before his 100th birthday, Isa returned to Brazil to join her brother Tom, an ordained missionary in Anapolis, but during a visit to the UK she died on October 10 1983 after a short illness, having given a lifetime of service to the country of her birth.

Development of Midwifery Training
Midwifery is a branch of medical care in which Christian hospitals have taken a leading part; in point of time it sometimes

took precendence over general nursing. Its development is well exemplified by experience in India. Here the needs of women in childbirth were so overwhelming that demands were made to meet them long before the dawn of emancipation of Indian women permitted nursing training. Miss Hewlett of the Church of England Zenana Missionary Society gained the first real success by training indigenous *dais* (midwives) in the Amritsar school. The profession of *dai* is hereditary. They are low caste, and force is the only remedy they know for sluggish or difficult labour. No wonder the public health commissioner of the government of India commented in 1938 that 'the percentage of women disabled as a result of pregnancy and labour may perhaps be taken as not less than 30 per cent in a country where 10,000,000 births are registered annually'!

Miss Hewlett insisted on: 1. Regular attendance at classes; 2. General good conduct; 3. Reporting of their cases; 4 Calling the teacher in all difficulties.

This plan is still the best of all attempts at training *dais*, according to Dr Ruth Young, principal of Lady Harding Medical College, Delhi but, unless the confidence and cooperation of the *dais* can be gained, and their remuneration assured, and unless they can be linked to a hospital, many feel that full midwifery training is more profitable and of more permanent value. This is being given increasingly in the many nursing schools attached to the 250 mission hospitals in India, Burma and Sri Lanka. Dr Kheroth Bose, who continued Miss Hewlett's work most successfully after her retirement in 1930, wrote:

'The fact is that, when women have had extensive experience and practice and are taught the theory of normal and abnormal labour intelligently, they are able to relate practice and experience in a way the other trained midwives are unable to with years of experience. Facts first and deduction and theories to follow is the ideal method of education for the students, but facts are often hard things for the patients.'

Simultaneously Dame Edith Brown, first in the Baptist Mission Hospital at Palwal, North India, and then from 1894 at the Brown Memorial Hospital in Ludhiana, taught and trained *dais*, paying them one rupee to report difficult cases and seek help. This was the firstfruit of one of the most forward centres of midwifery training in India, resulting in a network of domiciliary midwifery to all the homes in the urban and rural district of Ludhiana. Today the midwifery department is entirely in the hands of national professional staff, and training has risen to the level where one MSc Ludhiana graduate is teaching midwifery in the college of nursing, while another is doing practical domiciliary midwifery in the homes of the people around the city. To those of us who have had the privilege of watching the development of midwifery in Ludhiana, this is a story by itself of sheer grit and endeavour.

In Uganda Lady Cook, after acting as Matron of the Mengo Hospital for twenty-one years, devoted the rest of her life to the establishment and direction of the Lady Coryndon Maternity Training School. She was well backed by the government, which was becoming alarmed at Uganda's mortality statistics. Venereal disease was rampant, and infant mortality was three to four times higher than in Britain. To take young unmarried women and train them as midwives was a new venture, fraught with grave moral risks for the girls, and cutting right across native sentiment. Conservatism preserved the time-honoured old women (and trained them as midwives) whose masterly inactivity in normal cases was more helpful than their interference in abnormal ones. But the venture succeeded and a steady stream of certified midwives flowed from the School all over the African continent, proving their worth in values far higher than the traditional bride price.

No less noteworthy, but with far less help and support, has been the work of Miss Elms, of the CMS at Iyi Enu in Nigeria. For thirteen years, without a doctor, she successfully fought twin murder by means of her refugeee home, and infant mortality by the training of nurse-midwives. In 1926 she had a hospital of 100 beds ready for the doctor when he arrived. Women's conferences, baby shows and village maternity centres have all arisen from the inspiration and energy of this indefatigable worker. Today in Iyi Enu the midwifery training holds an honoured place in West Africa. Throughout Nigeria the resulting rapid spread of maternity homes caused a great demand for midwives, and every mission hospital able to provide sufficient facilities has been pressed into service. In this sphere the Methodist hospitals have played a leading role, and young trained midwives have shown great courage in travelling long distances through the bush and tackling really difficult deliveries.

In Sierra Leone midwifery training was pioneered by Sister Ivy Cook, with Dr E.E. Johnson, building on the foundations laid by previous nursing sisters such as Blanche Harper, Dorothy Heaf and Olive Robertson. The work was made possible by the building of a maternity unit, opened in 1949, funded (as a memorial to his late wife) by Alderman John G. Nixon, twice Lord Mayor of Newcastle-upon-Tyne and a life-long supporter of the overseas medical mission of the Methodist Church. At first it was largely in-service training, but successive sisters in charge, particularly Joyce Sorfleet and Linda Turnbull, introduced theoretical training until, in the 1960s, students were permitted to enter for the SCM examination and the national staff midwives on hospital staff were recognized as SCM (SL). At the same time training as maternity assistant was given to women who had taken at least one year's training in general nursing, but whose standard was not high enough for full midwifery training. In the 1970s a midwifery school was established in conjunction with the maternity unit of a nearby Roman Catholic hospital, the two units sharing one midwifery tutor. This was registered by the Central Midwives Board of the UK as a recognized training school.

Standardizing of School training

Over the years each country has gradually established nursing councils, which are the controlling bodies for devising the syllabus and the supervising of nurses' examinations. A uniform pattern has emerged in most countries, missionary nurses again leading the way. In Southeast Asia, India, China, parts of Africa, Brazil and, more recently, Bangladesh, Pakistan and Nepal, where British personnel were particularly involved, the pattern of the British General Nursing Council mode of examinations and uniform training emerged.

One of the early developments in this field was the formation of the Trained Nurses' Association of India in 1908. In India the period from 1920 to 1939 saw the extension of training for midwives and health visitors. The first Nurses Registration Act was passed in 1926, and by 1939 nursing councils were established in all the provinces except Assam. As there were no facilities for postbasic programmes in India, a number of nurses went to Britain for courses in nursing education, public health nursing and midwifery. In 1947 a Nursing Auxiliary Service was created which had a recognized nursing course of at least two years' duration with emphasis on midwifery. In 1942 a chief nursing superintendent was appointed to organize the service and to be nursing adviser to the director of medical services. The following year the government established a School of Nursing

Administration, and a one-year course was started to prepare nursing teachers. In 1946 courses leading to a BSc degree in nursing were established by the Universities of Delhi and Madras and the Christian Medical College, Vellore. The report of the Bhore Committee in 1946 advocated an Indian Nursing Council Act, and this was passed in 1947.

The All-India Nursing Council held its first meeting in 1949, and carried out a survey of a cross-section of training centres in India. A course was established for auxiliary nurse midwives. In 1954 a committee was appointed by the government to review conditions of service for nurses and midwives. Among its recommendations was the appointment of a superintendent in each state, and that there should be no separation between insti-tutional and public health nurses. A master's degree in nursing was established in the University of Delhi in 1959.

With the British withdrawal from India, partition made a great impact on the role of all Christian hospitals, particularly in North India. The new large Hindu and Sikh population, with Muslims ultimately in the minority, was more open and liberal in its thinking, so that general nursing training as we know it in Britain became acceptable. Small isolated training schools were able to link up with major teaching hospitals such as the Brown Memorial Hospital in Ludhiana, thus giving opportunities to many nurses to take the full Grade A training. Before 1947 there were two grades of training in India: Grade A and Grade B, the latter being confined to those nurses who had not nursed male patients, and could not be on the general register. This had meant that Christian nurses had to serve six months in a government hospital in order to obtain this certificate, which enjoyed full reciprocity with the General Nursing Council in Britain.

There also existed the examinations of the nursing auxiliary of the Christian Medical Association of India (CMAI) in which Miss Alice Chacke played such a prominent role. India being such a vast country, the CMAI examinations were taken by those in other states such as Hyderabad, Mysore, Baroda, and other areas. In 1949, I had the privilege of attending a conference of the Trained Nurses' Association of India in Calcutta; to one who had only been in the country for two years it was a revelation to witness the large number of educated national nurses taking a leading part. The president was Miss Adranwala, a Parsee, and the first director of nursing of India appointed by the Indian government. Later she became a staunch ally and friend, strongly supporting Christian hospitals the length and breadth of India. Mention must also be made of Miss Wilkinson of the SPG and Miss Hampton of the BMS, two early pioneers in the initiation of national nursing councils.

In China the initial progress of nursing was slower, but in 1912, under the stimulus of Miss Gage, a missionary nurse in Hunan, the Nurses' Association of China (NAC) was founded. This immediately placed nursing in China on a national footing, and set standards which were later to be accepted by the government as its own. The first national conference of the Association met in Shanghai in 1914. One of its functions was to coin a word for 'nurse'. With the help of an eminent Chinese scholar, two beautiful characters were associated to form the expression *Hu Shi*, meaning 'a scholar who cherishes life'. The following year Methodist hospitals in Central China were registered with the Association, and diplomas awarded to the first three successful students, the advance guard of an ever-increasing army bringing health and happiness to China.

The Nurses' Association developed rapidly, and in 1934 Sister Gladys Stephenson, the first president of the Association, was able to comment:

'Twenty years ago it was difficult to obtain any educated young people who would look on nursing as a worthy life's work. Now there are over 160 schools of nursing registered under the Nurses' Association of China, and nearly 4000 Chinese nurses have obtained the NAC Diploma. All our past work seems a preparation for the great day of opportunity that has come upon us.'

In 1922 the Association had been admitted to membership of the International Council of Nurses, taking precedence over France and Japan.

India, too, of course is affiliated to the International Council of Nurses, thus typifying how in many countries missionary nurses are taking the lead in setting standards, and constantly looking forward, absorbing the best of the West, and relating it in the training of nurses and midwives to the culture and benefit of the country in which God has placed them.

Degree courses in nursing
In 1963 I had the privilege of being seconded to the government of India to set up nursing services in the recently established Institute of Education and Research in Chandigarh, the completely new city, planned by the famous French architect, Le Corbusier, as joint capital of the Punjab and Haryana. Many

Christian nurses joined the staff, and it was not long before an active nurses' fellowship was formed. In addition, a group of Christian students from many parts of the world, who were studying in the University in Chandigarh, attended a weekly Bible study group. They came from West Africa, Thailand, Israel, New Zealand and many other countries. The Christian witness of those students had far-reaching effects, not least on the prominent government officials treated in the hospital.

After my return to Ludhiana as Director of Nursing, the University of Chandigarh, through its Institute, initiated plans for a degree in nursing. This, we felt, should be wholly hospital-centred at Ludhiana, and we set out to draw up a syllabus. In due course there was a link up with the Institute and after many months of negotiations we succeeded in evolving a joint syllabus for presentation to the University. It was a matter for deep thanksgiving when this was accepted. During all our deliberations we had been praying for guidance in working with the government so that the hospital-based syllabus, put forward jointly, but basically by Ludhiana, should be accepted, and not a sophisticated one which would distance the trainees from the Hospital. In 1972 the first students for the basic degree course were accepted for the College of Nursing in Ludhiana.

On my return to Ludhiana in March 1981 for the centenary celebrations of the Hospital, it was a great joy to witness the entire nursing department making such magnificent progress: highly qualified nurses holding masterships, many having specialized in branches such as paediatrics and community health. All were housed in a beautiful college of nursing built with generous gifts from USA and West Germany. In 1981 there were 160 taking the basic degree course, the majority of them Christians, 25 of them receiving their degrees from Punjab University, and for the third year running one of them receiving a gold medal. In addition, there were around 200 in the diploma course, 29 of whom received their diplomas on this occasion. It was a great privilege to return to the Institute at Chandigarh and find a strong faculty, several Christians in top posts, the College thriving and, perhaps above all, a strong Christian witness in the government hospital.

In encouraging and facilitating these developments in Ludhiana much is owed to the Vellore Medical College which pioneered the first degree course in a Christian college, and this close collaboration is being happily sustained. One of the notable features of the Vellore nursing training is the emphasis on community nursing and training nurses for outreach into the villages. This is now a characteristic of all nursing training, diploma or degree, in India, the aim being to meet the policy of the government to promote and complement primary health care programmes in order to achieve the World Health Organization goal of 'Health for All by the Year 2000'.

One wonders to what extent the early missionary pioneers foresaw that their God-given initiatives could reach out to such an extent, with such a width of vision, meeting the basic needs of mankind in caring and compassion and through skill and education, setting out to accomplish the ideals that Florence Nightingale repeatedly stressed: that skills must be learned.

Community health outreach

In many missionary hospitals all over the world Christians have led the way in pioneering community health, which now ranks high in the priority list in all developing countries. This is no new concept, as the early pioneers, both doctors and nurses, strove to reach out into the villages, but all too often this proved impossible since staff could not be spared from busy hospitals and teaching centres. In recent years, however, there has been a growing realization that there must be an organized outreach into the community. This is happening in many different countries as exemplified, for example, in the expansion from the Vellore Medical College in South India and the Ludhiana Christian Medical College in North India.

In the latter, for instance, teams consisting of doctors, public health nurses, auxiliary nurses and trained nurse dais radiate out into the rural areas from the central hospital and two satellite hospitals, each covering a population of around 4000. A similar programme is now under way in the urban area around the central hospital which is densely populated and where the people live in poor circumstances. Here the problem is not so much poverty, but lack of training in healthy living, in providing a healthy diet for themselves and their children and in taking full advantage of the facilities for antenatal, postnatal and child welfare clinics. So successful has this scheme been over the last decade that it has now been taken over by the Punjab Department of Health, with missionary and government personnel working in close collaboration. Nurses from the College of Nursing are not only heading many of these teams, but are also teaching community health to trainee nurses.

As a result, all over India, priority is now being given to the training of nurses in community health in order to meet the needs of the rural areas. Many smaller hospitals throughout India are at present playing a leading role in this sphere, doing a splendid pioneer task. Teams of young nursing students, with their leaders, are making their way in and out of the homes they visit. All too often, alas, they have doors slammed in their faces and they turn away saddened – but press on in their mission of compassion.

Retrospect and prospect

During the past century progress in nursing services has continued. Nursing leaders all over the world have gone forward with vision and purpose. Today in many countries, the entire nursing services are in the hands of well-trained and well-equipped national staff. The early pioneers could not have foreseen the wonderful network of medical and nursing programmes which has spread all over the world. Christian medical missionaries were the pioneers, leading the way in every field of service.

We have come a long way from the days of the untrained assistant nurse and nurse *dai*, as we realize when we view the current scene.

Colleges of Nursing granting degrees;

Post-certificate courses both at hospital and college level over a wide clinical area;

Great strides in child care and maternal and infant welfare;

Community nursing services penetrating from the main hospital to the very heart of the most backward rural areas;

Networks of domiciliary services;

Antenatal and postnatal services;

Advances in the nursing of leprosy patients, no longer shunned by national nurses, but treated with loving kindness and, thanks to medical research, having high hopes for the morrow held out for them;

Rehabilitation services pioneered by Christian doctors with nursing colleagues alongside;

The restoring of sight to the blind by the many eye camps held in the villages; the pioneering of ophthalmic training for nurses in the outlying small Christian hospitals.

When one pauses to think of the thousands and thousands of Christians all over the world who, by their giving and prayers, have made all this possible, one cannot but be filled with thanksgiving to Almighty God.

Sir Clement Chesterman wrote in 1936:

'It would be a sad twilight for medical missions if ever the day comes when they can no longer send out their offspring like the twelve and the seventy, and share their joy as they return to relate their conquests of healing.'

Today nurses are still going out to the far reaches of the earth, and bring succour and comfort to the ailing and the sick. The younger generation is still inspired by their Christian faith, and goes out to practise the healing art as exemplified by Christ himself. In this noble partnership, the profession of nursing has occupied a position of which it has every reason to be proud.

References

Chesterman, Clement (1936) In the Service of Suffering London: The Carey Press

Fanstone, Baird (Ed.) (1972) Missionary Adventure in Brazil Worthing: Henry E. Walter

Foster, W.D. (1978) The Church Missionary Society and Modern Medicine in Uganda. The life of Sir Albert Cook, KCMG (1870-1951) Privately printed.

CHAPTER 14

THE CONTRIBUTION BY
WOMEN MEDICAL MISSIONARIES

F.T. Davey and W.A.R. Thomson

In the annals of the history of the Christian Church, the medical profession and the service of women to humanity there are few, if any, more inspiring records than that of the contribution of women medical missionaries. For some reason these faithful servants have never received the gratitude and tribute to which they are entitled, and one of these days their tale will need to be told.

In this chapter the authors concentrate on India, China and Africa but recognize that other areas like South and Central America and the South Seas had their missionary heroines too.

India
The background is admirably exemplified by Dr Margaret Balfour, the first chief medical officer of the Women's Medical Service, India (Balfour and Young, 1929).

'In 1866, a civil surgeon, Dr Aitchison, opened a class for *dais* at Amritsar, which struggled on through many vicissitudes and changes of teachers, and became in the 80s the well-known Amritsar *Dais'* School, under Miss Hewlett of the Church of England Zenana Missionary Society, one of the first of the women pioneers who initiated relief for Indian women.

Most of the pioneers [they were medically unqualified] came to India as Zenana missionaries and, scattered in different parts of the country, came to the same horrifying realization of the fatal and almost unspeakable tragedies which were common events in the Zenanas they visited.

The missionaries soon realized the futility of trying to act as go-betweens, describing symptoms, and conveying bottles of medicine to and fro. Better to do what they could, as so many European officers did in those days, with their medicine chests, common sense, and the wisdom which experience soon began to give.

Medical books were begged from friends and the first

furlough was often the opportunity of haunting hospitals or friendly consulting-rooms in the endeavour to pick up all that might be used for the women of India.

Unfortunately, there were not many facilities in these days of the 60s and 70s for giving medical knowledge to women. One well-known missionary disguised herself as a nurse, and so was enabled to be present at her brother's clinics in a famous hospital. Institutions began to spring up where a short training in medicine and midwifery was given to missionaries. Many took advantage of this.

In any case the return after furlough usually showed more medical work. The Zenanas were still visited, but a room was taken where women were encouraged to come in and bring their babies for advice and simple remedies. Some bold spirits acquired pocket-cases and performed minor operations, and as time passed, major operations too. The need for a few beds for patients from a distance was soon apparent, and it was found that government officials were very ready to give what support and help they could.

Bible women were trained as rough and ready assistants with girls from Christian schools to help them. And in many cases the work, begun as a side issue and in response to the dictates of humanity, became a great success, the main purpose of the mission station, and requiring the employment of a large staff'.

The honour of sending the first qualified medical woman to India belongs to the United States of America. On January 2 1870 Miss Clara Swain, MD [Penn] arrived in Bareilly under the aegis of the Women's Foreign Missionary Society of the Methodist Episcopal Church. She opened a dispensary in 1873 and a hospital the following year. Such became her reputation that in 1885 she was asked by the Rajah of Khetri to become physician to his Rani and her ladies, an invitation she accepted on condition that she was allowed to continue Christian work. She finally left India ten years later. She died in 1910 at the age of 76.

The first qualified woman from the United Kingdom was Dr Fanny Butler, who was sent out in 1880 by the Church of England Zenana Missionary Society. Unfortunately, she died nine years later. One of her claims to fame is that she was one of the first fourteen women admitted to the London School of Medicine for Women when it opened in 1874 in association with the Royal Free Hospital. The roll of honour for women mission-aries of the Royal Free Hospital, composed by Professor Ruth

Bowden, with its 233 names, is a notable tribute to the services of those women who qualified at this hospital and then devoted their lives to the service of Christ (Bowden, 1975). Almost simultaneously a trickle of young women began to qualify from the Scottish Universities, particularly Edinburgh, and many went out to the mission field.

Another from the Royal Free Hospital was Dr Jennie Muller who qualified in 1897 and then went to Delhi. The task she took over was that founded by Mrs Winter, the wife of a missionary of the Society for the Propagation of the Gospel who was sent to Delhi in 1860, three years after the Indian Mutiny. Mrs Winter found the condition of the women so distressing that she opened the first dispensary for women and children in the notorious Chandri Chowk. In due course she set her heart on a hospital for women but never survived to see it, as she died in 1881. Four years later, St Stephen's Hospital was opened, and in due course Dr Muller joined it and gradually witnessed, and participated in, its growth without the city walls, to become in time one of the most prominent hospitals in the country.

Notable among these early Scottish recruits to India was Dr Agnes Henderson. She spent her life in Nagpur under the aegis of the United Free Church of Scotland. She was responsible for founding the Nagpur Hospital, called by Dr Margaret Balfour 'one of the best mission hospitals for women in India'. Dr Balfour described her as 'a woman of great ability, whose services to India met with their best award in the boundless love and devotion of the people among whom she worked'. When precluded by health from continuing her active hospital work, she took a house in Nagpur and carried on what has been described as 'a wonderful work' among the city *dais*. She also introduced the novel idea of training the children of the *dais*, for whom she introduced a Montessori school. She died in 1925. Writing in 1929, Dr Balfour commented: 'Dr Henderson's name is still one to conjure with in Nagpur and the surrounding districts'.

More dramatic, perhaps, is the tale of Miss Elizabeth Bielby, who arrived in Lucknow in 1876 under the Zenana Bible and Medical Mission. Although not medically qualified, she succeeded in opening a hospital for women, but in 1881 she decided to return to London to qualify at the Royal Free Hospital. Such was the reputation she had already achieved that she was asked by the Maharajah of Punna to visit the Maharani, his sick wife. Happily her medical knowledge, skilfully applied, effected a

complete recovery. On paying a farewell visit to the Maharani
before leaving for London, she was asked to: 'Tell the Queen and
the Prince and Princess of Wales, and the men and women of
England, what the women of India suffer when they are sick',
and to carry an appeal for more women doctors to be sent to
India. This message she was asked to give to the Queen in a silver
locket.

In due course, after her arrival in England, Dr Bielby was
admitted to a personal interview at Windsor Castle with Queen
Victoria, who listened to her with much interest and asked many
questions. In her journal the Queen wrote:

> 'Received a Miss Bielby, a medical missionary, who had
> attended the Maharani of Punna, and brought a large silver locket
> containing a petition from the latter, praying me to sanction
> female doctors being sent out to attend the ladies in the zenanas
> of India, many of whom died for want of proper medical atten-
> dance, no man being allowed to go near them. Miss Bielby gave a
> melancholy account of these poor ladies, and of the widows, or
> in fact, only betrothed women, who were treated like menials,
> from the moment their bridegrooms died. I expressed my deep
> interest and hope that something might be done in this matter'.

As the interview concluded, the Queen commented,

> 'we had no idea it was as bad as this; something must be done for
> these poor creatures', and she gave Miss Bielby a reply to take to
> the Maharani. She then made a statement which she said could
> be quoted wherever it might do good: 'We should wish it to be
> generally known that we sympathize with every effort made to
> relieve the suffering state of the women of India'.

In 1884 the Queen fulfilled her promise to the Maharani by
telling Lady Dufferin, the wife of the new Viceroy, that she must
do something to meet this demand for women doctors. This
Lady Dufferin duly did as best she could, and set up the National
Association for Supplying Female Aid to the Women of India. In
time Dufferin Hospitals were established but the supply of
women doctors was far from satisfactory. Why neither the
Indian government, nor the British government, nor the citizens
of the British Isles responded to the appeal of Queen Victoria is a
distressing commentary on the failure of a traditional Christian
people to ensure that the women and children of India should
receive the care so clearly expressed in the faith of the Christian
church.

Miss Bielby returned to India on qualifying in 1885 to take
charge of a hospital for women to be opened by the Lahore

Municipal Committee. Known as the Lady Aitchison Hospital, it was opened in 1888. After some fifteen years she resigned from the hospital and went into private practice in Lahore until she retired in 1927.

One more example will be quoted of the service of these women medical missionaries – that of Dr Ethel Douglas, who qualified from the Royal Free Hospital in 1908. Two years later she joined the staff of the Kinnaird Memorial Hospital in Lucknow as a member of the Zenana and Bible Medical Mission. Within nine months she was in charge of it and remained so until her retirement in 1946. Her description of the state of affairs at the hospital can never be forgotten:

'Poverty, ignorance, superstition, caste, the purdah system and the amazing contrast between poor and rich . . . Midwifery cases were brought in extremis when the untrained dai had done her worst. Surgical cases were few and even a simple abscess was allowed to go untreated until it became enormous and burst, rather than allow incision under an anaesthetic. Abdominal operations were always refused, the patient being taken to some hakim quack. It took many years for patients to have even hypo-dermic injections, and the Shia Mahommedans would always consult their beads to see if it was "the will of God". I remember patients leaving hospital rather than have an injection'.

To the inhabitants of Lucknow the hospital soon became known as the 'Douglas Hospital', to which they flocked in increasing numbers during the 36 years she was in charge of it. Over these decades her attraction was a combination of what has been described as 'all-embracing sympathy and devastating genero-sity, undoubted and great skill, all carried out in the Name of and for the sake of Him who came that we might have life'.

In 1927 she received the Kaiser-i-Hind Gold Medal, the cita-tion for which, when it was bestowed upon her in Government House, provides an apt tribute to a famous name in the annals of medical missions.

'Dr Ethel Douglas: as Medical Officer in charge of the Kinnaird Women's Hospital, Lucknow, you have by your devoted work, which has now extended over a period of sixteen years, raised that institution to a high degree of efficiency. Your able and sympathetic treatment of the poor and suffering has brought them in increasing numbers to your Hospital. In addition to this you have given unsparingly of your time to Committee work and to the furtherance of your child welfare movement. In the name of the King-Emperor and by His Majesty's command I have much pleasure in presenting to you today the Kaiser-i-Hind Gold

Medal, which has been conferred on you in appreciation of your eminent public services in India'.

In 1939 she was created OBE. At the time she was in England on furlough, but she asked if she might forego the presentation of it at Buckingham Palace in order that the investiture might take place in the grounds of the Kinnaird Hospital on her return to Lucknow. This request she was graciously granted as the reason she gave for this was that it was an award to the whole staff, and it was therefore fitting to all her many colleagues that the Order should be awarded in the grounds of the hospital in which she had spent her whole professional life.

One of the few women medical missionaries who have taken up psychiatry is Dr Marjory Foyle, who qualified at the Royal Free Hospital. She went out to Lucknow in 1949 under the Bible and Medical Missionary Fellowship. After a varied career there, in Bihar and in Nepal, she relates in 1965, 'I became sure that God wanted me to take up psychiatry'. She therefore returned to Scotland to take a psychiatric training. The tale is then best taken up in Dr Foyle's autobiographical note in *Royal Free Hospital Missionaries* (Bowden, 1975) (see also chapter 12).

'I had no clear idea initially of what was in God's mind, but by 1969 I was sure that I should return to Lucknow again, this time to work at the Nur Manzil Psychiatric Centre. I have been at the Nur Manzil for nine years now, initially as a psychiatrist, but for the last seven years as Director. Nur Manzil is a unique institution. Founded by Dr E. Stanley Jones, it is one of the only two psychiatric units in the world totally owned by a church, and offering the full range of modern psychiatric treatment. We try to concentrate on the whole person, to take time to hear the problem and to explore it in depth. The work is fascinating, rewarding, full of problems, but wonderfully satisfying. We have 33 in-patients and eight in a halfway home, the patients living as a large community.

I shall be retiring from Nur Manzil in 1981, aged nearly 60, but am planning a further two years' service in Asia. I hope to be a travelling missionary psychiatrist, helping missionaries and church personnel in their own countries on a three-month basis in each place . . . The idea behind it is to help the church'.

Looking back over this last century of service by women medical missionaries, one realizes the debt the women of India owe to medical missions, with its chain of mission hospitals stretching from the northwest and northeast frontiers to the very tip of the subcontinent. These missions, however, are notable, not merely for their extent, but also for the quality of the work performed. The hospitals have been staffed by women with the highest British, American, or other Western qualifications, many of them with international reputations for brilliant and successful surgery. One of the points stressed has been their work in training Indian girls as nurses, described by Dr Margaret Balfour as 'one of the most notable features of medical missionary work', which 'in after years will be regarded as second to none in importance'.

Another point emphasized by Dr Balfour is that:

'quite a large proportion of the first women medical students in Edinburgh and London took up the course with a view to becoming medical missionaries. Though the motive was thus one of desire to relieve human suffering, it must be kept in mind that the mission hospital was at that time regarded as an adjunct to mission work rather than as an object in itself . . . People soon became convinced that the hospital could do much for their physical ills, and the spirit of friendliness and trust this created introduced an atmosphere in which the missionary could attend to the moral and spiritual needs of her patients in addition . . . Evangelization was the aim, and the mission hospital was a means of opening doors which would otherwise have remained shut'.

In this memorable list of women medical missionaries in the Indian subcontinent, two names stand out supreme in the field of medical education of Indian women: Dr Ida Scudder (mother and daughter) in Vellore and Dame Edith Brown in Ludhiana. From their initial realization of the need for medical schools in the land to which they had promised (and devoted) their lives, there sprang two of the outstanding medical schools of the present day, the full story of which will be found in chapter 18.

In conquering the mountain vastnesses of Nepal, three graduates of the Royal Free Hospital played a pioneer part. The first of these was Dr Katharine Harbord who qualified in 1921. Her first posting was to India as a member of the Zenana Bible and Medical Mission, and it was in 1926 that she was allowed to work in some villages on the Nepal border. The following year the governor of West Nepal secretly asked her to attend his daughter in her confinement. This involved a hazardous mountainous journey. Arriving six weeks before what turned out to be a successful confinement, she made good use of her time in teaching the people in the local villages.

Thirty years were to elapse before the Zenana Bible and Medical Mission was to be allowed to send another member into what was tentatively attempting to become a constitutional monarchy. This was Dr Marjorie Foyle who, having qualified, went out to India in 1949 as a member of the Mission. In 1956 she was asked to go to Nepal, recently opened up to medical missionary aid. Here, as she records, she became the first woman doctor in the western part of Nepal. Of her five years there, she writes:

'I was stationed 16 miles away from the nearest road, involving a long walk to get to the nearest transport. It was a marvellous experience, involving every sort of medical care. Initially, we lived and worked in a haunted house which no-one else would use. Downstairs, we operated, housed infectious cases and had a few general and obstetrical beds. We lived upstairs. During these early years, I never saw one case of cross-infection, despite the fact that we had to house "dirty" cases in the room we also used for operations, X-rays and labour ward. Truly, God blessed us'.

The third representative from the 'Royal Free' was Dr Margaret Muddiman, who qualified in 1973. In the course of the vivid account she contributes of her experience to *Royal Free Hospital Missionaries*, she writes:

'Now I am in Nepal with United Mission to Nepal as a paediatrician . . . supported by the Church Missionary Society. I am responsible for the paediatric wards, but also help in the very busy outpatient department, where so many have often walked barefoot for many days and often have serious and very advanced illness. We have limited X-ray and laboratory facilities, but two very competent surgeons, who tackle almost anything involving orthopaedics (very many fractures and subsequent osteomyelitis in old, untreated wounds), abdominal surgery, eye surgery and plastic surgery, particularly in severely burned patients. It is tremendous to be part of God's family here, working with Nepalis and also with folk from America, Australia, Canada, Sweden, Norway, Scotland and England. Conditions are not so primitive as I had expected and scenery and climate are glorious.

I have already felt God's hand on me here . . . It is a privilege to work here in such beauty to try to improve child care and assist in diagnosis and treatment for the many poor, ill folk here of many ethnic origins, yet of one big family in God's world . . . I am so glad God can use even me in His purpose and that I can serve here in Nepal'.

China
The story of women medical missionaries in China has a characteristically mystic atmosphere of the orient. Dr D.B. McCartie, of

the Presbyterian Church of America, who arrived in Ningpo in 1844, adopted a foundling girl, named Yamel Kin. When she grew up she was sent to New York where she trained as a doctor, and became the first Chinese woman doctor trained abroad. It was an example that was followed soon after when four Chinese girls were sent for training to USA.

The first woman medical missionary to go to China was Dr Lucinda Combs, who arrived in Peking in 1873, sent by the Women's Missionary Society of the American Methodist Episcopal Mission. The following year she was followed by Dr Sigourney Trask, also sent by the same society, who settled in Foochow. Both opened the first hospitals for women in China: Dr Combs in Peking in 1873 and Dr Trask in Foochow in 1877.

The next decade witnessed a steady stream of women medical missionaries from the United Kingdom. Two of the first were Dr Isabella Mears and Dr Alice Marston, both of whom qualified in 1881 at the Royal Free Hospital. Dr Mears went to Foochow under the Church Missionary Society, and Dr Marston to Peking under the Society for the Propagation of the Gospel. Both of them were among the first women to qualify as doctors in Britain. Unfortunately, in spite of Dr Marston's pioneer work in Peking, which embraced teaching in medical schools as well as running dispensaries and working in hospital, her devoted work ended tragically early, in 1900, while on her way to England on sick leave. Dr Mears, along with her husband, who had been a lecturer in anatomy when they met, were spared for many years to carry on their good work.

Another pathetically short career was that of Dr Margaret Bennett who qualified from the Royal Free Hospital in 1898. After a postgraduate course she reached China in 1899 with the Wesleyan Mission. As there was no hospital ready for her in Wuchang, she remained in Hankow to study the language and hospital methods in China. The intervention of the Boxer trouble caused her evacuation to Japan. On her return there were inevitable antiforeign Mandarin checks, and it was not until February 13 1903 that the carefully planned hospital, the money for which was subscribed principally by herself and her family, was opened. Here, as recorded, 'Dr Margaret Bennett with her matron colleague, Miss Shillington, successfully laboured in healing and preaching for five months'. Then, alas, she developed dysentery and after only five days died on June 10. 'As she lay on her dying bed', it is recorded, 'near the close of her consciousness, in answer to a question, she replied, "No, I am not sorry, but glad that I came to China".' To commemorate her memory the hospital was named the Margaret Bennett Memorial. In 1906 she was succeeded by Dr Helen Randall Vickers.

Another of the Royal Free Hospital volunteers in the China field was Dr Ethel Gough, who went out to Hankow in 1895 as first woman medical missionary under the Methodist Missionary Society to help staff the hospital which had been built largely by money provided by an appeal by the Society at Queen Victoria's Jubilee in 1887. 'It was a great event', it is recorded, 'to welcome the first lady doctor to the small missionary circle in Central China'. She spent 13 years at the Jubilee Women's Hospital, which had been opened in December 1888 in the presence of the British Consul and four mandarins arrayed in their gorgeous official robes, accompanied by their retinue of soldiers and attendants. Subsequently Dr Gough spent many years up country at Anlu and then Wusuch. She died in November 1941.

One of the most remarkable records in this sphere is that of Dr Florence Cooper who qualified at the Royal Free Hospital in 1897 and served in China with the Church of England Zenana Missionary Society for 50 years until her death.

By no means the only medical missionary from the Royal Free Hospital to marry a bishop was Dr Eda Bryan-Brown who qualified in 1908. She spent forty-one years as a missionary in China, during which she married the Bishop of Chekiang. She died in 1964 at the age of 81.

As in India, this gallant company of women medical missionaries played a leading part in the inauguration and development of medical schools for Chinese women. Prominent among these was Dr Mary Fulton of the American Presbyterian Mission North, who in 1901 opened the Kwang Tung Medical School for Women in Canton, starting off with eleven students and teaching in Cantonese. In 1902 the name was changed to Hackett Medical College for Women. According to the Educational Number of the *China Medical Journal* in 1926: 'The Hackett Medical School continues its laudable activities up to the present day'.

An interesting commentary on the part played in China by medical missions in these early days is provided by the following excerpt from the issue of a well-known Chinese newspaper, the *Daily News*, dated September 7 1900.

'The growth of the people's confidence in Medical Missions and in educational work is remarkable. The Medical Missionaries are consulted by all classes from Viceroy to beggar, and their influence has helped much to break down opposition to non-Roman missions. In gratitude for the aid rendered to his wife by a lady doctor, Li Hung Chang [who has been described as 'the Grand Old Man of China, leading statesman until death' in 1901] built and equipped a fine hospital in Tientsin and placed it under the management of a medical missionary'.

Africa

One of the first of the women medical missionaries to enter the African mission field was Dr Jane Waterson, one of the first thirteen students to enter the Royal Free Hospital. She was over 30 years of age when she began her medical studies, having spent the previous eight years with Dr James Stewart as a missionary in the Lovedale Institution in South Africa. On her return to South Africa on qualifying in 1897, she played an increasingly important part in the sphere of health, not the least of her interests being sanitary reform. As an aggressive pioneer in this field her attitude did not enamour her to the powers that be. She died in 1932 at the age of 85.

Initially in Africa much of the healing contribution of the women missionaries was as nurses. Outstanding among these was Sister Mary Elms who arrived in Nigeria in 1901, where she was to stay until 1926. Typical of the conditions under which she had to work was the comment of Miss Maxwell who left for furlough shortly after the arrival of Miss Elms, regretting having to leave Miss Elms with 'an absolute dearth of dressings, very few medicines . . . and 6 shillings'. The vicissitudes of life were indeed trying, but her faith was unconquerable.

One of the hospitals in which she spent much of her time was the CMS general hospital at Iyi Enu at Onitsha in Eastern Nigeria (see also pp 38,114). It was rebuilt in 1924, and in 1925 Dr Sybil Batley, who had qualified at the Royal Free Hospital in 1925, arrived, the first doctor in the Nigerian Mission since the early part of the 1914-1918 War. Two years later she was joined by Dr Jessie Horne. In April 1926, Sister Mary Elms finally left Nigeria. In the official history of the Church Missionary Society it is recorded that

> 'she had kept Iyi Enu going against almost impossible odds; and by her writing and teaching she had prepared the way for a reformation in village hygiene in the Onitsha area which was already showing results in a reduction of infant mortality. She had also won over the years the sympathy and support of Government officials' (Hewitt, 1971).

In 1931 a third woman doctor, Dr Margaret Roseveare, arrived, to be linked initially with the new maternity block named after Mary Elms. In 1933 the Niger Mission appointed her to travel round the Ibo country, developing the opportunities Sister Elms had opened up in the field of village hygiene and maternity and child welfare. This work steadily expanded, and in 1939 Dr Roseveare reported that in the area she covered there were fourteen CMS maternity centres, each with a labour theatre run by a midwife, and wards for 8 to 20 women and babies. A fee of 5 shillings from each patient who could afford it was paid into local church funds.

One or two excerpts from *Royal Free Hospital Missionaries* giving personal reminiscences of missionaries who qualified, provide a fascinating kaleidoscope of the work encountered by those who dedicated themselves to the mission field in Africa. Thus Dr Phyllis Oxborrow, who qualified in 1974, was posted to Mvumi Hospital, Tanzania, of which she writes:

'Missionary work to me means a Christian working in a situation foreign to that which she is used to (preferably at the invitation of the local church in that new situation, who requires someone with particular qualifications to work in the diocese). I am employed by the Central Tanzania Church Diocese to work as a doctor in this hospital, and, to the extent that medical work is the same the world over, my job is identical to that of any doctor anywhere. The greater responsibilities I face here, the amazing medical conditions and the different life-style, do not affect the principle that, for me, as for any other Christian, my duty and my only way to inward peace is to do my job as God wants me to do it in the place of His choosing.

The realities of life here include a ceaseless battle against ants (in one's bed, food and operating theatre), a slightly unreliable electricity supply (the last breakdown was in the middle of an operation; at least despite the dark, we could hear the patient breathing steadily), lack of laboratory facilities and drugs . . .

I shall be here for just one to two years initially. But, whether or not I return, my understanding of Christian work abroad will be much greater and my own life, medically and spiritually, will have been enriched immeasurably'.

Dr Evelyn Nightingale, who qualified in 1941, arrived in the Kalene Mission in the northwest corner of Zambia in 1946. She writes:

'We tried to supervise infant feeding and immunizations, so that in all about 2000 children were under some form of observation in the area 100 miles around Kalene. Farther afield, kwashiorkor and malnutrition were common . . . these children suffer acutely and often fatally from measles epidemics. We were able to gather the children and their mothers with complete freedom for Bible teaching and chorus singing, which these little under-fives entered into with much action and great gusto. . .

I remember once operating with the sister and simultaneously giving directions to a second sister on the treatment of diabetic coma, and instructing the midwife on a difficult delivery. . .

Life was exciting and very fulfilling, but terribly stressful. Every talent we possesed, and some we did not, had to be put to use. . .

The days often started before breakfast with prayers in the Leprosy Settlement and it, too, was a time when some turned to the Lord and found salvation and forgiveness of sin. The night round was done at times to the sound of hymn singing, as the patients gathered together to thank and praise the God of the Universe who we know through Jesus Christ. We rejoiced with them, but at other times we wept with the mothers whose little children we had been unable to help'.

Dr Margaret Price, who qualified in 1933, subsequently becoming a Roman Catholic and joining the Community of the Daughters of Charity of St Vincent de Paul, did not go abroad until she was 60. She then went to Ethiopia intending to stay for six months, but remained for 14 years, and then, she comments, 'only left because missionaries of all kinds were expelled from the Province in which our little bush hospital was situated'. Of these days she recalls:

'Many thousands of patients were seen every year, besides which curative medicine, preventive measures, maternal and child health work, health education were all undertaken as opportunities occurred. . . Maternity work took up a fair share of our time. . . In the fourteen years we lost only one mother and saved every babe born alive, though resuscitation had to be pro-longed at times. A proportion of patients suffered from severe illness due to leprosy, malaria, typhus, tuberculosis and dysentery. . .

Only a small number of patients were Catholics, but of course Orthodox Christians, Protestants or Muslims were all welcome and if neither time nor talent enabled one to "spread the Gospel", love in action had its effect; and those Ethiopians working with us in the various clinics became truly dedicated Christians.

I can honestly say that my years on the mission were among the happiest and most fulfilling of my life as a doctor. Given a sense of humour, a lively imagination and unlimited confidence in Providence, a doctor in mission lands faces the greatest and most worth-while challenge in the world'.

On her way to Ruanda, Dr Decima Tracey, who qualified in

1929, was married in 1930 in Namirembe Cathedral in Kampala to Dr Joe Church who had already spent two years in the Ruanda Mission.

'In some ways', she writes, 'the marriage was a model for us, but conditions at Gahini, some 330 miles away, "in the blue" and in a completely primitive environment were very different. But, building up the work of Gahini Hospital gave many challenges, and the reality of that word, "cooperation", was seen to be so important. This was not only in the continual training of nursing and medical assistant staff, but in getting the Christian message through to be a working reality in the lives of us all.

Medically it was a life of tremendous interests, as being so isolated, all kinds and conditions would turn up and all had to be tackled as far as we were able...

We were soon to see the Spirit of God speaking to many... This was the beginning of what became known as the East African revival... One after another of the African staff were converted and the Christian witness of the hospital became widespread. The hospital became known as a place of caring people and patients would sometimes come from great distances, even from Uganda, where the non-mission medical services were much more developed, but where attention to patients often had to be secured by bribes.

I have been writing about the early years of Gahini Hospital, but the story has gone on with a succession of missionary doctors and nurses. We had the joy of one of these being our own eldest son, who took over the care of the hospital from us. We also had the joy of seeing our other two doctor sons coming to work in Uganda. Africa was "home" to them'.

It was an interesting coincidence that four years after Dr Church's marriage Kampala was also the site of the marriage of Sir Albert Cook's daughter, Marjorie, who qualified from the Royal Free Hospital in 1930, and then went out to spend three years in Kampala in the service of the Church Missionary Society. Here she worked in close collaboration with her father, subsequently, like him, settling in private practice in Kampala.

Throughout Africa are to be found representatives of the largest Roman Catholic Women's Medical Order, the Medical Missionaries of Mary. They began work at Anua in South East Nigeria in 1937 with a 12-bedded hospital which steadily developed into one of 300 beds. Initially the Order restricted its activities to Nigeria, but in 1947 these spread to Kenya, and subsequently to Tanzania, Malawi, Uganda, Ethiopia, and Angola.

What would most impress this regiment of pioneer women medical missionaries, were they to revisit the site of their earthly labours, would be the continuing service of the women medical missionaries of today in the name of Christ. Typical of them is Dr Ruth Coggan, daughter of Lord Coggan, the former Archbishop of Canterbury. Under the aegis of the Church Missionary Society she runs the zenana wing of the 90-year-old Pennell Memorial Hospital in Bannu in the famous North West Frontier, 25 miles east of the Afghan border. Until 1970 there was no woman doctor there, and purdah was so strict that many women would rather die than be examined or operated on by a man. Today, with Dr Coggan are two nurses and a midwife from England, and the number of women patients is steadily rising.

'The staff', it is recorded, 'say prayers before and after each operation, competing with the Moslem prayers chanted by the patients' relatives. But, apart from a daily prayer meeting in the stone-built hospital chapel, there is no attempt to proselytize'.

The satisfaction of service to the sick and suffering is the award received by this glorious army of the daughters of Christ. Their work still goes on.

References

Balfour, Margaret I. and Young, Ruth (1929) *The Work of Medical Women in India*. Oxford: Oxford University Press.

Bowden, Ruth E.M. (1975) *Royal Free Hospital Missionaries*.

Henderson, Agnes (1956) *Vision and Achievement 1796-1956*. London: Nelson

Hewett, Gordon (1971) *The Problems of Success. A History of the Church Missionary Society 1910-1942*. Vol.1 London: SCM Press Ltd.

Pollock, J.C. (1958) *Shadows Fall Apart. The Story of the Zenana Bible and Medical Missions*. London: Hodder and Stoughton.

Wong, K. Chimin and Lien-Teh, Wu. (1932) *History of Medicine in China*. Tientsin: The Tientsin Press.

CHAPTER 15

REHABILITATION OF THE DISABLED

Paul Brand

Medicine may conveniently be divided into three major divisions: preventive medicine, curative medicine, and rehabilitation. In situations where there is a general lack of medical resources, it is usually curative medicine that gets first attention, then preventive medicine and lastly rehabilitation. The area of Christian missions has been no exception to this. It is not hard to understand why this has been so, and why it remains so. Christian missionaries are motivated by one or both of two major objectives; a desire to preach the gospel and a desire to express love and compassion. It is when people are sick that they are most conscious of the need to be helped. It is at this time, when they are most obviously in need, that the missionary may be able to help them by means of medicine or an operation. Thus, in this face-to-face interaction of helper and helped it is possible and natural to speak of the love of God, and add a spiritual ministry to the physical. It has come about that all over the world Christian missions have organized medical clinics and have built hospitals and employed doctors and nurses and placed them in areas of need and in strategic locations.

Today the primacy of curative medicine is being questioned and preventive medicine is receiving more attention, and that for a number of good reasons. One is that those who treat patients in medical centres have come to realize that there is an unending stream of new sickness coming from the same rural areas. This sickness is largely preventable. It is caused by lack of clean water, lack of simple sanitation and lack of childhood immunization against the diseases that have long been eliminated from more affluent societies. It is frustrating and expensive to treat such a stream of sickness, but relatively simple to prevent. It requires a change of priorities, and a recognition that doctors and nurses may often be most effective by teaching and immunizing rather than by treating sickness. It restores the focus of Christian missionary work to the poorest of the people, and it forces the missionary to identify with the lack of facilities with which patients have to contend.

Thus the ideal in today's medical mission is to have a partnership between a medical centre, a hospital or referral base, and a wide network of village clinics where a pattern of community health is being developed and where village women, often almost illiterate, are being helped to undertake the sort of public health nursing role which their own culture has often assigned to them but in which their lack of knowledge of the causes of disease has made them ineffective. In this way we have a partnership between curative medicine and preventive medicine. What about rehabilitation?

It was a great shock to me, a cultural shock perhaps, when I first went as a missionary surgeon to India, to discover that there was no rehabilitation facility either in Christian medical missions or in the structure of medical care that was developing in India at that time. I could amputate a leg, but where could I get an artificial limb? I could treat a spastic child, but where could I send him or her for special education? If my wife, an ophthalmologist, could not restore sight to a blind man, where was a school for the blind? A victim of a stroke was unable to take care of herself, and there was no nursing home for the elderly infirm.

In India, and in many similar countries that we call underdeveloped, the whole of society is a rehabilitation facility. We from the West have much in the way of rehabilitation technology that we can teach, but in the great basic principle of rehabilitation, it is we who should be the learners, they the teachers.

The important thing in any medical missionary endeavour is to understand and to love the people and their culture first, and then to find out how best to bring the specific good that we know and add it or fit it into what is already there without disturbing what is already good. My own early mixture of good ideas and cultural mistakes in rehabilitation of leprosy patients may serve as an example of what I have been trying to say.

I was in India as a surgeon and to teach surgery. Rehabilitation was a need that forced itself upon me. The reason was that I was operating upon leprosy patients, and restoring their deformed hands to some extent so that they would be able to work. Many of them could not get work, because people were afraid of their disease. With a sense of urgency to meet a felt need, I therefore built a rehabilitation centre of mud-and-thatch huts to help these young men to learn to use their hands in a gainful way. They had to learn to work without injuring themselves because their hands were insensitive. So far so good.

I did not know much about farming in India, but had an impression that it was heavy work and that it would be bad for these insensitive hands. We therefore began to teach these boys and men the arts of light carpentry and the use of mechanical tools. We taught them to make rather beautiful wooden toys and puzzles that they could cut out of plywood and paint with spray guns. The products were good and they appealed at once to people who came to visit our centre. We found a ready sale among staff of the medical college and students and very soon we became known for this high-quality work. All our patients were kept busy and they earned money. As with this sort of work, it took time to learn, patients tended to stay on when they became skilled so that they could keep up our production needs and also teach others. All went well until we had a number of patients who really should be moving out. We arranged for them to buy tools and machines with their earnings subsidized by gifts. They were supposed to go back to their own villages and set up workshops there. One by one, however, they returned. There was no market for slick painted toys in the village. Children made their own toys in the village, and parents could not afford to buy. So our patients settled down near us and we bought and marketed their produce. We soon found that quite a colony was being developed. These were people whom we had made dependent on our type of culture. Many had families and a natural home in a village. There they would have been given farm work to do and would have damaged their hands in the doing of it, but they would have been secure in their own home environment. Now they looked to us, and if we left (or when we left) they would belong nowhere.

Today we have had much more experience. We try to keep patients in their own environment. The money we used to spend on housing and feeding and clothing patients in special centres we now save and spend it on sending our social workers and physiotherapy technicians to the villages. By teaching in the village we educate not only the patients but their families too. Most of our patients return to the farming occupations that they were in before, but they know that they should avoid some of the more traumatic jobs in farming; they also know that for ploughing and other heavy work they have to wear work gloves. They also know that if they do injure their hands they must strap a splint to keep the affected finger out of further harm or stress until it heals. They know all this. Some of them do it. Others do some of it, and all of it when they are not extra busy. Many of them do injure their hands, and get more injuries than they would if they had remained in the sheltered environment of our workshops.

We sometimes go back to the family when we observe recurrent damage in the hands of one of our patients. We try to persuade him to modify the work he does. We may even offer to help. For example, we sometimes buy a cow and a calf for the family. This is an investment which will encourage the family by providing a new source of income which does not involve stressful use of the hands. We make an agreement that the family will repay the cost of the purchase over a period of time as they are able to sell the milk. The patient's hands may be saved. He himself remains in the family and village unit. Self-respect has been maintained. The village learns that leprosy need not mean rejection and isolation, and need not result in progressive deformity. The Christian mission has spent less money per patient and has had more face-to-face interaction with people than under the old system.

I have wept to see the results of my own careful reconstructive surgery wiped out by misuse of an insensitive hand, but the patient smiles as he tells me that he now owns a pair of bullocks and a plough, and that he is kept busy working for a number of farmers. He is independent and lives at home. The price is progressive shortening of fingers. We patiently go over the lessons again, and we give him some new gloves and some spare finger splints, but we smile and pat him on the back because he can hold up his head, is better and more truly rehabilitated than the boys with good hands who work in the colony and remain dependent on us. We learn slowly, but we learn that it is people that we now aim to rehabilitate, or even families and not just a hand or a foot.

Christian initiatives in rehabilitation in different countries have emphasized different aspects of the problem. The first is the stage in which a damaged or crippled person, having been medically or surgically treated, is left with a need for training of the abilities that still remain to him. This often requires the help of physiotherapists, and is needed in cases of poliomyelitis, after muscle and tendon transfers, and in cases of stroke, to help patients to learn to use unparalysed muscles for actions they have never done before. The second is the stage in which a disabled person has received all the medical, surgical, and therapeutic help he needs, but still needs some mechanical device, such as an artificial limb, a wheelchair or adapted tools to assist him to become mobile and independent. This is an area where nearly all Third World countries need help. The third area is when the disabled person has received all the technical help that is available, and then has to learn to accept himself or herself as he or she is, and develop a new pattern of meaningful living. In this area Christian initiatives have been important in England in this century and have been a valuable corrective to the impersonal materialism that sometimes regards a worker as of value only for the amount of work he can produce.

A good example of this has been the development of the hospice movement. It may seem strange to call the care of the terminally ill by the title of rehabilitation but this is what it is. Most medical teams are so orientated to cure and to success that when a patient is known to be terminally ill there is a sudden loss of interest. There is no longer a challenge to further diagnosis or treatment, and the continued presence of the patient in the bed is a reminder to the doctors that they are finite and have had to admit defeat. They hurry past the patient and keep their eyes averted. All of this is devastating to the patient, and makes his last few months a misery. The initiative of the hospice movement has been to recognize these months as significant. The quality of life need not be diminished just because we have been unable to remove the disease. Thus an active programme is started which encourages the patients to use to the full all their potential. They participate in the care of other patients and so become coworkers. In some cases they are used as baby-sitters to set busy mothers free for work. The sense of responsibility and personal worth that is engendered by all this activity not only makes the patient feel good, it often also improves health and lengthens life. They need less care from others and can provide care for others, and in doing this they find joy and fulfilment. This is rehabilitation in the best sense of the word, and the whole movement has been a Christian initiative.

Technical aids constitute the field that has shown the most activity so far as Christian initiatives are concerned. Many medical missionaries whose background is the rich technology of the Western world find an outlet for their skills and their compassion when they see children crippled by poliomyelitis, crawling, or dragging themselves along the ground. As surgeons, they have tried to straighten legs, and transfer muscles and tendons, only to find that the paralysis was too severe or that the joints were too stiff and contracted. Then comes the need for braces and for artificial limbs and for wheelchairs and crutches. The cost of importing these things is often prohibitive; so a brace workshop is born and bracemakers are trained.

As I have travelled to many countries and visited many Christian mission hospitals, I have enjoyed being taken to these workshops by the British or American missionary and shown various devices and inventions and improvisations. I have enjoyed them, not least because they obviously provided enjoyment to the pioneers who have built them up. In most cases, there has been nothing new in the basic concept or design of any brace, but there has been much ingenuity and innovation in the attempts to make use of local materials and local crafts.

Kampala in Uganda was at one time a great centre for innovaive ideas in medicine and in teaching. The CMS hospital at Mengo and the Makerere Medical College with its government hospital at Mulago have had more than their share of pioneering spirits. It was there that the Professor of Orthopaedics, Ronald Huckstep, obtained help from the Kampala Round Table to devise simple splints and supports for children with various paralyses due to poliomyelitis. The enthusiasm that was developed and the ingenuity shown in making the braces inspired a great deal of imitation throughout East Africa.

In Nigeria, Dr Pfaltzgraff working in a leprosy hospital in Garkida, needed simple inexpensive artificial limbs to fit the amputees who had lost limbs because of neglected leprosy, or from accidents and disease. He found that even the best and most expensive imported legs did not fit well enough for the stumps that had no feeling. The patients just walked in them until new ulcers developed on the stumps. In the simple environment of the mission hospital, he took advantage of new plastic materials, and taught his helpers to mould an epoxy shell directly on the amputation stump, and on a cardboard cone below it. The result was a firm, well-fitting leg that allowed the patient to walk safely. It was not beautiful, because it had no moulded foot, but it met a need, and it was within the budget of a bush medical service. It has since been widely imitated and improved upon.

In India at the Vellore Christian Medical College, there was a critical need to provide a brace for spinal tuberculosis. Hundreds of cases were being seen and only a small proportion could be kept in hospital. Many could go home on medical treatment if only a firm supporting brace were available. Plaster casts were too heavy, and would not last. Appropriate plastics could not be imported, but India had a manufacturing plant for polyethylene granules. In the basement of the hospital a large oven was built, with a smooth metal shelf in the middle. Dusted with talc, layers of gauze were laid on the shelf and sprinkled with polyethylene granules over a pattern taken from the patient's back and sides. At the edges and wherever strength was required the granules were sprinkled thickly. Elsewhere a single layer was used. The critical decisions were made by a technician who could speak minimal English but who boasted the name of William Shakespeare. The patient meanwhile had his back covered by an even thickness of three layers of plaster bandage. When set and removed and dried in the sun it was just strong enough to support the softened heated polythene granules which were lifted on their gauze base and laid over the shell.

Those simple inexpensive shells were used by hundreds of patients, and I was amused when I saw an Indian patient who came to USA to be treated for spinal scoliosis thirty years later. She was wearing the identical type of brace, identifiable by the pebbled texture of the surface and the trouser hooks that were used for holding the laces.

Dr Mary Verghese, the Indian Christian doctor who became paraplegic after a motor accident, devoted her life to the development of a rehabilitation unit for spinal paralysis in India. She had noted that many wheelchairs imported from the West were unsuitable for an Indian village home. She therefore worked with engineers to develop an inexpensive lower-wheeled support that could be manufactured and serviced locally and that would enable a paralysed patient to participate in the life of an Indian village hut at the level where people ordinarily sit and work.

The term 'Christian Initiatives in Rehabilitation' must not be defined too narrowly. It is common for good programmes to be sponsored by secular organizations like the Red Cross; in many cases the moving force and stimulus to a particular programme is a member whose own life is based on loyalty to Christ. One such complex interaction gave fruitful results in Katpadi, India, when the Swedish Red Cross responded to requests from a committee for the rehabilitation of the disabled, called the Abilities Trust. The need was for a factory that would train and employ disabled people, especially leprosy patients, so that they could compete competitively in the field of mechanical engineering. The first need was for an Indian engineer who would run the factory and train the disabled people.

The manager of the English Electric factory in Madras informed the committee that he was in touch with a young Indian engineer, a Christian, who had been trained in the USA and had written his Master's thesis on 'Engineering in the Rehabilitation of the Handicapped'. The Swedish Red Cross provided the capital, built the factory and sent a succession of experienced engineers to get it started and to train the young Indian engineer. The Swedes then left India; for some twenty-five years the factory has trained generations of deformed and disabled people and sent them out to make their own way in the world of manufacture.

One of the sections of this enterprise has been the manufacture of wheelchairs, special beds, crutches, and other devices for the disabled. It is a case of the disabled who have been rehabilitated helping the disabled who need further help. Most factories and industries for the disabled fall into one of two categories. Either the workers are given special advantages and subsidies, and the work proceeds at a continuing cost to the church or the public; or the workers are exploited, because they have no alternative place to go to. The first category is kind, but works at a loss. The second makes a profit, but is unkind.

The Christian rehabilitation project tends to fall into the first category, and many of them fail when the financial subsidy fails. The Katpadi factory for the disabled (now called Worth Industries) is almost unique in that not only are the very severely disabled gainfully employed, but the whole enterprise makes money too. It is a non-profit organization; hence the money is ploughed back into the enterprise, and has financed the building of at least one new factory of the same type. In Worth Industries, high skill and intelligence are linked to real Christian faith. It takes faith for a man to persist in a non-profit industry when he knows that he could make big money in competitive industry.

I do not often weep, but I wept a few years ago when I toured Worth Industries, led by Antonysamy, the engineer, and saw an old patient of mine, John, who had only stumps for fingers and had lost sensation in his hands. Antonysany told me that John had just received an all-India prize, given by Swedish Typewriters to the mechanic who has the best production record with the fewest rejects in all their associated factories throughout India. John held out a handful of the little screws that he was making for the centre of a typewriter, and smiled with the half of his face that was not paralysed, and I wept because I remembered him as a problem patient. He was a problem from a physical sense, because of his paralysis, but more so because he felt himself rejected and hated because of his disease, and his only reaction was to hate in return. The proud and happy man who smiled at me now owed his true rehabilitation not only to the factory and the engineer but to the members of the little church in Vellore that had first accepted him into membership in spite of their fear of the disease. Rehabilitation is a complex thing. Its success is often due as much to a parent or a pastor or to a church member as it is to some programme or structured facility.

In many parts of the world, where it is difficult to obtain braces and limbs, Western mission organizations collect used braces and limbs and send them overseas where they may be altered to provide parts that are not available locally. A notable project of this type has been the campaign to provide used spectacles for patients who cannot afford to buy glasses of their own. The remarkable idea of 'eye camps' is essentially a Christian initiative. The surgeon removes the opaque lens. Then when the eye is healed he or she supplies the patient with glasses that focus the light and sight is restored. Not only are light and joy restored, but independence. As scores or hundreds of patients stream away from these village eye camps, it is obvious that men and women are now walking on their own, proudly, while the guides who led them to the camp are now free to do other things. That is rehabilitation.

Unfortunately many of the blind who seek help are beyond the reach of surgery or of glasses; their eyes are destroyed. One of the tragedies of malnutrition is that little children, just weaned from the breast, are subject to vitamin A deficiency. A slight infection, such as a conjunctivitis, may precipitate keratomalacia and be followed by total loss of sight. These blind children are a reminder of our responsibilities in the field of prevention and education. They are also a challenge to Rehabilitation. The village will help them and lead them by hand to where they can sit and beg, but Christian initiative should do more; schools for the blind have been established in many places. The School for the Blind in Palmanair in India is one example, and in Kenya the Salvation Army has a school for the blind at Thika. In Nigeria a major cause of blindness is onchocerciasis. The victims have to learn how to live in the dark. Meanwhile we have to think of those who can still see but who will go blind if we cannot learn how to control the black-fly that transmit the parasite.

Occupational therapy is an aspect of Rehabilitation that has been very widely practised in Christian mission hospitals and institutions. There are three good reasons for occupational therapy; one is to keep the patient busy and occupied while recovering from any illness that keeps him from doing what he would ordinarily be doing. Another is to provide an occupation that uses a part of the body that needs to be used in a certain way in order that it may become strong and well again. This is necessary for instance, after surgery on the hand. Another is to help a person to learn a skill that will be of use later on. This may be a skill that will earn money, or help to do a better job in house-keeping or in keeping the family clothed. A good therapist will devise projects that will fulfil all three objectives at the same time.

This is an area in which volunteers are useful. Ideally, a trained therapist will design the programme, and volunteers will implement it. Unfortunately trained therapists are rare in the Third World. In Christian missions this work is often done by women, perhaps wives of doctors or preachers. The fact that these women are not qualified in the sense of possessing degrees or diplomas in therapy or rehabilitation has made some people rather despise the work they do. Perhaps in some cases it was as much occupational therapy for the women who organized it as for the patients who were its object. However, there is something special about the woman who is an efficient wife and home-maker, who has brought up children, and who has learned to adapt to a new country and a new culture. If in addition she has the sensitivity to perceive a need and to be willing to do something about it, then indeed she is a professional. The usual crafts that are taught are needlework and knitting, or crochet or weaving. These are skills familiar to the teacher, but they can be done in bed or in a chair by a patient who is getting well but who is not yet strong enough to leave hospital. Moreover, these skills have a most useful part to play in the daily life of many patients when they return home and have to clothe their own families.

An impressive example of this kind of rehabilitation was organized in Addis Ababa in Ethiopia. The All-Africa Leprosy and Rehabilitation Training Centre was taking care of thousands of leprosy patients, and many of them had no means of support except begging. The hospital had beds only for the acutely ill and hundreds of others camped outside the hospital grounds in miserable shacks. In many cases, it was the husband who was sick, and the wife and perhaps the children had come with him. In this situation of real need the one occupational therapist, Jane Neville of the Leprosy Mission, was so busy with teaching and with health education that she could not spare time to devote to the many patients and families who should be learning skills to support themselves.

The wife of the Swedish research immunologist, and subsequently the wife of the United States ophthalmologist, Mrs Margaret Joffrion, took up the challenge and developed a programme of weaving and dressmaking and embroidery until it was an important feature of the whole training scheme, widely known for the quality of the goods produced. The success of this project is due in no small measure to the insistence of the organizers that it be an Ethiopian project. It would have been easy to teach the skills of Sweden or of North America, but this was Ethiopia, and the patients and wives had to live in Ethiopia; the leaders had to learn the authentic traditional methods of weaving and embroidery and clothing of that culture before they could embark upon their programme. The workplace had to have an Ethiopian setting; two Tukels, round mud-and-thatch village-style buildings, were therefore pressed into service. The next principle adopted was payment by piecework from real earnings. Beginners were slow, but there was to be no charity; they would earn more as they became more skilled. This ensured that there was an incentive and that, when the expatriate workers left, the work could continue. If patients had deformed fingers or paralysed hands, it was tempting to suggest that they would be paid more per unit of work because they were trying hard, but that way lies dependency. If they could not make money that way because of deformity, the very failure would prompt them to take action to change the situation. They might seek surgical correction of their hands, or they might choose a different type of work or different tools, but whatever it was, it must be they who did it, and the payment for the work must be a real reward for something accomplished.

This aspect of rehabilitation has been emphasized more than once because it is Christians who find it hardest to keep these rules. It seems wrong, somehow, to allow people to suffer poverty and disability when it would be so easy to supplement what they can earn with regular gifts. There are occasions, of course, when people are seen to be too old or too weak to take care of themselves. These people are quite rightly the object of Christian charity, but even these people are best taken care of by the local church, if they cannot be cared for by their own family or clan. The right way for a missionary to participate in such help is to contribute as a member of the church to the funds set aside for this purpose, and then let the church decide on whom and how to spend the money.

Having referred to the need to be uncompromising in insisting on the element of self-support in rehabilitation, I now go further and suggest that this may be the very heart of rehabilitation. The people who need rehabilitation are not merely patients who have specific physical disabilities; they are human beings who feel that they are failures. Their disease or accident has robbed them of the ability to fulfil their expected role in the family or in society. Their whole image of themselves is shattered, and they may not have the courage to rebuild their personhood. In this situation they need faith and hope. If they have faith in us, this is all to the good – better if they have faith in God. The test of either kind of faith so far as their present predicament is concerned, is whether it helps them to regain their belief that there is a future for them. It is only when they actually begin to see that they are able to accomplish something, when they see things growing under their hands, when they handle the coins they know they have earned, that they begin to believe that they have won.

This is why we have to resist the temptation to make the task seem easier than it really is. The Christian message is that God can live in us and through us. He accomplishes his purpose by having us do his will. It is our hands that move and lift the heavy weight. God rarely alters the weight of what we have to carry, but he does give us the strength to carry it. If we offer to carry the load that our patients should be bearing, except at special times of crisis, we only make it harder for them to carry it themselves later on.

The real message of Christians to the disabled person is that we sense the burden he bears; we work together with him to help him to use all he has to the best advantage. We do not laugh at him as he struggles, because we love and believe in him – in him and in our Lord.

CHAPTER 16

COMMUNITY HEALTH

J. McGilvray

Until recently the medical work of the Church through its overseas missions has been largely orientated towards individual care in a hospital setting. When the first national surveys of church-related medical programmes in less developed countries were undertaken in 1963, it was found that approximately 95% were hospital- and clinic-based, offering curative services to those who came for them. Little was being done for those who could not come because of distance, poverty or fear. Although curative services have been and are still being extended through the use of mobile clinics, their visits do not always coincide with the occurrence of illness and, apart from periodic immunization campaigns, they have done little to prevent disease or to promote health. Nevertheless, they were an acknowledgement of the limited impact that hospitals alone have on the incidence of disease when they lack an infrastructure of preventive measures and a filtering system of simple village clinics.

Another development has been the establishment of dispensaries, small clinics and maternity homes. Nevertheless, these extension services were still curative in concept and practice and left untouched vast areas of health needs. Cost has been an inhibitory factor in the development of preventive services and this led many missionary doctors to the conclusion that preventive medicine and community health were the primary responsibility of government. While the operating costs of clinical work can be subsidized by charging fees to patients according to their means, this was not considered feasible in the promotion of hygiene and healthy life-styles from which no immediate benefit was apparent. Furthermore, the overwhelming evidence of clinical need left little time for the more gradual approach of working *with* people, and seemed to justify the tendency of doing things *for* them.

This bias in favour of curative programmes is not at all surprising when one considers the enormous numbers of people seeking treatment and the scarcity of facilities and manpower available. There is usually an imbalance between urban and rural areas and in the latter there may be only one doctor to more than 50,000 people. While the majority of church-related hospitals are situated in the smaller towns, they have never been numerous enough to offset the national trend to concentrate medical resources in the largest cities. In Kenya, for example, as late as 1970, more than 80% of the available resources were allocated to Nairobi and Mombasa and their immediate environs. At the same time in those one-or-two doctor hospitals situated in the smaller towns of the less developed countries, the demands of a crowded outpatient department, the requirements of ward rounds and, frequently, a heavy surgical schedule left little time or opportunity for reflection about, or consideration of, alternative forms of health care such as an attack on certain endemic diseases or the promotion of better health and hygiene. Moreover, those physicians who have been trained in the West or in accordance with the Western system in their own countries are the products of a medical training that has a hospital bias and, by and large, assumes the existence of a sanitary environment together with adequate food, housing and education.

One must remember that the Christian pioneers who brought Western medicine to many areas of the world were moved by a compassion that was most naturally expressed in a one-to-one doctor-patient relation. This, in turn, was one of the motivating forces that gave rise to the missionary movement, which proclaimed a gospel of individual salvation that emphasized the worth and dignity of the individual in the sight of God. Individual medical care had a kind of theological sanction, and it was only later that this view was balanced by more emphasis on the community of which each individual was a part, contributing to the distinctive composition of the community while, at the same time, being partially shaped by it.

It was also compassion that gave rise to doubts in the minds of some of those early pioneers who questioned the effectiveness of over-crowded clinics and hospitals in which less and less time could be given to the more and more who came to be treated. There were some who were disturbed by the high proportion of admissions of patients with preventable conditions, and thought that programmes of disease prevention and health education would be a more effective service to be provided by the Western missionary doctor and nurse. While some early issues of the *China Mission Year Book* noted with pride the increasing number of mission hospitals and the establishment of

23 medical schools, later issues report on the growth of the Public Health Movement in China. For example, the 1924 volume records:

'It is extremely encouraging to note the increasingly prominent place which is being accorded hygiene in all phases of mission work . . . Medical schools reflect the trend of events in the creation of departments of hygiene . . . Mission hospitals are also reflecting the spirit of the times by evidence of the growing feeling that work limited to curative medicine is not as constructive a demonstration of modern medical science as would be the inclusion of disease prevention. An increasing number of medical missionaries are utilizing their furloughs to study hygiene. Several of these have returned to full-time preventive medical work.'

A Council on Health Education in China was founded by Dr W.W. Peter in 1912. Its aim was 'to promote health education among the people of the Republic of China by emphasizing all the aspects of health – physical, mental, social and moral. To present to them an ideal of health that is not merely freedom from disease, but a realization of the highest physical, mental and spiritual possibilities of the individual.'

In India, one of the bastions of 'medicine within walls', Dr Claire P. Thomson was untiring in her promotion of the claims of preventive medicine. Her appointment to the staff of the Christian Medical Association of India for her final years of service gave her the opportunity to travel extensively in that country, giving advice on methods of enlarging the spectrum of health care services. She also prepared several booklets that offered practical advice to rural workers on how to improve the health of village communities. Also, in India, Dr Douglas Forman of Allahabad had worked in close cooperation with the Agricultural Institute to develop a more comprehensive approach to health problems by setting them in the context of a multidisciplinary programme that linked the improvement of agricultural methods and production in order to combat malnutrition, together with public health measures and clinical treatment. Then, Dr Carl E. Taylor (later Chairman and Professor in the Department of International Health at Johns Hopkins University) introduced an even more comprehensive service at Narangwal in Northern India, associated with the Christian Medical College at Ludhiana. This emphasis on community health continues to be a feature of medical education in Ludhiana and also in the Christian Medical College in Vellore.

In Africa, Dr (later Sir Clement) Chesterman in the 1920s and, later Drs Raymond Holmes and Stanley Browne introduced a programme of comprehensive medical care in a circumscribed area around Yakusu in Zaire which took the needs of the total population into account, both healthy and sick. It mounted a concerted attack on the major endemic diseases, with notable success in the case of yaws and sleeping sickness, and instituted training programmes for auxiliaries to provide total coverage of a population of over 100,000.

Eighteen health centres were created, each of which had 20 beds for general cases and six beds for maternity cases. Each centre had the usual outpatient facilities with an adequate supply of drugs. In addition, there were 35 treatment centres linked to these health centres. The central hospital not only supplied the necessary drugs and equipment but regularly supervised the work of the Christian medical auxiliaries in charge of these smaller centres. This kind of close supervision together with frequent refresher courses ensured the success of this programme. The doctors from Yakusu, sometimes accompanied by a nursing sister, would visit the health and treatment centres every six weeks to see patients who might need to be transferred to the main hospital. They would also review the records and give short refresher courses.

The programme was outstanding in its comprehensive approach to the needs of the local population and was all the more remarkable because it was set up years before 'community health' was recognized as a distinctive approach in itself. In addition to an absorbing clinical and preventive medicine schedule, the doctors at Yakusu found time for research, teaching and epidemiological surveys of the prevalence of leprosy and other endemic diseases. Their success in eradicating sleeping sickness and controlling yaws ensured the co-operation of the people. Skin smears were taken from everybody suspected of having multibacillary leprosy and the records of these cases were updated annually. Meanwhile, all persons discharging ova of schistosomiasis were treated with antimony until the disease was brought under control. The gradual raising of general hygiene, beginning with school children, reduced the previously high prevalence of this and other water-borne diseases. (Browne, 1971).

Between 1938 and 1948 another interesting community health project was proceeding in Eastern Nigeria as part of the

Owerri Province Leprosy Control programme. Leprosy had reached epidemic proportions and there was no prospect of controlling it without the active cooperation of the people themselves. In over 30 areas where cooperation was offered the leprosy staff undertook to maintain clinics, combat infective disease and promote hygiene. In at least three of these areas the people quickly learned an important lesson: when a severe epidemic of bacillary dysentery arose, the local leprosy segregation village, constructed with simple sanitary precautions, remained unscathed with not a single death. At Ndi Oji Abam, the people were so impressed that they raised a levy on the adult population and built a dispensary which the leprosy staff maintained for two years until the government was able to take it over. In this area, effective campaigns against yaws and smallpox were undertaken and a great improvement in general health levels achieved.

Later, in Nigeria, Dr (later Professor) David Morley, deeply concerned with the frequent re-admission of malnourished children to the Wesley Guild Hospital in Ilesha, developed the first under-fives clinics (see chapter 6). Their initial success owed a great deal to the humility of Dr Morley who made a practice of deferring to the auxiliary or the nurse in order to build up the confidence of the local village people in their own resident health worker. Moreover, the health care of children, half of whom were likely to die before they were five years of age, provided an incentive to the community to participate. This, in turn, led to their first involvement in what came to be called community health.

There were two unique features of the under-fives clinics which had far-reaching effects. One was the involvement of the mothers themselves in the care of the children as they participated in the 'ceremony' of child weighing and witnessed the evident relation between nutrition and health. The other was the retention of the records within the community itself. The maintenance of health now had a direct connection to themselves and to their own activities.

Mention must also be made of Dr William H. Foege (previously a medical missionary of the Lutheran Church Missouri Synod in Nigeria), who later became Director of the National Communicable Disease Center in Atlanta, Georgia. He was so concerned with the mismatch between health needs in West Africa and the scarcity of resources available to deal with them that he decided he could be more effectively engaged in mass immunization programmes to eradicate some of the endemic diseases and provide protection against those that could not yet be eradicated. Later he became director of the smallpox eradication programme covering 20 African countries with a total population of 120 million. The majority of the people used in this programme were non-medicals trained in specific tasks such as health education, advance publicity, surveillance, vaccinating or assessing results, and each was educated to see his work in the context of the total programme. Dr Foege points out that, although the technical knowledge to eliminate smallpox had existed for more than 170 years, it took a major effort of will and a new perspective to eradicate the disease, concentrating on communities rather than individuals. In the community, medical interventions are often worthless unless something is done to create a sanitary environment, provide potable water and attack the causes of endemic disease.

These few examples illustrate what can happen when a compassionate imagination ranges over the total burden of sickness in a community and, with no ready-made prescription, seeks new answers to the alleviation of that sickness and its eventual elimination and replacement by positive health measures.

Four developments assisted this process. First, there were the national surveys of church-related medical programmes, which began in 1963 and by 1967 had covered 16 countries in Africa and Asia. These revealed the curative bias we have already mentioned and the fact that the cost of maintaining these institutions was rising rapidly because of the introduction of new drugs and technology. The location of the hospital had often been determined more by ecclesiastical and historical factors than by health needs. While these church-related medical programmes were providing between 15 and 40% of the total hospital needs, the available medical facilities, including those of governments, were reaching only about 20% of the population. The very slow economic growth in the less developed countries, part of which was absorbed by an increasing population, made it unlikely that the disparity between the 20% served by medical facilities and the 80% deprived would change in the near future if the prevailing medical system continued.

The second development was the publication in 1966 of the papers presented at a symposium held in Makerere University in Uganda (King, 1966). These provided a primer on the medicine of poverty, and emphasized a bottom-up rather than a top-down approach to the use of medical resources. This was important in countries where the choice lay between provision of rural health centres or of a sophisticated medical centre in the capital city.

The third factor was the growing interest in community development which took people rather than theories and systems into account.

Finally, from the People's Republic of China came news of the amazing attempt to offer medical services to a total population through the introduction of the 'barefoot doctor' who was selected, prior to training, by the local community itself.

One offshoot of this awareness of the need for change was the creation in 1968 of the Christian Medical Commission. A sponsored agency of the World Council of Churches and located in Geneva, it made itself available to all the churches – Protestant, Catholic and Orthodox – as a forum for promoting the coordination of their medical services with one another, and with national Ministries of Health in order to achieve a more effective mechanism for planning. One obvious objective of special interest to the Commission was to overcome the social injustice of a system which, by the ever-increasing cost of its technology, unwittingly deprived the bulk of the population of its services. It was ironic that those Christian hospitals that provided the highest professional level of care because they believed this to be an effective part of their witness, now had to price their services beyond the reach of the very poor whom they most wished to serve. It was therefore appropriate that Christians should develop experimental programmes of minimal cost medical care without any unacceptable increase in the risks. In this context, the physician is confronted with the realization that he cannot provide care for all and must find an answer to these most disturbing questions – for whom (or to whom) am I responsible? Can I show how a need can be met?

In some countries there were separate associations of Protestant and Roman Catholic hospitals and/or professional workers, but they lacked the corporate ability to engage in joint planning with governments. To some extent, the Tanzania Christian Medical Association was an exception to this since it brought Roman Catholic and Protestants together, but its decisions were not binding on individual agencies. Then in 1965 the churches in Malawi, both Roman Catholic and Protestant, formed an organization to plan joint services with the government for more comprehensive health care to the total population. The government in return offered accommodation in the Ministry of Health to facilitate joint planning. This has been copied in several other countries in Africa, the initiative usually coming from the churches.

Health and poverty are interrelated. If an individual or a community is poor, neither is likely to be healthy. If they lack resources for adequate food or protected water supplies, no medical intervention will improve their overall health. Conversely, poor health can be a major factor in preventing such a group rising above existing economic levels. Similarly, in many situations, better housing, sanitation, education and communication will have a greater impact on health status than medical care alone. While medical technology can influence the effects of disease, it has little impact on its incidence. A rapid increase in population also puts a strain on the available resources. Such conditions can only be alleviated through a concerted and carefully planned effort set in a multi-disciplinary context and with the cooperation of all.

The church has a special contribution to make because of its unique understanding of the importance of the individual. But it is also aware that people live in communities just as the Church itself is a gathered community. Its task, therefore, is to reach out to communities through its own community, the congregation, and see the task of health and development as the corporate responsibility of the congregation and not simply of its professional members alone. It also seeks to involve those it would assist in decisions about the kind of help they need and to ensure their participation in its provision. Only in this way will the community have respect for the help given and implement the programme as though it were its own.

The provision of health services is the constitutional and moral obligation of governments. When national resources are limited, the resources offered by churches and voluntary agencies are usually welcomed, provided they conform to national policy. There is a danger, however, that governments may ask churches to undertake expensive programmes that involve high recurrent costs beyond the resources of the national church, and which have to rely on external funding. Such programmes can distort the image and the rightful task of the church, and foster paternalism. On the other hand, the churches, with government approval, can most appropriately undertake experimental programmes in new forms of health services that foster self-reliance and local community participation and which are viable in the local economy. These would serve the areas of greatest need and could provide models for national adoption.

Directing attention to people and their needs, rather than applying a system to problems, opened up a whole new spectrum of resources that had seldom been considered. Among these were indigenous or traditional healers, herbalists and traditional birth attendants who, with some basic training in aseptic techniques, could be integrated into the comprehensive programme. This was a ready-made source of manpower. While, at first, physicians trained in the discipline of scientific medicine were often appalled by the mistakes made by some untrained practitioners, many of them came to appreciate the potential for more effective therapy inherent in some traditional approaches.

For example, there was the overriding interest of the patient and the relatives in the reason for the illness, and any explanation had to fit into their world view of causation. While we use what we call common sense to deduce the connection between snails and bilharzia, or between mosquitoes and malaria, they find it reasonable to attribute some diseases to unseen spiritual forces or to jealousies and hatreds and such like. The former must be placated and relations restored if healing is to take place. In addition to the indigenous practitioners, school teachers and other lay workers could assist in the provision of health education, vaccination, first aid and the maintenance of child weight records.

From the partnerships that resulted from the Commission's invitation, several new initiatives in community health emerged. Dr John Sibley, a missionary surgeon working in a large church-related hospital in South Korea, was increasingly disturbed by the high cost of hospital care, which excluded from care a large section of the surrounding population. He asked himself the disturbing question, "Ought we to exclude from our mortality and morbidity statistics people we cannot afford to care for?" After consultation with several of his colleagues and with the advice of faculty members in the Departments of Public Health in both Seoul National and Yonsei Universities, he drew up a proposal for a community-centred health project consisting of family planning, public health and a scientifically controlled curative programme coordinated with a community develop-

ment effort to encourage local residents to organize and participate in cooperatives and self-help projects. The programme was
adapted to the potential resources of the community so as to
make self-support a feasible objective and to involve the local
church congregations. Major capital investments were avoided
in the hope that, if the experiment was successful, it could be
reproduced in similar economic situations.

The island of Koje Do, off the south coast, was selected. It had
a population of 120,000, and an annual per capita income of less
than £60. There was one Western-trained doctor on the island
together with six indigenous practitioners and five Chinese
herbalists. It was hoped, eventually, to integrate them all into the
programme once their suspicions were allayed. A target area
with a population of 30,000 was selected initially, with the
expectation that this would be gradually extended to cover the
whole island. In the beginning, the project suffered somewhat as
its director tried to break away from being an institutionally
oriented general surgeon to a community orientated project
manager. Moreover, this approach to medical care was new to
Korea at that time and ran counter to several provisions of a strict
medico-legal code. The first break with tradition came when it
was realized that no national physician would respond to the
inducements offered to work with the project. They were not
willing to live in such an isolated place with no social amenities
and no adequate educational facilities for their children. For the
next few years attempts were made to train various types of
health worker who would provide basic medical services. While
auxiliary medical personnel had long been accepted in several
African countries, they were not generally recognized in most
Asian countries, with the later exception of China and then
India.

On Koje Do it was found that girls selected from the villages,
even though they had no more than primary education, could be
taught basic skills in medical care, family planning, health
education and first aid. Thus, they became the first-line resource
for health care in each village and they were linked to more
advanced services through a readily available referral system.
Initial supervision was provided by nurses who also ran the
well-baby clinics, tuberculosis home-visiting and mother-at-
risk programmes associated with their home nursing. Community coordination was achieved through meetings of the local
board of managers, who met with the project leaders each

month, often joined by the local township chiefs. Perhaps the
most significant contribution of this programme came through
the willingness of a Christian physician to break with a traditional system of medical practice in order to explore new forms
of service more appropriate to the cultural milieu and poverty of
the local people. Later, when two university medical colleges
rotated students and faculty for field experience in this programme, further experiments in community health became possible: these could avoid the growing pains of Koje Do, and
expanded considerably the access of the Korean people to medical care. As for Koje Do, it attracted the enthusiastic interest of a
former Minister of Health, who decided to extend the programme to the whole of the island and then to the mainland.

A new initiative which made the claims for promoting community health in less developed countries more cogent, and
indeed, imperative, was begun by an Irish Roman Catholic
Sister-doctor in Zambia. Sister Maureen O'Keefe chose the 70-
bed Mtendere Hospital for a study of the health of the community that the hospital believed it served. The population of
5500 which depended on the hospital for primary care lived in
scattered villages within a radius of 32 km from the hospital.
Taking a 10% random sample of this population, she divided
them into four categories: children under 5, children of school
age, 6-15; women of child-bearing age; the rest, adults. Information was collected in the form of a past history of sickness, noting
what the person regarded as serious disease; where treatment
was sought; previous attendance at the hospital and utilization
of under-fives clinics and antenatal services. To this information were added environmental factors such as availability of
food, water supply, housing, sanitation and the like. The sample
involved people from 16 tribes. Of those interviewed, 84% had
attended a hospital at one time or another and 42% had been
inpatients. The major diseases prevalent in the under-fives were
diarrhoea and dysentery, cough, malnutrition, malaria and
gastroenteritis. For the adults and older children, the pattern
was the same with the exception of gastro-enteritis, but in addition, there was a high incidence of schistosomiasis, chest infections and infected wounds. Forty-six per cent of the women had
lost one or more children under five, most of them after the first
six months. In one village, every woman had goitre and in one
primary school microscopic examination of a single specimen
of urine revealed that 65% of the children had *Schistosoma*

haematobium. The ratio of those at risk attending the hospital depended on distance. Within 5 km 1 in 2 attended; between 17 and 32 km the ratio dropped to 1 in 17; and from 33 to 40 km 1 in 46.

Sister Maureen O'Keefe ends her report with the following conclusions:

'Although the sample is too small to permit generalization, such an attendance gradient might perhaps suggest that utilization of medical care by communities with similar disease patterns depends not so much on the actual need for it as on the easy availability of medicine for the symptom of the present moment. While I have used only raw data and have not attempted to interpret these to any great extent, I think it is fair to say that the bulk of disease seen in the hospital and in the population is *community* disease. Since the hospital approach meets the needs of individuals, one cannot expect that, used as the sole vehicle of health care delivery, it will make a significant contribution to the health of the community as a whole.

In the long run, what difference will our Ambilhar and Sulphas make to a community where, as in the case of the study area, over 50 per cent of the people depend for their water supply on a bilharzia-infested source at least one kilometre away? Or where only two households in the sample group grow vegetables in an area which has the richest soil in Zambia? Or where, for almost half of the small number who rear poultry, tribal custom prohibits the eating of eggs? Where the problem is in the community and not essentially medical in its source, the solution would rightfully be sought within the community and in collaboration with those who are professionally concerned such as agriculturalists, community development personnel, school teachers, Water Departments, etc. I think we are becoming convinced that the health message must begin in the heart of the village and in a way that the people can make their own, so that they gradually – even if slowly – assume responsibility for their health care. With this growing conviction how salutary it would be if we endeavoured, even in a small experimental way here and there, to introduce health projects that have their roots in the community, so that in time the hospital will assume its rightful and more limited role in the health delivery system.'

While individual initiatives like this might previously have gone unnoticed, ecumenical cooperation became more possible as the churches coordinated their activities in health care so that information was widely disseminated. The journal *Contact*, published by the Christian Medical Commission in Geneva and issued free of charge, widened even further the spread of information of successful experiments.

The Bhore Committee which was set up by the government of India in 1946 recommended the following guiding principles:

1. No individual should fail to secure adequate medical care because of inability to pay for it.
2. Health programmes must lay special emphasis on preventive work.
3. There should be a change in emphasis from the urban to the rural population which bears the burden of famine and pestilence.
4. The doctor of the future should be a social physician, attracting the people and guiding them to a healthier and happier life.

Such guidelines should have provided a blueprint for an independent India to pursue a new approach to medical services. Instead, the government made spectacular 'progress' by increasing the number of medical colleges from 26 to 113 and expanding research facilities and urban hospitals. It is true that the number of primary health centres was greatly increased, but they were a far cry from the staff levels and population coverage recommended by the Bhore Committee. Even now four-fifths of the population has no access to medical facilities, according to Dr Bannerji of the Jawaharlal Nehru University in Delhi (1977).

This imbalance between those served and those deprived of medical services has stirred the conscience of a few Christian doctors in India who have experimented with alternative forms in order to reduce it. Mention has already been made of some who broke with tradition in a preceding generation. More recently, Dr William Cutting expanded the concept of the under-fives clinics into a more general form of community medicine in a circumscribed group of villages in Andhra Pradesh. Here medical care was no longer to be offered exclusively by the physician and his professional staff alone. The hospital became the apex of a filtering system of care which began in the house and spread through the village clinic.

The most significant initiative in pointing the way to a comprehensive system of health care in India has come from two Christian physicians, Rajanikant Arole and his wife Mabelle, both graduates from the Christian Medical College at Vellore in South India. They worked for five years in a church-related hospital serving a population of 100,000. At the end of this period, they realized that although they had taken care of the patients who came to the hospital, they had done little, if anything, for the general health of the communities around them. This disturbed them so much that they decided to take a course in public and community health as it is related to the needs of less developed countries. (It seems incongruous that they had to go to a so-called developed country for this, but this still sometimes obtains). On their way back to India, they visited the offices of the Christian Medical Commission in Geneva and discussed with the staff their proposal to begin a project in community health centred around the small town of Jamkhed in Maharashtra and covering several peripheral villages. Their target population was 40,000. The Commission staff promised to secure funding for the first three years of the project, and the Aroles returned to India.

Several accounts have been written about the Jamkhed programme (*Contact*, 1972, Newell, 1975).

The Aroles spent most of the first six months visiting the villages surrounding Jamkhed to discuss their proposals with the leaders of each community and listening to their reactions. It soon became evident that health was of little priority among the felt wants of the local people. Because of recent droughts, they were more concerned about water for irrigation and the production of better crops. Some expressed a wish for better housing and roads. There was concern about the health of their children, many of whom died before they were five years of age; otherwise, ill-health was accepted almost fatalistically because it had always been there.

By the simple act of listening to the local people, the Aroles discovered that there was a considerable difference between what they, as professionals, thought the people needed and what, in fact, they actually wanted. The Aroles took these people seriously and began by trying to meet their felt needs. First, they secured well-digging equipment, and the first instalment of the delayed grant was used to buy a tractor to be lent to the villagers for improving crop-production. They soon earned the respect and confidence of the people who were willing to listen to the Aroles as advice was offered about their health needs and how they could participate in meeting them. Instead of having to construct clinics for these villages, the Aroles were offered empty houses by the people themselves.

When irrigation enabled them to increase food production, the villagers used part of the surplus to provide a communal

meal for the children of each village. They were also taught how
to weigh under-fives regularly and watch for signs of malnutrition, and they themselves kept the records. The school teachers
or the village leaders were supplied with simple drugs and
taught how to use them. The Aroles deliberately avoided
holding separate clinics for leprosy patients, explaining to the
villagers the etiology of the disease and its reluctant transmission. Thus, they prevented the all-too-frequent social segregation of leprosy sufferers and were able to integrate them in the
community. These leprosy patients were organized into a goat-
breeding cooperative and soon paid back the original loan that
had enabled them to start. As a result, some of the leprosy
patients have now become the wealthier members of the community and others come to them for loans.

The Aroles were sensitive to the wants and needs of these
village people. They observed that when a nurse addressed a
gathering of women in the antenatal clinic the women would
later seek the advice of the clinic sweeper or watchman, who
were illiterates like themselves. There was a bond of community
and understanding among illiterates, so that an educated person
like a nurse, even though she came from that area, could not
easily find a bridge of communication to them. Thus it became
necessary to train illiterate women chosen by each village community to be their local village health workers. Each weekend,
they travel to Jamkhed to share their experiences of the
past week with those from other villages. It is like a clinico-
pathological conference at a lower level, the doctors and nurses
only intervening when they are asked to. The indigenous practitioners have now been integrated into the programme and are
regarded as colleagues, with the Aroles serving as consultants.
This programme has demonstrated that resources can be found
within the community, and people can be activated to identify
and help solve their health problems. As the Aroles say,
'Compassion for individual patients is an important component
of medical practice. The same compassion needs to be extended
to communities in areas not ordinarily covered by health professionals' (Newell, 1975).

The Jamkhed programme has attracted considerable interest
in India and beyond. (The Aroles have been appointed to the
National Planning Board for health services by the government
of India and have been asked to extend their programme to the
3 million people of the Ahmednagar District. They were recently

awarded the President Magsaysay Prize by the government of the Philippines.) Jamkhed has now become a training centre for physicians, nurses and others interested in developing community health care services, not only in India but also in several other Asian and African countries. The project was evaluated by an expert team appointed jointly by WHO and UNICEF, and their enthusiastic report was published under the lengthy title, "Alternative Approaches to meeting Basic Health Needs of Populations in Developing Countries." Later, Dr R. Arole, together with his wife, wrote an account of their experience, which was included in *Health by the People* (Newell, 1975). This book also contains descriptions of the initiatives of two other Christian physicians – Dr Gunawan Nugroho in Indonesia and Dr Carroll Behrhorst in Guatemala. Faced with the apparent hopelessness of the situation in which the rural people lived and suffered ill health, they were willing to live with them, learn from them and explore with them effective ways of securing and maintaining better health. They, with the Aroles, played no small part in moving the World Health Organization and, through the World Health Assembly, its member states to adopt the promotion of primary health care as their highest priority. Such care must be shaped around the life patterns of the people it serves and must meet their local needs and priorities. The services should also be fully integrated with those of the other sectors involved in community development, such as agriculture, education, public works, housing and communication. The workers are to be selected by the community and trained locally (WHO, 1974).

The Christian Medical Commission's initiative in promoting community and primary health care projects and, more especially, its ability to enable others to experiment, was acknowledged by the World Health Organization. A joint standing committee in 1974 made it possible for the Commission to use the expertise available in various technical units of WHO. It also facilitated joint activities in the field through the cooperation of WHO regional offices and country representatives. Making health services available to all by the year 2000, was adopted as a goal at a joint WHO/UNICEF-sponsored international conference for government representatives held in Alma Ata in the USSR in September 1978. A Christian physician with experience as a missionary in Africa, then on the staff of the Christian Medical Commission and of the health services of his own country, has now been appointed by WHO to oversee the implementation of this priority.

It has been noted that the first essential step in community health care is listening. The second step is a willingness to turn the familiar health-care pyramid upside down and to start with people where they are in their communities. The professional desire for 'excellence' has too often distorted the scope of the application of medicine to those millions who are still deprived of its benefits. A recent report to the Overseas Council of the Church of Scotland by one of its medical missionaries contains these revealing words:

> 'For myself I have been led, more and more, to see that the most realistic way of helping people medically and perhaps spiritually too, is not by sitting in hospital waiting for the seriously ill folk to come to us but to go out into the country areas and try to find out first of all what it is in their ordinary living habits which makes them so susceptible to illness and then try to persuade them to take such precautions as will prevent them from becoming ill. Some of the most obvious needs are clean drinking water, proper latrines and a more balanced diet, especially for babies – but I expect there will be lots more for me to learn. It is hard enough for me to think myself out of the whole concept of curative medicine, so how much more for those who hardly know what it means to be healthy as we understand it.'
> (Dr Janet C. Duncan, of Kalimbong, West Bengal)

Even more ambitious is the RUHSA project in Tamil Nadu near Vellore, based on the intensely practical acceptance of the principle that community health is the responsibility of government, but that in rural areas government is unlikely to have sufficient staff to make community health effective. Dr Daleep Mukarji began by becoming the first doctor ever to take a higher degree in the economics of the third world at the London School of Economics. With a group of dedicated colleagues he offered his services to government, to operate a comprehensive community health project in a substantial backwood area, realizing that agriculture, education and economic development must go hand in hand with improvements in health. They made no attempt to dictate to or to rival government and this won government support; their achievements are quite remarkable.

Even the collection of statistics, which one would consider a necessary basis for beginning community health work, has to be subject to this unique sensitivity to the feelings of those who are to be served. As Dr R. Arthur Hughes of the Welsh Presbyterian

Mission at Shillong in North-east India has to say:

'I had long realized that statistics could be either hypnotic or challenging, and at the administrative end, potentially vital. But from the villages' end of the story, official statistics were totally meaningless . . . In other words the statistics had to be their own figures, given by them, in terms they understood. Infant mortality rates, deaths per thousand live births, were totally irrelevant – who had ever seen a thousand live births in their village? Statistics must be the truth as they told it, and with this knowledge, which they couldn't deny, one could create the basis for active (participation) . . .'

From these quotations and the example of the Aroles in Jamkhed, it will be apparent that training programmes to equip people for community health service are very different from the familiar didactic teaching and training of other professional health workers.

One of the most successful initiatives in the training of community health workers was started by some Indonesian Christian physicians who designed a course of training along in-service lines. Those to be trained must first participate in exploring the needs, problems and potentials within the community in the field of health as well as other aspects of life in order to gain an appreciation of what they are being trained to do. Then they are to work out a simple programme designed to meet those needs, using the existing potentials within the community. Thus, the training is very practical, problem-solving and action-orientated in nature. The trainees are given various practical assignments to equip them with the necessary skills for identifying and solving health problems. This involves organizing people in the neighbourhood to clean their homes and yards; to keep the weight charts of the under-fives; to find and report patients who have a cough for more than two weeks, and so on. They are trained in the basic knowledge of diseases prevalent in the area, and priority is given to enabling them to identify such conditions as malnutrition, dehydration, bronchopneumonia and obstructed labour, and report these to the local health centre. In addition to these cognitive skills they are also trained in the treatment of minor ailments, emergency first aid, and simple diagnostic procedures.

The candidates for these courses are selected by the community, and many of them work as volunteers. From experience gained in the operation of these programmes, it is clear that one aspect of the training is to make the candidate aware of his or her limitations and to know where he can get help when needed. As front-line workers, they are indispensable agents of the local community but, by themselves, they are not sufficient. They must be taught to recognize their partnership in a total system of health services and understand their accountability in such a system. This will happen when other echelons of the health services accept their responsibility to support the community health worker.

References

Banerji, D (1977) *Formulating an Alternative Health Care Scheme for India. Community Health in Asia.* Christian Conference of Asia, Singapore.

Browne, S.G. (1971) *Contact* Geneva: Christian Medical Commission No.6.

Contact (1972) Geneva: Christian Medical Commission, No 10, p.28

King, Maurice (Ed.) (1966) *Medical Care in Developing Countries* Nairobi: Oxford University Press

Newell, K.W (Ed.) (1975) *Health by the People* Geneva: World Health Organization

O'Keefe, Maureen (1973) *Contact* No 17 October Geneva: Christian Medical Commission

World Health Organization (1974) *Promotion of National Health Services* Doc.EB.55/9 Dec.

CHAPTER 17

WATER, HYGIENE AND SANITATION

Roy Billington

'There is probably no single factor', says a writer in the *New Internationalist,* 'with a greater effect on the health and well-being of a community than the provision of an ample and convenient supply of clean water. Waterborne disease can account for half the illness-induced deaths in many under-developed countries, and could be prevented by such supplies. An efficient sewage disposal system is part and parcel of the water supply problem'. What gives such a sweeping statement its force and impact is the weight of evidence that dirty water and poor sanitation* account for an immense burden of preventable disease. The statistics are chilling indeed.

The World Health Organization estimates that as many as 80% of all diseases in the world are associated with water. The Brandt Report declares that 'between 20 and 25 million children below the age of five die every year in developing countries, and a third of these deaths are from diarrhoea caught from polluted water. All these deaths cannot be eliminated just by providing safe water and sanitation; but there can be no lasting improvement of public health without them.' And a United Nations statement adds: 'One could cut infant mortality by 50% with safe water and good sanitation'. The provision of clean water and the proper disposal of excreta are the two most important factors in improving health, but the difficulties of providing these services are immense.

In almost all developing countries the great majority of rural people use water that is either heavily polluted or distant from their home or both. Rural people often have no latrine and defaecate promiscuously wherever privacy is available (Feacham, 1981). It is estimated that 'half the world's population has no safe water and 75% of the population of developing countries have no sanitary facility'. In the rural areas of Africa, Asia and Latin America for instance, less than one third of the population

*Sanitation is used throughout in the sense of excreta disposal.

has safe drinking water and only 15% have adequate sanitation. The situation is at its worst in the 38 lowest-income countries, where only 28% of the population on average have access to safe water. The shanty towns are affected as much as the rural areas; so no wonder that Barbara Ward (1976) says: 'If any single physical service needs priority in the world's shanty towns, it is safe drinking water.'

To meet this gigantic problem the International Decade of Drinking-Water Supply and Sanitation was launched on November 10 1980. The declared aim of the Decade, which runs from 1981-1990, both inclusive, is to provide during that time clean drinking water and effective sanitation in every town and village in the world: a noble aim.

The programme will be largely carried out by the governments of the developing nations themselves, who will have to raise the bulk of the money from their own resources, but richer countries, the World Bank and other UN agencies are expected to help. The estimated cost is US $30,000 million a year, of which over $9000 million a year or $25 million a day will have to be given in aid. These sums seem vast at first sight but, when compared with the $1400 million spent every day on arms, and the $240 million spent every day on cigarettes, the cost of the Decade seems reasonable indeed, when the benefits are so great.

As Barbara Ward (1976) wrote years before the Decade began:

'There is an area of action that could and should be undertaken at once. It does more by itself to build up people's own capacity than perhaps any alternative . . . It avoids enormous human costs . . . This priority is simply to ensure to every village and city safe drinking water and reasonable sewage disposal. If there can be a commitment, let it be here . . . the release of hope, energy and resources might amaze the world . . . it would be a world reborn.'

What are the chances of success? Will the goal be reached in time? Almost certainly not. The task is a gigantic one indeed. New drinking water and sanitation facilities would have to be provided for half a million more people every day during the entire Decade. Water and sanitation are not top priorities with governments, and schemes for their provision in developing countries have failed in the past, the schemes sometimes breaking down faster than they could be built up. Donors are not interested in maintenance, and many government budgets cannot meet the running costs of much needed programmes.

Furthermore, it is not enough to provide a community with a new water supply or to encourage the building of latrines. Those who are offered these benefits must believe that the changes are worth the inconvenience of altering their personal habits, and must be willing to provide the money and effort needed to maintain the pumps, wells and other equipment. These changed attitudes cannot be adopted quickly, and can only come after much health education and discussion. Nevertheless, it is most encouraging that the Decade has been launched, and each place where progress is made can be a stimulus and challenge to neighbouring communities to do the same.

When drinking water is polluted or unprotected, or when water for washing is insufficient, the risks of contracting disease are considerable, as the following table, adapted from Cairncross *et al*, (1980) shows:

Transmission of Water-Related Diseases

Method	Examples
I *Waterborne* (carried in drinking water)	
(a) Classical	Typhoid, cholera
(b) Non-classical (transmission recently established)	Infective hepatitis
II *Water-washed* (washed away by plenty of water)	
(a) Superficial infections	Trachoma, scabies
(b) Intestinal infections	Shigella dysentery
III *Water-based* (parasite spends part of its life in water)	
(a) Water-multiplied (percutaneous entry)	Schistosomiasis
(b) Ingested	Guinea worm
IV *Water-Related Insect Vectors*	
(a) Water-biting (near water-holes)	Trypanosomiasis
(b) Water-breeding	Malaria

It must be noted that all water-borne diseases (Section I) can be spread other than by drinking water. The spread may be by contaminated food. Safe water supplies alone will not fully control the diseases in this group. In *Drawers of Water*, a study of domestic water use in East Africa, White and his colleagues (1972) conclude that an excellent water supply would reduce:–

Typhoid fever	by 80%
Urinary schistosomiasis	80%
Guinea-worm infestation	100%
Trypanosomiasis (*T. gambiense*)	80%
Inflammatory eye disease	70%
Gastroenteritis in children from 4 weeks to 2 years old	50%

The authors are nevertheless cautious in their conclusions. In the rural area they studied there are few villages, so it was difficult to estimate the total benefits obtained, and they stress that many factors influence the incidence of a disease. Nevertheless, rural water-users in East Africa stand to gain greatly from very modest improvements. As W.E. Wood (1978) has written:

> 'It is impossible to calculate the amount of sickness, misery and premature death throughout the world that can be attributed to man's ingestion of his neighbour's waste products. In practice, and on a worldwide scale, this is a problem of such magnitude as to be virtually insoluble, but it can be effectively undertaken within small communities.'

In many countries, it is the women and girls who carry water. This can take a great deal of time. In Mkuu, Tanzania, fetching water took an average of 4½ hours a day; in Masii, Kenya, it took 4 hours. In Bourkina Fasso (Upper Volta) women walk for two or three hours each way to fetch water. In the southern part of the Sudan during the dry season, when nearly all wells run dry, women and girls have spent eight hours of each day walking early in the morning and again in the evening to a stagnant pond in a river bed.

Water-carrying also uses much energy. In Zaire the average calabash of water holds 10 litres, each litre weighing 1 kilogram. In the Sudan, each woman carries an 18-litre (18 kg.) can while, astonishingly, in Bourkina Fasso mothers carry 25 kg of water back to their huts, which takes two or three hours. These are very heavy for a woman, since the greatest weight that a woman can carry in comfort is 15 kg – the weight of a heavy suitcase. More than one member of a family may have to share in carrying these loads. A family of eight – father, mother, grandmother and five children – needs 5 litres for each person daily just to survive: that is a total of 40 litres. No wonder a woman uses up to one-third of her total daily energy, namely 600 calories, in performing this burdensome task.

In addition, women do all the cooking in the home and face the stresses of pregnancy, childbirth and breastfeeding. And their small children run the risk of death from gastroenteritis. It is thus not surprising that the Venezuelan government has calculated that providing clean rural water will repay its cost five to seven times over in working days and human lives saved.

It is of interest that preventive medicine is scarcely mentioned in the early chapters of the history of medical missions, as exemplified in the records of the Church Missionary Society (CMS). For instance, at Old Cairo Hospital in 1905 2000 patients were treated for hookworm infestation, and at Gaza in 1903 there were 2300 deaths from cholera, but in neither case did medical missionaries undertake any preventive measures. From about 1912 onwards interest in promoting better hygiene slowly grew. In Peshawar in 1914 Dr Lankester worked with the government in formulating measures to prevent tuberculosis, and in east Nigeria in 1925 Sister Elms wrote a simple hygiene textbook which helped to reduce infant mortality. By 1918, when Old Cairo Hospital was treating 9000 hookworm patients a year, the staff gave weekly lectures to patients on its prevention and handed out explanatory leaflets when patients were discharged. In Kerman, Persia, in 1925 expatriate and Iranian doctors were recommending the provision of public latrines and an improved water supply; but unfortunately in 1930 the Kerman hospital staff had to report that 'there has been no improvement in local sanitation in the last 25 years'.

In 1935 Dr T.S. Williams, an Indian doctor working in Dornakal, South India, was writing simple booklets on village hygiene, dealing with clean air and water and the prevention of malaria and guinea-worm infestation. In Pachod, China, in the same year women were being taught health and hygiene. Up to this time, however, during years when the Medical Mission Auxiliary of the CMS (as the medical branch of the Society's work was termed) could be described as the largest medical missionary organization in the world, preventive medical work, though recognized as important, was virtually limited to antenatal care and child welfare, together with the teaching of hygiene.

A big change began at the World Missionary Conference at Tambaram College, Madras, in 1938. One section of the Conference was entitled 'The Christian Ministry of Health and Healing', and Dr E. H. Hume, missionary adviser to the Chinese Medical Association, and Dr P.V. Benjamin of the Christian Medical Association of India, urged medical missionaries to adopt a new attitude and a new policy. In 1939 Dr Benjamin wrote:

'There is a clear call to give greater attention to preventive medicine . . . health and welfare . . . and health teaching . . . Each hospital should be a centre of health . . . Its purpose cannot be considered fulfilled unless its influence permeates the community as a whole and is manifest in clean streets, a pure water supply, better sanitation and cleanly habits . . . We have scarcely crossed the threshold of such a quest as this.'

From about 1940 onwards mission or church hospitals became fewer, partly because of the increased cost of giving medical treatment, and partly because governments were providing these services widely. Church hospitals had to charge higher and higher fees and found it more difficult to treat the really poor, while subsidized government hospitals could give a free-at-the-time service. In some places government and Church hospitals existed side by side, providing the same service. Medical missionaries began to ask whether medical missionary work was only a pioneer task, to be given up when government services become established, or whether there was a specific Christian ministry of healing at all times.

To answer these questions Christian medical workers held the first of two consultations at Tübingen, Germany, in 1964 (McGilvray, 1981). Those present affirmed that there is indeed a Christian ministry of healing, and that this (taking healing in a wide sense) is the task of the congregation, the local fellowship of Christians, which should work towards restoring men and women to fellowship with God and with one another. This emphasis on the responsibility of the local Christian community, a responsibility for the health of its neighbours that could not be left to professional workers only, was a notable affirmation. In some way the Church now had to become a healing Church. In 1967 a second consultation was held at Tübingen, and more thought was given to ways in which a congregation could care practically for those with whom it lived.

Although these plans for truly church-based healing work were now being put forward, surveys showed that in 1967 95% of churches' medical work still focused on curative care in hospitals and clinics. Some change in direction was urgently needed and the World Council of Churches set up the Christian Medical Commission in June 1968, to find out how best the churches might give health care. The Commission urged that such care must centre on the community rather than on individuals, and that all those who wish to help others must work *with* people and not just *for* them.

Another big step forward was taken when the World Health Organization and the Commission established a joint committee in March 1974, to see how both bodies could work together. WHO studied some of the Commission's experiments in health

care, and then laid it down that primary health care at community level should be the foundation of all health services. In
this way the greatest possible number of people could benefit
from the resources available. But was even community medical
care the best way to improve health? The Commission recalled,
in further studies, that it was clean water, good sanitation, more
food and better housing that had changed the health picture in
the Western world a hundred years before. These environmental
changes had now to be striven for in developing countries if the
same great benefits were to follow. This concern of the
Commission for clean water and proper excreta-disposal has
been more than matched by WHO's support of the Drinking
Water and Sanitation Decade.

In addition, leading British aid agencies, such as OXFAM,
Christian Aid, and TEAR Fund have in recent years been asking
themselves what were the most important ways to improve
health in a disadvantaged community, and they conclude that
encouraging self-reliance, teaching skills to combat poverty,
helping with the growing of more food, and finding fresh water
supplies are vital steps to take. Their teaching has influenced
churches and missionary societies considerably and I draw
gratefully on their experience in the case-studies which follow.

Case-Studies

1. *Making the Desert Bloom* (1961-1976)

Winifred Coate was for many years a missionary in Zerka,
Jordan, and became very concerned about the unemployment
around her. In 1948, she bought tools for Zerka townspeople and
their morale rose immensely. But the problem of land workers
remained.

In 1960, she retired from CMS and stayed on in Zerka, 20 km
north-east of Amman. Waterless desert stretched out beyond the
town, but ruined castles suggested that there must have been
water in the past. She formed a company with a tiny capital of
£200 to bore for water. The company had six directors, five
Jordanians and herself.

Abu Nakleh, water diviner and tractor driver, advised pros-
pecting in a rocky area 43 km north-east of Amman. OXFAM
paid for a drilling rig, and, after one month, they struck water.
'Mabrook – (May it be blessed)', cried Abu. They put a submer-
sible pump in the well, built two-roomed houses and dug irrigation channels. The aim was to increase food production and give

employment. Any needy farmer could apply for a 2 hectare (5 acre) holding, and soon market gardens were producing tomatoes, cucumbers and onions. Water was piped into the houses, so that wives had time to join their husbands in the fields. Mechanics were employed to maintain the wells. Work was hard and there were many difficulties, with donkeys eating tree saplings and camels drinking the irrigation water. But 51 farmers settled in Abdelliyeh, the new village, and their crops were sold cooperatively.

The company built a school and then handed it over to the government. A clinic was started, shop-keepers arrived, and bigger commercial farms took shape. Then the company, which was never intended to be permanent, was wound up in 1975. The farmers reluctantly agreed to own their farms and shared five of the wells, with two mechanics staying on to maintain them (Coate, c.1977).

Comment. The coming of water – admittedly chiefly for irrigation in this instance – gave birth to a whole new community. Winifred was the innovator, but the company was mainly in Jordanian hands from the start, and when it closed down as planned, after 15 years, it left a flourishing independent farming group, which could support the water-supply mechanics.

2. Water at Matumbulu (CMS, 1980)

Matumbulu, like many other villages in the dry Central Region of Tanzania near Dodoma, has a water problem. In one way it is better off than other villages as it has a borehole, but the pump is powered by a diesel engine, and oil is expensive. Also there is no reservoir, nor is there piping to serve the spread-out Ujaama (self-help) village, so people on the far side have to walk a mile each way to fetch water. The village has many dry river-beds. One of them gets its water from a small reservoir 6 km away. In the dry season some of this lake water is let out on the first day of the month. The water runs down, losing much on the way, and arrives in the village as a very small stream which persists for one day only. Then it goes underground, and women dig small holes in the river bed. Dirty water slowly comes from the holes and then they fill their gourds.

Michael Hudson, a young missionary, obtained a water-filter unit in the form of a fibreglass rectangular box fitted with a slotted plate.* When buried open end down in the sea or river bed,

---

*Obtained from Sea Water Supplies Ltd.

and covered thickly with sand, the box-like structure becomes largely filled with sand and gravel which act as a filter, so that suspended matter, schistosome cercariae and most bacteria are trapped in it. A hose connects the filter to a hand pump at a little distance.

Michael buried his filter 2.5 metres deep in the river bed and covered it with sand. The pipe was joined to the pump. To everyone's surprise, water came pouring out. It was dirty at first from mud and sand, but in two days it was very clean. The women were bringing up over 3500 litres an hour, a quantity that would previously have taken many days.

Now the problem arose as to who should look after the pump. It could not be left unguarded, as it might be broken or stolen. At first Michael paid a church member, Kalebi, to work the pump for three hours each evening, after which it was disconnected and left overnight in the village shop. The village was asked to continue to pay him but nothing happened, and Kalebi lost heart and often did not come. Michael wondered what to do next.

Comment. The filter unit seems to be an excellent method for obtaining clean water from sandy-bedded rivers and lake sites. The box is robust and has no moving parts. A Patay hand pump is recommended for use with it, and this pump needs little maintenance apart from a new plastic diaphragm after every 400 hours' work.

3. *Christian Rural Service*

In 1965 Dick Lyth, a CMS missionary (who later became a bishop), launched a scheme to enrich the whole life of rural people in southwest Uganda. This beautiful part of the country has a large population, half of it under the age of 16. There is much pressure on the land, and many young people have never been to school.

The church is strong, but Dick wanted Christians to show greater caring for the spiritual and practical needs of their neighbours. He chose a team of 14 young men and women and trained them as evangelists and practical helpers in country parishes. World Neighbours, a North American aid group, and Christian Aid provided funds. Dick called his scheme 'Christian Rural Service'. The team learned how to mend their own bicycles and how to teach others to do the same; how to give health talks and help with government immunization campaigns; how to run young farmers' clubs and teach adults to read – and all in addition to the simple preaching of the Gospel. They encouraged families to use their latrines regularly. They urged rural communities to protect their springs of water. The government was willing to supply cement and piping for this, but the cement had gone dry in the storeroom for lack of anyone to accept the offer.

The young men – posted two by two to parishes – called local people together and encouraged them to dig a spring carefully and fill the space with graduated gravel and stone. They paid a mason to build the wall and set the pipe in place. Finally they put up a fence round the spring to keep cattle away. A 'good many score' were built in this way, says Bishop Lyth, and other groups did the same independently. In following years the work of Christian Rural Service spread all over Uganda as well as into neighbouring countries (Lyth, 1971).

In November 1980 the author and his wife visited Northern Uganda. The district had suffered greatly during Idi Amin's rule. Water had always been a problem; when we arrived, many of the borehole pumps were broken and wells blocked and clean water was 8 to 16 km walk away. Guinea-worm infestation was common and most painful and disabling, the victim being incapacitated for months.

Christian Rural Service is active in the diocese, and the parish workers are trying to protect springs, using mud retaining walls and bamboo pipes. In addition a nurse, Jean Williams, decided that a quick way to combat the guinea-worm menace was to teach housewives to strain their drinking water through a clean cloth, so that the tiny intermediate host, Cyclops, is caught in the material. CRS workers have been demonstrating this easy way of control, and the results are encouraging. Other agencies are planning more permanent ways of providing clean water in this district.

Comment. The CRS workers are motivators, and their concern to help others stems from their Christian character. Their practical efforts to provide clean water are part of a comprehensive plan for betterment of life in which local Christian groups take an active responsible part.

4. Benin Republic

Pastor Gabriel Doko, President of the Union des Eglises Evangéliques du Bénin, is interested in integrated development and improving water supplies. He invited Peter Batchelor, rural development consultant, to give him advice. 'I was horrified and moved', wrote Peter, after visiting some of the rural areas in February 1979. 'My lasting twin impressions are of people crippled with guinea-worm, and crowds waiting around almost dry, foul-smelling wells.'

Kéré village, 184 km from the capital Cotonou, is in a bad guinea-worm area. It had one government well which was virtually dry. Other nearby villages had practically no water supply. Water is extremely scarce in the long dry season. A.R. Meakins, an experienced water engineer, visited the area on behalf of TEAR Fund in February 1980. He reported that it would be difficult to solve this water problem: 75% of the hand-dug wells go dry each year, and open reservoirs easily become polluted and infected. Deep drilling might be needed. The Benin Government was about to start a drilling programme, but it would take many years to supply each village. A small church-based project would therefore have a place and bring much benefit.

So Jim Patterson, also a water engineer, with wide experience in Britain and developing countries, volunteered to lead the project, based in Kéré. In surrounding villages there were hopeful sites for hand-dug wells, for protecting a spring, or for enlarging a small reservoir, but the last would have to be protected, to avoid contamination by guinea-worm sufferers. Existing wells could be cleaned and deepened, and tanks built to collect water off roofs or rock-outcrops.

Jim was advised to train a team to work with him. Because the ground is so hard, hired men would be trained to do the digging and a compressor would be used. But local communities would be involved in the planning and would carry equipment and supplies and help with concrete work. His wife would explain to the women how illness is spread through polluted water, and how such illness can be avoided. She would also tell them how to look after the new water supplies. TEAR Fund agreed to finance the scheme, which was relatively expensive, and so Jim and his wife were launched on a difficult assignment.

Comment. The initiative here came from the Union Church, whose president shows great concern for practical issues. This is most encouraging. The felt needs were great, and the project was well planned, with expert advice and reminders to consult the local community and keep in close contact with government bodies. But perhaps the church communities should be asked to contribute to the cost, as in neighbouring Bourkina Fasso (see p.302).

5. *Deep-well boring in India*

In 1973 TEAR Fund received letters from Delhi describing the very serious drought in Maharashtra and neighbouring States.

More than 100,000 villages across India were without adequate water, and 200 million Indians were facing 'the worst famine in living memory.' The rains had failed for three years. The lack of drinking water was the worst effect of all.

Dr. Ben Wati of EFICOR (Evangelical Fellowship of India Committee on Relief) appealed for a drilling rig to be sent by air at once. It would be lent to CAN (Committee on Action Now), a Christian group in Pune (Poona) and supervised by the Rev John McLeod, a Church of Scotland minister with many years of drilling experience. It had to be able to drill down to 120 metres. The government was doing a ground-water survey that would help the drillers. The local community would maintain the pumps. Due to surface pollution, deep bore wells were essential. The rig was sent out and used for several years in the drought-prone areas. Later it was set up in Tamil Nadu State in the south, where again water shortage was acute. Women were then carrying water on their heads for 5 to 6 km.

EFICOR aimed to provide one well for each of the villages they served in the south, placing the well in the low caste area, and thus convenient for the Harijans ('people of God' – a name for the lowest caste) and the poorest people. No well was owned by any single person: they were accessible to all. Health teaching was given and training in pump maintenance. Spare parts were left in central places for villagers to use for repairs. The rig crew was small, and EFICOR worked closely with the state government's drinking water programme. Many of the people served were landless labourers earning Rs70 to 150 (£4-£8) a month, often with a family of eight to feed.

In 1979 94% of the bores were successful. Villagers had normally used an open well or pond as their water source, and the same pond was used for washing clothes and by cattle. A government survey some years previously had shown that after installing safe water the incidence of intestinal infections fell by 72%, and that of trachoma by 64% and the death rate of infants by 51%.

A local committee which included Church and government representatives decided where the needs were greatest, and where possible the local community paid for the pump. Several people in each village were trained in maintenance, and tools were left with them. A card was left with the village *panchayat* (committee) president, who could send for help if there was a major breakdown, and the crew then came at once.

Comment. This was a project started with much prayer and carried on as a Christian service. The drilling rig is a relatively expensive method of providing water and had to be funded from overseas but, in order to work fast in emergency situations and to go through hard rock, it was essential. EFICOR's cooperation with Church and government, its special care for the poorest and the Harijans, and its good maintenance plans are notable.

6. *Water in Karamoja*

In 1980 Karamoja in eastern Uganda, in common with other areas in eastern Africa, was suffering from disastrous drought and famine with much sickness and loss of life, especially among children. Massive aid was sent to the area, but it was soon realized that more than emergency help was needed. One urgent necessity was a better permanent water supply. Government boreholes had been neglected and an estimated 80% were out of action.

The diocese of Karamoja mounted a water development programme and Jim Rowland, a missionary of the Bible Churchmen's Missionary Society, decided to try Vergnet Hydropumps, which had been used successfully in Bourkina Fasso. TEAR Fund donated four such pumps. A French engineer, Arno Lescure, was waiting to set up a big French aid scheme in the district, using 40 Vergnet pumps, and in the meantime agreed to install three of the TEAR Fund pumps. Jim arranged meetings with the people at each site in or near Kaicheri, Karamoja. The purpose of the pump was explained and all were asked to prepare the site, build a fence and bring sand and stone. The scheme only went forward when there was full agreement to this.

The Vergnet pump is light, the piping being plastic. The pump top mechanism is fixed into a concrete plinth and a concrete block placed as a foot-rest. Then the piping and the pump body are lowered into the well, and pumping can begin. The pump is operated by foot, because, as Vergnet says, feet are stronger than arms. Each downward push on the pedal produces a jet of water. The pedal must be left to rise by itself, so the pump cannot be forced or used too fast. Very little maintenance is needed. The few wearing parts, pedal guide and piston rings, are cheap and easy to change. Spares will have to be imported.

After three months' trial Jim Rowland and Arno Lescure reported that the first pump was working well and was popular. The water in the second borehole was a little brackish but drinkable. The water in the third borehole was 49 metres below ground and this made pumping hard. The water was too brackish to drink but satisfactory for cooking and washing. In future, the only boreholes chosen for use will be those with the best quality water, and where the water level is less than 40 metres from the surface.

Comment. Again it was wisely made a condition that the community being served should contribute labour and materials. Somebody should also be responsible for the protection of the pump and replacement of worn parts. Karamoja is still in a very unsettled state, and keeping the pumps in repair will not be easy.

7. *Bourkina Fasso (Upper Volta)*

Here, in one of the poorest countries in the world, a Mennonite team based in North America has carried out a water supply programme for several years. Mennonite workers in developing countries are notable for their concern for human relations, their love of simplicity, their desire to foster self-reliance, and their care for the powerless.

Since 1975 they have been casing wells in rural areas, and a survey of them all in 1981 was very satisfactory. They give much time to selecting and training masons to do this work, making sure that they understand the difficulties and temptations of handling money, and emphasizing the need for conscientious and safe construction. They then expect the men to work on their own, earning their living and providing water for more villages. The Mennonite team has used compressors and jack hammers but prefers the simpler methods, leaving it to others to tackle the very rocky sites.

Much effort is put into 'village animation', motivating people to want the most suitable forms of water supply, and to participate fully in providing them. The team now asks church congregations not only to dig the well, feed the well workers and bring sand and gravel, but also to pay half the cost of skilled labour, transport and other materials. For a 20-metre deep well this means paying £200. This requirement will be increased each year until in five or six years' time villagers will be expected to pay the entire cost of a new well.

At a pastors' meeting, one pastor asked if this insistence on a realistic contribution to the cost was because the organizers could not afford otherwise, or because it was a matter of principle. After a few moments' silence the Mennonite worker replied that indeed the organizers were rich compared with the villagers themselves, yet compared to other aid bodies their means were limited. But the chief reason was to make adequate participation a matter of principle. It was a painful moment for the speaker, having to stick to his principles when faced with the contrast between his own background and the poverty all around him. But he was surely right.

Mennonite workers are keen to put forward a balanced programme of new proposals in addition to providing water supplies. They encourage the use of oxen, stress the importance of tree-planting, and hold basic health courses for Christian women. *Comment.* This emphasis on asking church communities to pay realistically for their wells is very important. It seems that many pumps and wells in India have become derelict because local communities were never involved in the planning or digging, and so considered these water resources as wholly a government responsibility. The evaluation survey of the work is admirable, as is the preparation of masons for independent work, which will steadily increase the number of wells provided.

. . . .

Fastank is the latest addition to the solution of this problem of ensuring the optimum possible water supply. It is a 9.12 cubic metre tank which consists of two elements: a tough durable PVC coated high tenacity fabric enclosure and an easily assembled frame of rugged aluminium. It can be erected in any climate on any suitable area of ground and without formal foundation requirements. No technical skill or special tools are required to make it operational in a few minutes, and it can be dismantled with equal ease for re-erection on another site. It needs no maintenance. Storing the water for several weeks destroys most of any disease-causing micro-organisms. If the water has to be drunk quickly, it can be sterilized by boiling or chlorination. Alternatively there can be two tanks which can be used in turn. An alternative method is to have a sand filter medium in the tank and an off-take tube at the bottom. The tanks are being supplied to an increasing number of missionary societies and other charity organizations throughout Africa and Asia.

Sanitation

The aim must be to encourage the proper disposal of stools and urine as well as the provision of clean drinking water. This calls for much tactful health education and, in particular, an understanding of traditional attitudes about defaecation.

In Jamkhed, Maharashtra State, India, Kondowe found that
most people defaecate in the open because 'one has not completely rid oneself of the impurity if one drops one's faeces on
top of another's.' In Zaire it is considered shameful to be seen
going to the latrine in the garden; it is better to relieve oneself in
the bushes. While in Tanzania the pit latrine is seen as a concentration of badness: faeces should be spread in the sun all round
the village. The sun is reckoned to sterilize everything.

Latrines and Toilets

What methods of excreta disposal should be encouraged?

The pit *latrine* is one of the oldest, cheapest and most effective latrines (Mara and Feachem, 1980). In southwest Uganda
the government insisted that all householders should build such
latrines, but many did not use them. Christian Rural Service
encouraged their use with the aid of clever puppet talks.

Small children seldom use pit latrines, although their stools
may be highly infectious. The opening is too big and a small
child might fall in. At Luteete Family Health Centre, Uganda,
Stanfield and Church put up a children's latrine with a small
opening, and demonstrated its use on clinic days. In Gahini,
Ruanda, parents were shown a clay pot cut in two. One half is
put over the latrine opening, so that children can sit on it and use
it safely: the other half acts as a lid to keep off flies.

Pour-flush toilets

These are common in India. Dr Gladys Jeffree, a CMS missionary
in Kasner, Maharashtra State, worked for thirty years and produced a simple inexpensive variety of this latrine, designed to be
flushed with 0.5 to 1 litre of water. It consisted of a squatting slab
and bowl with water outlet, made by pouring concrete into
plastic moulds supplied by Friends Rural Centre, Rasulia,
Madya Pradesh. Instead of building a septic tank, a locally made
water-storage pot or 'ranzan' was sunk in the ground and the slab
and bowl placed on top. A soakage pit was dug close at hand.
The owner digs the two pits and brings the stones.

The bowls were put in the staff living quarters and the
Nursery School at Kasner. Later each of the Christian families in
the village had one. At first the adults only poured bath-water
down them, but after realizing that staff and children used them
contentedly, the families did the same. Later, caste people in the
village asked for them. 'Herein,' says Dr Jeffree, 'lies the value of

an intimate and very small health set-up'.

Comment. Improved pit latrines and pour-flush toilets are the cheapest methods of sanitation and will be needed for many years to come. Ways must be worked out to dispose of toddlers' stools safely, and to make pit latrines safe and easy for children to use. Much careful education will be needed, by word and example, on the right use of latrines.

Lessons to be learned

These case studies are brief and limited in range. But what are the lessons to be learned from them?

Perhaps the first is that, fortunately, water is often a *felt need*: an urgent one in times of drought, and a longstanding one at other times. Communities therefore welcome the idea of an improved supply, even if the health benefits are not immediately obvious.

Planning together is essential. Here a Christian group wishing to help has the great advantage of an immediate link with church congregations, where fellow Christians learn to trust and understand each other. A programme can be explained and attitudes discussed. Some people do not like the taste of borehole water, and collecting water off the roof deprives women of social gossip at the well. These difficulties must be faced.

If a well has to be dug or a spring capped, are church members willing to work voluntarily in digging or bringing materials? And will they pay part or the whole of the cost – a big challenge in Bourkina Fasso or anywhere else? If there are several possible sites for a well, which would they prefer? Are they willing to keep it off private land and make it easy for the poorest and neediest to use it as part of the witness of the Church, as was done in Tamil Nadu?

Will the Church be responsible for maintenance, choosing volunteers who would learn how to do simple repairs and know when to call for more help? Will the Church meet the cost of this, if the government cannot help? These decisions are costly.

In addition to providing a good water supply, latrines or lavatories should be made and used. Gladys Jeffree worked hard to have wells dug in and around Kasner and also installed the pour-flush toilets. As well as giving simple teaching to maintenance volunteers, it may be necessary to train some men more thoroughly, so that they can case wells, install pumps and help build latrines. Such men would be of permanent benefit to any country, as was foreseen in Bourkina Fasso.

Some evaluation is most useful, whether it be of health improvement as was done in Tamil Nadu, or of the condition of the wells or springs after installation, as the Mennonites did in Bourkina Fasso. In all this work, good relations with local and central government are essential. New projects should fit into government plans. Indeed such projects should be regarded as pilot schemes that could be copied, and which in the end will be taken over by government. Water supply and sanitation should be two items in a general betterment of life. Better farming, co-operative marketing, teaching about a good diet, planting trees (important for water conservation) and much more besides, should become the concern of the church, in the way that Christian Rural Service has pioneered.

Finally, is there still something more that urges Christian health workers to provide clean water wherever it is needed? Surely it is the great example of our loving Father, who supplies all our needs so bountifully. And what of the Lord Jesus Christ, who so freely gives us 'life-giving water' (Jn. 4.14) to cure the thirst that nothing else can satisfy? As we have received so much, we must long that Christian groups everywhere will demonstrate the same spirit of loving generosity, so that fresh springs and wells of water will be the means of strengthening relations of love and care between man and man, and giving welcome relief to the poorest and neediest.

References

Billington, Roy (Ed.) (1978) *Health has many Faces*, London: Edinburgh House

Cairncross, Sandy, et al (1980) *Evaluation for Village Water Supply Planning*. Chichester: Wiley

Cairncross, Sandy and Feacham, Richard (1978) *Small Water Supplies*, Bulletin 10. London: Ross Institute

Coate, Winifred A (c.1977) *Abdelliyeh 1961-1976*, Abdelliyeh Village Project, Jordan. Jordan: Box 49, Zerka (Privately published)

Feacham, Richard (1981) *Journal of Tropical Medicine and Hygiene*, **84**, 47-48

Feacham, Richard and Cairncross, Sandy (1978) *Small Excreta Disposal Systems*, Bulletin 8. London: Ross Institute

Lind, Tim (1979) *Biblical Obedience and Development*, Akron, Pa: Mennonite Central Committee

Lyth, Richard (1971) *Mission to the Under-Loved*, London: Ruanda Mission

McGilvray, James G. (1981) *The Quest for Health*, Tübingen: German Institute for Medical Missions

Mara, D., and Feacham, Richard (1980) *Journal of Tropical Medicine and Hygiene*, **83,** 229-240

Stern, P.G. (1975) *Hand-Dug Wells*, Southampton: Gifford and Partners

Ward, Barbara (1976) *The Home of Man*, Harmondsworth: Penguin

Watt, S.B. and Wood W.E. (1977) *Hand Dug Wells and their Construction*, London: Intermediate Technology Publications

White, G.F., Bradley, D.J., and White, A.U. (1972) *Drawers of Water*, Chicago and London: University of Chicago Press

Wood, W E (1978) *Tropical Diseases Bulletin*, **77,** 2114

CHAPTER 18

MEDICAL EDUCATION

Stanley G. Browne

Medical missionaries were the pioneers in bringing medical education to the countries where they worked. For the most part, the beginnings of such education were modest and unstructured; they were a response to the local situation, the local needs. And the doctor had to make do with the human material available: often keen young lads bubbling over with an enthusiasm that compensated for their lack of formal education. This state of affairs has persisted until quite recently. For instance, not so long ago in the highlands of Papua New Guinea (Kettle, 1979), aid-post orderlies had to be recruited from those who had had but one year of primary schooling. On the other hand, today in India there is a glut of university graduates who are eager to train as medical auxiliaries and to accept any employment opportunities open to them.

Historically, the Western-trained doctors who went as missionaries, or as physicians and surgeons to the Armed Forces, to commercial undertakings (like the East India Company) or into government employment, took scientific medicine with them and began to train nationals. This training took diverse forms (Moorshead, 1929). For instance, most doctors – as soon as their reputation was established – began training likely youths in the elements of diagnosis and treatment of the commoner ailments that brought people flocking in crowds to the primitive dispensaries and hospitals. Then, when inpatients were admitted and operations performed, ward- and theatre-orderlies received some training from doctors and nurses. For the control of insect vectors of disease, 'fly-boys' became adept at the capture, identification and elimination of anopheles mosquitoes, tsetse

308

flies, blackfly, snails, and so forth. For mass vaccination campaigns, young men achieved high levels of efficiency and dependability. Others became uncannily skilful in finding minute subcutaneous veins for intravenous medication, such as for sleeping sickness and yaws, or for the parenteral introduction of intravenous fluids in cholera epidemics. Their good eyesight and ability to concentrate without being distracted made them first-class microscopists in spotting the single trypanosome in material obtained from lymph-node puncture, or the malarial parasite in a stained thick-drop preparation.

When Dr Clement Chesterman arrived at Yakusu in the former Belgian Congo in 1920, he found a population being rapidly decimated by a sleeping sickness epidemic that had already led to the complete disappearance of many riverside villages; yaws and leprosy were rife; undernourishment was widespread; malaria was holo-endemic (Chesterman, 1940; 1978). Realizing that he could never tackle the huge problems alone, he began training youths to help him. This is how a model training institution started, which sent out a total of over three hundred certificated auxiliaries before it ceased functioning in the early 1960s. With government approval, a School for Medical Auxiliaries was founded in 1931 and upgraded in 1935. Health centres (18 of them) and 35 dispensaries eventually provided skilled medical care over the whole area of 10,000 square miles, each health centre being manned by a Christian medical evangelist. When these medical outposts were staffed, Christian young men came for training at Yakusu from fifteen Protestant missions to the east and south of the former Belgian Congo, and returned to the sending mission after gaining the government diploma or to employment with the government or a concessionary company, mining or agricultural. Thanks to the practical training they received, they made a tremendous impression on the control of endemic disease, and raised the standards of hygiene and nutrition in the whole district and beyond (Browne, 1971).

Medical auxiliaries have been recognized as the key to medical services in many African countries, and missionary doctors have been the pioneers in their training and deployment. In that part of Zimbabwe then known as Mashonaland, Dr Tommy Steyn gained a great reputation for the training programme he inaugurated at the Morgenster Hospital (Du Toit, 1975/76). 'The local people must be trained to help themselves' was his watchword, and he was justly renowned for the efficiency and dedication of the many trained husband-and-wife teams that went out to serve their fellows in distant dispensaries. From 1920 they received a local certificate of proficiency; from 1936 they qualified as government-certified nursing orderlies; and finally they sat for the medical or midwifery assistant qualification registrable with the Medical Council. The mission hospital pioneered the way and set standards for the official diploma.

A similar tale could be told in many other parts of the world, where the vision and drive of a charismatic personality had far-reaching effects through the training of auxiliary medical workers. A counterpart to the Yakusu School for Medical Auxiliaries was in Sona Bata (in Lower Zaire) where the American Baptists established a similar school. This has now been superseded by the Institut Médical Evangélique at Kimpese. The existence of these two training institutions stimulated the government to create official schools in provincial capitals, so paving the way for the founding of medical schools of university rank.

Nowadays, government recognition of training schools attached to mission institutions depends on the maintenance of minimal levels of suitably qualified staff as well as on the provision of minimal numbers of beds for inpatients – requirements that may be difficult to achieve and to maintain.

Medical education in China and India owes much to the initiative of Christian doctors and nurses (Balme, 1921). They were responsible for the founding and funding of the medical schools and schools for nurses, for the introduction of Western medicine into these countries (Wong and Lien-teh, 1932), and for the translation and publication of standard medical text books. By their exemplary courage in facing epidemics of cholera, pneumonic plague and other scourges, they reinforced the theoretical teaching given in the context of Christian ethical ideals, and they also stimulated gifted national doctors to devote themselves to research.

In China, from the earliest days of the introduction of Western medicine, the training of Chinese nationals was a primary commitment. Peter Parker, the first medical missionary to China, having arrived in Canton in 1835 (Balme, 1921) and opened the Ophthalmic Hospital in that city in the same year, began two years later to train three assistants in the hospital. During 'the next fifty or sixty years similar classes for students were organized in various parts of the country, in connection with different mission hospitals'. In 1866 a medical school in Canton was opened by the American Board of Missions. The first medical school in China in which instruction was given along modern lines was founded by Dr J.K. Mackenzie in 1881 in Tientsin; this afterwards became the government medical college. The university of Taiyuanfu, which later saw the addition of a medical faculty, was established by a non-medical Baptist, Dr Timothy Richard. In 1884 Dr Dugald Christie was responsible for the institution of medical education in Mukden (Manchuria); five years later, the medical school at Nanking was founded. In 1894, the Soochow Medical College came into being three years after a women's hospital had opened its doors for training students. The dream of William Lockhart recounted in his book *The Medical Missionary in China. A narrative of 20 years' experience* (Lockhart, 1861) was coming true. As he had written:

'The education of Chinese youths in the principles of the medical profession will prove a powerful agent in spreading a knowledge of service among their country men, and in carrying out the objects we have in view . . . Young men thus instructed will gradually be dispersed over the empire . . . and will dispense the benefits of a systematic acquaintance with the subject whithersoever they go'.

Perhaps the most notable of the Christian initiatives in medical education in China was the Peking Union Medical College. A small mission hospital (Aitchison, 1983), which had been in existence for some years, was destroyed during the Boxer Rebellion, and in 1902 was housed in 'a tumble-down grain shop, and behind that was some stabling. The shop kitchen was his dispensary and another small room with a floor of cracked bricks and a paper window was his surgery. The waiting room *pro tem* was a leaking building with a mud floor'.

Despite these daunting conditions, Dr Thomas Cochrane (who, with his wife and family, had managed to escape through the Boxer lines) set to work to transform the place and eventually to erect on the enlarged site a suite of distinguished buildings to house the Peking Union Medical College, the cost being defrayed by grants from the Boxer Indemnity Funds. A most fortunate happening was the professional attention that the Empress Dowager received at the hands of Dr Cochrane. In response to his request for help in building the projected medical college, she gave a donation of 10,000 ounces of silver. Many court officials then made generous donations for the same purpose.

A consortium of missionary bodies, American and British for the most part, made themselves responsible for staffing the hospital and the college. The college was 'solemnly opened' on February 12 1906. More than 30 students were admitted for training. The instruction was given in Mandarin, but students were required to learn English. The first dean of the school, who remained for five years in this position, was Dr Thomas Cochrane himself. Thus was created hospital and college that became the foremost in the whole of Asia. In the first year of its work, the hospital gave over 20,000 treatments, and a great number of opium addicts were helped to break the habit. The college flourished. High academic standards were encouraged, and an International Examining Board assured the standing of the medical degrees given.

Within a couple of years, the Peking Union Medical College for Women was founded. Women students had been admitted to the Canton Medical School since 1879 only five years after the London School of Medicine for Women had opened its doors.

In the Peking college, instruction was given in English as well as in Mandarin. In Central China, at Soochow (Balme, 1921), a pioneer women's hospital school was established in 1891, which united three years later with the college for men to form the Soochow Medical College. In 1923, however, the Peking Union Medical College for Women was merged into the Medical Department of the Shantung Christian University.

Meanwhile, the Rockefeller Foundation of New York was taking an increasing interest in medical education in China. Its president, Dr George E Vincent, wrote:

'The great need of China is scientific knowledge and technical skill dominated by idealistic loyalty to the highest and best things in human life; and that idealism that is most enduring ... is an idealism based upon a deep and abiding religious conviction'.

The Foundation despatched two influential commissions (in 1914 and 1915) to China 'to enquire into the conditions of medical education, hospitals and public health'. Their Report, entitled 'Medicine in China', exerted a wide influence on medical education in the whole country.

The Peking Union Medical College came under the aegis of the China Medical Board of the Rockefeller Foundation; 'the most beautiful modern building in the whole of China' was erected on an extensive property, and 'one of the best-ordered and best-equipped medical schools and hospitals to be found anywhere in the world' came into being. Instruction was still given in Mandarin, and the Rockefeller Foundation recommended that another such college (already functioning since 1908 in Tsinan) should be enlarged and upgraded as the school of medicine of the newly fledged Shantung Christian University. Under the dynamic leadership of Dr Harold Balme, this school developed into a remarkable cooperation between denominations and nationalities in achieving a standard of medical excellence unsurpassed in the world. In 1923, the college was opened to women students, and the following year the Canadian government accorded the university a charter giving it the right to confer degrees.

The translation of standard medical texts (from English) into Chinese has been a feature of the Christian contribution to medical education from the early days of the introduction of Western scientific medicine into China. William Lockhart (1861) was full of praise for missionaries like Hobson who translated medical texts into Chinese, and himself wrote a series of medical books in Chinese destined for national students. Benjamin Hobson, who arrived in China in 1839 as a missionary of the London Missionary Society, devoted the greater part of his life in China to translating medical and scientific textbooks into Chinese. Writing in 1858, he commented:

'It is still quite practicable to make every subject with which we are ourselves acquainted as clear and expressive in Chinese as in English . . . The great desideratum for a translator is a good and fixed nomenclature on every branch of science. The language admits of a satisfactory and distinct explanation of most new terms'.

Hobson was outstandingly successful in his efforts, which placed succeeding generations of medical teachers in his debt. Such forbidding tomes as Gray's Anatomy were done into Chinese by Lawrence Ingle, a Baptist missionary. By 1907, no fewer than 91 medical textbooks had been translated into Chinese and published (Broomhall, 1907).

The training of nurses and paramedical workers was similarly due to the initiative of Christian doctors. It is difficult for people brought up in the Western world to picture the primitive state of the early mission hospitals in China. As Balme (1921) puts it:

'No suitable premises to work in; no apparatus nor equipment; no nurses nor trained assistants; possibly not even an educated

Chinese helper willing to be trained for such a work: not the least semblance of sanitation, nor of intelligent measures to prevent the spread of disease . . . There have been few events in China within recent years which have marked so fundamental a change of mental attitude on the part of the people as the fact that it has now been found possible, in many centres, to introduce into Chinese hospitals the practice of nursing on a modern basis. The old-time hospital . . . flagrantly broke every law of hygiene which it did not ignore'.

Into this situation came the missionary nurse, with her tradition of care and skill, ready to overcome prejudice and misunderstanding: not a ward coolie, nor was she an unqualified or second-rate doctor.

The first nursing sisters in China were Christian missionaries who arrived in the 1880s. Before long these early nurses wanted to train suitable persons in the skills they themselves exercised. But the only ward orderlies available came from the menial uneducated classes, many of them Christians – a far cry from an educated nursing profession. Yet that was the vision and the ideal that actuated those nursing pioneers. Systematic training had to await the arrival of educated school girls into hospitals and the appearance of a spirit of Christian service among the new generation of young people. When the need and the opportunities for training were publicized among pupils in the best of mission schools, doubts were slowly dispelled as Christian girls responded to the challenge to a worthwhile life-work. The menial tasks of bathing verminous patients, cleaning the incontinent, and feeding the uncooperative began to be shouldered by these Christian girls. Teamwork and attention to detail were encouraged, and theoretical lectures were combined with clinical instruction.

A new profession was born: essentially a Christian profession. In 1909 the Nurses' Association of China came into being, at first predominantly expatriate and overwhelmingly Christian, but gradually Chinese-trained nurses assumed the majority and non-Christians were welcomed into its membership. High standards were set and imposed. In the matter of the training of midwives, too, Christian hospitals took the initiative – in Hong Kong, Hangchow and elsewhere.

Another aspect of training in China in which Christians took the initiative is that of laboratory technicians (Chinese Mission Year Book, 1925). The need for such trained staff is obvious to anybody acquainted with hospitals, yet for many years mission doctors – even those engaged in medical education – had to be content with virtually untrained or only half-trained auxiliary staff in laboratories. When the importance of microscopy in the diagnosis and management of tropical diseases is realized, the delay in the inauguration of such training is all the more surprising. However, the Medical Missionary Association of China addressed itself to this problem, and sponsored the creation of the Institute of Hospital Technology in 1924 to fill the gap. The Institute aimed to help particularly the smaller and isolated hospitals, and train men and women in the necessary auxiliary skills of various kinds, such as laboratory technology, administration and radiography. In Africa, too, laboratory technicians have been trained in many mission hospitals and in a few special Schools. Alumni have served a variety of institutions and have rendered valuable help in the control of endemic and epidemic diseases.

Korea is another country in which medical education has been associated with Christian doctors since its inception (Yonsei University College of Medicine, 1977/78). In 1885 the Emperor presented to Dr H.N. Allen, a Presbyterian missionary, a hospital in Seoul picturesquely called The House of Extended Grace. The hospital became the first in Korea to practise modern medicine and to train medical students: the first group of young Koreans began their studies in 1889. After the world missionary conference held in New York that same year, a wealthy Christian industrialist named L.H. Severance provided funds for the upgrading of the hospital and the establishment of a medical school on Western lines. The first class of students who had followed the government-approved curriculum graduated in 1908. Even during the difficult years of the Japanese occupation, Severance College managed to maintain its teaching standards. Despite the loss of 80% of its buildings and equipment as the result of damage sustained in the tragic Korean war, teaching in refugee hospitals continued. In 1957 the Severance Union Medical College united with the Chosun Christian University to form the Yonsei University, and five years later the greatly enlarged Medical College was opened on the new site.

The Severance College has been the inspiration for the foundation of much of the training of doctors in the whole of what is now South Korea. The Christian basis has been openly maintained in the modern complex in Seoul and is implicit in other medical schools, government and private, in other cities in Korea.

Turning to India, we see a rather different development of medical education. The medical services of the Army were coming into being at the same time as the growth of the Indian Medical Service. Medical education was emerging in an unplanned and desultory fashion, responding to local need and epidemic diseases. Beginning with Dr John Thomas, Carey's colleague (Drewery, 1978; Moorshead, 1925), Christian doctors were more concerned with responding to the overwhelming clinical challenge than with instituting formal training of doctors. They did, however, train men to help them with translation and with screening the crowds of outpatients. Because of the density of the population and the extent of acute and chronic illness, the hospital itself became the centre of the work, and the training of auxiliary staff was geared to the curative practice of the hospital – medical, surgical, obstetric.

Before formal medical education in India was ever contemplated, a number of doctors began training some of their highly intelligent helpers in things medical. Such a one was the well-known Scots missionary, Dr Alexander Duff. Not content with his own local efforts, in 1834 he persuaded a reluctant government to accept converted Brahmins for medical training, even to the extent of sponsoring some to follow the full medical course at a school in Great Britain.

Christian missionaries have played an important role in establishing colleges for training Indian doctors. The earliest was that at Miraj, in Bombay Presidency, which was founded in 1897 by Dr (later Sir) W. J. Wanless (Richards, 1971). Twenty years later, the college was registered by the University of Bombay and its diploma was recognized as a valid licence to practise.

In 1834 Dr Alexander Duff induced government to give full medical training to his ablest students, who afterwards served in the army and as teachers in medical schools.

It is a curious fact that the two major medical educational institutions in India with a Christian foundation were both founded by women. At first they trained only women as doctors but eventually admitted men on the same basis as women. Both are cooperative institutions, both have attained high academic standards, and are recognized by neighbouring university medical schools as offering equivalent courses of graduate instruction. The two institutions are Ludhiana, associated with Dame Edith Brown, and Vellore with Dr Ida S. Scudder. What appealed to both of these medical pioneers was the pitiable state of India's women. Denied medical attention because of the widespread practice of *purdah*, they suffered not only from the rampant endemic diseases but also from anaemia, the complications of pregnancy, osteomalacia and the psychoses inseparable from their unnatural exclusion from sunlight and contacts outside the home.

In 1882, Edith Brown enrolled as an honours science student at Girton College, Cambridge, having gained a scholarship in mathematics (Reynolds, 1968). She subsequently entered the Royal Free Hospital, London, for the clinical part of her medical course. Denied as a woman the opportunity of graduating in medicine at Cambridge, she took the Licenciate of the Scottish Colleges and then the MD of Brussels. On October 17 1891 she left England for India to work under the auspices of the Baptist Zenana Mission. Having observed the government medical schools in Agra and Lahore, and noting the difficulties experienced by girls in these male-dominated institutions, Edith Brown considered that the only way to ensure a supply of well-motivated Christian lady doctors willing to work among women in India's villages was to train them in a Christian college. That was in 1893. At a conference she called in Ludhiana of representatives from various missions working in India, it was unanimously resolved to found a college for training women doctors – and at Ludhiana. Thus was born the North India School of Medicine for Christian Women. In October 1894, the School was opened and the first students enrolled.

Non-Christian students were first admitted in 1909, and the first men in 1957. Two years later, the Medical School was upgraded to conform to university and government requirements. Nurses, medical technicians and other grades of auxiliary staff were trained, and specialist departments manned by first-class staff were inaugurated. True to its original purpose, the college still trains doctors (of both sexes) to help women and their families living in the villages of India. The college has pioneered in community health, mobile eye hospitals, cobalt-bomb therapy for malignancies, and the domiciliary care of women being delivered in their homes. Many of Ludhiana's graduates are serving the less privileged rural communities through mission hospitals.

Entering into a long family tradition of generations of missionary service to India, Ida S. Scudder was the youngest child and the only sister to five brothers when she was born in India in

1869. It was the plight of India's women that impelled her to enrol for the medical course in Philadelphia and then Cornell. On the first day of the new century she landed in India to begin a life of unusual dedication and fruitfulness. She soon had to face an epidemic of bubonic plague, and then one of cholera. Her surgical skills were tested in almost impossible conditions, but she never lost sight of the needy masses in the villages near Vellore.

In 1913 she determined that a medical college for women was needed, but she had to wait five years before she received official permission to start. Fourteen of the original class of eighteen completed the medical course, and all of them graduated at the Presidency examination in nearby Madras, most of them very creditably. Despite difficulties of various kinds, the Medical College on its newly acquired campus, and the enlarged hospital, continued to expand and to improve. In 1942, the diploma course in medicine was abolished in Madras, and Vellore found itself obliged to upgrade the curriculum, the staffing and the standards in lecture rooms, laboratories and wards so as to attain the requirements for MB, BS degrees. Men were first admitted in 1947 to an institution up to then predominantly female.

From the beginning, finance and members of staff came from several countries and several Protestant traditions. From 1942 the national and denominational contributions were more numerous and more diverse. New specialist departments were added and new equipment purchased. With continuing emphasis on meeting the needs of India's village folk, while raising academic standards all the time, Vellore was achieving a reputation as the hospital with the greatest concentration of medical expertise in India. Today most of its graduates serve in mission hospitals in India; others go into government service. While the majority of staff and students are Christian, there is no discrimination on grounds of creed or caste. It is not only in the education of medical students that Vellore has pioneered the way. It was the first Indian college to introduce a BSc nursing course; its postgraduate nursing course began admitting male students in 1947. Postgraduate courses leading to the MD and MS degrees were duly inaugurated. More recently a Department of Community Health has been organized to be incorporated into the undergraduate course and provide an integrated programme of health care. As a Christian institution, Vellore has played a highly significant role in medical education not only in India but throughout southern Asia.

Although there are over 1500 hospitals and dispensaries in India run under the auspices of the Roman Catholic Church, until recently that Church had no medical college for the training of doctors for its own hospitals and for the community. Following a decision taken by the Roman Catholic Bishops' Conference of India in 1954 and later in 1959, St John's Medical College, Bangalore, came into being in 1964. From about 12,000 applicants every year, the College is able to admit only 60. Intended primarily for Roman Catholic students, men and women, the College is open to applicants irrespective of religion, caste or community. The admission policy shows a definite bias towards the acceptance of dedicated persons (like Religious Sisters) likely to devote themselves to service for the rural poor, and in the context of community health. All students are bonded to serve in such situations for two years after graduation. To this end, and within the limits imposed by government authorities, the curriculum and the clinical experience available are heavily weighted in favour of rural health; the emphasis is on maternity and child welfare programmes and on community participation. Postgraduate and in-service courses are available for graduate doctors and paramedical community health workers of various categories. The Ross Institute of Occupational Health is an active and integral part of the medical college.

In Africa, the outstanding training institution that has its roots in a Christian Hospital is the Makerere Medical School in Kampala, Uganda. Thanks to the vision and first-class medical work of the brothers Cook, CMS missionaries, with their meticulously kept medical records, the development of a national medical school related to a mission hospital (Foster, 1979) seemed logical and inevitable. The standard of training of nurses and medical auxiliaries was so good that the government did not need to look beyond the CMS hospital at Mengo for a model for teaching and clinical training when it was decided to create a modern hospital and attached medical school in the capital of Uganda. The ethical foundations of the old mission hospital provided the firm basis for the new venture, and the Christian initiative was everywhere evident – in the staff, the relations with patients and with the government, and the practical nature of teaching and training.

A lower grade of medical training is provided at Kimpese, in Lower Zaire. After exploratory discussions extending over several years, a group of Protestant missions decided in 1946 to investigate the possibility of creating a joint medical project to comprise a training school for African auxiliaries in association with a hospital, and also possibly a small hospital facility for missionary patients. The British and American Baptists and the Swedish Lutherans, who already had a considerable medical presence in Lower Zaire, agreed to cooperate in planning, financing, and staffing the proposed complex and undertook to provide funds for upkeep. The Congo Welfare Fund made generous grants, and the government authorities proved most helpful and cooperative. In 1951 work was begun, both constructional and clinical. The Institut Médical Evangélique is now a going concern, training Christian medical auxiliaries of both sexes, and maintaining standards of real ecumenical commitment and cooperation. Its orthopaedic and leprosy work is recognized by the government as being of exemplary worth. Now that doctors are being trained in the nearby government school, Kimpese acts as a proving ground for medical graduates.

A similar institution is the Institut Médical Chrétien du Kasai, organized by the American Presbyterian Congo Mission in 1954, and having a government-approved school for nurses. Since the disturbances following the granting of independence to Zaire (in 1960) this Institute has made notable progress in the training of medical auxiliaries, nurses and dental aides for service in dispensaries and health centres within its own immediate sphere of medical responsibility, and beyond. Where government health authorities are unable to provide this service, Christian initiative does so, with commendable thoroughness and despatch.

In East Africa, a good illustration of a cooperative effort to provide a clinical service attached to a training facility is provided by the Kilimanjaro Medical Centre in Tanzania. After an uncertain beginning, complicated by political difficulties, this fine hospital not only serves as a referral centre for major surgery, ophthalmological conditions and heart diseases, but also provides excellent training for high-grade medical auxiliaries.

A more recent trend, encouraged by the Christian Medical Commission of the World Council of Churches, has been the creation of joint councils representing all Christian missions in the countries that have medical work. These councils ensure collaboration and prevent overlapping; they can speak with one voice to government health authorities, and they foster understanding between Protestant and Roman Catholic, between mainline denominational medical missions and Seventh Day Adventist groups. In matters of staffing and bulk purchase of drugs and equipment, in medical education at all levels, they certainly point the way forward. In Malawi, Tanzania and Sierra Leone they are proving their worth and value.

Over the years Christian doctors have made many notable contributions to knowledge and have published numerous articles in medical journals. From medical schools and universities and from 'bush hospitals' (Browne, 1976) they have pioneered and encouraged others to investigate local problems. Among the many publications written by Christians as textbooks or source books for the instruction of doctors and medical auxiliaries, mention must be made of the *Tropical Dispensary Handbook* by Sir Clement Chesterman. Intended primarily for medical auxiliaries in Africa, this book has been translated into French, Spanish and Portuguese; the English version went through several editions. The influence of Maurice King's *Medical Care in Developing Countries* in the 1960s was equally great.

Christian doctors are maintaining their interest in medical education, although their strategic input may not be so initiatory as in the past in countries of the Third World. However, in the light of the current debate on the implementation of the widely publicized WHO 'Health for all by the year 2000', the Medical Committee of the Conference for World Mission (representing the main denominational missionary societies) joined with the Evangelical Missionary Association in sponsoring in 1983 a consultation to consider the essential Christian contribution to the ongoing discussions. Unless the spiritual component of any health programme is recognized, the best laid plans will certainly go awry.

The revived interest of Mission Boards in community medicine is now seen to be a return to the original purpose of medical missions. All too few medical programmes were in the past geared to preventive medicine in the community: the majority therefore made little impression on the general level of health and nutrition, despite their undoubted success as curative institutions. The Christian Medical Commission of the World Council of Churches is now popularizing these modern concepts, particularly through its influential periodical *Contact*.

Education of Christian doctors, Mission Boards and the whole Christian community of the West is still necessary if the new insights in medicine are to be implemented for the benefit of the vast and needy populations of the Third World.

References

Aitchison, M. (1983) *The Doctor and the Dragon.* Basingstoke: Pickering & Inglis.

Balme, H. (1921) *China and Modern Medicine.* London: The Carey Press.

Browne, S.G. (1971) Comprehensive medical care delivery through a Church-related rural health programme in the former Belgian Congo. Contact No. 6. Christian Medical Commission, Geneva.

Browne, S.G. (1976) Research in a "bush hospital". *Tropical Doctor* **6,** 187.

Browne, S.G. (1979) The contribution of medical missionaries to tropical medicine. *Trans. R. Soc. trop. Med. & Hyg.* **73,** 317.

Broomhall, M. (1907) *The Chinese Empire. A general and missionary survey.* London: China Inland Mission.

Chesterman, C.C. (1940) *In the service of suffering.* London: The Carey Press.

Chesterman, C.C. (1979) The medical missionary. *Trans. R. Soc. trop. Med. & Hyg.* **73,** 360.

Chesterman, C.C. *Tropical Dispensary Handbook.* London: Christian Literature Society. Many editions in English, French and Spanish.

China Missions Year Book, 1911, 1913, 1925 and 1931. London: Church Missionary Society.

Drewery, M. (1978) *William Carey.* London: Hodder & Stoughton.

Foster, W.D. (1979) *Sir Albert Cook.* Privately published.

Kettle, E. (1979) *That They Might Live.* Sydney: F.P. Leonard.

King, M. (1966) *Medical Care in Developing Countries.* Nairobi: Oxford University Press.

Leprosy Review. (1981) Higher medical education in China. **52,** 190.

Lockhart, W. (1861) *The Medical Missionary in China.* London: Hurst & Blackett.

Moorshead, R.F. (1929) *Heal the Sick.* London: The Carey Press.

Patterson, M.C. (1980) A medical survey of a South American Indian tribe in the Paraguayan Chaco. *Tropical Doctor* **10,** 124.

Reynolds, C. (1968) *Punjab Pioneer.* Bombay: GLS Press.

Richards, M. (1971) *It Began with Andrews.* London: Salvationist Publications & Supplies Ltd.

St. John's Medical College, Bangalore (1971) Information brochure.

du Toit, D. (1975/76) John Helm Memorial Hospital Morgenster, Annual Report.

Wilson, D.C. (1965) *Ten Fingers for God.* New York: McGraw-Hill Book Company.

Wong, K. Chimin and Lien-teh, Wu (1932) *History of Chinese medicine*. Tientsin. The Tientsin Press.
Yonsei University College of Medicine and Severance Hospital, Bulletin (1977-78) Seoul, Korea.

CHAPTER 19

CO-WORKERS – NATIONAL AND INTERNATIONAL

F. T. Davey

From reading the biographies of the early pioneers in medicine in Asia and Africa, one could easily gather the impression that they went alone into impossible situations and performed remarkable feats all by themselves. This was never the case. What of the people who provided accommodation, rendered them day-to-day service, taught them the language, and came and assisted them in their work? In many instances these colleagues remain nameless, and it is a sad commentary on the times that this should be so. The truth is that behind every foreign pioneer, behind every achievement in medical research, there were sons and daughters of the soil who chose to throw in their lot with the foreign medical workers, and contributed to the enterprise in ways so important, so diverse and so numerous that volumes would be required to do any justice to their story.

Almost everywhere the decision to join a foreign worker or group entailed the crossing of a wide culture gap. References are often made to the culture shock experienced by Europeans when they go and live among the people of an Asian or African country, but the reverse process is equally difficult, and goes far beyond personal habits and customs. What of the Nigerian nurse called upon to foster twin babies, when all the teaching of her people has been that one of them possesses an evil spirit, and no-one can tell which one it is? That teaching was not just mindless superstition, but had its origins in the struggle for existence in a hostile environment, where milk from a cow or any other source was non-existent. What of the Indian nurse called upon every day of her life to cross age-old barriers of caste, and perform duties for patients which would fill her family with horror at the very thought? One of the key workers at Faizabad leprosy home was Prem Nath Dube, member of a priestly Brahmin family. Cobbling is normally regarded as a job for the despised lower castes, considered unclean because the handling of leather is essential to it. Protective footwear is vital to sufferers from leprosy, and in defiance of many centuries of tradition, Prem Nath chose to learn this trade and give himself to it for their sakes, his motivation the love of Christ.

The very travels to which national colleagues were committed could be a deep cause for anxiety in a way that few Europeans could comprehend. When one's homeland is a village and at most ten miles of territory around it, a journey of 20 miles is a major adventure. Crossing the no-man's land between one language group and another was thought to be taking one's life in one's hands, and not without reason. Yet the fact remains that none of these problems deterred the first Asians, Africans and South Sea islanders from joining the early medical missionaries, forerunners of what was to become a great army, embracing people of many races and all classes of society. Equally remarkable is the fact that in every continent they caught the vision that inspired the pioneers whom they joined, and in due time many were destined to become pioneers themselves, worthily carrying on the responsibilities bequeathed to them by the first bearers of the Christian message.

Everywhere they brought to the foreign compound not only their personal qualities but also something precious of their own tradition and culture. Wherever the foreigners were prepared to listen and learn, a respect for the people developed which ripened into love, and there emerged a new creation, a mutually enlightened understanding which uplifted the work itself, encouraged the development of medical services, and indeed influenced many young nations seeking to find their place in the modern world.

Here it is possible only to indicate some of the important directions in which national colleagues made their special contributions, and illustrate these by examples from different continents.

The story of David Livingstone and his devoted African helpers has been told round the world. It enshrines for all time the sweetness of the relation that can exist between people of different races under the influence of the Christian faith. Susi and his companions were as sensitive to the faith and deep humanity of Livingstone as any of his own countrymen could have been, and it is fitting that the names of these worthy sons of Africa, typical of so many of their people, are recorded on his tombstone in Westminster Abbey.

Right across Africa and Asia there are numerous examples of

generous and tenderhearted persons who facilitated the opening
up of medical work by the offer of gifts, land and facilities. Their
own religious background was immaterial; their concern for the
sick was the overriding consideration. Chief Nwoji of Uzuakoli,
Nigeria, is a typical example. When it was proposed to establish
a large leprosy hospital in the neighbourhood, all the ancient
fears of the Ibo people regarding leprosy rose to the surface in the
minds of local chiefs and land-owning people, and very strong
opposition developed. There were, however, several people
with leprosy in Chief Nwoji's own village, and in defiance of the
feelings of the heads of adjacent villages, he offered the use of
some of his village land. This broke the deadlock; other chiefs
followed suit, and the hospital was founded. Nwoji was a traditional animist. Sadly, six years later he himself contracted
leprosy and died in the very hospital he helped to found.

A generation before Livingstone undertook his African journeys, the medical pioneers in China were encountering the same
kind of dedication among their first Chinese colleagues. It was a
recipe for danger to life for any Chinaman to ally himself with
the 'foreign devils', but from the very beginning the pioneers
were joined by Chinese colleagues and helpers whose invaluable qualities often made the continuance of the work possible.
Morrison, the great pioneer missionary and Chinese scholar,
arrived in Canton in 1807, at a time when torture and execution
were the inevitable lot of any Chinese discovered helping
foreigners with language or translation work. Nevertheless,
heroic Chinese did in fact come to his aid as teachers, block cut-
ters and printers, and continued doing so for several years.

None of the pioneers of Western medicine in China could
have achieved what he did without Chinese help. The great
Lockhart, medical pioneer in Shanghai, Tientsin and Peking,
once said after 20 years in the country that 200,000 Chinese
patients had passed through his hands, a scale of work that
would have been utterly impossible in the absence of Chinese
assistants.

Medical work in Formosa was begun by Dr James Laidlaw
Maxwell, who arrived there in 1864, together with three Chinese
assistants. He opened a dispensary in Tainan and soon was
seeing over 50 patients daily. Driven out with the evangelist
whose words had provoked hostility, they moved to Takow.
Maxwell wrote of the aged janitor 'Bun', whom he had taken
with him, praising him for 'his ceaseless warmth of affection for

the work of the gospel and his calm confidence in its power. I do not know that I have seen a finer type of Christian character than in this old man.' At Tainan the hospital was re-established and aborigines from interior villages, well treated there, invited them to extend their work into the rural areas. This led to a hospital at Chiang Hoa, and in time medical students were trained both there and at Tainan.

When the intrepid William Elmslie set off from Lahore in April 1865 on his first journey into Kashmir, he was accompanied by two Indian assistants who faced with him the dangers of his arduous life in Srinagar, including coping with a cholera epidemic. They also accompanied him on tours from Srinagar into surrounding districts, travelling as far as Islamabad. Both were orphans brought up in a children's home in Lahore. Elmslie died at the age of 40, eight years after his first trip to Kashmir. It was said that 'God chose some of his choicest disciples to be his successors in after years.'

The first women medical worker in the area of Madras recruited by the Wesleyan Methodist Missionary Society in 1884 was Miss A. Palmer, an Anglo-Indian with medical training who soon afterwards qualified as a doctor and gave a lifetime of service to the women of the district. In recording the opening of this work, her Society linked with the name of Miss Palmer that of Salome, an Indian assistant, whose services were thereby officially acknowledged. This little incident could be multiplied a thousand times. When I visited Mother Teresa in 1962, soon after her home for the dying was opened in the Kali temple precincts in Calcutta, one of the most moving of many impressions was to see her Indian colleagues, 16 of them, caring in an amazing way for well over 100 patients admitted in the last stages of neglect and malnutrition, many of them incontinent.

The first nursing sister in charge of Ama Achara hospital in Eastern Nigeria recalls one of her early helpers.

'Bernadine Dibue was the first girl to take her midwifery certificate in a Methodist Hospital in Eastern Nigeria. She had been a pupil teacher and was the first standard VI girl I had been able to acquire for our staff. She passed with very high marks and gave us splendid loyal service. I remember one midwifery case. Bernadine had been called when the patient was admitted at 3.30 a.m. and had called me at 6 a.m. All day we worked with the patient, the Government doctor from Umuahia coming five times to try to avoid surgery. Finally at midnight he said we must do an extraction. We finished up at 2.30 a.m., the most difficult case I had ever seen up till then. As soon as he finished, the doctor turned to me and said "You must go straight to bed, Miss Godfrey." "Oh! I couldn't, I must stay and watch the patient", I replied. "Bernadine will do that," said the doctor. "No," I said, "she has been up longer than I have." "Yes Ma," Bernadine said, "That is true, but the patient (a teacher's wife) is my friend, and if I went to bed I should not sleep." I was finally over-ruled and went to bed at 3 a.m.

At 7 a.m. I got up and sent Bernadine off duty, telling her to stay until called for, but she was back at 1 p.m., "refreshed and ready for duty". The patient recovered, largely I am sure due to Bernadine's unremitting care and love.'

A pioneer nursing sister from the Nixon Memorial Hospital, Segbwema, Sierra Leone, tells of Alihu, one of their first medical assistants. Quite early in its life the hospital began to develop local clinics farther into the interior, and from one of these a little girl aged seven or eight named Mahun was brought to the hospital suffering from infantile cataract. She had been blind from early childhood. Considerable difficulty had been experienced in persuading her family to allow the child to come to hospital for operation, and the reputation of Western medicine was at stake. The operation was finally performed.

'We had by then a few more helpers, but no night nurse, patients' relatives staying in the ward at night. As Mahun had no relative with her, this was a problem. Alihu came to the rescue when it was explained that Mahun's head must not be moved as it might impair the operation. He sat by her bed every night and kept the sandbags which immobilized her head in their place, until the time came when the bandages were removed. Alihu's black hand and the doctor's white hand were placed in turn before her eyes, and she said in Mende, "Black and white." There was a most joyous scene in the ward and helpers danced each other up and down.

During an outbreak of smallpox in the district, a very old lady was left on the path to the hospital suffering from confluent smallpox. We did not know who brought her and never did find out to whom she belonged. The doctor was away, so Alihu again came to the rescue – all the other helpers were too afraid of this sickness. He built a little shelter for her as far away from the hospital buildings as practicable, and nobody but Alihu and I went near her and cared for her. She did not live very long. Alihu dug a grave and we wrapped her in a native cloth and mat, and he and I lifted her into it. Nobody ever enquired for her, and all our enquiries came to naught. I shall never forget Alihu's wonderful help.'

Following the pioneer work of Dr Elmslie in Kashmir, opportunities began to arise for Christians to introduce Western medicine in a number of cities and towns on the North West Frontier in what is now Pakistan. There was no settled government administration at the time in this mountainous and fanatically Muslim area, and the Church Missionary Society had insufficient expatriate doctors to respond to the situation. They therefore turned to the Indian medical profession, and several Indian Christian doctors responded to this appeal and joined the mission at considerable personal self-sacrifice.

Most famous of these was John Williams, who in 1869 started a hospital at Tank on the Afghan border, and worked there for over 20 years. There are repeated references to this saintly and devoted man, whose medical skill and humility quickly endeared him to the local population. His small medical centre was soon visited by fierce Waziri tribesmen from the surrounding mountains, commonly suffering from gunshot wounds, and his reputation spread among them also, so much so that when ten years later Waziri tribesmen sacked the town of Tank, Dr Williams and his unit were spared. The government dispensary was sacked.

A year after Dr Williams' arrival, a visitor reported:

'From early morning until after midday or later if necessary, the "native" doctor is unceasingly employed prescribing for, and with the aid of helpers, dispensing medicine to all comers. After his first or midday meal he has a constant succession of visitors till late at night.'

Another fellow-missionary colleague wrote:

'Here I gained an incidental testimony to the widespread influence of Tank medical mission and of our "faqir doctor", who every one of these rough hill-rangers knows, and knowing loves. Many a time had they sought to make him their mediator to negotiate terms with the British Government; but without offending them he prudently refrained from associating himself with either party. During 1883 there were new patients to the number of 8057 – a great many of these from beyond the Afghan border, and all have had the opportunity of hearing something of the Good Physician and of the glad tidings of salvation.'

Dr Williams died in 1898, and Robert Clark, another great CMS pioneer said of him:

'By his gentle and winning manners, his kindness to the people and his medical skill, he won his way amongst the Waziri clans, and he was probably the only Christian man in India who could in those days travel unarmed and without any escort uninjured throughout the length and breadth of that mountainous country of wild Mohammedans. It was said that his solitary grave in the hospital grounds would have become a Mohammedan shrine had it not been placed within a Christian compound. So passed a humbly great descendant of Francis Xavier's converts.'

At Clarkabad, a village in the Punjab named by the government after the Rev. Robert Clark, it is recorded:

'A small hospital-dispensary was built in 1894 and placed under the supervision of an Indian Christian doctor, and has continued to this day, though now under a compounder. In this case, however, it was not local hostility but shortage of missionaries which decided its manner of staffing. The work was locally supported moreover and never a charge on Church Missionary Society funds.'

Similar stories can be told of the Near East.   In 1883 a dispensary was opened at Salt in Palestine and a Christian Arab doctor was put in charge. In the first six months there were 2558 attendances, and 228 patients were visited in their homes. In spite of Salt being a very antiforeign centre, a succession of Lebanese doctors kept the work going.

In 1936 the Church of Scotland appointed Francis Ibiam, a young Nigerian medical graduate of St. Andrews University to open up medical work at Abiriba, a rural area about 20 miles from Uzuakoli, in Eastern Nigeria, where I had recently arrived. As at that time there were only two doctors for the whole Bende Division (or county) with its population of 250,000, there was plenty of scope for Dr Ibiam. I met him there at his lonely temporary hospital and it was obvious that he was welcomed by the local people. Dr Ibiam was destined to become governor of Eastern Nigeria, and knighted for his services to his country.

Farther south, deep in the Niger delta, midwifery work had been established at a place called Bethel by two English nursing sisters, but their constant ill-health prompted its transfer to Nigerian colleagues. The 1936 report of the Iyi Enu hospital contains the following, referring to work at Bethel:

'The place is unfortunately very unhealthy for Europeans, and after the continued ill-health of Miss Jewitt and Miss Inge, who has helped her for over 2 years, it has been decided to transfer the training centre to Warri, and to leave Peter Okoro, the dresser, Dorcas Abighe, the midwife and Emily Obieki to carry on the dispensary, the maternity work and the charge of the motherless babies at Bethel. Miss Jewitt writes of the disappointment of having to retire from Bethel, but she goes on: "The sting of disappointment is largely removed in the joy of seeing young Africans rise and shoulder unexpected responsibility in a very capable manner, giving of their best without reserve in an effort to keep the dispensary and maternity work alive." So African Christians are taking up the task of proclaiming the Gospel by their actions as well as by their words.'

The 1930 Decennial Report of the London Missionary Society Central African Mission contains the following:

'The mission has one bit of medical work entirely carried out by a native medical orderly. At Niamkolo where he lives on the shores of Lake Tanganyika, this orderly has been so successful in his treatment of both ordinary cases and injection cases, that those unable to reach Niamkolo begged him to visit the district. He made several journeys both preaching and healing . . . This orderly has 26 lepers under his care whom he regularly injects. He has also in the last year given 550 injections for yaws and has treated over 3,000 outpatients.'

It was a salutary experience, when I was first posted to a rural area in Eastern Nigeria, to discover that British medical qualifications meant nothing to the local people. One was just another medicine man setting himself up in rivalry to the local exponents of the genre, to be judged entirely by results. To be frank, there were some aspects of medical practice in which the newcomer had nothing startling to offer. Uncomplicated fractures hardly ever came our way, but it was in relation to surgery and the treatment of certain widespread and serious infections, malaria and yaws in particular, that the reputation of Western medicine was made.

In the early stages, medical centres were few and far between, but once the virtues of Western medicine were discovered, the pressure for development became enormous, and applied in two directions. First came the appeal, often rising to a clamour, for the multiplication of medical centres in the surrounding countryside. Simultaneously came an almost intolerable pressure for enlargement and increased facilities at the original centre. Hardly anywhere could voluntary agencies or colonial governments rise to these new opportunities with more than token increases in foreign staff, but in numerous places major and sometimes spectacular development did occur, made possible by the work of national colleagues who proved themselves not only apt pupils but often also capable of carrying heavy and varied responsibilities. Indeed time has proved that in relation,

for example, to community health, no foreigner can achieve anything comparable to that which is possible to the dedicated
national with his own understanding of the background and
problems of his people.

The role of national colleagues in the development of health
services cannot be exaggerated. It made possible the introduction of modern medicine into thousands of localities where no
foreign doctor or nurse was available. The heavy loss of life
among foreign workers in some parts of Africa indeed forced
missionary societies to abandon these areas as far as foreign staff
were concerned, replacing them by national colleagues who
possessed some immunity to those great killers, yellow fever
and malaria. It was the same urge for development that prompted many missionary medical centres to initiate medical,
nursing, midwifery and laboratory training. There was usually
no dearth of candidates.

With the passage of time increasing numbers of trained
national colleagues began to appear. It was usually nurses and
midwives who led the way, and gradually the entire responsibility for the nursing services of many a hospital was taken over by
nationals. Doctors posed a more difficult problem. Armed with a
medical qualification acceptable in the West, he would be a
determined and dedicated young doctor who could resist the
lure of affluence abroad, and choose instead to live and work
among his own people, especially in rural areas. Nevertheless
there have always been doctors of this calibre, both men and
women, with their sacrificial motivation and their own
Christian faith. Some have accepted life in a rural hospital,
others have joined the staff of larger city hospitals and risen to
the highest office. Yet others have made the various aspects of
community health their life's work and have rendered service of
great importance to their countries. One example from each of
these groups must suffice us here.

On the south bank of the Godaveri river in central India lies
the little town of Dudgaon. Here in 1926 a British lady doctor
founded a mission hospital, especially for women and children.
It was never intended to develop this country hospital beyond
the scope of a single doctor, but within its limitations the hospital came to be very precious to the 100,000 village people
whom it served. A succession of foreign lady doctors worked
there and in due time retired. In 1954, the diocese of the Church
of South India for the first time had an Indian doctor available in

the person of Dr Daniel, a young graduate from Vellore, who had been sponsored by the diocese. He accepted an appointment at Dudgaon, and rapidly won the confidence of the local people, with inevitable expansion on the men's side of the work. A born surgeon, he excelled in emergency surgery and obstetrics. A democrat, a good administrator, sensitive and tenderhearted, he won the deep affection of his staff, and the hospital flourished. A devoted Christian, he sought no more advantageous situation.

In 1966 the government of India embarked on a major hydro-electric scheme for harnessing the waters of the Godaveri river to irrigate an enormous area, and located this at Pochampad, two miles from Dudgaon. Almost immediately heavy additional burdens fell on the shoulders of Dr Daniel as the result of the employment of hundreds of workers on this project. No additional professional help was forthcoming, however. Rural medicine, alas, holds little attraction for most doctors in India. Nevertheless, Dr Daniel accepted the situation, received workers from the project into his practice with total courtesy, and organized his time to cover the influx of patients as well as possible. He continued to work at the hospital until his death in 1980, mourned by the entire community, a shining example of Christian service.

Some 200 miles above Shanghai, at the confluence of the Yangtse and Han rivers, lie the three major cities of Hankow, Wuchang and Hanyang, a conurbation of great importance to the industrial, commercial and administrative life of central China. The first doctor to penetrate so far up the Yangtse was a Methodist missionary, Dr Porter Smith, who arrived at Hankow in 1861, and with great difficulty established a dispensary in the heart of the city. This small beginning was destined to develop into a major general hospital. By 1935 the hospital had a Chinese superintendent with two European doctors working under him. The same process had occurred at a sister hospital, the Union Hospital, located four miles away close to the foreign concessions. Within a few years both hospitals were engulfed in the trials and disasters of war, and it was their dedicated Chinese leadership that enabled both to continue their work. Some details of this extraordinary story are given later. This is another example that could be multiplied a hundredfold, demonstrating how competent and dedicated national colleagues continued and developed the work of their foreign predecessors into new and often dangerous times, maintaining an international outlook wherever possible.

In Chapter 16 the pioneer community health work of Dr and Mrs (Dr) Arole is described, as is that of Dr Daleep and Mrs Mukarji, remarkable examples of what can be achieved by nationals applying the Christian spirit in traditional rural areas and in entirely new situations.

The development of medical services in Africa in general came at a later date than in Asia. Precisely the same story has unfolded, though with one important additional feature, namely the Christian influence within government medical services in several African countries, and the effects of this on both medical research and administration. Conditioning factors were the serious health hazards for Europeans living in areas where malaria and other serious diseases were hyperendemic, so that those who went to work there needed a strong motivation, and also the absence of religious alternatives in areas outside the dominance of Islam. There are outstanding examples of leadership and initiative among African colleagues with the same vision that inspired the most dedicated Europeans.

Nigeria has a particularly honourable record in this respect. The names immediately come to mind of Sir Samuel Manuwa, the first Nigerian Director of Medical Services, and Sir Louis Mbanefo, Chief Justice, Eastern Nigeria, Chancellor of the Anglican diocese on the Niger, chairman of the board of governors of Iyi Enu Hospital, a vice-president of the World Council of Churches and the first Nigerian to serve at the International Court of Justice at The Hague, 'a great man in every sense of the word, with the dignity and humility that is characteristic of his kind.' Sir Francis Ibiam, whose medical practice became engulfed in greater public service to Nigeria, a great Christian, Chairman of the Bible Society in Nigeria, came to Britain to speak on behalf of the Bible Society

Nigeria also has nurses of great distinction, none more so than Miss Grace Ifeka, matron of the large Anglican hospital and nursing schools at Iyi Enu, Onitsha. Miss Ifeka entered the nursing profession and mission service out of a sense of Christian vocation and is believed to have been the first Nigerian doubly qualified staff nurse, midwife and nursing sister. A senior colleague adds:

'During the Nigerian civil war, when the hospital had to be evacuated into two boarding schools, more than anybody else she held the staff together, maintaining morale and discipline. Iyi Enu was the only mission hospital which was evacuated from its own premises and yet maintained a full service to the surrounding population from its place of refuge until the end of the war. Miss Ifeka then spearheaded the return of the hospital to its devastated compound, and has worked ever since to develop and sustain it.'

Miss Ifeka has received wide recognition and a national honour for her outstanding service.

The Mende people of Sierra Leone have sons and daughters who have gained distinction in medicine. Regina Sao Kallon, eldest surviving child of a town chief at Segbwema, determined to work at the newly developing mission hospital there in the late 1920s, trained as nurse and midwife in the early 1930s and became a senior member of the nursing staff. In 1945 her father died and the people called her home to be their chief. There she proceeded to build a maternity unit and child care rooms in the town where she worked unstintingly for 30 years and trained many midwives. Samuel Jusu, a colleague of hers, had become staff nurse at the hospital in charge of the men's ward by 1943 and his sterling qualities led to a series of promotions to business manager and medical assistant. He was awarded the British Empire Medal for services to medicine in Sierra Leone. Thomas Conteh became senior nursing officer at the hospital in 1973, and gained international diplomas.

So the story goes on. There are numerous mission hospitals in Asia and Africa which have been served by dedicated and highly competent members of staff such as these, many of them carrying heavy burdens of responsibility, and all of them united in a common motivation – their personal experience of Christianity.

Times of stress, of natural disaster, epidemic, revolution and war inevitably threaten the continuity of medical services and test the quality of those engaged in them. Most developing countries are familiar with such events, but time and again the sadness of them has been redeemed by the extraordinary heroism of ordinary medical workers who have continued their life-saving vocation even in desperate situations. National colleagues figure prominently in the roll of honour created by such emergencies.

The turbulent history of modern China provides many remarkable instances of this. During the Sino-Japanese war some hospitals managed to survive, their spirit undiminished under Japanese occupation. Others transferred themselves from one place to another before the advancing Japanese and continued their work amid extraordinary hardship.

Fatshan is an industrial city close to Canton and was an important Japanese objective, captured early in the war. The historic Methodist hospital there already had a Chinese superintendent, but the hospital was not taken over, and was allowed to continue under its Chinese superintendent because of its reputation in the city. The hospital remained open throughout the war in spite of many and grave difficulties, the continual threat of being requisitioned by the Japanese, neighbouring properties becoming military camps and targets for allied bombing, the loss of staff to Free China, great problems with finance, medical stores, food and fuel, armed robbers and the kidnapping of better class patients, problems of police protection which had to be paid for. Yet the doors of the hospital never closed.

A different story comes from Lingling in Hunan Province. The story is best told in the words of Dr Kenneth Leese.

'In May 1944, the Japanese captured Changsha, and as this directly menaced the town of Lingling, it was decided by the staff of the Methodist hospital there to evacuate to Tao Hsien, 180 kilometres away. The staff were divided into four parties. The first party, with medicines left almost immediately by boat, under the business manager Chen Yu Ming. A second party taking the hospital equipment and families left a short time later under a senior nurse, Yu Ping. This party suffered great difficulties. Robbers were very active on the river, and children were always falling ill. The boats took 18 days to get to Tao Hsien. On the way Sung Hai Tao's baby was taken ill and died three days after they arrived. The third party with half the Nursing School went by road. The fourth party included Dr Huang, Superintendent of the hospital and the remainder of the Nursing School. On arrival at Tao Hsien great difficulty was experienced in finding somewhere where they could work. The beds were set up in a family temple. About 40 outpatients a day were seen elsewhere, and staff camped out where they could. Yu Ping's mother died two weeks later and was buried there.

Within a month the Japanese had broken through to Henyang and were advancing on Tao Hsien, so it was decided to evacuate again. Amid the panic and turmoil Yu Ping performed the almost miraculous feat of getting three small boats for the party. He rationed each family to two pieces of luggage per person and ordered them aboard. The women folk refused to go. They hired their own coolies and set off to walk to Chiang Hua, 45 kilometres away. The boats eventually took the hospital equipment, although the beds were left behind. One party from Lingling with hospital equipment had still not arrived at Tao Hsien, so the departure of the rest of the staff was left until the last moment, Yu Ping and one colleague remaining until the very day that the Japanese arrived. When they did leave, they found the Chiang Hua road entirely blocked with refugees, and taking by-roads they arrived in Chiang Hua to find it deserted, with everybody in hiding except Dr Huang. The hospital equipment was some-where on the river; Yu Ping insisted on seeking it by foot, and at great peril to his life he succeeded in tracing it. By this time there were some who felt that the whole unit should disband. Coolies were almost uncontrollable and much of the hospital equipment had been stolen, but Dr Huang, Yu Ping and some colleagues held the party together, and after desperate adventures the hospital came to life again at Ma T'ou O'u. Seeking lost equipment, Yu Ping repeatedly risked his life, and at one stage was six days without food and slept in the mountains, where it was so cold that each morning there was frost on his hair. About this time, following a Japanese defeat, Chiang Hua became open again, and the Government asked the hospital to return there. A clinic was quickly opened, and within two months 50 patients a day were being treated. All this time the Nursing School had been scat-tered, but gradually they came together again, and in due course after extreme privations the hospital returned to Lingling, Yu Ping being the last to leave Chiang Hua.

Hospital after hospital can tell a story like this. Many Chinese members of staff and their relatives lost their lives, but all the time the extraordinary heroism of colleagues like Yu Ping glows like a rich jewel amid all the horror of those days.'

The story of the celebrated Union Hospital at Hankow is equally dramatic. As the Japanese advanced into central China they approached the key city of Hankow on the River Yangtse. With experience at other captured hospitals to go by, it was felt that the Union Hospital, located on a main road near the foreign legations, was certain to be taken over by the Japanese. Four miles away, deep in the Chinese city, the hospital possessed a branch dispensary, and it was decided to move the work of the hospital bodily from its vulnerable position right into that crowded Chinese area where the hospital could become anony-mous. This novel decision was in fact put into practice, thanks entirely to the very high regard for it felt by the Chinese popula-tion. Accommodation was secured in a large warehouse, and the hospital, renamed the Ho Chi hospital, carried on for over two years, its whereabouts concealed by the loyalty of the Chinese people who helped in a multitude of ways to keep the hospital open right under the prying eyes of the occupying Japanese authorities. Financial assets and stores were distributed for safe keeping among responsible friends who released them as required.

The first hospital report after hostilities ended (1945) continues the story:

'The Union Hospital building on the Chung Cheng Road was eventually occupied by a Japanese military infectious diseases hospital unit which is still in occupation. The Ho Chi Hospital, however, carried on uninterruptedly for over two years. It had been planned that a local Supervisory Committee should exercise a general oversight; but very shortly after the final expulsion of the British residents from Hankow the Japanese seized the Hospital and handed it over to the control of the puppet Municipality. (This development had been anticipated and preparations had been made to meet it.) Although nominally the Ho Chi was now a Municipal Hospital and had even to change its name again, Dr Liu was left in charge as promised. Official evangelists could no longer appear on the staff roster; but the Christian impact of a hospital in China does not depend solely on its official evangelists. The Hospital continued its general work for the sick and its midwifery services, and was successfully financed with the help of its accumulated stores and its private ward patients. Its nurses' training school carried on its valuable training work.

At some point, probably early in 1944, Dr Liu was transferred to another hospital, leaving in charge his assistant, Dr Wang. On 10th December 1944, Hankow which had for some time been under heavy bombardment by American planes based on Chungking, suffered a terrific bombing, and a considerable part of the city was set on fire and destroyed, including Mr Klein's block of warehouses just across the road from the Ho Chi Hospital. The staff carried on. But on 18th December there came a more terrible bombing still which laid waste the whole business section of the city, and this time the Hospital itself was burned down and destroyed together with the whole block of buildings in which it stood. There were many hospital casualties, but no list is available.

This gallant little Christian staff, the heirs of the Union Hospital tradition, for the sake of its work had endured privation, hardship and danger of death, the threats and misery of the Japanese occupation, the taunts of its friends in Free China, and the loss of its entire foreign leadership; and yet it had cheerfully carried on, true to type, faithful and undismayed. It had borne a triumphant witness to the faith that was in it: but now it had finished its course and was scattered, leaving it to its survivors to carry as individuals its message far and wide.'

Maieogaru, a Papuan nurse, was honoured by H.M. the Queen of England for outstanding bravery during the 1939-45 war.

Middle-aged, and with a limited knowledge of English when she began to train, she was a natural nurse, and highly motivated. Her story is told by Miss Ellen Kettle as follows, in *That they might live.*

'Maieogaru had completed her two years of training and was based at Divinai on the northern shore of Milne Bay when the Japanese invaded on August 26th 1942. It was a furious battle; the Australians had anticipated the Japanese move and set an ambush for just days before they were attacked. The following day the people of Maieogaru's village saw what appeared to be a log on the beach of a nearby island; Maieogaru thought otherwise, and paddled across in a canoe to find a seriously injured Australian airman. He had been in the water many hours before the tide washed him ashore. She brought the airman back to the village and cared for him there, until she realized that he needed more care than she could provide if he was to survive. This brave woman replaced her nurse's uniform with a grass skirt, put the airman in the bottom of her canoe and covered him with vegetables. To reach Gwavili, where she knew the Australians were, meant passing through the Japanese lines and crossing Milne Bay itself, a distance of about 24 kilometres. A Japanese boat pulled alongside to investigate and accepted her bluff as a village woman taking home supplies. The airman's life was saved.'

China is also the scene of appalling and recurring flood disasters. Here is a report from Anlu on the Han River, 100 miles above Hankow, following a major disaster when widespread flooding resulted from the breaking of the river banks in 1926. Mr James K.C. Liu was the first graduate of the school of nursing at Anlu hospital, and was recruited by Dr E. Cundall as a boy of about 14. After qualifying he was retained on the hospital staff.

'During the troubles of 1925 the hospital was boycotted and the work closed for the summer months. It was then that James returned from Peking after a post-registration course at Union Medical College, proceeded inland to Anlu, and re-opened the hospital. When the missionaries reached the station after the summer, James was awaiting them, the hospital was spick and span, the staff gathered together, patients had been admitted and were waiting for the doctor, and all was in readiness for him to begin work at once.

At the time of the disaster on the Han river it was James who enabled the Mission to do relief work among the refugees. The breaking of the river embankments was an appalling disaster. Whole villages were swept away and an enormous area was flooded, leaving thousands of people homeless and destitute. Children who managed to scramble into trees and up to their top branches gradually lost their hold and dropped into the floods below and were drowned. Famine followed, the cold weather came on, and the suffering was intense. It was obviously impossible for the one doctor to leave his patients at the hospital, so James volunteered to go. It meant some months of living among the refugees while the banks of the river were repaired.

A little dispensary was opened, medicines were given out, preventive treatment given, wounds and injuries were attended to, the more severely injured and most seriously ill patients were assisted with transport facilities to hospital, milk was served to the babies and rice given out to the adults, bath sheds were opened and fitted up for use, and work given to the able-bodied.

When he at last returned, the work finished, he was asked one day by a friend as to what had impressed him most during this experience. Was it the long hard days and cold nights, the lack of his ordinary food and comforts, the horrid sights and nauseous smells, the strain of dealing with hundreds of destitute and homeless people, many of whom were embittered and hopeless? No, it was none of these things. He had caught the vision of service and he replied, "I thought it was a great opportunity to witness for Jesus".'

Grave epidemics are another feature of the history of China, none more dreadful than the outbreaks of plague which have continued right into modern times and have been a frequent threat in city after city. Reference is made to this in chapter 7, but here is a report from Fatshan hospital near Canton written in 1908.

'There have been several instances proving the devotion of our Fatshan students to their work. About three years ago we were in the middle of a severe epidemic of plague. People were dying all around. It was a sad thing to see the despair which is a feature of the disease. Oftentimes the patient makes no effort and at once accepts that death is inevitable. One day we went into the town to see a little boy in the last stage of the disease. He was the only son and all the women in the house were wailing bitterly. The poor mother was ready to grovel on the ground in the hope that something could be done but only a miracle could have saved her child. Upon our return, there was a boat anchored by the river steps outside the hospital containing an old student and local preacher, who was lying on a couch suffering from the same disease in its pneumonic form, the most virulently infectious of all. Somebody had to nurse him, and one of our students, Kwok A Yam, offered to take the risk. As a student he had always been an active member, and ready to speak at the services to the heathen. Being clever and reliable, he had just been promoted, after completing his course, to the position of house surgeon. During the short time he occupied this post he proved very useful and learnt enough English to read prescriptions and so take much work off the hands of Mr So, the dispenser. He was shortly to be married, and we were looking forward to a long life of happiness and usefulness for him. But God had ordained otherwise. Three days after attending to his friend, he himself began to show signs of the terrible scourge, and went rapidly downhill. When first attacked, he declared that he knew he would die, but that he had "prayed to the Heavenly Father, and was not a bit afraid." Just before death he again said that he had no fear. The end came very soon, and surely it was a noble one, for he had surrendered his life for the friend whom he had tried to save. Nobody could give a better dying testimony. His trust and fearlessness were in marked contrast to the horror shown by most plague patients, and this contrast taught a lesson to at least one observer which it will take a long time to forget.'

The first medical missionary of modern times was a German, Dr Schlegelmilch, who went to India in 1730, 80 years before the first doctor went from Britain to practise medicine in the Third World. During the interval a succession of medical workers went in the service of continental societies, notably the Moravians and the Basel Mission. The first woman doctor to follow in their steps was an American, who went to Peking in the 1860s. These facts are a reminder that the contributions of British societies to the health of mankind is only part of a much wider spectrum of sacrificial service in which continental Europe, America and Australasia have played a very important part. The scale of this is well brought out in the periodic editions of the World Missionary Atlas. The 1925 edition of this gave the accompanying statistics (see Table 1) for medical work. They apply to Protestant missions only, and so are incomplete.

These figures give ample evidence of the importance of medical missions in developing health services in many Third World countries but, in spite of their great scale, they do not do justice to the continental societies, many of which had not recovered from the disruption of the 1914-18 War, and by 1925 were still excluded from some territories where they formerly had had important work. Even as they stand, these figures indicate that British based medical mission enterprise represented approximately one-third of the total being undertaken in 1925. This proportion did not increase with the years. There are major territories in which British societies have never done any significant medical work, but the people there have not been neglected.

Table 1: Christian Medical Missions Worldwide in 1925. (Protestant only and therefore incomplete).

SOCIETIES BASED IN	FOREIGN STAFF			NATIONAL STAFF				Hospitals	Dispensaries
	Doctors Male	Doctors Female	Nursing Sisters	Doctors Male	Doctors Female	Trained Assistants Male	Trained Assistants Female		
America (USA & Canada)	489	172	423	262	52	573	1503	400	648
Australasia	8	8	28	8	1	28	32	12	43
Continental Europe	50	11	125	18	2	184	204	61	126
Britain	218	146	345	176	22	1032	940	316	544
International and Local	33	19	83	49	24	184	239	68	242
TOTAL	798	356	1004	513	101	2001	2918	857	1603

The true picture emerges if a single territory is used as an example. Thanks to the work of Miss Ellen Kettle, accurate details are available for Papua New Guinea. New Guinea was annexed by Germany in 1884 and by Britain in 1883 and 1884 through the Government of Queensland. Even before that time, in a country full of dangerous hazards to the life and health of foreigners, several societies had tried to start missionary work, with care of the sick as part of their activities; but with most of the pioneers killed by malaria or by local inhabitants, progress was very slow, especially with the population fragmented into small warring groups and with 700 different languages. When colonial administrations did begin to operate, they turned to Christian societies to initiate medical services for the people, and an outstanding contribution to the development of health services was the result, made really effective because of the international range of the societies concerned. Australians, British, French, Germans and Pacific Islanders were all involved. As government medical services developed, official recognition of the mission institutions continued when they were invited to accept responsibility in the training of midwives and medical orderlies, and to staff special hospitals for sufferers from leprosy and tuberculosis.

The Report of the Church Missionary Society in China for 1865, referring to the treaty port of Ningpo, includes the following:

'At the close of October a proposal was made to us by Dr McCarter, an old and well-known member of the American Presbyterian Mission, to commence a gratuitous dispensary in our rooms, if we would guarantee a small stock of medicines for the purpose. The dispensary has been at work now for some 7 or 8 weeks. The rooms are altogether too small for the numbers of medicines, which have risen from about 50 to 150.'

This early example of cooperation, both international and across denominational frontiers, could be multiplied a thousand times. In Third World situations the distinctions between one brand of Christianity and another are often revealed in their true perspectives and irrelevancies. There are always extremists in all religions, as in all political parties, who are blind to any approach other than their own, but for the most part the experience of overwhelming need has tended to draw Christians together in carrying medical work forward most effectively, and at every level. An example has already been given of a Christian government doctor coming to the aid of a missionary nursing sister. There is nothing unique about this, just as there are numerous examples of missionary doctors being invited to participate in government projects, especially in emergency situations.

This process accelerates very rapidly when work founded by missionaries becomes the responsibility of national churches. The Victoria Leprosy Hospital at Dichpalli in Central India was a Protestant foundation, absorbed in 1947 into the Church of South India. I worked there between 1968 and 1973 and it was a joy to discover that the hospital by then had no truer friend than a Roman Catholic priest, while a dispensary maintained in a village 5 miles away by an Order of nuns was visited one afternoon weekly by a doctor from the hospital. At diocesan level, the Church of South India welcomed the idea that a celebrated Roman Catholic social worker should be based at the hospital and another Order of nuns should undertake rehabilitation work there.

Cooperation, both international and denominational, has been of outstanding importance in the sphere of medical education. The great centre at Vellore became what it is because during the years of development the hospital and medical school were supported by 42 missionary societies from several countries, representing all shades of theological opinion. The same principle applied widely, and became the forerunner of cooperation on an even wider scale. In one country after another nowadays, government and voluntary agencies are coming together in establishing Health Associations under the influence of the World Council of Churches, with the object of promoting cooperation on a broad front, but most importantly, in the sphere of community health, a development that augurs well for the future.

CHAPTER 20

THE COST AND THE VISION

Stanley G. Browne

Nobody reading through the previous chapters can imagine that the task of bringing health and healing to needy people in developing countries could be other than costly. For many decades, the unfolding story has been punctuated by tragedy, as tropical diseases and strife have taken their toll of life and health. Of course, medical missionaries have not been alone in facing these risks and succumbing to these diseases; their nonmedical colleagues and nonmissionary fellow-exiles from their homelands (soldiers, administrators, planters and merchants) have shared with them the exigencies of life and work in a tropical climate (Warren, 1965). They all had to be highly motivated in one way or another, to serve (for instance) in the countries of West Africa. Otherwise, why go to an area so dangerous to health, with the reputation of being 'the white man's grave'? Government agents were instructed to provide themselves with a coffin, to be kept over the rafters in the living room, 'just in case'. Many failed to survive their first tour of duty. Doctors and nurses by reason of their being brought into close contact with the sick were subject to extra risks of infection.

The cost – the toll of tropical diseases

In the earlier years especially, a not inconsiderable number of medical workers died on the job. They succumbed to malaria (before the days of prophylactics) and blackwater fever, to typhoid and typhus, to plague and dysentery. They endured privations of many kinds in a climate as hostile as the people they were trying to help. They lacked the amenities of civilized life – adequate shelter from the elements, safe water, nourishing food. Uncomplaining, they battled on against chronic sickness and bouts of 'fever', and gave themselves day after long day to their task of succouring others more sick than themselves – 'for the sake of the Name'.

The pages of the Golden Book of those who gave their lives for the hope that was in them did not close in the apostolic age. They

345

are still open, and contain the names of many medical workers. Some died violent deaths. More succumbed to disease and privation. Like their Master, they 'learned obedience through suffering'. The world is not worthy of them.

In the Roll of Honour of the Royal Free Hospital, we see that some of these courageous heroines served only a short time at their posts. Dr Janet Hoare was dead within three months of arrival in India: 'Why this waste?' was the evocative title of a pamphlet issued by her missionary society. Dr H.A. Rachel died within a year, and five others within five years. It is amazing that 23 of them served for more than 10 years, and that Dr Florence Cooper worked abroad for 50 years before she was called to higher service in 1947 (Royal Free Hospital, 1980).

Dr Gavin Russell arrived in Formosa in 1890. Two years later he died of typhoid at the age of twenty-five. 'Even on his deathbed', we read, 'he frequently regretted his inability to render any further service to some patients on whom he had operated a few days before his illness began' (Band, 1948).

In the CMS Hospital at Bannu on the Northwest frontier of India, Dr Barnett died in 1912 of septicaemia, contracted while operating on a patient. Treating his sick colleague, the renowned Dr Pennell caught the infection and was dead within a few days (Band, 1948). In Bannu Hospital there is a bed inscribed 'In memory of Captain Connolly, beheaded at Bokhara'. When Afghan patients are admitted to the bed, they are shown the plaque and told that the care they receive as inpatients is the kind of 'revenge' that Christians love to show to those who injure them. 'Greater love has no man than this'.

Dr Cecil Robertson died of typhus in China in 1913, and within three weeks his colleague, Dr Stanley Jenkins, was dead of the same disease (Moorshead, 1929). Robertson had served for less than four years and Jenkins for nine. Such was their reputation that funds were raised by public subscription for a Memorial Hospital in Tsinanfu, to be named after them.

Dr Arthur Jackson arrived at Moukden at the height of a plague epidemic. He volunteered to serve at a 'strategical danger point', caught plague and died (Hewat, 1960; Costain, 1911).

More recently, medical workers, expatriate and national, have died in harness while caring for those fatally ill from Lassa fever in Segbwema Hospital (Sierra Leone) and in Nigeria. National colleagues shared in the nursing duties, often forfeiting their status in the community by so doing and putting their own health, and life itself, at risk. They died in circumstances of great heroism.

The cost – violent death

It was not only tropical diseases that exacted their grim toll of medical missionaries. Dr Harry Wyatt was gunned down and killed by Communist bandits in China, the Union Jack he displayed affording no protection (Payne, 1939). Dr Hilda Bowser was lost at sea in 1941 as the result of enemy action while on her way back to India.

In China doctors were often in danger from violent mobs. In one report we read: 'Our house surgeon Mr Anderson was severely injured by an attack made by upwards of seven hundred delegates of secret societies. One of the stragglers of the band inflicted on him with a sword such a serious wound that, but for prompt action, it would have most probably been fatal. Our doors have not been closed for a single day during the riots' (Davey and Davey, 1964).

Also from China (in Cheng-fu), comes the story that 'the doctor and his assistants were beaten with sticks and rifles and tied up for an hour' (Band, 1948).

In 1897, Dr Roderick McDonald was in high spirits as he made his way home from Synod, having announced that he had secured a site for a new hospital at Wuchow. He was never to see the hospital, for the boat on which he was travelling was attacked by pirates; Dr McDonald was shot at point blank range and killed while he was tending the wounded captain (Davey and Davey, 1964).

Few experiences of medical missionaries can be as harrowing as those of Dr Thomas Cochrane who, with his wife and three young sons, escaped death at the hands of the Boxers in 1900. Thanks to the courage and devotion of their Chinese servant and sympathetic Christian villagers, they managed to pass through the Boxer lines unscathed (Balme, 1921; Aitchison, 1983). In Christian 'revenge', Dr Cochrane became Physician to the Empress Dowager Tzu-Hsi and the éminence grise who had together encouraged the Boxers to kill missionaries and Chinese Christians. That 'the blood of martyrs is the the seed of the Church' has been exemplified times without number in the history of medical missions, in China especially.

Dr Cochrane may have renounced the medical prizes in the Western world that his professional gifts merited, but he

accomplished a far greater work in China than if he had
remained in Scotland. He founded and was the first President of
the Peking Union Medical College. He had the joy of seeing his
son Robert become the world's leading leprologist, and he
himself used his considerable experience as a medical missionary to sponsor such organizations as the World Dominion Trust
and the Missionary Aviation Fellowship.

Nearer our own time, during the Civil War in Nigeria,
Dr Elizabeth Edmunds of the CMS Iyi Enu Hospital was
wounded by federal soldiers.

National medical workers face danger, too. In August 1977 a
paramedical leprosy worker attached to Manorom Hospital,
Central Thailand, heard another motorcycle coming up behind
him. As it passed him, with three youths on it, they fired at him.
He was hit in the chest by three bullets; he fell off and lay for
dead, while one of the thugs drove his motorcycle away. Then he
managed to get a lift from a passing lorry, eventually walking
into the outpatient department of the Manorom Hospital saying
'I've been shot'. Examination showed three wounds – two
bullets had just missed the lung, and one the heart. He recovered, and was soon back on the job (Leprosy Mission, 1977).

The cost – broken health

A much larger number than those who actually died on the field
was invalided home broken in health, some of them to die pre-
maturely as the result of disease contracted abroad: chronic
malaria, tuberculosis, poliomyelitis and prolonged nervous
strain accounted for most of these cases of invalidism following
residence in the tropics.

This devotion to duty made great demands on the conscientious doctor faced with such appalling needs and unrelieved
suffering. Dr Maxwell, describing his second visit to Srinagar in
1874, writes as follows: 'I had over 50 patients on the first day,
they rapidly increased, and one day, after I had seen 170, I
fainted!' (Band, 1948).

The lonely doctor in a pioneering situation was frequently
overwhelmed by the huge task he was trying to tackle single-
handed. It is understandable that the idealistic missionary
doctor often felt himself obliged to work for long hours day after
day to cope with demands that were really beyond him. He
could not see that his first priority should be his own personal
survival and integrity. Since his usefulness increased with local

experience and acceptance by the people, a disciplined conservation of energy should have been regarded as absolutely essential. Unfortunately, no senior experienced colleague was there to turn to for advice and help, and to point out that there is no particular virtue in killing oneself through overwork, however piously it might be represented. Home Boards were not blameless in this. In the briefing of doctors about to sail for China, the exhortation was expressed like this: 'You may not live long, but . . .' Some individuals made increasing demands on themselves and their colleagues, became more and more impervious to advice, and eventually had to be repatriated before their useful missionary career had really begun.

Nothwithstanding the risks, many missionary doctors have demonstrated that a sensible regard for the ordinary principles of personal health and hygiene, coupled with adequate relaxation and a genuine interest in people and their problems, and cultivating some hobby – can go far to minimize the undoubted constraints and restrictions of a demanding vocation. Some doctors have developed an interest in language or in anthropology; others have become very knowledgeable about local birds or butterflies; some have found time to pursue a bent in music or botany, or have given rein to their questioning and questing disposition.

The cost – to missionary wives

Far too little tribute has been paid to the noble band of missionary wives who shared the rigours of life with the men they loved and followed (Miller, 1981). Hazards of extremes of climate – heat and cold, floods and drought, hurricanes and tornadoes and earthquakes – difficulties in finding suitable food and cooking it, the perils and discomforts of travel, the peculiar risks of pregnancy and childbirth, the loneliness and lack of female companionship – they faced it all, with a smile and a sublime trust in God. Their unmarried sisters might get a goodly portion of the limelight, but those missionary wives will receive a crown incorruptible (Thompson, 1982).

In the matter of family life and children, it was the wife and mother who bore the brunt of the burden and who paid the highest price. She was nursemaid and babyminder, overseer of milk formulae and transitional weaning foods, kindergarten teacher and inculcator of general knowledge. She protected her children from the bites of innumerable arthropods and from infections from a variety of pathogens, tropical and temperate. She and her children had to share the hazards of the life chosen by the father of the family; sometimes they found it hard to share the ideals that inspired him or the vocation that drove him on. When necessity or custom decreed that the children should pursue their education in the homeland, the deep pains of separation left open wounds of anguish and loneliness. This was the most poignant price the missionary wife and mother had to pay. In the first flush of married life she rarely realized how costly this separation would be, but when it had to come it hurt, and hurt deeply. By painful personal experience these missionary mothers were admitted into the select fellowship of those who did not love son or daughter more than they loved their Master.

The cost – to the children of missionaries

For the children, too, this separation was costly. After all, they had had no say in their choice of parents or in their father's calling. They had not chosen for themselves a life of renunciation, of deprivation, of denial of the legitimate expectations of family and home. At boarding school in India (Ootacamund or Darjeeling), and in China (Chefoo) (Miller, 1981), these missionary children rubbed shoulders with the privileged offspring of well-to-do merchants and administrators, who outside school enjoyed a much higher standard of living than they could ever aspire to. Little wonder that some of these missionary children grew up estranged from their parents, rebellious even, resentful, anti-Christian and delinquent. On the other hand, despite all the agony and loneliness of years of separation and the inadequacies of substitute parents, many of these children came to appreciate the spiritual motivation of their natural parents who had made great sacrifices in order to serve others and their Lord. Such children came to have a deep personal faith, and second generation missionaries – and medical missionaries – are by no means rare.

The cost – voluntary or involuntary celibacy

Unmarried medical missionaries of both sexes, particularly nurses, have made a tremendous contribution to health in developing countries (Anderson, 1956). Unhampered by the demands of children, they have pioneered in medical care for women in purdah, in training doctors and nurses, in commending scientific medicine and the Gospel by means of community health care. Many have faced loneliness and danger, and the prospect of lifelong celibacy in the absence of suitable male contacts, but the outworking of their sublimation is apparent in the many 'children' they have begotten – orphans cared for, nurses trained, opium addicts rescued, neonatal mortality reduced, mothers saved. Some of these women found suitable suitors and married, continuing their work with the advantage, in the eyes of many communities, that the married status confers (Thompson, 1982).

The cost – professional

Another real part of the cost borne by the medical missionary is in his professional career. He cuts himself off from his university or hospital alma mater and from his medical peers. He renounces worldly advancement and prospects of promotion. In most medical missionary situations, he becomes a kind of glorified general practitioner. He must be ready to be a jack-of-all-trades and master-of-few. He must turn his hand to everything medical – from general and tropical medicine to obstetrics (often complicated) and major surgery. He must be good at dealing with eyes and skin diseases. He must be able to make do and to improvise. He should be able to fashion his own splints, fit up his own anaesthetic apparatus, make his own bricks and cut his own timber in the forest. He is laboratory technologist and perhaps radiographer, too. He should be a good teacher and organizer, able to teach, able to inspire.

And all this in an isolated hospital, far from peer stimulus and from consultant opinion at the end of a telephone line. The wonder is not that some doctors find that the demands of the task are beyond them, but that so many over the years have responded magnificently to the challenge of these demands and have proved adaptable and capable of initiative and improvization. Through it all they have not only shown professional competence of no mean order, but have demonstrated the love of Christ that constrains.

They may have renounced the world's glittering professional prizes but they have gained much of enduring worth. Many of them had been distinguished students, outstanding in their academic careers. Dr Cecil Robertson was the best student in his year, gaining every prize, and then went to China as a Baptist missionary doctor (Chesterman, 1940). For Dr David Grant the tempting offer of a Professor's Chair did not deflect him from serving his Master in China (Band, 1948). When he announced his confirmed intention, one of his teachers said to him: 'A medical mission? – good gracious, Grant, is that all?' Yes, that was all, but men have died for less. After fourteen years' service, 'a strong devotion to duty kept him at Chuan-chow longer than was medically advisable', and in 1894 he was invalided home.

Who has not heard of Eric Liddell, the Olympic Gold Medallist who ran a good race for his heavenly Captain, and died in a Japanese prisoner-of-war camp in China, having devoted himself to the physical and spiritual welfare of his fellow-prisoners? (Magnusson, 1981).

Part of the cost to the medical missionary is the burning of his professional boats. When obliged to return to his home country – most commonly because of family commitments or breakdown in health – he finds it increasingly difficult to secure an appointment commensurate with his seniority and experience. Unless he has been so fortunate as to assure his future re-insertion on the professional ladder by means of an anticipatory arrangement with hospital authorities, he may find himself as a trainee assistant in general practice. In the past, many ex-medical missionaries became medical officers of health or general practitioners. Some few have managed to achieve consultant status in accident departments or in general surgery or geriatrics, but the fact remains that the cost of a period of devoted service as a medical missionary has frequently to be paid in subsequent years of less glamorous practice.

The cost – financial

From time to time, concern is expressed about the financial sacrifice of the medically qualified man or woman, or the certificated nurse or therapist, who goes to work abroad. Most missionary societies offer a stipend that covers modest living costs, with an additional weighting the size of which is related to the local cost-of-living. They also provide housing (with a minimum of heavy furniture), transport, medical care, and eventually a small contributory pension after many years of service. Compared with commercial or government professional scales, salaries for medically qualified people (usually the same as for their nonmedical colleagues) are ludicrously low. But as long as relief from financial anxiety is assured and expectations are reasonable, the stipend is adequate, especially if extra allowances for children are generous. There is admittedly this huge difference in financial reward, but to most motivated missionaries, these materialistic considerations are of little interest or importance. In fact, the standard of living necessarily adopted by a missionary household is a positive advantage when it approximates to that of the people they try to serve.

The cost – doctor or evangelist?

Until the turn of the present century medically qualified men and women were not sympathetically welcomed into the ranks of missionaries unless they were willing to subordinate their professional work to the claims of evangelism and church work (Moorshead, 1926). Home Boards sought to limit the work of doctors to 'taking care of the health of colleagues' or 'of some Europeans or natives who may be ill and send for help'. They suggested that medical work could be done without buildings or equipment. Naturally, this attitude was not conducive to the recruitment of well-qualified doctors who saw in their professional activities a means of demonstrating their Christian faith in a practical, understandable way. Happily, with the appointment of medical secretaries, the missionary societies shed many of these old prejudices, and medical work began to be valued in its own right (Moorshead, 1929).

Compensations

If medical missionaries are at risk more than their nonmedical missionary co-workers because of their contact with nationals and colleagues suffering from infectious diseases, they have been able to build up a personal reputation precisely because of their courage in the face of dangerous men and pathogenic microorganisms. Such a one was Dr Theodore Pennell, who was described by an administrator as worth two divisions of soldiers in that turbulent area peopled by fanatical Moslems. When he lay desperately ill (in 1909), we read that the whole town of Bannu came to a standstill. All work ceased, and all shops closed, even in the bazaar. Everywhere, everybody could think of nothing but the fact that their beloved doctor was ill, very ill. People of all religions – Muslim, Hindu – and of none 'poured out their hearts in prayer for his recovery'. In a few weeks, he was on his feet again, busy as ever, helping and healing.

Notwithstanding the cost of medical missions in terms of life and health, of broken families, of surrender of professional career prospects, there would be no doubt in the minds of those most directly concerned – whether the medical missionary himself or herself, or those who benefited from their care and example – that it was all abundantly worthwhile. In many a strategic situation, they have been able to exert a tremendous influence by their medical practice and example, an influence far outweighing anything they could have expected had they remained in their homeland. Costly it may be, but costly experiences are beyond price and of eternal worth.

Some UK medical missionaries have been honoured with the accolade of knighthood, their work having been already recognized by colleagues and governments as of more than local renown. These include Sir Albert Cook, founder of Mengo (CMS) hospital out of which grew the Makerere Medical School in Kampala, Uganda; Sir James Wanless, the pioneer in tuberculosis control in India; Sir Henry Holland, the beloved eye surgeon of Pakistan, pioneer of eye camps; Sir Wilfred Grenfell 'of Labrador'; Sir Clement Chesterman, the pioneer in organizing programmes for comprehensive health care. Some Christian doctors have profoundly influenced government health policies by virtue of the offices they held; the names of Dr Samuel Hynd, formerly Minister of Health in Swaziland, and Dr A. M. Merriweather, Speaker of the Botswana House of Representatives, come to mind. And a Christian Minister of Health in India, Raj Kumari Amrit Kaur was able to guide the young Republic along the right health lines during its formative years.

Some medical missionaries have received worldwide publicity and acclaim. Perhaps Dr Albert Schweitzer is the best-known in modern times. His brilliant academic attainments in theology, music and philosophy were left behind as he devoted himself in Lambarene to founding a hospital and serving the sick African. His selfless renunciation in response to the ideal of helping to discharge the debt incurred by the West towards the African has made its appeal to many who have been blinded by the godless materialism of the 20th century. In addition to running the busy hospital he continued his writing on musical and philosophical topics and earned the high praise of the Nobel Peace Prize (Schweitzer, 1934).

The social and medical services of Mother Teresa (another Nobel laureate) and the Missionaries of Charity have deservedly received wide publicity, and have stimulated the Indian government to refurbish its attitude to the poor and deprived.

Improvisation
The difficulty faced by medical staff in trying to run a hospital on the slenderest of financial grants from the Home Boards is as remarkable as the hope of some nationals that when the local church took over the hospital it would benefit from the income derived from patients' fees. Sometimes this preoccupation with making ends meet has distorted the image of the mission hospital so that it seemed to neglect the poor and cater for the rich.

If the principal yardstick of success is the ability to pass on to national medical colleagues the Christian spirit of initiative and a willingness to adapt to changing circumstances, then it must be admitted that many medical institutions called Christian have not been conspicuously successful. What was right and admirable in 1880 may not be so in the '80s of this century. Furthermore, it is undeniable that in an attempt to bring the best to the hospital, the expensive facilities provided are beyond the reach of the poor who should benefit from them unless heavily subsidized from outside (Anderson, 1956). In our Lord's day 'the common people heard him gladly'. He seemed more concerned with the poor and needy than with the rich. His heart went out to them 'as sheep without a shepherd'. It must be admitted that some mission hospitals may have failed in this respect; they have priced themselves out of the reach of the poor and needy in their striving for medical excellence and the installation of elaborate equipment, expensive to purchase and costly to maintain.

Most missionary doctors and nurses had to make do. This they did in many ways. Extremely meagre resources necessitated recourse to improvisations by imaginative minds and nimble fingers. Here is an example from Eastern Nigeria. Dr. Frank Davey writes: 'Confronted with thousands of leprosy patients all to be treated at local clinics by intradermal and intramuscular injections of hydnocarpus oil, and negligible financial resources, how was asepsis to be achieved?' . . .

'An ordinary locally made cooking pot was kept half full of boiling water throughout the session. A round tin of suitable size which had contained milk or any other food was inverted in the pot, a ring of thirty small holes having been pierced

around the inside of the rim. The level of boiling water was
always maintained just above the top of the tin. Into the holes
were inserted twenty injection needles. After the water had
boiled for ten minutes, the work began. The trained Nigerian staff
took, with sterile forceps, a needle from one end of the chain, replacing it after use at the other end. It was about ten minutes
before that needle arrived again at the sterile end of the chain. By
this simple procedure, it became possible to give millions of
injections every year with virtually no case of sepsis'.

Books and articles by Christian doctors have had a tremendous
influence on the thinking of government health planners and of
missionary doctors (Somervell, 1936). Maurice King (1966) and
David Morley (1973) have been prolific writers in these subjects,
and instruction in laboratory techniques has been made available to the many through the book by Monica Cheesbrough
(1981, 1984).

The vision for today, and tomorrow

The destiny of medical missions
In one sense, the days of the traditional 'medical missionaries'
are over. They have fulfilled their task, and governments in general are to an increasing extent assuming their role (Anderson,
1956). In their time, they contributed something essential to a
pioneering medical service – the spirit of altruistic, compassionate and conscientious care. In the changing situation of
today (Wilkinson, 1981), the average surviving medical mission
cannot compete in material terms with the well-equipped and
well-staffed government hospital unless, of course, it can offer
the 'something more' that may make all the difference when
added to mere medical efficiency. And this it does, and it does
so convincingly. It is the sheer goodness and kindliness of the
staff, expatriate and national, that more than atone for material
shortcomings in buildings, equipment and facilities. When this
goodness is accompanied by medical competence and a genuine
outreach into the community, then the Christian institution may
regain the initiative and demonstrate its vitality and relevance
both to the people it serves and to the government authorities
under which it works. Far from succumbing to the creeping
paralysis of senility and irrelevance, the revived medical
mission, adaptable and alert, faces the unknown future with a
confidence that comes from its divine Master. The challenge of
change evokes a response that continues to meet a real need in

the spirit of the Great Physician himself.

The vision that inspired most of the early medical missionaries was compounded of a response to an overwhelming physical need in the spirit of our Lord's second commandment, 'Love your neighbour as yourself', and a sharing of the Gospel of Christ. As the work developed, medical missions came to be seen as part of the whole Christian message of reconciliation, demonstrating in an intensely practical and obvious way God's concern for his suffering children. But in the nature of things, and in the light of these activities, they could not be regarded as other than transitional. Ultimate responsibility for health rests with governments acting for the wellbeing of their people. Christians could show the way, and they did in country after country.

They pioneered in bringing to needy peoples the obvious benefits of Western medicine; they introduced medical education for men and women; they initiated nursing services and founded schools for nurses; they established standards of excellence, and showed that it was possible to do first-class medical work with second-class equipment and facilities in third-class buildings; they pioneered in community medicine years before the term became current or fashionable; they created a climate of acceptance, both of Western medicine and of social responsibility, and they introduced the ideals of compassionate caring for the unwanted, the rejected, the outcast. In all this, they inspired a devotion that was as remarkable as it was unexpected.

Breaking down opposition

A remarkable instance of the way a medical mission broke down opposition to the Gospel was seen in the English Presbyterian Mission at Cheg Pu, 40 miles north-west of Amoy. In 1889 (Band, 1948) Dr Howie reported as follows: 'the successful amputation of the leg of a poor beggar who had been laid down at the door of the doctor's house to die, filled the city with amazement. To devote such pains and care to a beggar was as wonderful as the operation itself, and when the hospital was built and operations and cures more marvellous were multiplied, all opposition ceased. And no wonder'.

It is a truism that developing countries are passing through a phase of rapid transition. In the newly emerging

administrations there is much to admire, and also much to regret
and deplore. Political expediency seems often to control
medical policies and priorities. Rural health services suffer;
endemic diseases return and spread; curative medicine in
palaces of healing seems to take precedence over health facilities
for the mass of the people, and the newly qualified doctors find it
easier to employ the medical techniques of the West than to
absorb and practise the ethical principles that underlie Western
medicine.

In some provinces in China, the reputation of Christian hospitals was such that no military guard had to be provided. Such
was the case of the Jenkins and Robertson Memorial Hospital in
Sianfu, when students had pledged themselves to riots and
demonstrations on Christmas Day 1925 (Moorshead, 1929). Two
months later a leading Chinese physician, a Dr Yen, at a meeting
of the National Medical Council of China, praised the medical
service manned by British doctors. He said, 'British medical
prestige had been established through medical missionaries and
Chinese physicians educated at British universities'.

A similar tribute comes from Hupeh (China); 'If in some ways
the official atmosphere is unfavourable to Christian work, in
other ways it presents unique opportunities, especially for the
medical missionary (whether male or female) to gain access to
the households, often of great influence, who naturally regard
missionary work with something of supercilious indifference
and contempt. Again and again I have had occasion to thank God
for the entrance of my medical colleagues into the houses of the
highest officials in the city, and for the object-lesson that they
have been able to give of Christian love, sympathy and self-
sacrifice, over and above any mere physical relief that they have
brought to their patients' (Broomhall, 1907).

As recently as 1947, the staff of the Fatshan Hospital of the
Methodist Mission in China were planning larger buildings to
meet the growing need revealed by the hospital's increasing outreach. They wanted more inpatient beds, a larger nursing school,
and facilities for refresher courses for local general practitioners;
they were encouraging cooperation with neighbouring communities, and were building health clinics in several nearby
villages. Seminars on 'preaching and healing' open to anyone
interested were organized. Although the expatriate missionaries
had to leave within a year or two, the government took over a
well-functioning hospital and a medical service that was

reaching out into the community (Davey and Davey, 1964).

That is past history. Is the old vision still clear and sharp and relevant? Is it still valid in the rapidly changing context of newly independent governments in the developing countries and of new thinking in the corridors of medical power? In the light of the new nationalism, aggressive ideologies, the urge to self-sufficiency and the resentment of medical and religious 'interference' now apparent in many countries, is there a continuing justification for medical missions and medical missionaries?

Many instances could be cited of mission hospitals inspiring governments to assume responsibility for the sick, and providing the foundations of a community health service (Hewat, 1960). One of the basic functions of this Christian ministry is to pinpoint and respond to need not hitherto recognized as important.

In Nigeria the government has taken over many of the mission hospitals, but in most cases has engaged the expatriate and national staff in order to maintain continuity and standards.

In some other countries, missionary medical institutions are permitted to retain their identitiy within the government's overriding medical programme. This is the case of Tanzania, for instance, where this kind of working together is encouraged – to the lasting benefit of all. Government services profit from the cooperation of highly qualified and highly motivated expatriate personnel, and strategically important links are maintained and strengthened.

In India, on the other hand, the Indian church has largely taken over the medical institutions that were formerly administered and financed from abroad. This arrangement poses many problems – some of them well-nigh insuperable. The local church is quite unable to shoulder the financial burden and face the administrative complexities of these institutions. Some subsidies in cash and drugs may be forthcoming, but problems of many kinds are still unresolved.

As the Report of the World Council of Churches states, 'Overseas churches, with no imperialist connections and closer in mind and spirit with Jesus Christ, have increasingly brought pressure to bear on long established and rigid churches so that there is once again a growing impetus towards reform and rediscovering of the unique Good News for all mankind, which was the substance of the life and teaching of Jesus Christ'.

New ways forward
In some countries, mainly as a result of inspiration and pressure from the Christian Medical Commission of the World Council of Churches, local Christian Medical Associations have come into being, on which Roman Catholic as well as Protestant medical institutions are represented. In addition to working together in matters of staffing and bulk purchase of drugs and equipment, these Associations speak with a united voice to Governments on such questions as: the recognition of medical qualifications, work permit requirements, and legislation. In Malawi, Zambia, Tanzania and Nigeria, as well as in India, this cooperation in matters concerning the contribution of voluntary agencies to the health of the countries is proving invaluable.

A very useful innovation of proven worth is the work of ECHO (Equipment of Charity Hospitals Overseas). Under its enthusiastic Director, Dr James Burton, a former Baptist missionary in Africa, ECHO supplies hospital equipment and apparatus, drugs and (more recently) vaccines to mission hospitals. Through bulk purchase of galenicals and acquirement of discarded hospital equipment of various kinds, ECHO is able to supply anything medical at very advantageous prices (Burton, 1976, 1979). Because of its resources and experience, ECHO can respond to emergency appeals in cases of famine or natural disaster. Similar bodies exist in the USA, West Germany and Holland.

Another mode of perpetuating Christian ideas and the medical standards associated with mission hospitals consists in the secondment of Christian medical workers to teaching hospitals and medical schools. The influence of these Christians, working in centres of strategic and academic importance, cannot be overrated (Browne, 1980).

There is another possibility that presents itself. Many governments realize that there must be proper motivation of medical staff at all levels if the World Health Organization slogan 'Health for all by the year 2000' is to have any real chance of implementation. They refer to 'the missionary spirit', thus tacitly acknowledging the importance of the nonmedical, the nonmaterial. It may well be that the new insistence on primary health care and a juster distribution of medical facilities will provide the opportunity for medical missions to regain the initiative and emphasize those factors that have made them so outstandingly successful in the past. It seems providential that this new attitude on the part of governments and international organizations coincides with a turning away from curative medicine concentrated in relatively few centres of excellence such as the traditional mission hospital, and a turning towards the mass of the people through programmes of community health care. The new emphases, especially when coupled with genuine reassessment of priorities, and set in the larger context of population control, adequate nutrition, the provision of clean water and the hygienic disposal of waste, will do far more good to far more people than the old ways of curative medicine for the individual. The acceptance of these emphases will make real demands upon the expatriate staff trained in the traditional mould in the medical and nursing schools of their homelands, but the opportunities now presenting themselves for making a real impact on the health of the whole communites will be well worth the taking. The cost of these measures in hard cash – only partly met by government subsidies – may at first sight appear somewhat intimidating, but ways and means will surely be found to finance them. The Drs Arole in Jamkhed (India) have shown how such a programme, deeply rooted in the local population and enthusiastically endorsed by them, can be made to be self-supporting.

An area of relative failure is related to this; in general there has been too much concentration on curative medicine for the individual and too little outreach into the community. The result has been a growing reputation of the hospital but minimal impact on the health of the people. This understandable attitude is compounded of the traditional training of most medical workers and the appalling dimensions of the need confronting them. It is easier to look back with critical hindsight than to suggest what should have been done.

Cooperation with governments
In 1935, when the Chinese government announced its intention to organize a national health service, mission hospitals were invited to cooperate (Hewat, 1960) – a far cry from the official attitude of only 35 years previously (the time of the Boxer rebellion).

In countries like Uganda and Kenya, official recognition of the government's indebtedness to medical missionaries was publicized in official reports, mentioning specifically the disappearance of smallpox, cancrum oris, yaws and tropical ulcers

(Fraser, 1927). Traditional customs such as the treatment of measles conjunctivitis with the urine of the mother, and the abandonment of twins and babies born with teeth or other abnormalities, were becoming rarer as the mission hospitals pursued their quiet work of healing and teaching.

In India before World War I, a leading non-Christian government official paid tribute to medical missions in the following terms: 'What we dread is your women's missions and your medical missions, for in your women's missions you are winning homes, and in your medical missions you are winning our hearts, and when homes and hearts have been won, what is there for us to do but to do what you tell us?'

A new pattern of co-operation between mission hospitals and between these hospitals and governments, is exemplified by the Emmanuel Hospital Association in India. Responding to pressures from several quarters – increasing government requirements, escalating costs of hospital services, and the limited financial resources of the newly-formed Church of North India – a dozen mission hospitals agreed to organize together an indigenous comprehensive health care ministry. At present, some twenty hospitals in the Association, all under Indian control, provide a wide range of general and specialist services through 50 doctors and 275 nurses, with government-recognized training schools for nurses and nursing auxiliaries, and various in-service training courses. Outside finance is still needed for capital expenditure and for 25% of running costs.

Conforming to Government policies and cooperating especially in community health programmes, the member bodies of the Association demonstrate the value of working together to provide a service that is both needed and acceptable, maintaining a distinctive Christian witness in the community.

If, as some suggest, medical missions received less than their due recognition at the World Congress of Missions held in Edinburgh in 1910, subsequent international gatherings have been most forthcoming in recognizing the unique contribution made by medical missionaries to the ongoing work of the Church of Christ. The Jerusalem Council (1928) Report has this to say (Moorshead, 1929):

'As the Christian Church, animated by the same spirit of divine compassion, seeks to follow in His footsteps, it should attempt, whenever needed, to carry on effectively the ministry of healing. Work done in this spirit is spiritual service'.

And

'The Christian Church can never expect, should never dare to compete with national medical institutions in the service of healing, save only in the quality of the work achieved . . . The personality of the doctors and nurses in mission hospitals is of supreme importance . . . They can create or mar the spiritual atmosphere of the hospitals'.
'We lose the mission content of the medical work at our peril'.

The way forward is indicated by the findings of a Joint Consultation organized (in September 1983) by the Medical Committee of the Conference for World Missions, together with the Evangelical Missionary Alliance, with a contribution from the World Health Organization. This Consultation was convinced that a spiritual component was essential to the successful implementation of the WHO slogan 'Health for all by the year 2000'. In programmes for primary health care, in the training of health staff, in the supervision of auxiliary workers in rural or urban situations, it is honesty and integrity that make for success; it is the dependability and trustworthiness of staff that count.

References

Aitchison, M. (1983) *The Doctor and the Dragon*. Basingstoke: Pickering and Inglis.

Anderson, H.G. (1956) *The New Phase in Medical Mission Strategy*. London: Church Missionary Society.

Balme, H. (1921) *China and Modern Medicine*. London: The Carey Press.

Band, E. (1948) *Working His Purpose Out. The History of the English Presbyterian Mission*. London: Presbyterian Church of England Publishing Office.

Billington, R. (1978) *Health has Many Faces*. London: Edinburgh House.

Broomhall, M. (1907) *The Chinese Empire. A general and missionary survey*. London: China Inland Mission.

Browne, S.G. (1980) *Medical Missions – regaining the initiative*. Rendle Short Lecture. London: Christian Medical Fellowship.

Burton, P. (1976) *Flying Forceps*. Eastbourne: Victory Press. (1976).

Burton P. (1979) *Cheaper by the Million*. Worthing: Henry Walter.

Cheesbrough, M. (1981, 1984) *Medical Laboratory Manual for Tropical Countries*. Vols. I and II. Doddington, Cambridge: Tropical Health Technology.

Costain, A.J. (1911) *Arthur Jackson of Manchuria*. London: Hodder & Stoughton.

Davey, F. and Davey K. (1964) *Compassionate Years*. London: Cargate Press.

Foster, W.D. (1979) *Sir Albert Cook*. Printed privately.
Fraser, D (1927) *The New Africa*. London: Church Missionary Society.
Hewat, E.G.K. (1982) *Vision and Achievement*. London: Thomas Nelson.
King, M. (1966) *Medical Care in Developing Countries*. Nairobi: Oxford University Press.
Leprosy Mission (1977) News release. London.
Magnusson S. (1981) *The Flying Scotsman*. London: Quartet Books.
McIndoe, B. (1974) *God's Man for China*. London: Hodder & Stoughton.
Methodist Missionary Society. (1946). Report 1939-46. London.
Morley, D. (1973) *Paediatric Priorities in the Developing World*. London: Butterworth.
Miller, S. (1981) *Pigtails, Petticoats and the Old School Tie*. Sevenoaks: Overseas Missionary Fellowship.
Moorshead, R.F. (1926) *The Way of the Doctor*. London: The Carey Press.
Moorshead, R.F. (1929) *Heal the Sick*. London: The Carey Press
Payne, E.A. (1939) *Harry Wyatt of Shansi*. London: The Carey Press.
Royal Free Hospital missionaries – a centenary study. Duplicated. For private circulation (1982).
Schweitzer, A. (1936) *On the Edge of the Primaeval Forest*. London: A. & C. Black.
Somervell, T.H. (1936) *After Everest*. London: Hodder & Stoughton.
Thompson, P. (1978) *Sent to Heal*. London: Medical Missionary Association.
Thompson, P. (1982) *Each to Her Post*. London: Hodder & Stoughton.
Warren, M. (1965) *The Missionary Movement from Britain in Modern History*. London: SCM Press.
Wilkinson, J. (1981) *Health and Healing*. Edinburgh: The Handsel Press.
Wesleyan Methodist Missionary Society (1982) Annual Report, 1892.

INDEX OF NAMES

INDEX OF PLACES

INDEX OF SUBJECTS